Uncle John's
BATHROOM
READER.

The WORLD'S GONE CRAZY

By the Bathroom Readers' Institute

Bathroom Readers' Press
Ashland, Oregon

P9-DJK-579

*Dedicated to the memory of Zephyr the cat,
who was crazy in all the right ways.*

UNCLE JOHN'S BATHROOM READER®
THE WORLD'S GONE CRAZY

For information, write:
The Bathroom Readers' Institute, P.O. Box 1117,
Ashland, OR 97520
www.bathroomreader.com • 888-488-4642

Cover design by Michael Brunsfeld, San Rafael, CA
(*Brunsfeldo@comcast.net*)

ISBN-13: 978-1-60710-101-7 / ISBN-10: 1-60710-101-7

Library of Congress Cataloging-in-Publication Data
Uncle John's bathroom reader world's gone crazy.
   p. cm.
   ISBN 978-1-60710-101-7 (pbk.)
1. American wit and humor. 2. Curiosities and wonders.
I. Bathroom Readers' Institute (Ashland, Or.)
   PN6165.U5295 2010
   081—dc22

                             2009041841

Printed in the United States of America
Second Printing: September 2010
2 3 4 5 6 14 13 12 11 10

THANK YOU!

The Bathroom Readers' Institute sincerely thanks the people whose advice and assistance made this book possible.

Gordon Javna	Jef Fretwell
Jay Newman	Jodi Webb
Amy Miller	Les Weishar
Thom Little	Sue Newman
Brian Boone	Adam Bolivar
John Dollison	Christine DeGueron
Michael Brunsfeld	JoAnn Padgett
Angela Kern	Melinda Allman
Claudia Bauer	Dan Mansfield
Claire Breen	Lilian Nordland
Malcolm Hillgartner	Pam Morlett
Jahnna Beacham	Monica Maestas
Michael Kerr	Lisa Meyers
Paul Seaburn	Amy Ly
Sue Steiner	Ginger Winters
Judy Plapinger	Jennifer Frederick
Megan Todd	Sydney Stanley
John Scalzi	Tom Mustard
William Dooling	R.R. Donnelley
Mark Thorburne	Media Masters
Kyle Coroneos	Publishers Group West
Cam Dokey	Raincoast Books
Jack Mingo	Porter the Wonder Dog
James Greene Jr.	Thomas Crapper

CONTENTS

Because the BRI understands your reading needs, we've
divided the contents by length as well as subject.
Short—a quick read
Medium—2 to 3 pages
Long—for those extended visits, when something
a little more involved is required
* Extended—for those leg-numbing experiences

YOU ARE ENTERING ANOTHER DIMENSION

CRAZY TOWN
It's called "Planet Earth," and it may be the strangest place in the entire universe. The dedicated team of trivia nuts at the Bathroom Readers' Institute (led by yours truly, Uncle John) has spent more than 20 Earth years making *Bathroom Readers*. All our books are odd in their own special ways, but none has been odder than the one you hold in your hands right now (it's even odder than a book we did a few years ago called *The Wonderful World of Odd*).

Quite simply, this book turns the crazy dial up to 11. We plunged deep into the depths of pop culture, current events, and all-around oddballery to bring you strange-but-true stories of everything weird under the sun...and over the moon. Just flip this book open to any page. You never know what you'll find...

• **VSPs (very strange people):** Behold the man who thinks he's a carpet, the woman who spent two years in a tree, the teenager who wants to be a zombie, and the celebrated painter who's *blind*.

• **Arts and entertainment:** The Sinatra song to kill for, cheating on reality shows, Lady Gaga's true gender, and that homeless bum called Superman.

• **Conspiracy theories:** Is the government poisoning our skies? Is there a secret "Planet X" about to lay waste to our existence? Is the food in your refrigerator riddled with deadly chemicals?

• **Animal oddities:** A snake with a foot, gay penguins, a bear that ate an airplane, and a doctor's dose of medicinal parasitic worms.

• **Professionals gone crazy:** Lawyers, police officers, teachers, scientists, doctors, politicians, and the clergy. (No one gets a free pass.)

• **Science on the edge:** Human-animal hybrids, a human-caused earthquake, and a remote-control sphincter.

• **Myths and legends:** An elf school in Iceland, the Lemurians of Mt. Shasta, the Mayan Prophecy, alien deities, and how to capture irrefutable evidence of the paranormal. (Good luck.)

• **Looking crazy good:** Botox for your armpits, jewelry for your eyeballs, and bagels for your forehead.

There's so much more we could tell you about, but you'll have to dive in to see for yourself. And a word of warning: Some of what you'll read may make you feel a bit…squeamish. Don't worry—it made us feel squeamish, too. But our goal was to seek out really weird stuff and then share what we found. So have fun, but read with caution.

As we're now mere hours away from sending this behemoth of a book off to the printer, I'd like to send a gigantic thank-you to my barely sane team of writers and editors for all of their hard work. (They were barely sane when we started. Now that we're finished, forget it.)

But as always, I save my last and biggest thanks for all of you. It is because of your quirky dedication and support of such a bizarre book series that we get to keep coming up with new ways to entertain you. We hope we've succeeded!

Happy reading and…

Go with the Flow!

—Uncle John, the BRI Staff, and Porter the Wonder Dog

A YEAR OF WEIRD

Real (and really odd) wall calendars we've spotted.

Naked Clowns Calendar: Good news: It's published by San Francisco Clown College, and proceeds go to multiple sclerosis research. Bad news: It's pictures of naked clowns, with their faces painted and their naughty parts obscured.

Odd-Eyed Cats Calendar: Each month features a cat with crossed eyes, strange-looking eyes, or eyes that are different colors.

My Zombie Pin-Up: Dressed in vintage 1940s and '50s clothing, blood-covered, gore-oozing men and women pretend to be happy zombies posing with their dead victims.

Pets Rock: Dogs and cats are dressed in costumes and makeup to look like famous rock stars, such as Elvis Presley and KISS.

From Girls Calendar: *Association Fromages de Terroirs* is a French organization devoted to "cheese awareness." This annual calendar is part of their campaign and depicts female dairy farm workers and farmers' wives in revealing outfits, holding their favorite kinds of cheese.

Men on a Mission: This calendar features young, male Mormons who have gone on their required religious mission and have now returned home…to pose shirtless.

Credit Crunch Calendar: Produced in England, this one features photos that symbolize the economic recession, including abandoned factories, jobless people, and boarded-up businesses.

The Lindner Calendar: Lindner is a Polish casket manufacturer. Each year they put out a promotional calendar featuring young women in swimsuits or underwear posing on top of the year's hottest new coffins.

Toilets of the World: Just johns—modern, primitive, and exotic.

Pointless Calendar: Indeed, it's completely nonfunctional. Each month has 40 days, each week consists of 10 days, and no days of the week are listed. For each month, there's a photo of a random object, like a peeling wooden wall or a pile of bricks.

21st-CENTURY FADS

*Uncle John told us he just doesn't get all these new
fads, so we told him to go pet his pet rock.*

BAGEL HEADS
This "beauty treatment" fad got its start in Tokyo dance
clubs in 2009. Using disposable syringes, teenagers inject
saline solution (a common hydrating fluid) into their foreheads. A
few moments later, the saline disfigures the forehead, creating a
large, bulbous growth with an indentation in the middle. In other
words, it looks like a giant bagel (or possibly a tumor) growing out
of the forehead. Food coloring is sometimes added to the saline to
turn the "bagel" green or blue. Thankfully, it's not permanent—
the bulge deflates in about a day.

IKEA DINNER PARTIES
IKEA sells modern-looking furniture that's very popular with the
young and hip. So popular, in fact, that some can't wait to get
home to enjoy IKEA merchandise. In Sacramento in 2008, a small
group of young people began holding "dinner parties" inside an
IKEA store, and the fad has since caught on at locations around
the U.S. After dining on lingonberry jam and meatballs in the
store's Swedish-themed cafeteria, partiers retire to the living-room
furniture displays to play board games. IKEA managers don't seem
to mind—the partygoers are paying customers, after all, and the
publicity doesn't hurt.

FINGER MUSTACHE TATTOOS
In a trend that's taken off around Brooklyn, New York, college-age
men and women get a permanent tattoo of a tiny handlebar mustache on one side of their index finger. Why? When they hold it
up to their face, above the lip, it looks like they have a tiny, silly
mustache. (*Superbad* star Jonah Hill showed his off on *Saturday
Night Live*.) The one drawback to a finger mustache tattoo (other
than actually having a finger mustache tattoo) is that the joke
doesn't work if you're wearing gloves. Problem solved: You can
now buy gloves preprinted with a mustache.

South Africa fad: Some boys in Cape Town have their upper front teeth extracted to look cool.

CELEBRITY ISSUES

1. Become famous. 2. Act weird. 3. Get mentioned in a Bathroom Reader.

EWW! Actor Ryan O'Neal was the longtime companion of Farrah Fawcett. Moments after Fawcett's burial service in 2009, O'Neal was taken aback when "a beautiful blond woman" came up and hugged him. Despite having just put the love of his life in the ground, O'Neal asked the woman if she wanted to go get a drink. She did not. "Daddy, it's me," replied actress Tatum O'Neal, his estranged daughter.

UNCAGED. Nicolas Cage once collected rare and exotic animals, including an octopus, a saltwater shark, and two king cobras named Moby and Sheba. He would probably still own them today had he not mentioned his collection during an appearance on *The Tonight Show*. Cage's neighbors saw the interview and notified animal control, who came and took his pets away.

HEY, BABY. In 2010 workers at the Mondrian Hotel in Los Angeles reported that one of the strangest guests they'd ever had was Britney Spears. While living in the penthouse, she watched the DVD box set of the Fox cartoon *Family Guy*. For days, Spears would speak only in the voice of Stewie, the sarcastic, football-headed, English-accented baby. "It's a bit weird," said a hotel worker, "especially when she's in the gym speaking like a Brit."

HAAW MINNY RUADS MUSS AMANN WAWK DEWN? Two homeowners in Long Branch, New Jersey, called police during an August 2009 rainstorm after spotting a ratty-haired, disheveled man peeking in through the windows of a home for sale across the street. Cops questioned the drifter, who turned out to be Bob Dylan. He said he was just "looking around."

HE COULD PLAY CENTAUR FIELD. New York Yankees shortstop Alex Rodriguez has two paintings of himself hanging on the wall over his bed. In both, Rodriguez is depicted as a centaur—the half-man, half-horse creature from Greek mythology.

At last count, the U.S. had 612,020 fast-food cooks and only 393,730 farm workers.

END ALIEN MIND CONTROL NOW!

Get out of my head, you damn dirty alien!

PROTECTION
In 1998 Michael Menkin, a former technical writer for NASA, invented the "Thought Screen Helmet," a hat made out of Velostat, a kind of metallized plastic produced by 3M. On his "public service, nonprofit website," *www.stopabductions.com,* Menkin offers instructions for building your own helmet. Here are a few excerpts from the site.

THE THOUGHT SCREEN HELMET STOPS ALIENS FROM ABDUCTING HUMANS. IT'S A TESTED DEVICE THAT WORKS.

• Aliens cannot immobilize people wearing thought screens nor can they control their minds or communicate with them using their telepathy. When aliens can't communicate or control humans, they do not take them.

• Adults and children all over America, all over Australia, in Canada, the United Kingdom, and in the Republic of South Africa are wearing thought screen helmets to stop alien abductions.

• Only four failures from standard thought screen helmets have been reported since 1998. A third failure in 2005 was from a cloth helmet with a smaller square area of Velostat and a Velcro strap which was easily removed by an alien-human hybrid.

• Other shielding material was tried in previous models with less success. Only thought screen helmets using Velostat are effective. Large leather aviator hats lined with Velostat with secure straps are recommended for making effective helmets.

• You can make a thought screen helmet (or thought screen base-ball cap) for $30 if you purchase Velostat by the yard.

Here's a customer testimonial from John Locke, alien abductee:
"Since trying Michael Menkin's helmet, I have not been bothered by alien mind control. Now my thoughts are my own. I have achieved meaningful work and am contributing to society. My life is better than ever before. Thank you, Michael, for the work you are doing to save all humanity."

Did they tank the Academy? Sean Connery and Lionel Richie both keep their Oscars in the bathroom.

WHAT A VERY STRANGE PERSON

You may consider yourself a strange and unusual person. If so, see how you measure up against these oddballs.

Strange Person: Nileen Namita of Brighton, England
Background: In the late 1980s, Namita became convinced that she was a reincarnation of the ancient-Egyptian queen Nefertiti.

Very Strange: Namita decided that being a reincarnation of Nefertiti wasn't enough; she had to also look like her. So she started having plastic surgeries. Using the famous 3,300-year-old bust of Nefertiti, which sits in a Berlin's Neues Museum, as a model, Namita has had eight nose jobs, three chin implants, nine facelifts, two lip surgeries, five eye surgeries, and several other facial procedures—adding up to 51 operations in all. She turned 49 in 2009, and so far has spent more than $330,000 in her quest to look like the ancient queen. Did it work? By all accounts, no. She looks like...well, someone who's had a lot of plastic surgery.

Strange Person: Japanese truck driver Yuuki Oshima
Background: One day in August 2009, 22-year-old Oshima was driving through the city of Noda when he saw a woman walking...and fell instantly in love with her. He discreetly followed her to her apartment, and over the next couple of months, tried to get up the courage to tell her his feelings...but he was too shy to do it face to face. Then he got an idea.

Very Strange: Oshima went to the woman's house in the middle of the night...and peed through the mail slot in her door. That, not surprisingly, didn't cause the woman to fall in love with him. She called police. Oshima was arrested, and explained, "I absolutely went crazy for her the first time I saw her, and just did it." He was charged with property damage.

Strange Person: Rick Murray, a teenager from Montreal, Canada
Background: "When I was a kid, I wanted to be a Teenage

A heated jawbreaker can explode when bitten into.

Mutant Ninja Turtle and live in the sewers," said Murray, "But as I got older, I fell in love with zombies and wanted to become one."

Very Strange: Now Murray is known as "Zombie Boy." His entire body is covered with tattoos that make him look like a zombie. Black ink surrounds Murray's eyes; his "teeth" and "jawbones" can be seen beneath his cheeks, his "brain" appears from beneath his bald head; and his "guts," "skeleton," and several ghoulish designs are inked all over the rest of his body. When asked if people are bothered by his appearance, Murray said, "It's like if you met someone with purple hair, after 10 minutes you'd think, 'Oh yeah, they have purple hair. So what?'" He's not done yet—Murray said that he's planning on removing one of his ear lobes as well as the tip of his nose to complete the look of the undead.

Strange Person: Melanie Renfrew of Burbank, California

Background: In 2007 Renfrew, 54, saw local meteorologist Fritz Coleman on television. Renfrew, a geography professor at Los Angeles Harbor College, called the station to tell Coleman that he had confused "onshore" winds, which blow in from the sea, with "offshore" winds, which blow out. (She was right.)

Very Strange: When she got no response, Renfrew called again, demanding an apology. When *that* didn't work, Renfrew became obsessed—and over the next year called and e-mailed Coleman thousands of times, trying to get him to apologize to her on the air. In March 2008, Coleman got a restraining order against Renfrew, preventing her from coming within 100 feet of him, e-mailing him, or calling him. Renfrew kept harassing him anyway, and in October 2009 was convicted of violating the restraining order. She was given a year to comply, after which time, if she is still harassing the weatherman, she could be sentenced to jail. "I don't feel obsessive," she said in an interview. "It's about the truth." (She added that she is currently working on a book, titled *What It Took to Convince NBC the Winds are Coming From the West.*)

✳   ✳   ✳

"You're only given a little spark of madness; you mustn't lose it."

—**Robin Williams**

Exhibits at Washington, DC's Newseum include the Unabomber's cabin & Saddam Hussein's poetry.

DANCING BALONEY

A few of the latest phrases that have made their way, mostly via office workers and the Internet, into the English language.

GOOD Job: This acronym refers to a "Get Out Of Debt job"—a decent-paying job that you take just to pay down your debt, then quit.

Social Jet Lag: The exhaustion felt after staying up too late doing social networking on sites like Facebook.

PEBCAK: When your tech person grumbles this, the "Problem Exists Between Chair And Keyboard." And if the problem is an "ID-Ten-T," they're calling you an "ID10T."

Seagull Manager: A manager who flies in, makes a lot of noise, poops on everything, and then leaves.

Chips and Salsa: Nicknames for hardware (chips) and software (salsa), e.g., "Is the problem in the chips or the salsa?"

Keyboard Plaque: The disgusting stuff that builds up on your computer keys.

Chainsaw Consultant: Hired by a company to figure out the easiest way to reduce the number of employees.

Telephone Number Salary: The kind of salary we all wish for: one with seven digits.

Yuppie Food Stamps: The $20 bills that are spewed out of ATMs, as in "Oh dear! I didn't know the Chard and brie were going to cost so much! Better go get some more yuppie food stamps."

Nomophobia: Short for "no-mobile phobia," this is the terror that takes hold when you're without your mobile phone, or simply out of signal range.

Assmosis: A way to soak up success—not by doing actual work, but by being very good at kissing the boss's ass.

Crapplet: An "applet" is a computer application written to perform one task. (Example: the QuickTime movie player.) A "crapplet" is a crappy applet.

Dancing Baloney: Unnecessary and garish animation on a Web site, which amateur designers love—and the rest of the world hates.

Uninstalled: Fired.

BACON FLOSS

*Even though we're told it's bad for us, bacon
seems to be more popular than ever.*

• **Bacon salt.** This is the product that launched the fad in 2007:
flavored salt crystals that "make everything taste like bacon."

• **Gummy bacon.** It's just like gummy bears or gummy worms, but
it looks like bacon (and, fortunately, tastes like candy).

• **Bacon vodka.** For years, vodka has been available in berry- and
vanilla-flavored versions. But now there's Bakon: premium vodka
infused with the flavor of bacon. Maybe it's not such a stretch—
vodka is often made from potatoes, which do taste great with
bacon.

• **Bacon-flavored envelopes.** Instead of getting a taste of glue
whenever you lick the flap of one of these pink-and-white-swirled
envelopes, you get a mouthful of artificial bacon flavor.

• **Bacon-flavored dental floss and toothpicks.** Because bacon
tastes better than string and wood.

• **Bacon wristbands.** A parody of the yellow Lance Armstrong
"Livestrong" cancer-awareness bracelets, these are marbled pink
and white, and emblazoned with the word "bacon" to promote
awareness of…bacon.

• **Bacon soap.** At one time, most soap was made from animal fat,
and bacon is just salted pork fat and meat. Fragrances and chemicals are added, so you shouldn't eat it, but it's still bacon you can
wash with.

• **Baconnaise.** Two of the world's unhealthiest foods—bacon and
mayonnaise—combined into one fatty concoction.

• **Bacon action figures.** These come in a set of two: the heroic,
all-American, strip-shaped "Mr. Bacon" and his nemesis, the evil,
cube-shaped "Monsieur Tofu."

NEW DISEASES

Just when you think you've got a handle on swine flu or
E. coli, the medical community discovers a new bug.
Great—something else to worry about!

New Disease: *Progressive inflammatory neuropathy*
Symptoms: Numbness, tingling, and/or burning in the
arms and legs; fatigue; weakness in the limbs; temporary
paralysis.

Discovery: In February 2008, a translator at a medical clinic in
southeastern Minnesota noticed that three different Spanish-
speaking workers at a nearby pig slaughterhouse had recently
come in complaining of fatigue and strange sensations in their
arms and legs. She told a doctor, and the resulting investigation
found that 12 people at the slaughterhouse had similar symptoms,
and a few others at a pig slaughterhouse in Indiana did as well. All
of the victims worked in similar locations in the plants: near the
"head table"…where the pigs' brains are removed from the carcasses with high-pressure air hoses. (The brains are then sold to
food markets in Asia.) Researchers from the Centers for Disease
Control (CDC) in Atlanta are still conducting studies on the disease, but they believe it may be a brand-new illness. How do they
think people catch it? By inhaling tiny pieces of pig brain, like
those floating in the air at slaughterhouses. The body produces
antibodies against the foreign brain bits, and the antibodies then
attack the body's own nerve fibers—resulting in this neurological
illness.

New Disease: Yet to be named
Symptoms: Fever, malaise, lack of appetite, muscle aches,
headache, nausea, vomiting, stiff neck, joint pain, chest pain, tes-
ticular pain, propensity to infection, enlarged heart, bleeding in
the brain, and death
Discovery: In December 2006, three people in two hospitals in
Melbourne, Australia, received organ transplants from the same
man, a 57-year-old who died of a brain hemorrhage after returning
from a long stay in Europe. Within weeks, all three transplant

patients were dead. Local testing found nothing linking the deaths of the three victims to the organ donor, so samples were sent to the Greene Infectious Disease Laboratory at Columbia University in New York. There, in 2007, using the latest in gene sequencing technology, researchers found a previously unknown virus in each of the transplanted organs. It's related to a well-known virus called *lymphocytic choreomeningitis* (LCMV), which is tested for in organ transplant cases, but the new virus is genetically distinct enough that had never been detected. The researchers say the virus may explain why many organ transplants have failed in the past, and the unfortunate deaths of the three Australians may help prevent more fatalities in the future.

New Disease: *Chapare virus hemorrhagic fever*
Symptoms: Fever, headache, muscle and joint pain, bleeding disorders, shock, and death
Discovery: In 2003 a young man in a small village in Bolivia became sick. Over the next few days, his condition worsened, and a few other people in the area came down with the same illness. Two weeks later, the man was dead. Every test for known diseases came up negative, so a local doctor, Simon Delgado, sent specimens from the man's body to the CDC. Researchers in the CDC's most secure lab studied them, and five years later they announced that the man had been killed by an *arenavirus*—a strain of virus that causes hemorrhagic fever (the Ebola virus is another). But it was one they'd never seen before. Only that one death occurred, and it's still the only known outbreak of what came to be known as the *Chapare* virus illness (after the young victim's home province), but CDC doctors say it's probably only a matter of time before it spreads. "There are lot of arenaviruses we don't know," Dr. Pierre Rollin said. "Are they going to be the new pandemic virus that's going to wipe out the planet? I don't think so." (How reassuring.)

*　　*　　*

HE WAS NEITHER

In July 2008, police in Tampa, Florida, arrested a man for selling cocaine within 1,000 feet of a church, a first-class felony. The man's name: God Lucky Howard.

BRITISH BREACHES

And here we thought "breaches" were really nice pants. Turns out that in the secretive world of British Intelligence, it's something completely different…and it's not nice at all.

DOWN THE TUBE

A British cabinet member (name withheld) often commuted on the London Underground subway and passed the time by reading work documents. One day in June 2008, he was going over the latest version of the government's top-secret Al-Qaeda profile…and left it on the train. A passenger turned it in, not to the authorities, but to the BBC. The news agency reported the find online, and added that it would be "tragic" if the documents had fallen into the wrong hands.

STATUS UPDATE

In 2009, when Sir John Sawyer was appointed head of MI6, the British government's spy agency, his wife, Shelley, posted the good news on her Facebook page. Unfortunately, Mrs. Sawyer hadn't enabled any of the social networking site's privacy features, meaning that anyone with Internet access could see her page, which contained sensitive information about her and her husband, including where they lived, places they frequently visited, and photos of their children. After the leak was discovered, Mrs. Sawyer hastily made her Facebook page accessible to "friends" only.

PIC OF THE LITTER

An English postal worker bought a digital camera on eBay in September 2008 for about $30 U.S. After he'd used it a few times, he looked through the camera's memory and found, along with his vacation pictures, photographs of terrorist leaders, missiles, rockets, fingerprints, and snapshots of documents detailing a spy computer system that were so revealing that they could have been used to hack into the network. The postal worker contacted the British government, and after he was interrogated for a few hours and released, he was told that he'd accidentally been sold a camera used by an MI6 agent, whose name was never released to the public.

MOMMIES...

How much do they love their daughters? THIS much!

FAILED. All Caroline McNeal of Huntingdon, Pennsylvania, wanted for her daughter, Brittany, was for her to get ahead... of her classmates. So Caroline, the high-school secretary, used stolen passwords over the course of three years to improve more than 200 of Brittany's grades and test scores—and even *lowered* the grades of two of her daughter's classmates. Brittany would have been the 2008 valedictorian, but a guidance counselor found a 360-point discrepancy in the school's record of her SAT score. Brittany graduated, though not as valedictorian, and Caroline was convicted of unlawful use of a computer and tampering with public records. She faces seven years in prison and a $15,000 fine.

STUNNING. LeShawn Fisher of Warr Acres, Oklahoma, insists she was just trying to reason with Bethany Lorenz, her daughter's cheerleading coach, in Putnam City High School's parking lot. But despite Fisher's plea, Lorenz wouldn't add her daughter to the team. So Fisher yelled, "Look over there!" and when the coach turned her head, Fisher zapped her on the neck with a stun gun set at 100,000 volts. Fisher's lawyer argued that she wasn't thinking clearly because she was on pain medication for a back injury. Fisher insists it was her "love of children" that inspired the attack. She was sentenced to five years in prison.

AWFUL.COM. After her nine-year-old daughter got in a fight with another girl in Hauppauge, New York, in 2009, Margery Tannenbaum was so enraged that she vowed revenge. Tannenbaum, a licensed social worker, posted an ad on Craigslist: "I need a little affection. I am blond and very cute! I'll be waiting." The men who responded to *Lacethong23-@***.com* were actually e-mailing Tannenbaum, who replied to them with the name and phone number of her daughter's rival. Nearly two dozen men called the little girl's house before Tannenbaum was arrested and charged with aggravated harassment and endangering the welfare of a child. In addition, she lost her position as "room mother" at her daughter's elementary school.

In 2009 a 10-year-old British girl placed her "moaning" grandmother for sale on eBay for 99¢.

...AND DADDIES

Three tender moments between fathers and sons. Isn't bonding great?

WHAT WAS HE INKING? During a backyard barbecue in spring 2009, Eugene Ashley, 24, of Floyd County, Georgia, decided that his three-year-old son needed a tattoo. So Ashley (who had been drinking heavily) fetched his tattoo gun and got to work inking the shoulder of his toddler (who was crying heavily). Neither the boy's mother nor the Floyd police were amused by Eugene's antics. "You keep thinking you've seen everything," said the arresting officer, "and then, *voilà!*" Eugene was charged with child cruelty and lost custody of his son—who now sports a tattoo that reads "Daddy's Boy."

DESIGNATED DODO. A 41-year-old father from Clio, Michigan, was too drunk to drive one night in 2007, so he gave the keys to his 13-year-old son. A patrolman later found them in a park with their pickup truck stuck in the mud. The officer gave the father a breathalyzer test. He failed and was cited for DUI. But then the officer noticed that the boy didn't look quite right, either...and administered a second test. The son turned out to be just as drunk as the father, and was also charged with a DUI.

THE BIG LIGUES. In September 2002, 34-year-old William Ligue Jr. and his 15-year-old son, William III, were attending a Kansas City Royals baseball game. Standing 25 feet away from them on the infield was Tom Gamboa, the Royals' 54-year-old first-base coach. For some reason, the Ligues—both shirtless—jumped the fence and rushed Gamboa during a play. "It felt like a football team hit me from behind," Gamboa said. "Next thing I knew, I'm on the ground trying to defend myself." The Ligues pounded the hapless coach until players in the dugout rushed out and broke up the scuffle. Father and son were led away in handcuffs. And to this day, it's still the proudest moment in young William III's life (judging from how much he brags about it on his MySpace page). More good news: "I'm expectin' a little shorty." Watch out world, here comes William IV!

The American Psychiatric Assn. lists four different caffeine-related mental disorders.

ELF SCHOOL

Ah, Iceland! Home of hot springs, fermented cod,
hard-to-pronounce names, and...invisible people?

LITTLE COUNTRY, LITTLE PEOPLE

Magnus Skarphedinsson believes in fairies—and dwarves, gnomes, pixies, and trolls. Just about anywhere else in the world, he'd be considered a bit crazy. But not in Iceland. In fact, more than half the country's nearly 300,000 citizens say they also believe in fairies and other mythical creatures. That statistic may seem at odds with the global perception of Iceland as a hip, techno-savvy Nordic country—until you consider that modernization came to Iceland only recently.

For most of its 1,000-year history, the island was a frigid, isolated outpost of European civilization. Stuck in the Dark Ages long after the rest of the continent had been "enlightened," Iceland didn't even have a major city until 200 years ago. And though most Icelanders have embraced the modern world, they continue to cling to the old ways—including, for many, a guarded belief in mythical creatures. Says Olafur Stephensen, former editor of *Morgunbladid*, Iceland's principal newspaper, "Many Icelanders say they don't believe in elves, but often consider it safer to behave as if they might exist. That way they don't risk offending them."

ÁLFASKÓLINN

That was Skarphedinsson's thinking in 1991 when he opened an *Álfaskólinn*, or "Icelandic Elf School," to educate the world about his country's unique heritage. A tall, paunchy man in his 50s with short white hair and a well-trimmed beard, Skarphedinsson teaches classes and leads tours to sites where elves or other strange creatures have reportedly been sighted. According to Arni Bjornsson, head of the Ethnology Department at the National Museum of Iceland, Icelandic folklore contains tales of more than 500 supernatural beings.

Although some scholars come to the Elf School to study Icelandic legends in depth, most students are tourists. For about $60

U.S., you can attend a lecture given by Skarphedinsson and then ride along with him on a tour of local elf sites. You'll receive a diploma, which states (in Icelandic) that you now know more than most people about Iceland's "other" inhabitants. To date, more than 9,000 people have graduated from the Elf School.

HIDE AND SEEK

According to the school's textbook, Iceland is home to 25 different varieties of elves, gnomes, trolls, fairies, and the curiously named *huldüfolk*, or "Hidden People." According to the Elf School, the huldüfolk were once human, the descendants of Celtic settlers who were already in Iceland when the Vikings arrived in the 9th century. Rather than be enslaved by the Norse invaders, the huldüfolk slipped away into a shadow world, a sort of parallel universe, where they remain today. According to Skarphedinsson, as many as 20,000 huldüfolk may still exist. A few Icelanders, mainly children, claim to be able to see and talk with them, and report that the huldüfolk look pretty much like us, except for their old-fashioned, traditional clothes. (One branch of the huldüfolk is notable for their blue skin.)

Although Skarphedinsson himself has never encountered the huldüfolk, he remains a true believer. "I have spoken with over 500 people who say they have seen them," he says. "Many swear that the huldüfolk cured illnesses and saved their lives." A trade union leader, Tryggvi Emilsson, insists that when he was a young man, he was saved by a beautiful huldüfolk girl when he fell off a cliff. There are even rare stories of people who fell in love with huldüfolk and vanished with them into the shadow world. These tales have inspired more than a few single women to enroll in Elf School in the hopes of a romantic encounter with a "shadow man."

MAINTAINING ELF CONTROL

For the most part, folklore enthusiasts say, Icelanders got along well with the elves, dwarfs, fairies, gnomes, trolls, and huldüfolk—until humans started building roads, neighborhoods, and Taco Bells in the forests and lava fields where the creatures live. Result: They've fought back. Mysterious equipment failures, strange accidents, bizarre illnesses—there have been so many worksite mishaps in recent years that the Icelandic Public Works administration has resorted to some drastic measures. "Our basic approach is not to deny this phenomenon," explains Birgir Gudmundsson, an engineer with the Iceland Road Authority. "Fortunately, there are people who can negotiate with the elves, and we make use of that."

These negotiators are known as "elf-spotters." Their job: to ensure that the land is clear of the creatures before any work begins. One of the most respected elf-spotters, Erla Stefansdottir, has drawn up several maps charting known locations of Hidden People for Reykjavik's Planning Department (as well as for the tourist authorities). That's not all elf-spotters do.

• Developers building Iceland's first shopping mall utilized a folklorist's knowledge to make sure that electrical cables and other underground equipment was placed far away from suspected elf homes.

• An elf-spotter halted construction of a highway to relocate a boulder called the *Graustein*, purported to be a dwarf home.

• When a crew building a golf course outside Reykjavik moved a rock, their bulldozers stopped running and a rash of injuries disabled the workforce. Finally, on the advice of the local elf-spotter (who had already told them the rock was home to some elves), the chief engineer returned the rock to the field and apologized out loud. He swore that his crew would not bother them anymore. The bulldozers started up again, and there were no more accidents. The course was completed on schedule.

Stories like these make Magnus Skarphedinsson proud. "My mission," he declares, "is to get the elves and Hidden People the respect they deserve."

FOOTNOTE: IT'S MAGIC

Another curious attraction in Iceland is the Icelandic Phallological Museum in Husavik, more commonly referred to as the "Penis Museum." The institution's mission is to catalog and display penises from every mammalian species, living or extinct, native to Iceland—272 specimens, representing 92 species. In between displays of mummified horse and polar bear members sits a small jar filled with murky embalming fluid. It is labeled "Elf's Penis." Its contents are, of course, invisible.

CRAZY WORLD RECORDS

*Uncle John holds the world record for the most pages ever
read on the throne (234,815 and counting). Here
are some other dubious achievements.*

• Christian Adam of Germany set the distance record for riding a
bicycle backward while playing the violin: 37.5 miles. It took him
a little more than five hours. He played J. S. Back...er, Bach.

• For 20 minutes of "every waking hour" for 16 years, Australian
Les Stewart spelled out every number from one to one million
on his typewriter. He went through seven typewriters and 1,000
ink ribbons. Now he not only owns a world record but a 19,890-
page book consisting of every spelled-out number up to one
million.

• On May 6, 2009, Eric "No Class" Matyjasik of Arizona
unzipped his pants 162 times in 30 seconds, breaking the old
record by 27 zips.

• Artist Maria Reidelbach built the world's largest garden gnome
in 2006. It stands 13 feet, 6 inches, and lives on a miniature golf
course in Kerhonkson, New York. The gnome's name: Gnome
Chomsky, a play on the name of linguist and philosopher Noam
Chomsky (who is only about half as tall as Gnome Chomsky).

• The unofficial world record for staying awake: 18 days, 17 hours,
set by Maureen Weston of England while participating in a rock-
ing-chair marathon. Although she hallucinated quite a bit, she
says she hasn't suffered any long-term health effects.

• An exotic dancer who goes by the name Maxi Mounds is the
proud owner of the world's largest augmented breasts. Each of
Mounds's mounds weighs 20 pounds; her bust measurement is
about 60 inches.

• Naya Ganj of India has the world's longest ear hair. "Making it
into *Guinness* is special for my family! God has been very kind to
me!" said the guy with 5.25 inches of hair growing from his ears.

THE BIG DUMP CONTINUES

*And other actual headlines ripped from news
stories of the recent, strange past.*

Main Street merchants
want crack at market

**9-Year-Old Stops
Carjacking**

**Man shot in head
'not popular'**

*Some 40% of female gas
station employees in Metro
Detroit are women*

A-Rod goes deep, Wang hurt

Hotel cancels jihad
conference, citing
safety reasons

MPs seek answers
on Nutt sacking

*Scientists Find Sand
on Sea Floor*

*Hippies Face Horror
at Weekend B.O.*

Courtney Love Banned
From Using Hole

*Federal judge likes
sentencing freedom*

*How Scientists Are
Helping Cook Inlet's
Little White Whales*

Jimmy Carter's hometown
excited over burial plans

*Cop Tasers One-Armed
Legless Man—Twice!*

Church Kids Raid Pantys
For Food Bank Supplies

MISSING BABY FOUND
IN SANDWICH

*Naked Jacqueline
Onassis Photo Found
With Warhol's Junk*

State population to double
by 2040; babies to blame

17 Remain Dead in
Morgue Shooting Spree

MISSIPPI'S LITERACY
PROGRAM SHOWS
IMPROVEMENT

**Missing wall allows
escape from new jail**

Stool pigeons: A company called Avian Fashions makes diapers for pet birds.

POLLY WANTS A LAMB CHOP

The latest in true—and truly strange—
news from the world of animals.

UP, UP, AND MEOW

In August 2008, a cat in the Chinese city of Chongqing started growing what were described as "bumps" on its sides. They kept growing, and in less than a month they resembled a set of furry wings, each several inches long. (The owner claimed that the cat, a male, grew wings because he was being harassed by too many female cats.) Surprisingly, reports of winged cats have been circulating for at least 150 years. American writer Henry David Thoreau wrote about one that his neighbor had: "This would have been the right kind of cat for me to keep, if I had kept any, for why should not a poet's cat be winged as well as his horse?" Experts say that the phenomenon might be the result of genetic mutations, or it might have a simpler cause: poor grooming, which can lead to skin diseases and extremely matted fur.

PAGING DR. SHARK

One afternoon in November 2009, tourists at Kelly Tarlton's Underwater World in Auckland, New Zealand, reported that one of the aquarium's sharks had just bitten another one in the belly—and that baby sharks were swimming out of the resulting gash. Staff quickly isolated the shark—they didn't even know she was pregnant—and the babies, along with four more that were still in the mother's womb. According to staff members, the attacking shark had apparently bitten the pregnant shark in order to help her have the babies—a sort of shark cesarean section. "It had to bite a certain part to let the babies out," said staffer Fiona Davies, "and do it without killing the babies or the mother." No other "shark cesarean" had ever been reported, she added, and extensive study would be needed. (She also said that the mother and the babies were doing fine.)

The Las Vegas Golden Nugget hotel's swimming pool encircles an actual shark tank.

TOUGH BIRD

Someday when you're out walking through the alpine mountains on New Zealand's South Island—with your pet sheep—you'd better watch out: A vicious parrot might rip out out your sheep's guts while it's still alive. The region is home to the *kea*, a species of parrot known as one of the smartest, most inquisitive—and most savage—on the planet. Keas normally eat things that wouldn't surprise anyone: seeds, leaves, roots, insects, grubs, and the occasional chicks of other birds. But during the winter months, when food is scarce, the kea turns to something else: sheep. Groups of kea will swoop down on a herd of sheep, pick out one unlucky victim, and take turns jumping onto its rump. There they use their curved, strong beaks to tear away the wool, pierce through the skin, and bore into the sheep's innards. (The bleating sheep is usually running around in terror at this point.) From there, the birds stick their heads inside the sheep and rip out chunks of succulent fat from around its kidneys. Given the chance, they'll even eat its organs and intestines. Sheep that have been attacked by keas sometimes die during the attack; more often, they die later of infection.

LOUSE GOT YOUR TONGUE?

The tongue-eating louse (*Cymothoa exigua*) is a marine *isopod*, a type of crustacean related to woodlice that lives in ocean waters and grows to about two inches in length. Why is it called a "tongue-eating louse"? Because it crawls into the gills of a rose snapper fish, makes its way to the base of the fish's tongue, sticks its claws into the tongue, and sucks the fluid out of it. The tongue eventually withers away completely, and the louse then attaches itself to the nub that's left. Surprisingly, the fish is not harmed by this process. More surprisingly, the louse actually becomes the fish's substitute tongue—the fish can even move it around using the muscles in the old tongue's nub. Open the mouth of a fish infested by *Cymothoa exigua*, and you'll see something you'd expect to see in a science-fiction film: a whitish creature with beady little black eyes looking out at you, wiggling its clawed legs. They're normally found only in the waters of the Gulf of California, but one was recently spotted in the mouth of a snapper...in London, England.

Barbie dolls sold in Japan have their lips closed, with no teeth showing.

SOCIAL NUTWORKING

Strange and crazy stories from the virtual worlds
of Facebook, Twitter, and MySpace.

TERRORISM IN 140 CHARACTERS OR LESS

Twenty-six-year-old Paul Chambers of Ireland was trying to catch a plane home, but it was delayed due to heavy snow at Robin Hood Airport in South Yorkshire, England. Chambers logged on to his Twitter account (a blogging site that allows you to "tweet" updates in 140 characters or less) and wrote an "amusing" message for his friends:

> Robin Hood airport is closed. You've got a week to get your s*** together, otherwise I'm blowing the airport sky high!!"

Another Twitterer saw the tweet and alerted police, who deemed it a threat and arrested Chambers a week later under the U.K.'s Terrorism Act. He said that he spent seven hours trying to explain Twitter to detectives before they released him. He was banned from Robin Hood Airport for life, was suspended from his job, and his iPhone, laptop, and home computer were confiscated.

@ THE ALTAR

Tracy Page was surprised when her brand-new husband, Dana Hanna, pulled out his cell phone—while their wedding was still going on—and posted this update to Twitter:

> Standing at the altar with @TracyPage where, just a second ago, she became my wife! Gotta go, time to kiss my bride.

Before he kissed her, the groom updated his Facebook status to "married." Then he pulled out Tracy's cell phone (which he'd also brought to the altar) and updated *her* Twitter and Facebook accounts. Only then did Dana kiss the bride. Said the priest: "If it's official on Facebook, it's official in my book."

DUMB AS A POST

A woman in Fort Loudoun, Pennsylvania, arrived home one afternoon in 2009 to find that someone had broken in to her house: A window was broken, cabinet doors were ajar, and her two diamond rings were gone. Then she noticed that her computer had been

---

That's all? A study by a U.S. research firm found that 40% of Twitter messages are "pointless babble."

turned on, and there was a Facebook page on the screen—belonging to one of her neighbors, 19-year-old Jonathan Parker. The woman called police, and they arrested Parker and recovered the two rings. During the burglary, Parker had stopped to check his Facebook page...and forgot to log off. He faces up to 10 years in prison.

IT'S NOT JUST *YOUR* SPACE
In 2009 a man robbed a bank in North Augusta, South Carolina. After a surveillance photo of the robber ran on the local news, police received a call from a viewer who said the suspect looked like his friend Joe Northington. On a tip, the cops checked Northington's MySpace page and saw this message running across the top:

> On tha run for robbin a bank! Love all of yall.

Northington's status was listed as "wanted." He was arrested and convicted.

COME ONE, COME ALL
In 2009 police were alerted to this invitation posted on Facebook by siblings Chris and Cassandra Phalen in Papillion, Nebraska:

A History Making House Party!
> Liquor, six kegs of beer, a DJ, professional photographer, and shuttle service. P.S. Don't worry about the cops, I have a police scanner so I will have the heads up if they come.

Undercover cops showed up at the party and arrested nine underage guests, along with the Phalens.

THIS THING DOES MORE THAN POST UPDATES?
Two girls, aged 10 and 12, got stuck in a storm drain in Australia in 2009. Despite their yells for help, no one came to their rescue. Finally, one of the girls had an idea—she took out her cell phone and used it to update her Facebook status:

> We're stuck in the storm drain! Call for help!

More than an hour later, firefighters showed up and freed the girls. Said one of the rescuers: "They could have just called us directly and we could have gotten there quicker than relying on someone being online and replying to them and eventually having to call us anyway."

MIGHTY UNICORNS VS. KONKRETE KIDS

Actual high-school team names.

PUNS
- **Poca Dots** (Poca High School, West Virginia)
- **Hot Dogs** (Frankfort, Indiana)
- **Deaf Leopards** (Arkansas School for the Deaf)
- **Fightin' Planets** (Mars, Pennsylvania)

SOUNDS DIRTY, BUT ISN'T (OR IS IT?)
- **Butte Pirates** (Arco, Idaho)
- **Cornjerkers** (Hoopeston, Illinois)
- **Purple Pounders** (Harrison, Tennessee)

NOT THAT INTIMIDATING
- **Pretzels** (New Berlin, Illinois)
- **Nimrods** (Watersmeet, Michigan)
- **Syrupmakers** (Cairo, Georgia)
- **Jugglers** (Utica, New York)
- **Bumblebees** (Little River, Texas)
- **Tractors** (Dearborn, MI)
- **Kewpies** (Hickman, Missouri)
- **Poets** (Montgomery, Alabama)
- **Mighty Unicorns** (New Braunfels, Texas)
- **Orphans** (Centralia, Illinois)

JUST ODD
- **Wooden Shoes** (Teutopolis, Illinois)
- **Sugar Beeters** (Chinook, Montana)
- **Golden Goblins** (Harrison, Arkansas)
- **Konkrete Kids** (Northampton, Pennsylvania)
- **Millionaires** (Williamsport, Pennsylvania)

In 2008 South Africa passed a law making it illegal for kids under the age of 16 to kiss.

ECCENTRIC WRITERS

We don't think it's so weird to do this stuff.
But then, we're writers.

• Poet **John Donne** (1572–1631) kept a coffin in the office where he wrote. Occasionally, he'd climb inside it to remind himself how fleeting life can be, a major theme in his poetry.

• **Jonathan Swift** (1667–1745), author of *Gulliver's Travels*, always walked around his house while he ate because he believed that moving around while eating would cancel out the food and help him keep weight off.

• In 2009 Sotheby's of London auctioned off a series of largely unpublished letters of the famous Romantic poet **Lord Byron** (1788–1824). In them, Byron criticizes the Portuguese, who he says have "few vices except lice and sodomy." And, in a display of bathroom humor well ahead of his time, he calls his rival William Wordsworth "Turdsworth."

• The Irish poet **William Butler Yeats** (1865–1939) suffered from chronic sexual dysfunctions. After dealing with the problem for many years, he did something about it—he had the "Steinach operation," a surgery that claimed to provide a "reactivation" of the male organs. It was basically just a vasectomy, but Yeats claimed that both his sex life and literary output greatly improved.

• American poet **James Russell Lowell** (1819–91), founding editor of *The Atlantic Monthly*, once attended a dinner party where he carefully removed each flower from a bouquet centerpiece and, with a knife and fork, ate every single one.

• Novelist **John Cheever** (1912–82) owned only one suit. He put it on each morning, then took an elevator down to the basement of his New York apartment building, where he rented an office. Once there, he took off the suit, hung it up, and wrote all day sitting in his underwear. At the end of the day, he'd put the suit back on and take the elevator home.

It is illegal to die in the U.K.'s Houses of Parliament, or to enter wearing a suit of armor.

ARE YOU A "DEAD PEASANT"?

Even if you don't think you have life insurance, a policy may have been taken out in your name. So is that good news? Probably not. Here's a look at one of the craziest tax-avoidance schemes in U.S. history. It's still legal and still in widespread use.

PAPER TRAIL

Not many people realized it at the time, but by the early 1990s it had become a common practice in many American corporations for the company to contact the estate of any employee who died and request a copy of the death certificate.

It made no difference if the death was work related or not. The deceased didn't even have to be a *current* employee—so what if they'd quit two years earlier, after only a few weeks on the job? The company wanted a copy of the death certificate just the same. Few companies bothered to explain why they needed the death certificates, and considering what they were up to, it's no wonder they kept it a secret. Not many bereaved families had the presence of mind to ask; those few families who learned what was going on usually found out by accident.

In the case of a banker named Dan Johnson, who died of brain cancer in 2008, that accident came when a letter addressed to Amegy Bank, his former employer, was damaged while being sorted at the post office. Johnson's name was listed on the letter, and the post office mistakenly forwarded it to his widow.

The letter contained a check for nearly $1.6 million. But it was payable to Amegy Bank, not to Johnson's heirs. The check was just one installment in a $4.7 million life insurance policy that Johnson's former employer had taken out on him—the company was cashing in on his death.

JANITOR INSURANCE

For decades it has been common for companies large and small to take out "key-person" life insurance policies on company presidents and other valuable employees who are difficult to replace.

Dan Johnson was hardly indispensable: The bank proved that when it demoted and then fired him after he got sick. By then, it was too late for him to buy his own insurance. But it wasn't too late for Amegy Bank: By pooling him with 40 other executives, the bank was able to take out a multimillion-dollar policy on him *after* he'd been diagnosed with terminal cancer.

In years past, it would not have even been possible for Amegy to take out a policy on Johnson because the bank had no "insurable interest" in him: It didn't stand to lose much if he died. But thanks to years of intensive lobbying by insurance companies, all that began to change in the late 1980s. In many states, regulations were loosened to allow companies to take out policies on any employee, no matter how lowly or unimportant, often without their knowledge or consent. Such policies became known inside the insurance industry as "janitor insurance" or "dead peasant insurance."

DEATH AND (NO) TAXES

Dead peasant policies had a lot to offer: The payment balance grew, tax-free, until the insured party died, and the after-death payout to the company was also tax-free, just as if it had gone to a widow or an orphan. If the company borrowed money to buy the policy, or borrowed against the policy's cash value, the loan payments were tax deductible. Under certain circumstances, a corporation could reduce its taxes by more than a dollar for every dollar it spent on dead peasant insurance.

With no requirements for disclosure, either to the employee or to corporate shareholders, it's difficult to know how many policies were taken out by the time the practice peaked in the mid-1990s. According to one insurance industry estimate, as many as six million American workers may have had policies taken out in their name.

Keeping track of employees after they quit or were fired was not a problem; all a company had to do was conduct quarterly "death runs" of insured employees' Social Security numbers to see if anyone had died, then collect death certificates from the next of kin and forward them to the insurance companies to cash out the policies.

ARE YOU DEAD YET?

Dead peasant policies created some appalling and cynical conflicts of interest: What's the incentive to provide a safe work environment if you collect a $400,000 payout every time one of your hourly employees falls off a creaky ladder or drops dead from a heart attack loading a big-screen TV into a customer's car? Why should a company improve its prescription drug coverage if doing so would make its insured employees live longer?

Dead peasant policies may actually have cost some workers their lives. In the early 1990s, Texas' Diamond Shamrock convenience-store chain upgraded security at its stores with bulletproof glass and other improvements, while a competing chain took money that could have been used for such upgrades and insured its store clerks for $250,000 each instead. Between 1991 and 1995, Diamond Shamrock had one on-the-job fatality; the competitor had nine.

THE PARTY'S OVER?

The IRS began to disallow some dead peasant tax deductions in the late 1990s, and Congress and state legislatures began closing the loopholes. And in many states, the next of kin retained some legal claim to life insurance policies where the purchaser of the policy had no insurable interest in the deceased. That wasn't much of a problem when the policies were a well-kept secret, but as the publicity generated by one horror story after another brought the policies out into the open, more families of the deceased began to sue. So did many "peasants" who weren't dead yet: Because life insurance policies have a cash value even while the insured is alive, many employees who'd had policies taken out against them without their consent filed suit to claim some of the cash for themselves.

FREEING THE SERFS

For many companies who held them, dead peasant policies became a nightmare. The publicity was devastating, and when all the closed loopholes and lawsuits were tallied up, many policies were now money losers. Wal-Mart alone lost $150 million on the 350,000 dead peasant policies it purchased between 1993 and 1995.

Dead peasant policies are still alive and well in the states that allow them. But federal law now requires companies to obtain the written consent of the insured; in all, it's estimated that today companies hold policies on as many as five million workers. At least these dead peasants have been informed that they're dead peasants, and have given their consent.

But does it really make them feel any better?

CRAZY WORD ORIGINS

*You'd be insane not to want to know where all these nutty
words for "crazy" came from—and how to properly
use them, so people don't think you're batty.*

CRAZY / CRACKED / CRACKPOT

The verb "to craze" originally meant "to violently shatter," and most likely came from an Old Norse word. It was first applied to people in 1555 to describe one who was "in ill health." The use of "crazed" and "crazy" to describe the mentally impaired came about 40 years later. The term "cracked," from the same root, was first applied to mental derangement around 1611. "Crackpot" is more recent, first appearing in the late 1800s. Often used to describe people with unusual ideas, it was short for "cracked pot"—"pot" having been a common slang term for "head" since the 16th century.

INSANE

The Latin word *sanus* means "healthy," but in English, the term "sane" wasn't attributed to a "healthy mind" until about 1600. About the same time, its opposite, "insane," also came into use. The term is no longer used by the medical establishment, who instead refer to a patient's specific mental illness (such as obsessive-compulsive disorder or schizophrenia). So, technically, no one can be clinically diagnosed as "insane."

BATTY

There are a few theories as to where this term came from. A popular one says that it was named for Fitzherbert Batty, a prominent English barrister known for being eccentric, who was certified insane in 1839. London's newspapers widely publicized the diagnosis, and ever since, "batty" has been used to describe anyone who is harmlessly crazy. Another possible origin is that "batty" is short for "bats in the belfry" (or bell tower), an Americanism dating to at least 1899, when it appeared in William J. Kountz's *Billy Baxter's Letters*: "The leader tore out about $9.00 worth of hair, and acted generally as though he had bats in his belfry."

NUTS

"Nut" in its original sense—peanuts and cashews, for instance—is a very old word, most likely coming from the Indo-European root *knu*, which meant "lump." The English word "nut" first appeared around A.D. 875, but wasn't used to refer to a person's head until the mid-1800s. Around the same time, anyone who acted a little off kilter was said to be "off his nut" or just "nuts." However, referring to a crazy person as a "nut" wasn't common until around 1903. (The British form, "nutter," didn't appear until the late 1950s.)

GIDDY

These days, we associate being giddy with being silly or in love. But at one time, being giddy could have gotten you locked up. It first appeared in Old English as the word *gydig*, meaning "insane" or "possessed." The root of "giddy" is, in fact, the same Germanic root that gave us the English word "god"—and originally, to be giddy was to be possessed by a god or other supernatural being.

BERSERK

Thought to be a combination of the Icelandic *ber* ("bear") and *serkr* ("shirt"), Berserkers were Norse warriors who wore bearskins into battle and were known for their terrifying, uncontrollable bloodlust. They were thought to have suffered actual fits of madness, referred to as *bärsärkar-gång* ("going berserk"), described here in Howard Frabing's *On Going Berserk: A Neurochemical Inquiry*:

> Men who were thus seized performed things which otherwise seemed impossible for human power...which at last gave over into a great rage, under which they howled as wild animals, bit the edge of their shields, and cut down everything they met without discriminating between friend or foe.

Today, we use "berserk" to describe out-of-control behavior.

Crazy for word origins? Go to page 226 for
"bonkers," "wacky," "madcap," and more.

THE SKIES HAVE EYES

Google Earth is a downloadable computer program that lets you view the world via satellite images, aerial photography, and a close-up "Street View" feature. It's great when you need to find a donut shop, but not so great when something unexpected gets caught in the photo.

• After photographing several U.K. cities for Street View, Google fielded hundreds of complaints from citizens who inadvertently wound up in photos—including a man caught exiting a sex shop, a man throwing up outside of a pub, and a group of teenagers getting arrested.

• Sharp-eyed Google Earth users noticed a collection of 40-year-old buildings in southern California that, from above, resembled a Nazi swastika. The owner of the structures: the U.S. Navy (the buildings were barracks on a military base). The Navy spent $600,000 to redesign the facility.

• While photographing for Street View in Melbourne, Australia, Google's car-mounted cameras captured a man passed out in his mother's front yard. The man, who'd had too much to drink after a funeral, later complained. Google removed the photos.

• Users scrolling through pictures of upstate New York on Street View noticed a deer fawn standing in the middle of a rural road. But in subsequent shots, the deer was lying in the road, dead, with blood-soaked tire tracks leading away from it. Google's camera car, it turned out, had accidentally hit it. The company kept the images, but edited out the deer.

• If you look closely, you can spot hundreds of photos that caught people urinating in public, including one with a French bus driver photographed relieving himself on the side of his bus.

• One Google Earth user was looking at photos of a female friend's house—and spotted her own husband's Range Rover out front. Divorce proceedings followed.

• At least one person was ready for the cameras: At Google's headquarters in California, a software engineer named Michael Weiss-Malik held up a large sign as the camera passed overhead. It read "Proposal 2.0: MARRY ME LESLIE!!" (Leslie said yes.)

The FDA announced in 2008 that milk from cloned cows may already be in the nation's food supply.

TERROR IN TOILET TOWN

In the last episode of Terror in Toilet Town, *we brought you "Snakes on a What?!," the true story of a woman in China who was bitten by a snake hiding in her toilet. Now, sit back for some brand-new episodes about the scariest room in the house.*

Episode: "Curses!"
Setup: One night in October 2007 in West Scranton, Pennsylvania, Dawn Herb was at home when her toilet started overflowing. As she tried to unclog it and clean up the mess, she let out a stream of bawdy curse words.

Terror! Herb's neighbor, off-duty police officer Patrick Tillman, stuck his head out his window and told her to "shut the f*** up." Not true, says Tillman; he simply told her to stop swearing, and Herb told *him* to "f*** off." In any case, Officer Tillman called in some fellow police officers—and Herb was arrested for swearing inside her own house. She was told that she faced up to $300 in fines and 90 days in jail for disorderly conduct. But at the hearing the judge ordered the charges dropped, ruling that swearing at a toilet in your own house was not illegal. Afterward, Herb sued the city of West Scranton for improper arrest—and they ended up awarding her $19,000, plus her legal fees, to settle. (Hopefully she got a new toilet.)

Episode: "Out with the Train Water"
Setup: In October 2009, a crowded train was rolling through the countryside of West Bengal, India. A pregnant passenger, Rinku Roy, felt a sudden pang that she thought might be a labor pain. She left her husband, Bhola, in his seat, went to the restroom… and had her baby.

Terror! In the cramped restroom, and in an awkward position, Roy had trouble grasping the slippery newborn and dropped it— straight down the toilet and onto the tracks below. She ran out of the toilet screaming for help, dashed to the closest exit, and jumped off the moving train. Quick-thinking passengers pulled emergency cords, stopping the train—and allowing Roy and her

---

Designer Amigo Zhou invented a Love Seat Toilet—attached potties for two to use at the same time.

husband to retrieve the baby. Mother and child were taken to a hospital, and, amazingly, both of them were fine.

Episode: "Toilet May be Armful to Your Health"
Setup: This story took place on a high-speed train traveling between the French cities of La Rochelle and Paris. But instead of a baby being dropped into a toilet, a 26-year-old Frenchman dropped his cell phone into one of the train's commodes. And he reached into the toilet to get the phone back.
Terror! The ultramodern train had an ultramodern toilet, equipped with a powerful, ultramodern, automatic suction system—and it pulled the man's arm into the drain nearly up to his shoulder. He yelled for help, attendants quickly arrived, and the train was stopped in order to shut off the suction system. But the man's arm had been pulled into the toilet with such force that he was still stuck. EMTs worked for two hours to remove the toilet from the floor, then took it—along with the man—to a hospital. It took several more hours to saw the toilet off the man's arm. (No word on whether he ever got his phone back.)

Episode: "(Cork)Screwed Again"
Setup: It was a dark and drinky night in Vershire, Vermont, in October 2009. Nazeih Hammouri, 53, was at home, drinking. Late in the evening, his 19-year-old son came home. Then someone used the toilet.
Terror! The toilet became clogged, and the intoxicated Hammourt and his son got into an argument about it. The fight escalated and finally ended with the elder Hammourt stabbing his son in the stomach…with a corkscrew. Hammourt was arrested on charges of first-degree assault. His son was treated and released at a nearby hospital.

Episode: "The Man *Under* the Moon"
Setup: In September 2009, a boy on a family camping trip in New Hampshire's White Mountain National Forest ran off to use the park's restroom, a rustic "pit toilet" with a large sewage container under the seat.
Terror! As the boy approached the toilet, he was amazed to see a

---

soaking-wet man climbing up out of the pit. The boy ran back to his parents, who called police. They easily caught Gary Moody, 49, (presumably by the smell). Moody told police that he put his shirt on the toilet seat for sanitary reasons before sitting down, and it had fallen in. He'd climbed down into the pit, he said, simply to get his shirt back. Police had trouble believing that—especially since the man had been arrested in the same park in 2005 for doing the same thing. Moody eventually admitted to having a pit-toilet fetish. He was arrested. (Bonus: Moody is from the town of Pittston, Maine.)

Episode: *"That's Cold!"*
Setup: One day in July 2008, Martin Bierbauer of the Austrian city of Eisenstadt was sitting on the toilet in his apartment. Everything was fine until…
Terror! …Bierbauer was blasted off the toilet by huge hailstones that came shooting out of it. "I heard the pipes rumbling a bit," he said later, "and suddenly hailstones the size of golf balls started exploding out of the toilet like it was a popcorn machine." The ice balls eventually covered the bathroom floor, then the entire apartment. The same thing, it turned out, was happening all over the building. The region had been recently struck by unusually high temperatures followed by a sudden cold snap, which resulted in violent hailstorms. City officials said the hailstones had clogged local drain systems, a heavy rain had followed, and pressure in the sewer system had built up. The hailstones had to go somewhere, so they started flying up out of toilets. Bierbauer and other residents demanded that the city pay for the extensive damage the toilet-stones had caused to their apartments.

*　　*　　*

FOR THE LOVE OF ANIMALS

In 2009 the Florida state senate was debating enforcement of bestiality laws, and the subject turned to animal husbandry—which simply means the breeding and raising of livestock. Senator Larcenia Bullard, however, thought it meant something else, and blurted out, "People are actually taking these animals as husbands?"

JUNGLE SPA

*Animals—they're not just for petting. They can help
you relax and make you pretty, too!*

SNAKES. For about $80, a California king snake will massage your shoulders at Ada Barak's health spa in Talmey El' Azar, Israel. At the same time, a corn snake will crawl all over your lower back, providing a deep-tissue massage. Then turn over, and small garter snakes will massage your face muscles. According to Madame Barak, "People either like having snakes slither around all over them, or they hate it."

CARP. $45 will buy you 15 minutes of "doctor-fish therapy" in a Tokyo spa. Here's how it works: You dangle your feet in a tank full of tiny carp called *chinchin yu*, or "doctor fish." They eat the dead skin flakes and calluses, leaving your feet soft and beautiful. But don't worry; these fish have no teeth and only dine on *dead* cells. The most common complaint about the therapy is that it tickles.

"VENOM." The poison of the Malaysian temple viper paralyzes its victims by blocking the nerve signals that cause muscles to contract. A new anti-wrinkle cream called BioVen is a "gently synthesized" version of the venom. Marketed as an alternative to Botox injections, BioVen does basically the same thing: It prevents your face muscles from contracting when you laugh, smile, or frown. "No wonder Hollywood celebrities are waiting in line for it!" says the commercial.

LEECHES. *Hirudo medicinalis*, the "medicinal leech," is black and slimy, measures four inches long, and has three jaws, each of them containing more than 100 tiny teeth. When attached to your skin, the leeches are said to suck out toxins, leaving you feeling fresh and revitalized. Leech therapy, which costs up to $600 and dates back to Ancient Egypt, was given a big boost in the U.S. after actress Demi Moore appeared on *The Late Show with David Letterman* in 2008 and bragged about having leech treatment in Austria. "It really detoxifies your blood," said Moore. "I'm feeling very detoxified right now."

ERNIE CHAMBERS SUES GOD

Only someone totally crazy would try to sue the Lord Almighty, right?
Certainly not a state senator with nearly 40 years' experience.

THE "ANGRIEST BLACK MAN IN NEBRASKA"
That's a label Ernie Chambers has worn proudly since he was first elected in 1970 to represent Nebraska's 11th district in the state legislature. Never one to shy away from controversy, Chambers, an Independent, once called the U.S. a "hypocritical society," saying, "The public doesn't look for politicians to tell the truth or to deliver on their promises, and politicians know this." Another favorite target was the Catholic Church, which Chambers once said was "more effective as a criminal enterprise than the mafia." Yet he still managed to get reelected eight times.

In the 2000s, Chambers didn't let up. But after the Nebraska legislature voted to limit state senators to two terms, Chambers was disqualified from running again in 2008. "They had to change the constitution to get rid of me," he said.

SUFFERING THE WRATH

But Chambers had one more big fight in him: In September 2007, he filed a lawsuit against "God Almighty," which sought a permanent injunction against the Lord from creating "fearsome floods, egregious earthquakes, horrendous hurricanes, terrifying tornadoes, pestilential plagues, devastating droughts, genocidal wars, birth defects, and the like." Chambers claimed these horrors affected his constituents, thus making it harder for the senator to do his job.

Case dismissed, right? Not so fast. Courts must take all lawsuits seriously, however ridiculous they seem. Dismissing it by denying the existence of God would have obvious PR ramifications in a deeply religious state. With this in mind, the judge needed a good reason to toss it out. The reason seemed clear enough: God was not a resident of Douglas County, so the court had no power to compel God to appear, and the case could be dismissed. So the case was dismissed, right? Not so fast.

A woman in France married her boyfriend in 2009. What's so odd about that? He died in 2008.

SEEKING THE LORD

Chambers refused to give up. He argued that God exists in all places, so it stood to reason that He should be considered a resident of Douglas County. The court countered that since God had no address, there was no way to send Him papers informing him the lawsuit had been filed. "As an all-knowing being," said Chambers, "God should already know that the lawsuit had been filed against Him." This back-and-forth continued as the courts tried every trick in the book to shut down the lawsuit: Did Chambers and God first attempt to resolve the issue out of court? Chambers said he'd tried to contact God on several occasions, and met with failure each time: "Despite reasonable efforts to effectuate personal service on Defendant, God has been unable to do so." Did God even exist? Chambers drew attention to the fact that in Nebraska, few state employees would be willing to deny the existence of God outright.

Was anyone taking this case seriously? Chambers said he was: "This is a lawsuit against a Defendant who has perpetrated much harm on the human race." Ironically, he said he actually wanted to bring attention to all of the frivolous lawsuits that were currently bottlenecking the judicial system. "Anybody can sue anybody, even God," he said. But both his proponents and his critics were unsure if Chambers was saying that was a good thing or not.

JUDGMENT DAY

The judge dismissed the case on the grounds that God could not be located and compelled to appear. Chambers, of course, appealed—and the arguments continued. Finally, in February 2008, Nebraska's Court of Appeals tossed out the lawsuit a second time, ruling that courts decide "real controversies, not abstract questions or issues that might arise in a hypothetical or fictitious situation or setting."

Chambers let the matter go, believing that he had successfully made his point. However, a few days later, a mysterious piece of paper appeared on a desk at the Douglas County courthouse. It contained a neatly typed, two-point response to Chambers' suit: 1) "God is currently outside the jurisdiction of a Nebraska state court." 2) "God is not subject to earthly laws." The document was reportedly signed by the almighty Himself, and witnessed by one "St. Michael the Archangel."

DEMENTED DENTISTS

It takes a special kind of person to take up a profession that involves putting your fingers inside strangers' mouths all day. And while most dentists are really good at what they do, the ones in this article may make you want to switch to false teeth.

BOGUS UNIVERSITY
A 2004 investigation in Italy discovered that you can't count on your dentist's diploma being real. Officials uncovered a ring of scammers, involving two dental schools in Rome, that sold fake diplomas to dental "students" for as much as $220,000 each. Investigators found evidence of false school-attendance records as well as test answers and term papers provided to students for a fee. Other university staff members were bribed with vacations, gifts, and bonuses to keep them quiet about the scam. Investigators are still trying to locate the dozens of dentists who are practicing without a degree.

TORTURE CHAMBERS—WITH FREE SWEATSHIRTS!
In 2004 twenty dentists in California's Central Valley area were accused of defrauding the state Medi-Cal health system of $4.5 million by performing unnecessary—and cruel—dental work. To lure low-income patients, these dentists went to homeless shelters, shopping malls, and schools and offered gift certificates, sweatshirts, and electric toothbrushes. The patients were then given unnecessary dental work, including root canals. Some dentists were accused of holding crying children down in the dental chair and using straps on elderly patients. Then they charged outlandish amounts of money for the work and sent the bills to Medi-Cal. "In every single one of the 300 files we checked," said an official, "we found fraud." In 2008 the two lead dentists in the scam were sentenced to one year in jail and forced to repay $3 million.

LAUGHING MATTER
On Long Island, New York, a patient (name not released in press reports) showed up for his dentist appointment, but the waiting room was empty. "Is anyone here?" he asked. No one answered, so

---

British businesses lose $260 million of productivity per day from workers surfing the Web.

the man walked into the back, where he found the dentist, Norman Rubin, lying on the floor. According to police, "He was unresponsive and drooling, and had the gas mask on his face." Rubin was later charged with "inhalation of hazardous inhalants." He blamed the incident on a migraine, but admitted, "It was a mistake." An investigation found that his license had been suspended several times, which he blamed on "six disgruntled patients."

WHAT A TOOL

Donna Delgado of Tampa, Florida, had dental surgery in 2008. In the weeks and months afterward, she suffered from frequent nosebleeds and sinus infections. A year later, Delgado was still in pain, so she went to another dentist…who discovered that a one-inch steel dental tool had been left inside her right maxillary sinus. It was removed, and Delgado's symptoms disappeared (although she may have nickel poisoning). A lawsuit is pending.

AT LEAST HE'S NOT A PILOT

In June 2004, Dr. Colin McKay of Halton, England, drank six glasses of wine at lunch and then performed a tooth extraction on Andrea Harrison. It didn't go well. It took McKay two tries to inject the anesthetic into her gums, then he started the procedure before Harrison's mouth became completely numb. "I was in a lot of pain and yelled, but he carried on," she said. "Then he seemed to fall over me. I ended up running out." Another dentist finished the extraction; McKay was found guilty of professional misconduct.

YANK!

"Dr. Allena Burge pulled teeth so hard and fast, the patients' blood would spray," her assistant, Janet Popelier, told investigators. "Sometimes parts of the jawbone or mandible would break." Why did the Florida dentist have to work so fast? "She was trying to make $12,000 a day from Medicaid. I saw many half-conscious, bleeding patients led out the back door soon after their surgeries to make room for new patients." Burge was charged with fraud and malpractice. (She even let her 12-year-old son administer anesthesia.) In just four years, she filed more than 57,000 Medicaid claims totaling $6.6 million. No word on the investigation's outcome, but at last report, Burge was still practicing dentistry.

OVEREXTENDED

Just because a company is good at selling one thing doesn't mean consumers will buy something else from them. While some "brand extensions" make sense—Hershey's chocolate milk, for example—others, like these, are just weird.

- Cheetos lip balm

- Colgate frozen dinners

- Tootsie Roll earphones

- Humane Society Dog Lovers' Wine Club

- Sony PlayStation snacks

- Harley Davidson perfume

- LifeSavers soda

- Donald Trump steaks

- Bumble Bee chicken

- Frito-Lay lemonade

- *Cosmopolitan* yogurt

- Smith & Wesson bicycles

- Burger King underwear

- *Girls Gone Wild* clothing

- Jeff Gordon wine

- Sylvester Stallone's High Protein Pudding

- Disney's *Sleeping Beauty* executive fountain pen ($1,200)

- Snoop Dogg pet accessories

- Barbie clothing…for adult women

- Pierre Cardin cigarettes

- Hooters Airline

- Salvador Dali deodorant

- Willie Nelson biodiesel fuel

- Diesel Jeans wine

- Starburst shampoo

- Precious Moments coffins

- Disney milk

- *Chicken Soup for the Soul* dog food

AHHHH!!!

And we don't mean "Ahhhh" as in, "this feels really good," but "Ahhhh!!!" as in, "Something just scared the @&# out of me!"*

SETUP: One night in November 2009, a thief in Wuppertal, Germany, decided to steal a Mercedes Transporter van. What the thief didn't know was that…

AHHHH! …an African lion was in the back of the van. The vehicle belonged to an entertainment company called Circus Probst and was fitted with a special cage in the back. The lion, a five-year-old male named Caesar, was being transported to a new circus site. Police found the van the next day, a few miles away from where it was stolen. Whoever had taken it had crashed it into a road sign and run away, leaving the engine running. Police said they assumed that Caesar had stayed quiet at the beginning of the escapade, then suddenly roared and scared the wits out of the thief. The thief was not caught; Caesar was fine.

SETUP: In September 2009, Mike Cunning and his five-year-old daughter, Caleigh, were fishing from a dock in Vancouver, British Columbia. Cunning was cleaning fish; Caleigh was sitting on the edge of the dock a short distance away, when…

AHHHH! …a seal jumped out of the water, grabbed Caleigh's hand in its mouth, and pulled her into the water. Cunning only heard the splash and looked over to see that his daughter was gone. Caleigh popped up out of the water a few seconds later, screaming "Daddy! The seal! The seal!" Cunning scooped up the girl, who was bleeding profusely, and rushed her to an emergency room. She was treated for four deep puncture wounds to her hand. Caleigh asked her father why the seal would do such a thing. Cunning answered that maybe the seal wanted to go swimming with her. "She thought about that for a second," he later told reporters, "and said, 'Well, I think the seal was rude for not asking first.'"

SETUP: On the afternoon of November 9, 2009, eight-year-old Brianna Adams of New Market, Maryland, came home from school and told her mother that there was something in her eye. Her mother told her it was probably just an eyelash, but a short time later, Brianna complained again. Her mom agreed to have a look. She gently pulled Brianna's upper eyelid open and...

AHHHH! ...saw a tick in her daughter's eye. "When I opened up her eye and saw a tick and all the legs were moving," mom Christina Beachner said, "I almost fell on the floor." It was stuck tight, so she rushed Brianna to the hospital, where doctors—who said they had never seen or even heard of such a thing before—put some ointment in the eye and covered it with a patch, hoping the tick would back itself out. (It was actually embedded in the *fornix*, a thin membrane between the eye and eyelid.) By the next day, the tick hadn't moved, so the medical team had to anesthetize Brianna's eye, pry the eyelid open, grab the tiny creature with forceps, and pull it out. Brianna's eye was fine—and she even asked to keep the tick to show her classmates. (She named it Hurt because "it hurt my eye.")

SETUP: A pilot for the Silver Falcons, an aerobatic-flying group affiliated with the South African Air Force, was giving a civilian friend a ride in one of the group's two-seater jets. During a tricky and stomach-turning maneuver, the friend, apparently trying to steady himself, accidentally pulled a lever near his feet and...

AHHHH! ...found out that it was the emergency ejection lever when he was instantly blasted out of the jet's canopy and shot into the sky. After he and the rocket-propelled seat had flown about 300 feet, a parachute deployed, and the man floated unharmed (if embarrassed) down to the ground. Air Force officials reprimanded the pilot for taking a civilian on one of their planes, and they'd make whatever changes were necessary to the ejection system to ensure that such accidents would not happen in the future.

*   *   *

"I feel pretty lucky. Thousands of people die every single day, and it's not me."

—Sarah Silverman

Scientists have created a genetically modified mouse that can run nonstop for five hours.

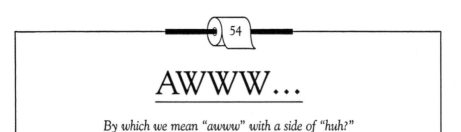

AWWW...

By which we mean "awww" with a side of "huh?"

SETUP: A 21-year-old college student and Army reservist was walking home from work in Milwaukee, Wisconsin, late one night in 2009 when four men confronted him. They dragged him into an alley, held a gun to his head, forced him to lie facedown on the pavement, and took his cell phone, wallet, keys, and $16 in cash. But then...

AWWW: ...as the muggers were about to leave, one of them ordered the others to stop—and told them to give the young man his belongings back. And the robber apologized. Why the change of heart? While he was going through the wallet, the mugger had seen his victim's Army ID. He said he would never rob a soldier, and the other muggers thanked their would-be victim for his service and walked away—and one of them even gave him a fist bump. (The soldier's name was not released; the robbers still had his keys, which he hoped to get back.)

SETUP: A cat named Arthur, owned by Robert and Mavis Bell of Wigan, England, passed away one day in January 2008. The couple's 18-month-old dog, a Lancashire Heeler named Oscar, whom they described as Arthur's "best friend."

AWWW: The day after Arthur died, the Bells woke up to find the deceased cat lying in Oscar's basket at the dog's side. The dog had snuck out through the cat door during the night and dug up Arthur from his backyard grave. Oscar had then dragged him back inside and cleaned him up. "Arthur's coat was gleaming white," Robert Bell said. "Oscar had obviously licked him clean. It must have taken him nearly all night." The Bells got Oscar a new friend—a kitten named Limpet—and reburied Arthur in what they said was a much more secure grave.

SETUP: In 1944 British soldiers participating in the invasion of Normandy, France, found a 20-year-old German soldier hiding in a foxhole. Heinrich Steinmeyer, a member of the notorious Nazi combat force Waffen-SS, was sent to a maximum-security POW camp in Perthshire County, Scotland, where only the most dangerous Nazis were imprisoned. At the end of the war, Steinmeyer was released, but decided to stay in Scotland and ended up living in the village of Comrie, not far from the site of the camp, for seven years before returning to Germany.

AWWW: In 2009, 65 years after he was captured by the British, the ex-Nazi notified Comrie officials that he was planning to leave his fortune, about $670,000, to the little Scottish village. He said he wanted the money to be used to assist the town's elderly residents. "I always wanted to pay something back," Steinmeyer said. "The people were very kind to us German POWs. They did not treat us as the enemy." Steinmeyer also left instructions that when he dies, he wants his ashes scattered in the hills around the site of the former Scottish war prison.

SETUP: In March 2009, 55-year-old woman named Montse Ventura boarded the Number 64 bus in Barcelona, Spain. A woman seated across from her looked at her for a few minutes, then leaned forward and told Ventura that she'd better get to a doctor. She needed to be tested for a condition called *acromegaly*, the woman said, which causes an excess in growth hormone due to a tumor on the pituitary gland. "She wrote something down and said, 'Have the analysis done as soon as possible,'" Ventura later told a Spanish newspaper, "because if you wait until you feel the need to the consult your doctor, you may already be in a very bad state.'"

AWWW: Ventura showed her doctor the note and asked for the tests that the stranger had recommended. The results came back abnormal…and further testing found a tiny tumor on her pituitary gland. It was successfully removed.

FOLLOW-UP: A media campaign to find the woman Ventura called her "guardian angel" followed, and several months later, a 60-year-old endocrinologist named Maria Gloria Prat finally came forward. She said she had made the bus-seat diagnosis based on the shape of Ventura's hands. "The hands gave me a lot of clues," she said. "I wasn't sure whether to say anything—but I am a very spontaneous person." The paper said that the two women would meet after the media hype had died down.

ODD THEME PARKS

*You could go to Disneyland and have fun...or you
could go to one of these perplexing places.*

BON BON LAND

Bon Bon is a Danish company that makes candy with a toilet-humor theme (its most popular product is something called "Dog Fart"). Bon Bon Land, the fourth-largest amusement park in Denmark, takes all of Bon Bon's cartoon-animal mascots and turns them into rides and attractions. The signature ride is the Dog Fart roller coaster, which winds around giant mounds of dog doo, pooping dogs, and giant speakers that play fart noises. Other attractions include a roller coaster through a sewer filled with (fake) feces and vomiting rats, and statues of buxom cows and dogs lifting their legs.

DICKENS WORLD

Almost all of Charles Dickens's literature takes place in a grimy, drab 19th-century England plagued by disease, starvation, and dirty orphans. And at Dickens World in Chatham, England, you can relive that horrible era. In addition to rides based on bleak Dickens books such as *Oliver Twist*, there's a *Great Expectations* boat ride, the Haunted House of Ebenezer Scrooge, a pawnshop, and a debtor's prison. Throughout the park, hired actors pose as hungry, filthy street urchins.

LOVE LAND

The claim to fame of this park, located on Jeju Island in South Korea, is its 140 giant, sexually explicit sculptures. It's designed to be educational; neither South Korea's schools nor its popular culture offer much in the way of sex education, and arranged marriages are still commonplace. So this park was opened by the art department of Hongik University as a honeymoon destination. Theoretically, newlyweds are supposed to study and learn from the imposing white sculptures of giant reproductive organs and people engaged in various sexual positions. No kiddie rides here; you must be 18 or older to enter.

SPACE JUNK

Imagine a shiny screw—just a screw—tumbling through space. Ahead is a man, oblivious, protected only by his spacesuit. He takes a break from his work to admire the view of the blue-green Earth hanging in the blackness of...WHAM!—the screw pierces the man's leg and shoots out the other side! He screams as the oxygen is sucked from his lungs... and the blood-red screw continues on its way.

OUT OF SIGHT, OUT OF MIND

A vast junkyard of potentially lethal projectiles surrounds our planet, and it's been accumulating since the 1950s. For decades, space programs in the United States, the U.S.S.R., and other nations followed a similar process: Build a satellite, attach it to a rocket, and blast it into space. Once out of Earth's atmosphere, the satellite separated from the rocket and went into its planned orbit. But what happened to the rocket? No one gave it too much thought; after all, space is big, and rockets are tiny in comparison. And so, too, are the satellites, which had only limited battery life to begin with. So all that equipment floated in space, and there was no plan in place to dispose of it. Occasionally, left-over fuel would build up pressure in an unventilated tank and cause an explosion. When that happened, what was once a rocket transformed into a cloud of floating debris. And as more countries joined the space race, even more rockets and satellites were launched into orbit.

Today, in addition to about 900 operational satellites, there are nearly 2,500 derelict ones up there. The oldest of them is the second satellite the United States ever launched, *Vanguard 1*, which has been orbiting Earth since March 17, 1958.

TOO MANY ODO'S IN THE LEO

The part of space that is most crowded with old junk is, not surprisingly, the part that's easiest to get to and the most useful to us. More than half of all satellites—along with the International Space Station and any spacecraft that happen to be flying—circle the planet within a range of altitude called *Low Earth Orbit* (LEO), which stretches from about 124 to 1,240

Eeew! International Space Station astronauts change their underwear only twice a week.

miles up. (By comparison, the moon is more than 200,000 miles away.)

The problem with filling this most useful of altitudes with junk is that the junk doesn't just float around harmlessly up there; it's actually moving incredibly fast—at an orbital speed of up to 17,000 miles per hour. At speeds like that, even the smallest debris particle can cause significant damage to whatever it hits; tiny flecks of paint and pieces of grit have been shown to pit the surface of expensive satellites. And a direct collision with any-thing larger than about a half-inch in diameter could actually destroy a satellite—or, for that matter, a manned spacecraft.

To counter these dangers, NASA and other space agencies try to catalog and track every piece of junk they can. The United States Space Surveillance Network monitors the location of more than 19,000 individual orbital debris objects (ODOs). But, unfor-tunately, the network can't track anything smaller than about four inches across. NASA estimates there could be as many as 500,000 ODOs that are big enough to wreck a spacecraft but too small to track from Earth.

THE KESSLER SYNDROME

It wasn't until the late 1970s that the space program looked at this problem head-on, after NASA scientist Donald Kessler and his colleagues warned that LEO could become so crowded that it would no longer be safe to launch new missions. If an item as small as an old bolt or screw could destroy a spacecraft, Kessler told them, imagine what an entire defunct satellite could do.

In February 2009, scientists had the opportunity to find out: A 2,000-pound decommissioned Russian satellite crashed into a still-operational 1,200-pound American model, obliterating both crafts and turning them into a dense cloud of dangerous debris. That event—the rendering of two large objects into thousands of small-er ones, each capable of going out on its own to destroy other spacecraft—is called the *Kessler syndrome*. Space junk multiplies at a constantly accelerating pace: More junk equals more collisions, and more collisions mean more junk. Even if humans never launch another rocket, the number of ODOs will still continue to multiply.

Not helping matters, in 2007 the Chinese government shot

down an old communications satellite, presumably just to show they could do it. The test, which was deemed a success by the Chinese, added thousands of objects to the catalogue of ODOs. The following year, the United States also shot down one of its own satellites—supposedly because it was on a course to crash back to Earth with a full tank of toxic fuel. Now it's 1,000 toxic bits and pieces.

In 2009 the danger of space junk made big news when three crew members aboard the International Space Station had to evacuate into a waiting spacecraft because a five-inch chunk of an old rocket was heading straight for them. Thankfully, it missed. Afterward, NASA acknowledged that debris comes close enough to the station to cause concern several times per month, and the station has to take evasive action to avoid a collision about once a year.

FAR OUT

Unfortunately, the technology to clean up LEO doesn't exist yet. But there is good news: The closer an object is to Earth, the less time it will last up there. The reason: The planet's atmosphere, thin as it is at very high altitudes, exerts drag on objects in orbit, causing them to slow down. As they decelerate, they fall and typically burn up as they enter the thicker lower atmosphere.

Moving farther away from the planet, however, that atmospheric drag decreases exponentially—just a small change in altitude translates into a large difference in how long an object can expect to remain in orbit. A piece of space junk that would last only a few months at 150 miles up could last for years at 600 miles, decades at 800 miles, and centuries at 1,000 miles.

Because of this, most new satellites are designed to fire their rockets one last time when they come to the end of their operational lives. The blast moves them either low enough that they will crash back into the atmosphere, or up into a "graveyard orbit" of more than 22,000 miles—high enough that they are thought to be out of the way (for now).

MORE DIRT ON SPACE JUNK

Along with old satellites and booster rockets, there's a lot of other random stuff hurtling through space. For example:

- **480 million copper needles:** Launched by the U.S. military in 1963, the needles, which were only the width of a hair, were meant to disperse around Earth and act as a sort of giant space antenna. It was hoped that this system would replace undersea cables for transatlantic communications, and it worked...for a while. Then the needles drifted a little too far apart and the radio signal gradually weakened, rendering the needles obsolete.

- **Nuclear reactors:** The United States put only one nuclear reactor in space, in 1965, but it's still orbiting about 700 miles up. The Soviet Union, on the other hand, shot more than 30 nuclear-powered spy satellites into orbit between 1967 and 1988. Aside from a few accidents (including one that crashed into Canada in 1978), the reactor cores were shut down and boosted into a grave-yard orbit at the end of their lives.

- **Tiny droplets of radioactive liquid:** When those Russian spy satellites shot their reactor cores into a graveyard orbit, there was often some coolant loss...leaving behind millions of globules of radioactive goo.

- **Stuff dropped by astronauts:** In 1965 Ed White became the first American to walk in space. Tethered to his Gemini space capsule, White lost his grip on a spare glove and could only watch as it floated away. Spacewalking astronauts have been dropping things ever since. Among the lost items: cameras, springs, screws, bolts, grease guns, pliers, and, oddly enough, a spatula.

- **Other astronaut "stuff":** On manned spacecraft, urine and fecal matter is (to use a nautical term) "dumped over the side." In September 2009, the Space Shuttle *Discovery* discharged 150 pounds of waste (about 10 days' worth that had built up while the shuttle was docked with the International Space Station). Viewing conditions were just right—the liquid portion of the waste crystallized into a majestic plume that was visible from Earth.

*   *   *

"Transported to a surreal landscape, a young girl kills the first woman she meets and then teams up with three complete strangers to kill again."

—The *San Fran. Chronicle's* TV listing for *The Wizard of Oz*

The Dinner in the Sky company offers fine dining at a table suspended 150 feet in the air.

BAD LIARS

This article was originally attributed to William Faulkner but turned out to be the work of a BRI office drone, Fern Gurgleman. Nevertheless, enjoy these other stories of blatant fakery.

WARHOL'S BALDWIN PERIOD

In February 2008, a fine-art collector bought six Andy Warhol paintings from a pair of art dealers at a bargain price of $100,000. But after the sale, the collector started wondering about the low price, so he took one of the pieces to an appraiser. Almost instantly, the appraiser could tell it was a fake because of two clues: First, it was signed "Andy Warhol, 1996"—nine years after Warhol's death. And second, the painting was not, as the sellers had claimed, a portrait of Matthew Baldwin, of the famous Baldwin acting family. How did he know? Because there is no Matthew Baldwin of the famous Baldwin acting family.

IT'S A HORSE (OF COURSE)

Shenyang Botanical Park, a small zoo in China, scored a major coup in 2007 when it acquired a zebra. They proudly showed it off and charged visitors the equivalent of 60 cents to have their picture taken with the exotic African animal. One problem: It was obvious to almost anyone that it was a white horse with black stripes sloppily painted on it. When pressed by a reporter, a zoo official said, "It's from Africa. What do you call it if it's not a zebra?" The "zebra" is still available for pictures and rides.

FOXY FOOTAGE

In 2009 Fox News host Sean Hannity showed video from a November anti-healthcare reform rally in Washington, D.C. that had "20,000 to 45,000 protestors." The next night, Jon Stewart observed on Comedy Central's *The Daily Show* that in the video, the colorful fall leaves switched to summer green: "Did they just put two different rallies together?" Stewart was right; Fox added footage from a much larger summer protest to make it appear that more than a few thousand people showed up to the fall protest. "It pains me to say this," said Hannity, "but Stewart was right."

A Japanese company offers a "Dial-A-Flattery" service for people who need a compliment.

TWIN TOWN

IItt"ss aa mmeeddiiccaall mmyysstteerryy..

PAIR-ADISE
For parents expecting a baby, finding out that they're having twins can be both a joy and a financial burden. And no one knows that feeling better than the residents of a village called Kodinji in Northern India, also known as "Twin Village." The town is home to nearly 250 sets of twins…out of only 2,000 families, giving it, by far, the highest ratio of twin births in the world—six times the global average. But why? A local group called TAKA (Twins and Kins Association) is trying to figure out what's going on.

WHAT'S GOING ON?
No one knows for sure why Kodinji has become the twin capital of the world. "It's an amazing phenomenon. The people are not exposed to any kinds of harmful drugs or chemicals," said Dr. Krishnan Sribiju, who's working with TAKA to study the village. The locals don't eat a special diet, either. And genetic causes seem unlikely, since people who grew up elsewhere and move there as adults are also more likely to have twins. But many women raised in Kodinji who then moved to other places have continued to have multiple births.

DRINK IT UP
So with all of the usual suspects of twin-making ruled out, there is one prevailing theory: It's the water. Kodinji is almost surrounded by it, and during monsoon season, the village is often completely cut off. But so far, tests of the water supply have proven inconclusive.

It appears, though, that scientists will have plenty of time to study the phenomenon—because the twin birth rate in Kodinji is actually *rising*. As of early 2010, five more women in the village were pregnant with twins. "The more the merrier," says Bushara Mohammed Kutty, the mother of a set of twins *and* a set of triplets. She then adds, "provided you have the wherewithal."

Fastest-growing language in the galaxy, according to *Time* magazine: Klingon.

LET'S DO A STUDY

However you describe these research projects—goofy, offensive—
they all beg the question: Did someone really need to spend
all that time and money to tell us that...

D UCKS LIKE RAIN
Says Who: Marian Dawkins, Oxford University,
2009
Study: British scientists gave a group of ducks full access to a
pond, a water trough, and a shower. They found that the ducks
preferred standing under the shower to standing in still water. The
three-year study cost more than half a million dollars.

BARTENDERS ARE LIKELY TO DRINK TOO MUCH
Says who: Eric Goplerud, George Washington University
Medical Center, Washington, D.C., 2008
The study: Fifteen percent of bartenders and cocktail waitresses
abuse alcohol—the highest level of any industry. By comparison,
only 5.4% of teachers, nurses, and social workers are problem
drinkers. The likely cause, according to this statistical study:
"Proximity to and availability of alcohol."

DISTRACTIONS MAKE IT HARDER TO LEARN
Says who: Russell Poldrack, UCLA, 2006
The study: Subjects were given a set of cards and asked to mentally keep track of shapes drawn on the cards. In a separate test,
they were given a new set of cards to sort but were also fed a series
of low- and high-pitched beeps through earphones. They were
then asked to keep count of the high-pitched beeps while they
sorted the cards. The results showed that subjects had better recall
when they performed only one task at a time.

MEN PREFER TO PEE ALONE
Says who: R. Dennis Middlemist, Eric S. Knowles, Charles F.
Matter, Journal of Personality and Social Psychology, 1976
The study: Researchers asked 60 men to urinate in a public lava-

---

Scientists in England built the world's smallest snowman—smaller than the width of a human hair.

tory and measured their *micturation times* ("time of intent" to "start of flow") according to how closely an assistant unknown to the subject stood nearby. Three "personal space" comfort levels were used: adjacent, one urinal removed, and out of the room. With no one there, it took an average of 4.8 seconds for subjects to start peeing. With someone one urinal away, 6.2 seconds. With someone right there: 8.4.

STUPID FLIES LIVE LONGER

Says who: Tadeusz Kawecki, Joep Burger, University of Lausanne, Switzerland, 2008

The study: One group of fruit flies was left alone; the other group was given tasks, and the flies who showed the most intelligence were bred to each other to produce more "smart" flies. After generations, the flies in the "stupid" colony lived an average of 80 to 85 days, but the "smart" flies lived for only 50 to 60 days. Why? Because, the study concluded, a more active brain requires more fuel…and therefore burns out its body's reserves faster (at least if you're a fruit fly).

UGLY DEFENDANTS GET CONVICTED MORE

Says who: Sandie Taylor, Bath Spa University, England, 2007

The study: Ninety-six volunteers were asked to read a transcript of a mugging case. Half were shown a photograph of an attractive suspect, the other half a picture of a not-so-attractive suspect. Both groups were asked to render a verdict. The good-looking subject was let off far more often than the less attractive suspect.

JAMES BOND DOESN'T PREFER BLONDES

Says who: Kimberly Neuendorf, Cleveland State University, 2009

The study: For a 2009 article in the journal *Sex Roles*, Neuendorf and her team analyzed the physical traits of 195 female characters from the first 20 James Bond films. Of the 97 women he was "intimate" with, only 27 percent were blonde and 15 percent were redheads. It turns out 007 prefers brunettes—59 percent of "Bond girls" had black or brown hair.

Smallest Texas state park: The .006-acre zone around the grave of Davy Crockett's second wife.

CANADIAN GANGLAND

*Canada: the land of big lakes, lots of snow, friendly people—
and a whole bunch of dangerous, violent gangs.*

BACKGROUND
Most people don't think of Canada as a place where violent gangs roam the streets, but in the past two decades,
the number of gangs in the country has grown exponentially.
Today there are today literally thousands of them, and their turf
wars and drive-by shootings make the headlines more and more
often. Here's a rundown of some of the most notorious—and
dangerous—of them all.

Gang: Indian Posse (IP)
Base: Winnipeg, Manitoba
History: Indian Posse, believed to be the first "aboriginal gang"
(or "First Nations" gang), was founded by a handful of disaffected
teenagers in Winnipeg around 1990. IP quickly grew from a petty-
theft operation into a criminal powerhouse specializing in drug
trafficking, robbery, and prostitution on reservations, in cities, and
inside prisons. Today it's the largest of the many existing aboriginal gangs, with hundreds of full-fledged members and many more
"associates" who can be identified by their red bandannas and "IP"
tattoos. IP members are believed to be responsible for hundreds of
violent crimes, including many murders, mostly of rival gang
members in drug wars. Co-founder Richard Wolfe was sentenced
to 19 years in prison for armed robbery and attempted murder in
1996, and still maintains a leadership position from his cell.

Gang: The Galloway Boys, or G-Way
Base: Scarborough, a section of Toronto, Ontario
History: In 2000 this small but deadly gang was founded by a
youth named Tyshan Riley, who, at the age of 18, became one of
Scarborough's leading gangsters. In 2002 a high-ranking G-Way
associate was shot to death by members of their main rivals, the
Malvern Crew, from Toronto's nearby Malvern district. That led
to a gang war that saw dozens of drive-by shootings and several

murders. In 2004, after a two-year undercover police investigation, Riley and 16 other G-Way members were arrested. Riley alone was charged with 39 offenses, including three murders and five attempted murders. He and two other members were convicted of first-degree murder in July 2009, and each was sentenced to two consecutive life sentences.

Gang: Mad Cowz
Base: Winnipeg, Manitoba
History: This gang formed in the early 2000s around crack dealing in Winnipeg's crime-ridden west end. Members are African Canadians, most of them refugees from nations ruined by decades of civil war, such as Somalia and Sudan. New members are recruited from recently arrived immigrants, mostly teenagers already accustomed to violence. The gang quickly became a successful, wealthy, and dangerous force in the city. In late 2005, their success led to a split, and a new rival gang, the African Mafia, was born. That same year, the son of a prominent Manitoba surgeon was shot and killed in the streets by battling Mad Cowz and African Mafia members. His death dominated local news for weeks, and a resulting police crackdown put most of the Mad Cowz' leadership behind bars. Still, they continue to operate in the city and in prisons.

Gang: Ace Crew
Base: Ottawa, Ontario
History: Formed sometime in the early 1990s, the Ace Crew was involved in activities common to most gangs, including drug dealing and extortion, but they became infamous all over Canada in August 1995 when they abducted four teenagers in retaliation for a perceived slight to the gang by one of the teens. They tortured all four and murdered 17-year-old Sylvain Leduc. Ace Crew member John Wartley Richardson was sentenced to life in prison for the murder, with an additional 73 years added for other crimes. The gang faded, but some members are still active in Ottawa.

Gang: The Independent Soldiers, or IS
Base: Vancouver, British Columbia
History: IS became an organized gang in the early 2000s and is

---

The 9/11 attacks in New York and the 2004 train bombings in Madrid were 911 days apart.

now one of Canada's most well-known gangs. The membership is multiracial, but the leaders are Indo-Canadians; the gang grew up out of Vancouver's large Punjabi Sikh community. Dealing in drugs, prostitution, gun-running, and money laundering, the gang has spread across British Columbia and into several towns in neighboring Alberta. IS has been linked to hundreds of shootings and dozens of murders, mostly in Vancouver, since 2005. In January 2009, a crackdown on Mexican drug cartels led to a brutal war between the IS and other Vancouver gangs over dwindling drug supplies, with more than 100 shootings and stabbings and more than a dozen murders in just two months.

EXTRAS

• A 2008 report by the Royal Canadian Mounted Police (RCMP) said that gang members involved in international drug smuggling had infiltrated airports in major cities around the country. Most were working as baggage handlers.

• More than 130 gangs are based in Vancouver alone, vying for a drug business estimated to be worth more than $6 billion per year.

• In the late 1990s, Toronto police arrested four members of the Spadina Girls, a short-lived, all-female gang led by a 16-year-old girl. The gang consisted entirely of high schoolers, who, among other things, charged other students for protection. The arrests came after gang members brutally assaulted a fellow student at a billiard hall.

• A much more dangerous all-female gang has formed in recent years: the Indian Posse Girls, an offshoot of Indian Posse. They're believed to be in control of the sex trade in Winnipeg and Edmonton.

• Canada's Criminal Intelligence Service estimates that more than 11,000 Canadians are members of street gangs.

*   *   *

WE'RE IN THE WRONG BUSINESS

Most cell-phone carriers charge customers 20 cents for each text message. Actual cost to the provider: about a third of a cent. That's a markup of 6,000 percent.

Philips Design sells an emotion-sensing bracelet. It lights up when you're stressed.

CAN WE PLEASE HAVE OUR (BLANK) BACK?

*If you guessed the missing word was "lung,"
you're on the right track.*

Can We Please Have Our ROAD SIGNS Back? Police in Lincoln, Nebraska, went to a garage sale in May 2009 at the home of 42-year-old Bradley Hillhouse. And they arrested him. Why? Because he was selling road signs, 47 of them, that were owned by either local cities or the state of Nebraska. Possession of road signs is a Class II misdemeanor in Nebraska, punishable by up to six months in jail and $1,000 in fines (for each sign). Police had learned about the signs because Hillhouse had posted photos of them, and himself, on the Web site Craigslist to advertise the garage sale.

Can We Please Have Our TWO-HEADED TURTLE Back?
Sean Casey, owner of the Hamilton Dog House pet shop in Brooklyn, New York, reported in August 2008 that the store's pet turtle, which had two heads, had disappeared from the shop. Casey had gotten the yellow-bellied cooter turtle from someone in Florida, he said, who had hatched it from rescued eggs after the mother turtle was killed by a car. Two-headedness is very rare in turtles, Casey said, adding that he'd take the turtle back without asking any questions because he was worried that it wouldn't get the special care it needed. It had to be kept in shallow water, for example, and because the two independently thinking heads didn't work together, it was unable to right itself if it flipped over. And it had to be fed by hand, one head at a time—otherwise the two heads would fight over the food. Casey offered a $1,000 reward for the turtle, and at last report, it was still missing.

Can We Please Have Our ALMOST EVERYTHING Back?
One day in March 2008, an ad appeared on the Craigslist Web site saying that a man in Jacksonville, Oregon, needed to move

---

How about you? About 15,000 Americans are currently in a coma.

away suddenly and was leaving all of his possessions behind. Everything he owned, it said—including a horse—would be left at his house, free to anyone who wanted it. The problem was that the owner of the house, Robert Salisbury, didn't place the ad. And he wasn't moving. He was staying at a worksite about 50 miles away when he got a call from a local woman who tracked him down because she thought the ad seemed suspicious. As he rushed home, Salisbury flagged down a truck that was full of stuff he recognized—ladders, a lawn mower, and work gear from his job as a contractor. The truck got away, but when Salisbury got home, he found 30 people ransacking his house. After subpoenaing Craigslist for posting records, police located and arrested Brandon and Amber Herbert, who had posted the ad to cover up the fact that they'd stolen some saddles and other materials from Salisbury's property at an earlier date.

Can We Please Have Our LUNG Back? In October 2009, "Bodies: The Exhibition," a traveling science exhibit featuring human cadavers, was visiting Lima, Peru, when they announced that a lung had been stolen while it was on display. The Atlanta-based owners of the show offered a $2,000 reward for the return of the stolen organ. A few days later, an anonymous tipster called and said they could find it outside the exhibit in a plastic bag. No one tried to collect the reward. "In the whole world," an exhibition spokeswoman said, "this has never happened."

Can We Please Have Our TOILET SEAT Back? In August 2009, Trev Inwood, owner of the Belfast Tavern in Christchurch, New Zealand, called police to tell them that someone had stolen a "very significant" 20-year-old plastic toilet seat from the pub's restroom. Why was it so important? The Belfast Tavern is a regular watering hole for celebrities, he said, and the butts of many famous people had sat on the seat. "It's got a lot of history," he said. "Prime ministers have sat on that thing." Inwood offered a $100 reward for information leading to the return of the toilet seat, which he described as "well-used, with a few burn marks and stains."

POINT & SHOOT

Three stories to reinforce the fact: Guns are not toys!

NOT QUITE SUPERMAN
In 2009 a Falmouth, Massachusetts, man bragged to a friend that if the friend shot a BB gun at him from across the room…he'd catch the pellet with his bare hand. So the friend picked up the gun and pulled the trigger. Good news: The man actually did snatch the BB out of the air with his hand. Bad news: The BB ended up lodged *in* his hand. He later explained to police at the hospital that the whole incident was just an "accident gone wrong."

RUSSIAN TO THE HOSPITAL

Two teenage boys—William Rafferty, 18, and a 16-year-old friend (not named in press reports)—were at a girl's house in Norwell, Massachusetts. The boys decided to go back to Rafferty's house, but before they did, they stole a snub-nosed revolver from her father's safe. Then they decided to play a game of Russian roulette. Rafferty pointed the gun at his head and pulled the trigger. Nothing happened. He handed it to his friend. Showing a *little* more sense, the boy aimed the gun at his thigh…and shot himself. Louellyn Lambros, Rafferty's mom, drove him to the hospital, where she covered up for the boys, telling police that an intruder shot her son's friend. When the girl's father showed up to report the stolen gun, police arrested mom and son on a long list of charges.

BIG SHOT

Lukas Neuhardt, 27, of Saarbruecken, Germany, wanted to impress his friends with "something big." He thought carrying a loaded pistol would be pretty impressive, so he hid a gun in his pants pocket. Only problem: He forgot to put the safety catch on. Sure enough, the pistol went off, blasting a hole in Lukas' pocket (and his "manhood"). To avoid embarrassment, he told paramedics that he'd been shot by a masked attacker. But the cops noticed that Lukas had a bullet hole inside his pocket and not on his pants. Doctors got his parts back in working order, but now he's facing three years in prison for breaking Germany's strict gun laws.

The International Pole Dancing Fitness Association is trying to make pole dancing an Olympic sport.

THAT GUY IN THE UPPER DECK IS GYRATING

He entertains most of the fans in the stands—and frightens a few.
And he's everywhere. Just who is this mysterious sports nut?

FAN-SPASTIC

When Cameron Hughes attends a sporting event, he never goes unnoticed. It's not just that he's a husky, six-foot-tall man with fiery red hair sitting in the cheap seats. No matter how well or badly the home team is doing, he cheers into his megaphone, jumps up and down, pumps his fists—whatever it takes to get the fans around him excited. And in really desperate times—like when the home team is getting shellacked—Hughes does his infamous "stripper dance": Slowly, he removes one of his 10 or so layered T-shirts, holds it up over his head, twirls it in the air, and then throws it. Then he starts gyrating. "I'm *that* guy," he says, "the funny, happy, dancing, possibly very drunk guy you've seen at the ballpark at least once."

Is he crazy? You might think so—and you might think he owns his own jet if you've noticed him cheering wildly at a Los Angeles Lakers game one night, a Toronto Blue Jays baseball game a few days later, and a Detroit Red Wings hockey game a few days after that. And then he's off to do his thing at a high-school football game in Duluth. And at every venue, it's always the same schtick: Cheer, jump, and dance.

And he never has to buy a ticket.

ALL THE STADIUM'S A STAGE

For 15 years, Hughes has been a "fan for hire"—teams pay him anywhere from $1,000 to $2,500 just to show up and be himself. It adds up to a lucrative career: Working more than 80 games per year, Hughes earns somewhere in the "six figures" (he won't say how much).

It all began, quite humbly, when Hughes didn't make it onto his high-school basketball squad in 1989. Still wanting to help the team, he played his part from the bleachers by painting

Oregon, New Mexico, and Alabama all have annual UFO festivals.

the school's colors on his face, waving homemade signs, and cheering louder than anyone else. Later, at Bishop's University in Quebec, Hughes took the job of "Melonhead," the team's mascot.

And then destiny found him at an Ottawa Senators hockey game in 1994. More than a little drunk at the time, Hughes recalls, "I started dancing to 'We Are Family,' and everyone was like, 'What is he doing?' Then they all started clapping and cheering, and I thought, 'Uh-oh, what did I just do?' After the game, the team communications guy came up to me and said, 'We want to hire you.'" Hughes took the gig, and then got another job (at $300 per game) cheering for the Toronto Maple Leafs. Hughes knew he'd found his true vocation—a professional sports nutcase.

The theory goes this way: If the fans sitting around him start acting a little nuttier, then the fans near *them* might get more excited as well. And hopefully that energy will transfer down to the home team and will translate into more wins. That's what the teams who employ him hope, anyway.

WORKPLACE HAZARDS

The job may look like nothing but fun, but it isn't easy. To stay in shape, Hughes trains by doing high-intensity aerobic workouts. And though he appears drunk when he's doing his routine, he isn't; his klutzy moves are all carefully choreographed, and three Red Bull energy drinks are usually enough to get him through the game. And with all the gyrating, Hughes gets his share of blisters, bleeding palms, bruises, sprains, and twisted ankles. At one game, he had to be rushed to the hospital suffering from dehydration. He's also been known to upset grumpy fans, who have retaliated with hot popcorn, boos, and, in some cases, violence. Once, security didn't get to him in time and Hughes was pushed down a flight of stairs.

So does all this effort actually help the home team play better? Hughes believes it does. So does Amanda Greco, a team official for the NBA's Cleveland Cavaliers: "Having Cameron there adds just a little extra energy to the crowd, and it definitely gives the players an extra advantage."

"It's not just a job," Hughes insists, "It's something I live to do."

Anton-Babinski Syndrome is a rare condition in which a blind person doesn't realize they are blind.

MODERN PIRACY

The Somali pirates that we see on the news are a far cry from the peg-legged, parrot-shouldered, arrrr-sayin' marauders of yesteryear. Instead of swords and periscopes, these new pirates carry assault rifles and satellite phones. And, as twisted as it may seem, they've become folk heroes to a nation in turmoil.

THE MOST DANGEROUS PLACE ON EARTH

Few countries are more unstable and chaotic than Somalia. Located on the Horn of Africa, the continent's easternmost point, Somalia lies right next to the Gulf of Aden and its busy shipping lanes, carrying passengers and cargo from all over the world.

In 1991 Somalia's government collapsed, leaving its nine million citizens to endure two decades of insurgencies, civil war, genocide, famine, drought, corruption, and crime. In 2008 more than 1,800 civilians were killed in violent clashes, and by the next year, more than 1.3 million people were displaced within Somalia and another 330,000 had fled to neighboring countries. Thousands more died from starvation and disease. Although there's now a U.N.-backed government in power, it's spending most of its resources fighting a fringe Islamic insurgency. And with no navy patrolling Somalia's waters, other nations have taken the opportunity to overfish the waters and dump their toxic waste there. But it's in those same waters that many Somalis see their salvation.

SEEKING NEW OPPORTUNITIES

With little hope at home and few prospects if they flee, some young Somali men have taken to a life of piracy. It's not much more dangerous than trying to survive on the war-torn streets, and the pay is a lot better: A pirate can make $10,000 for a successful raid. (Somalia's average wage is below $650 per year.)

Attacking from speedboats and armed with AK-47 assault rifles and rocket-propelled grenades, pirates stop ships and rob them of cash and equipment. The real prize, however, comes from taking hostages and collecting ransom for their release. The practice has become so profitable that at any given time, there are at least 200

Chinese gym coach Xiao Lin rents himself out as a punching bag for stressed women.

hostages being held in the Gulf of Aden by Somali pirates. "They have a great business model," according to Admiral Rick Gurnon, head of the Massachusetts Maritime Academy. "See ships, take ransom, and make millions." Says one young pirate, "Foreign navies can do nothing to stop piracy."

DAVID VS. GOLIATH

Just how brash *are* Somali pirates? No ship is too big to take on, and no ransom demand is too high. But that doesn't mean they don't sometimes bite off more than they can chew:

• In 2005 the U.S. cruise ship *Seabourn Spirit* was carrying 311 crew and passengers through the Gulf of Aden. Two speedboats carrying 10 pirates raced up and started firing machine guns and grenades at the liner. The *Spirit's* security team blasted the pirates with a high-pressure water cannon and then pierced their eardrums with an LRAD, or Long Range Acoustic Device, which emits a debilitating sound wave. The confrontation ended when the massive cruise ship simply ran over one of the speedboats.

• In 2006 two U.S. Navy warships spotted a suspicious vessel towing two fishing boats 25 miles off Somalia's coast. This is a standard tactic for pirates: One medium-size "mothership" tows two smaller boats, which carry out the raids. The warships tailed the pirates through the night, and at dawn the Navy sent two boats to investigate. The pirates opened fire on the boarding party. It was the first attack on a U.S. Navy ship in the 21st century. The destroyers easily disabled the fishing boats.

• Seven Somali pirates spotted what appeared to be a commercial tanker on the horizon in March 2009. They approached it and started firing at its hull. But it wasn't a commercial ship...and it wasn't alone. Belonging to the German navy, the heavily armed tanker was participating in "Operation Atalanta"—a military operation designed to combat piracy. The pirates turned around and fled, but by then they'd attracted the attention of an international fleet that included two Greek warships, a Dutch frigate, a Spanish warship, a U.S. Navy amphibious assault ship, several Spanish fighter planes, and two U.S. Marine Cobra helicopters. The armada easily captured the pirates.

• On November 29, 2009, about 800 miles off Somalia's coast, pirates closed in on the *Maran Centaurus*, a Greek vessel carrying a crew of 28 people...and two million barrels of crude oil, worth $150 million. The pirates boarded the ship and captured the crew—who didn't dare fight back because a single shot could have ignited the oil and blown up the ship. What followed was a month-and-a-half-long standoff, which lasted until the ship's owner agreed to the ransom demands on January 18, 2010. But shortly before delivery, a rival group of pirates sped up to the ship, firing their weapons, determined to grab the ransom for themselves. The pirates onboard the *Maran Centaurus*, knowing how combustible the cargo was, actually radioed an anti-piracy task force for help. A nearby warship dispatched two helicopters to protect the ship *and* the pirates. A short time later, a plane flew over and dropped a package containing $9 million—the largest haul in the history of Somali piracy. The hostages, all unharmed, were released. And the pirates took their loot back home.

BIG BUSINESS

As violent as these pirates are, they're fairly tame compared to other crime syndicates. According to Steve Rosenbush of Portfolio.com, "For their part, at a time when terrorists and global drug cartels from Mexico to Brazil have pushed violence to mind-numbing levels, the Somali pirates seem positively businesslike, avoiding unnecessary gunplay and raising capital in an orderly fashion on a small stock exchange." Stock exchange? Yes—in Somalia investors can buy shares of pirate operations and collect dividends after ransom money is delivered. This is the new face of piracy: well-organized plunderers who employ accountants...and even publicists to make statements to the media. And the well-insured shipping companies have come to expect piracy as a cost of doing business in the Gulf of Aden, so they're likely to quietly give in to the demands rather than risk losing a crew, passengers, or cargo. The emboldened Somali pirates have even started patrolling their shores as a makeshift coast guard, running off fishing trawlers and capturing boats that dump their waste.

, And much of the hundreds of millions of dollars made by Somali pirates each year goes straight back into the country's tattered economy. As a result, poor coastal towns are starting to thrive again...and the pirates are looked upon as heroes in a country that has had little to cheer about for decades.

REALITY BLIGHTS

Even "normal" reality shows are weird. But
these are not normal reality shows.

S*uperstar USA* **(2004, The WB)**
Contestants on this show were told that they were in a singing competition, but they were actually being judged for their *lack* of singing ability. The show's producers also told the live audience that the singers were terminally ill patients who were getting their last wishes fulfilled by the Make-A-Wish Foundation. The "winner," a tone-deaf woman named Jamie Foss, won $50,000.

Mr. Personality (2003, Fox)
This derivation of *The Bachelor* featured a woman choosing from a series of men. The twist was that she could judge potential mates only on their personalities—because all the men wore gruesome masks. The show was hosted by Monica Lewinsky (famous for her scandalous relationship with President Bill Clinton).

Dating in the Dark (2009, ABC)
Another *Bachelor* variation, this show asked single people to pick partners based on personality instead of looks, but it upped the ante even more: They had to choose each other entirely in the dark. The show was shot with night-vision cameras, allowing viewers to watch the contestants not only flirt, but also bump into walls and each other.

My Bare Lady (2006, U.K.)
Four American adult-film stars attempted to become legitimate actresses by performing scenes from classic musicals (including *My Fair Lady*) alongside British theater actors.

Gimme My Reality Show (2008, Fox Reality)
Contestants from *other* reality shows competed on *this* reality show to win a contract to star in *another* reality show. It aired on the Fox Reality Channel, a short-lived network that showed only reality shows. Really.

KILLER 'ROOS

*As Australia's population grows and more space is needed to put a
couple shrimp on the barbie and throw back a few coldies, boomers
are getting hopping mad at the humans encroaching on their
territory—and they're starting to fight back.*

Date: October 27, 1996
Victim: Steven Shorten, 13, of Grafton, New South Wales
Attack! Steven was playing a round of golf at the Grafton
District Golf Club when he hit a wayward shot into some tall grass.
As he wandered into the grass to find the ball, he heard a sound
"like the growling of a dog." He looked up…and just a few yards
away was a six-foot-tall "boomer," or large male kangaroo. Before
Steven could react, the animal leapt at him, grabbed him, threw
him to the ground, and began to stomp on him with its powerful
hind legs. Another golfer finally scared off the animal and Steven
was rushed to the hospital, where he was treated for a fractured
cheekbone and deep gouges all over his body. He couldn't open
one eye for a year, but eventually recovered from his wounds.

Date: June 2003
Victims: Doug and Pauline Lawson of Monto, Queensland
Attack! Pauline Lawson looked out a window one day and saw
her husband Doug running toward the house, screaming, with his
face covered in blood. Doug ran into the house, and a large kangaroo hopped in after him—and began attacking both Doug and
Pauline in their kitchen. The duo fought back with hands, feet, a
broom, and a water hose until it finally left. The Lawsons were
both badly bruised and scratched but not seriously injured. And
that same animal is believed to have struck again…

Date: July 2003
Victims: John and Helen Crouch of New South Wales
Attack! During a vacation in Monto, the site of the previous
attack, the Crouches were standing outside their motor home
when a huge kangaroo seemingly appeared out of nowhere and
pounced on Helen. It gouged her on the face, back, and groin

(kangaroos have stout, sharp claws on both their front and back legs) before John was able to get the animal off her. Then the kangaroo turned on him. "It was kill or be killed," said John. He grabbed an axe and struck the kangaroo several times before finally killing it. Authorities believe it was the same animal that had attacked the Lawsons. It was probably driven by hunger because the area was suffering a severe drought.

Date: July 18, 2008
Victim: Rosemary Neal, 65, of Mudgee, New South Wales
Attack! As Neal was walking through a horse pasture on her farm about 160 miles northeast of Sydney, a 6 ½-foot-tall kangaroo "just jumped up and launched straight at her," according to her son, Darren. The Neals' dog was able to chase the kangaroo off, but not before Rosemary suffered extensive cuts as well as a concussion. The attack brought a heated response from residents of the area, who called for the police to find and kill the offending 'roo. "How do you propose we do that?" Mudgee Police Inspector Greg Spinks asked. "By doing some kind of kangaroo lineup?" A hunt for the animal was not attempted.

Date: July 3, 2004
Victim: Christine Canham of Canberra, New South Wales
Attack! Canham was watching her four dogs swim in a pond in a city park one day when a large kangaroo appeared on the shore. Then it jumped into the water, swam up to one of her Golden Retrievers (kangaroos are excellent swimmers), and, as Canham watched in horror from the shore, held the dog underwater until it was dead. "The kangaroo just stared back at us," Canham told the *Canberra Times*. "I will never forget that." Surprisingly, reports of kangaroos trying to drown dogs and other perceived predators are not uncommon.

*   *   *

"You have to run as fast as you can just to stay where you are. If you want to get anywhere, you'll have to run much faster."
—**Lewis Carroll**

YOU'RE SICK? *I'M* SICK!

*What do you call a panic that causes an imagined illness
to spread over a population? Mass hysteria.*

THE SWEET SMELL OF PANIC

In 2009 a worker sprayed herself with perfume at the Bank of America corporate office in Fort Worth, Texas. Apparently, two people nearby were allergic to it, reported feeling dizzy, and went home. Soon after, a public-address announcement instructed that any worker who was also feeling dizzy should go outside for some fresh air. Within a few hours, more than 140 people reported feeling ill, with symptoms including dizziness, shortness of breath, and hallucinations—the symptoms of carbon-monoxide poisoning. As the news spread throughout the building, more than 30 people rushed to the hospital, while others were treated at the scene. The fire department sent in a hazardous materials unit, but they never detected any carbon monoxide—only perfume.

SOAP SICKNESS

Morangos com Açúcar is a popular Portuguese soap opera. On a May 2006 episode, all of the characters were stricken with a mysterious disease whose symptoms included dizziness, difficulty breathing, and a rash. A few days later, more than 300 students at 14 high schools throughout Portugal suddenly came down with the exact same symptoms. All of the kids quickly recovered, and the federal health department dismissed the outbreak as mass hysteria.

ONE THING LEADS TO ANOTHER

In 1999 large quantities of animal feed in Belgium were found to be tainted with the poisonous compound dioxin. The reports set off fears over contamination of the food supply, although scientists reassured the public that it was "unlikely" to be a threat to humans. A few weeks later, 26 children at a Belgian school were hospitalized with severe fatigue and upset stomachs after having consumed Coca-Cola. Soon, hundreds of people claimed that they'd felt sick after drinking Coke, and they blamed dioxin. The Belgian Health Council briefly banned the sale of Coca-Cola, but never found dioxin in any samples. The scare was attributed to mass hysteria.

No joke: Studies show that 80% of adult laughter is unconnected to any joke or funny situation.

THE ONE MILLION GUESSES QUIZ, PART I

Here's how it works: We'll tell you an actual news story and leave out one important piece of information—and you have to guess what it is. And we'll give you one million guesses, because you'll need at least that many to get it. Good luck!

STORY: 27-year-old Jens Wilhelms of Frankfurt, Germany, was climbing the stairs to his top-floor apartment one night in April 2008 when he noticed that the door to an elevator was open. The elevator had been broken for some time, and he peered in through the door to see if it was finally being worked on. Then he slipped—and fell 25 feet to the floor of the shaft. But he wasn't injured, because he landed on something. What?

ONE MILLION GUESSES LATER: He fell on a woman who had fallen down the same shaft a day earlier. The unidentified 57-year-old woman was unconscious and bleeding internally, and Wilhelms managed to climb out of the shaft and call emergency services. And although he made her injuries worse by falling on her, police said she was lucky—because she almost certainly would have died if Wilhelms had not landed on her and then gotten help.

STORY: A woman pulled into a Winona, Minnesota, auto repair shop in August 2009 with a broken fan belt. The mechanic told her it would take an hour to fix, and the woman let him in on a secret: She had something special in her trunk. What was it?

ONE MILLION GUESSES LATER: Did you guess "a live goat that had been painted purple and gold, the colors of the NFL's Minnesota Vikings, with the number 4, the number of new Vikings quarterback Brett Favre, shaved into each of its sides"? Then you were right. She told the mechanic that she planned to butcher it later. The mechanic called animal control, and police arrived shortly afterward to arrest the woman on animal-cruelty charges. The goat was saved and was eventually given a new home on a Wisconsin farm. Its new owners named it Brett.

Experts say: The best badminton shuttlecocks are made of the feathers from a goose's left wing.

STORY: In April 2009, Artyom Sidorenko, 28, of Izhevsk, Russia, started coughing up blood and having seizures. He was admitted to a hospital, where doctors told him that he had a cancerous tumor in his lung and would need surgery to remove it. He was operated on—and doctors discovered that the growth in his lung wasn't a tumor. What was it?

ONE MILLION GUESSES LATER: Hopefully one of your guesses was "A piece of a fir tree." Dr. Vladimir Kamashev opened Sidorenko's chest and, he said later, was about to remove most of the lung but decided to analyze the growth first. He cut into it and found what looked like a needle from a pine tree. "At first I thought that I was seeing an illusion," he said. "I asked my assistant to check it out, and he confirmed it. There was a fir tree in his lung." They removed the approximately two-inch-long piece—complete with several needles—and were able to save Sidorenko's lung. Even stranger, the doctors actually believe that it was a tiny tree *growing* in his lung. Kamashev said that Sidorenko must have inhaled a fir tree seed or bud, and that it had somehow germinated and started growing. Botanists said that that's not possible because trees, like all plants, need light to grow. Sidorenko, they say, must have somehow inhaled the tiny branch as it was. (The question is: Wouldn't he have noticed that?)

STORY: In September 2009, Tatiata Kozhevnikova, a 42-year-old housewife and fitness enthusiast from the Russian city of Novosibirsk, made it into *Guinness World Records*. What was her world record?

ONE MILLION GUESSES LATER: Kozhevnikova set the record for having "the world's strongest vagina muscles." Fifteen years after she had children, she explained to reporters, she developed an exercise for what she called her "intimate muscles." It involved a specially designed device that she clamps down on with—well, you get the idea. The other end of the device is attached to a set of weights. Her record lift: 14 kilograms (just over 30 pounds).

If you've got a few more million guesses in you, we've got some more quiz questions on page 313.

MADOFF WITH THE GOODS

Here's a news item from the future: "June 29, 2159: 231-year-old former stockbroker Bernard Madoff was released today after his 150-year prison sentence ended. His first words to reporters: 'I want my stuff back.'"

EVERYTHING MUST GO
Over a career of more than two decades, stockbroker—and scam artist—Bernie Madoff bilked thousands of investors out of nearly $20 billion in what is considered the biggest Ponzi scheme in history. He was arrested in December 2008, and pleaded guilty to securities fraud, mail fraud, money laundering, perjury, theft, and six other charges four months later. In November 2009, while Madoff was beginning a 150-year prison term, the U.S. Marshals Service attempted to return some of that money to his victims by holding a series of auctions. The first one was held at the Sheraton Hotel in New York City. Purses, ashtrays, dishes, jewelry, golf clubs, stationery, duck decoys, and a Wayne Gretzky action figure were among the 200 items stacked on folding tables or leaned against walls, ready to go to the highest bidder. What did these things all have in common? They belonged to Madoff and his family, and were seized from their Manhattan penthouse and Montauk, Long Island, vacation home.

As collectors from around the world queued up to bid on the items from the New York sale, the auctioneers estimated they'd fetch about $500,000. Turns out they grossly underestimated just how crazy some people will go for anything (no matter how seemingly insignificant) that has "celebrity" status.

HEY BIDDER, BIDDER...SWWWING, BIDDER!

Auction item: A blue satin New York Mets baseball team jacket with "Madoff" stitched on the back in orange. (Ironically, team owner Fred Wilpon was one of Madoff's victims.)
Estimated value: $720
Sold for: $14,500

New definition of "ladylike?" King Henry VIII's ladies at court...

Auction items: A Lady Hermes brown suede handbag that belonged to Madoff's wife, Ruth, plus two other purses.
Estimated value: $210
Sold for: $1,900

Auction items: Three boogie boards, one with "Madoff" written on it with a black marker.
Estimated value: $80
Sold for: $1,000

Auction item: A set of Madoff's personalized golf clubs (irons only).
Estimated value: $350
Sold for: $3,600

Auction item: A pair of Ruth Madoff's diamond Victorian dangle earrings.
Estimated value: $20,000
Sold for: $70,000

Auction item: A 1960 Hofstra University ring engraved with "BM."
Estimated value: $360
Sold for: $6,000

Auction item: A black leather Mont Blanc wallet embossed with "BM."
Estimated value: $100
Sold for: $2,200

EVERYTHING ELSE MUST GO

At later auctions, Madoff's 61-foot yacht, *Bull*, fetched nearly $1 million; his 38-foot-long boat, *Sitting Bull*, sold for $320,000; and his 21-foot-long *Little Bull* brought in $21,000. Some other Madoff items that collectors made off with: hockey trading cards, a "Bernard Madoff Investment Securities" pen, a Tiffany silver key ring monogrammed "BLM," and the Madoffs' Christofle flatware engraved "RMB." And then there was Madoff's 18-carat-gold Rolex "Prisoner Watch," inspired by the steel watches given to

Allied prisoners of war in Germany during World War II. The Prisoner Watch sold for $65,000 (or about the cost of two years' worth of room-and-board to imprison Madoff).

In the end, the auctions earned about $3 million for the victims—a tiny fraction of what Madoff had stolen from them.

SWINDLER'S TWIST

Following on the heels of the official Bernie Madoff auctions, several *unofficial* "Bernie Madoff Auctions" took place around the country...in much less posh hotels and community centers. Each of these auctions promised bidders a piece of the Madoff pie. The only problem: None of them offered any items that had actually belonged to Madoff. Atlanta-based Southern Star Auctioneers—which held a sale in Syracuse, New York—said they never claimed to be selling Madoff's personal items, just stuff that belonged to his *victims*. But an investigation by the U.S. Marshals discovered that the items didn't even belong to the victims. In some of the other bogus auctions, organizers forged the stockbroker's name on the items: They sold $20 fountain pens for hundreds, even thousands of dollars...proving that even though he's behind bars, Bernie Madoff is still able to part people from their money.

*   *   *

CRAZY WORLD RECORDS

• At an Illinois summer camp in 2001, 297 people flossed their teeth...with a piece of dental floss that measured 1,500 feet long.

• Ten Royal Marines from England hold the record for pushing around an adult dressed up like a baby: 271.7 miles in 24 hours.

• In 1999 Dustin Phillips of Los Angeles sucked an entire bottle of Heinz ketchup through a straw in 33 seconds.

• As part of a stunt on *The Ricki Lake Show* in 2001, a couple kissed for a record 31 hours.

• Timothy Badyna ran the Toledo (Ohio) Marathon in 1994 backward—that's 26.2 miles in four hours, which would even be an excellent time if he ran it forward.

ZOMBIES IN THE NEWS

*With flesh-eating monsters devouring everything from Jane Austen
to Louisville, Kentucky, it seems like dead is the new living.*

THE ZOMBEES ARE COMMING!

In April 2009, the BBC's news site reported that the swine
flu virus, H1N1, had mutated into "H1Z1." It could
…restart the heart of it's victim for up to two hours after the initial
demise of the person where the individual behaves in extremely
violent ways from what is believe to be a combination of brain
damage and a chemical released into blood during "resurrection."

The story prompted a few concerned calls to the BBC, but the bad
grammar, along with the date it appeared (April 1st), was a dead
giveaway that this was a fake Web site designed to look like the
BBC's real site. No panic ensued.

THEY'RE EVERYWHERE!

For one crazy night each August, up to 3,000 zombies gather in
Louisville, Kentucky, and stagger through downtown, swarming
pedestrians, cars, even city buses. It's the "Louisville Zombie
Attack," billed as the U.S.'s "first and oldest" undead gathering
(started in 2005 by three friends who love zombie movies).
Although the event—which also features zombies dancing to DJ
music—is all in fun, the organizers ask that you plan ahead with
your friends so that "only consenting participants are attacked."

NOT EXACTLY THRILLER

In 2006 a group of staggering partygoers dressed as zombies raised
the suspicion of police in Minneapolis, Minnesota. Why? These
"undead" were carrying backpacks that had wires sticking out of
them… so police arrested them on suspicion of possessing "simulated weapons of mass destruction." It turned out that the wires
were part of a stereo system for their "Zombie Dance Party." Once
they convinced officers that they weren't carrying explosives, the
weapons charges were dropped. But a few were cited for disorderly
conduct for stumbling down the street like they were in "some
kind of Michael Jackson video."

SIGN OF THE DEAD

In early 2009, after an unknown trickster hacked into computerized road signs in Austin, Texas, motorists saw signs that warned them: "CAUTION! ZOMBIES AHEAD!!!," "RUN FOR COLD CLIMATES!!!," and "THE END IS NEAR!!!" Although most commuters said they were amused by the sign, the City of Austin was not. If caught, the culprit faces jail time and a $500 fine. "When you change a sign, you're endangering people," said one city official. (And in the future, citizens might be less inclined to believe the signs in the case of an actual zombie attack.)

UNDEAD AUTHOR'S SOCIETY

In 2009 author Seth Grahame-Smith took Jane Austen's 1813 masterpiece *Pride and Prejudice* and added his own "zombie mayhem." Result: *Pride and Prejudice and Zombies*, a surprise best seller. The hybrid novel is 85% Austen's work and 15% Grahame-Smith's gory sensibilities, staying true to the original plot of star-crossed lovers, except for a few forays into zombie-killing, corpse disposal…and ninjas.

Z-SCHOOL

Harvard University psychiatrist Dr. Steven Schlozman's fascination with movie zombies led him to write an academic paper on the subject. The study analyzes years of (movie) data and details why zombies behave the way they do. His findings:

• Zombies are slow-witted because they have only enough frontal-lobe activity left in their brains to "sense" other zombies or humans.

• The *amygdala* (the part of the brain that controls emotional reactions) also influences zombies, so they "can only be fueled by rage." And reasoning with them is useless, Schlozman notes, because it's like "being mad at a crocodile" for wanting to eat you.

• Other cerebral deficiencies account for their slow walk, lumbering movements, lack of fear, and insatiable appetites.

• Why do zombies moan? Because they're constipated, writes Schlozman: "They never seem to poop."

FINE, JUST FINE

Just last week, Uncle John got fined $50 for letting his duck off its leash. He thought that was weird—until he saw what these people got fined for.

In September 2009, Mishka Gamble of Cairns, Queensland, Australia, was fined $200 for owning two unregistered dogs. The problem: They were fiberglass dogs that were standing in her yard. "I've got a fiberglass pig and sheep," Gamble said. "Do I need to register them, too?" She refused to pay the fine.

• A waitress in the city of Klagenfurt, Austria, was fined the equivalent of nearly $800 after serving a table of guests industrial-strength cleaning detergent. She claimed that she thought it was schnapps. One of the guests (the one who wasn't already drunk, we're guessing) refused to drink the shot of liquid because it "smelled funny." But the rest of the party drank the toxic drinks and had to be taken to the hospital. The waitress said she was simply overworked and had grabbed the wrong bottle.

• A Charlotte, North Carolina, guitar teacher named Bob Teixeira spent $1,200 converting his 1981 diesel Mercedes to make it run on vegetable oil. His reward for making his car more environmentally friendly: The state of North Carolina fined him $1,000—because he wasn't buying gasoline, and therefore wasn't paying gasoline taxes. The federal government fined him an additional $1,000. To top it off, North Carolina officials told Teixeira he owed the state a $2,500 fee imposed on "small fuel users." The fines were later reduced, but Teixeira still had to pay $2,500.

• In March 2008, Boulder, Colorado, hairstylist Joy Douglas was fined $1,000 for dyeing her poodle pink. A Boulder law says that "No person shall dye or color live fowl, rabbits, or any other animals." Douglas fought the fine, saying she used natural products like beet juice to dye the dog in support of a campaign for breast-cancer awareness. The city later ruled that Douglas wouldn't have to pay the fine...as long as she refrained from dyeing animals for the next six months.

CLAPPERS, SNAPPERS...

...and other weird achievements that rhyme with "-apper."

CLAPPER. Kent French has beaten his own hand-clapping speed record several times. It's currently 721 claps in one minute—about 12 per second. Navneet Singh of India set the record for clapping with *one* hand in 2007. Number of single-handed claps: 284 in one minute.

SNAPPER. Scott Woodson, a teenager from Mountville, Pennsylvania, developed a way to manipulate his joints so that every finger snap becomes three snaps. Woodson holds the record for finger-snapping, with 162 snaps in 10 seconds.

SLAPPER. At a 2009 event for the World Record Appreciation Society (an organization whose members set mundane records), a man named Lawson Clarke took a record 46 slaps to the face, from 46 different people, in one minute.

RED SNAPPER. In 1996 Doc Kennedy was fishing in Port Fourchon, Louisiana when he caught a 50 lb., 4 oz., 41-inch red snapper—the largest one on record.

GIFT WRAPPER. Ann Erickson of Utah won the 2009 "Scotch Brand Most Gifted Wrapper" contest for her speed and accuracy in wrapping a toy helicopter, jigsaw puzzle, bicycle, and sailboat.

RAPPER. Twista, who had a #1 hit in 2004 with the rapid-fire rap song "Slow Jamz," made *Guinness World Records* in 1992 for fastest rapper, able to enunciate 11.2 syllables per second.

CRAPPER. Avant-garde artist Michelle Hines decided in 1995 that she wanted to produce the largest poop possible. Working with nutritionists at the University of Michigan, Hines ate a fiber-rich diet and took fiber supplements for a week before finally producing —on a bowling alley that donated its floor for the event—a turd measuring 26 feet long, the entire length of Hines' digestive tract. (To prevent any premature evacuations, Hines wore a "plug.")

11 GREAT MOMENTS IN THE HISTORY OF MADNESS

The world didn't become crazy in a day. It took eons of war, famine, plague, and board meetings to get this way. Here are a few milestones of insanity through the ages.

5th century B.C.: The Greek physician Hippocrates (460–370) believed that the human body contained four types of fluids called *humors*: blood ("sanguine humor"), yellow bile ("choleric humor"), black bile ("melancholic humor"), and phlegm ("phlegmatic humor"). Hippocrates considered these humors to be the source of moods and behavior, making him the first recorded doctor to reject the idea that mental illness was caused by supernatural forces. Instead, he considered it the result of environmental factors such as diet and lifestyle. Treatment consisted of trying to restore the balance of the four humors—for example, using citrus to elevate the sanguine humor (blood) when there was thought to be too much phlegm.

A.D. 705: The first psychiatric hospital was founded in Baghdad, followed by other such asylums in Morocco, Egypt, Syria, and Turkey. In the Muslim world, sufferers of mental illness were treated much more humanely than in Europe. Instead of chains and isolation, patients were prescribed baths, drugs, music, and recreational activities.

9th century: The Muslim physician Ali ibn Sahl Rabban al-Tabari (838–870) became the world's first known psychotherapist. He believed that mental illness was caused by delusions and imagination, and should be treated by "wise counseling" from physicians who first build a rapport with their patients.

11th century: In one of the first documented cases of a mentally

Roughly half of all North Americans with a genius IQ (140 or higher) never graduate from high school.

ill patient being cured, a psychotherapist named Avicenna (980–1037) treated a Persian prince who believed he was a cow. The prince refused to eat and begged to be slaughtered. So Avicenna approached the prince with a knife, pretending to be a butcher, but stopped short, saying the cow was too lean and not ready to be killed. The prince was offered food and began eating again, until he gradually regained his strength and overcame his delusion.

The Middle Ages: In Medieval Europe, the idea that mental disorders were caused by an imbalance in the four humors was steadily being replaced by the idea that they were the result of sin, evil spirits, and Satan. Many "cures" were attempted: bloodletting, purging the bowels, whipping, fasting, prayer, and exorcism. In extreme cases, *trepanning*—drilling a hole in the top of the skull to allow the demons and excess humors to escape—was recommended.

1200: England's King John sent his royal messengers to the village of Gotham to scout locations for a new hunting lodge. When the king's men rode into town, the townsfolk were acting strange: Some were attempting to drown an eel (which is impossible); others had joined hands and formed a circle around a thorny shrub to "keep trapped the cuckoo bird hiding within." The messengers informed King John that the townspeople were mad. At the time, many believed that insanity was contagious, so the king decided to build his hunting lodge elsewhere, far away from the "Fools of Gotham." But it was the king and his men who were the fools—the Gothamites had known in advance about John's plan and didn't want to pony up the taxes to build the hunting lodge. So they feigned madness. (Also works on IRS auditors.)

1330: The oldest continuously operated hospital for the mentally ill, London's Bethlem Royal Hospital—better known as Bedlam—was founded in 1247 as a *priory*, or monks' residence. It became a hospital in 1330, and soon after, a hospital for the insane. The facility was basically a prison where inmates were cruelly restrained with manacles and chains. The screams and moans coming from inside were so loud that "bedlam" entered the English language as a

---

David Smith Sr. has been shot out of a cannon 9,000 times without breaking any bones.

word meaning uproar or confusion. It took several centuries for conditions to improve (in the 1700s, visitors paid a penny to stare at the "freaks" and poke them with long sticks), but Bedlam still functions today as a mental-health facility, more than 750 years after its founding.

1494: The phrase "ship of fools" dates back to the medieval practice of herding people considered insane or depraved onto boats, putting them out to sea, and abandoning them. In 1494 French satirist Sebastian Brant wrote a poem on the subject, depicting a happy crew wasting time pursuing idle pleasures—drinking wine, eating fruit, singing, and playing the lute—while no one was steering the ship. The poem, in turn, was the inspiration for a famous painting by Hieronymus Bosch.

15th–17th centuries: The persecution of people accused of witchcraft led to as many as 100,000 executions in Europe and the New World. This deadly example of "mass hysteria" mostly occurred in rural areas without a strong central government, where townspeople believed wild stories of witches killing and eating babies and conspiring to overthrow Christianity. The accused were put on trial and subjected to various forms of torture (hot pincers, thumbscrews, immersion in water) until they confessed...or died. Those fortunate enough to survive the trial were burned at the stake, hanged, or decapitated. By the time the famous witch trials occurred in Salem, Massachusetts, in 1692, the European witch hunts had nearly become a thing of the past.

1600s: One of Bedlam's most famous inmates was Moll Cutpurse (1584–1659). Born Mary Frith, Cutpurse got her nickname from her prowess as a London pickpocket. But her clothing, speech, and mannerisms brought accusations—mostly from men—that she was insane. Instead of wearing conventional women's clothing—constricting bodices, petticoats, and puffy gowns—Cutpurse wore trousers. She also smoked a pipe, swore in public, and sang risqué songs on stage—something only men were allowed to do. By the 1620s, she was working as a pimp—not only supplying female prostitutes to men but also procuring handsome young men for middle-class housewives. Cutpurse was eventually arrested and confined to Bedlam. She was released in 1644 after being "cured" and went on to live another 15 years.

Early 1800s: King George III (1738–1820) is best remembered in the U.S. as the tyrant who imposed unfair taxes that led to the American Revolution. Throughout much of his life, George suffered from mental illness. In 1788 he had a particularly bad episode, causing him to rant nonsensically for hours until he was foaming at the mouth. He addressed his court as "my lords and peacocks," and it was even rumored that he shook hands with a tree, believing it to be the King of Prussia. Many theories have been put forward as to the cause of King George's madness. Some suggest it was a result of the genetic disease *porphyria*, which is known to run in the royal family. But a 2005 study of a sample of his hair revealed high levels of arsenic, a common component of medicine and cosmetics in that era, which may have caused the king and countless others to suffer bouts of insanity.

*   *   *

TWO DUMB CRIMINALS, ONE FUNNY GUY

In 2005 two English crooks, Kenneth Speight and Craig Reeves, convinced a friend who worked at a bank to access an account belonging to Ricky Gervais (who is extremely famous in England ever since he starred as David Brent, the obnoxious boss on the hit comedy series *The Office*). Speight and Reeves then transferred about $320,000 of Gervais's money to an account at another bank and used it to buy a large amount of gold bullion. When the men attempted to pick up the bullion, one of them showed his passport—in Gervais's name—as identification. The clerk noticed that the man didn't look much like Ricky Gervais, and that the passport photo was obviously a cut-out of David Brent from the sitcom's DVD sleeve. The clerk immediately called authorities; Speight and Reeves were arrested and later sentenced to prison terms. Perhaps no one found the scam more humorous than Gervais himself: "It's a picture of David Brent sitting at his desk with that little smug look on his face! I tell you what, I was laughing for 10 minutes!"

JAPAN GONE CRAZY

*If you ever decide to make a trip to the weirdest places on Earth,
don't forget Japan. Here are just a few reasons why.*

BIG BABIES

In April 2009, more than 80 Japanese sumo wrestlers and 80 Japanese babies born in 2008 (along with their parents) showed up at the Sensoji temple in Tokyo for the annual "Baby Cry Sumo Festival." Two at a time, the sumo giants, dressed in their traditional loincloths, sit on a stage facing each other, each holding a baby. A Shinto priest then approaches and, by making loud noises and scary faces, frightens the babies until they cry. The sumo wrestlers then hold the babies up to make them cry louder— while hundreds of people clap and laugh and cheer. According to Japanese tradition, this is good for infants—their wails are regarded as prayers for health. The baby who cries the loudest is deemed the "winner," and that baby, so the tradition goes, will lead a long and healthy life (and, presumably, will have a lifelong terror of priests and sumo wrestlers).

HAVE A BALL WITH YOUR KIDS

If you're in the market for a sexually suggestive toy for your child (and who isn't?), the Hokkaido Marimokkori, a doll made in the northern Japanese state of Hokkaido, may be just the thing. "Marimokkori" is a play on words: *marimo* is a type of algae that grows in a ball shape and is found on Hokkaido's shoreline; *mokkori* means "mound." That explains the doll's round, green head (like the algae balls)…and possibly explains the *mound*: a round, pink ball on its crotch. The pink ball is attached to a string that you can pull. You then let go of the string and, as it retracts, the doll vibrates and emits a giggling sound.

YOU'RE VIRTUALLY UNDER ARREST

In May 2008, a 43-year-old Japanese woman was playing an online virtual-reality game when she found out that her "virtual husband," played by a 33-year-old Japanese man she had never met, had divorced her. "I was suddenly divorced, without a word of warning," she later said. "That made me so angry." She was *so* angry, in fact, that she logged on to the game, somehow figured out the man's password…and deleted his character. When the man discovered that his virtual self, which he'd been developing for more than a year, had vanished, he called the police. They tracked the woman down, arrested her, and put her in jail for what the media dubbed a "virtual murder." The woman faces up to five years in a real prison and a $5,000 fine for manipulating electronic data.

THE OTHER DIMENSIONS

In October 2008, a man named Taichi Takashita launched an online petition that, he said, he would present to the Japanese government when it had one million signatures. What's the petition for? A change to Japan's marriage laws—because he wants to marry a cartoon character. He has fallen in love, he says, with the famous Japanese *manga* cartoon character Mikuru Asahina, and wants to change Japanese law to allow marriage between humans and fictional people. "I am no longer interested in three dimensions," he wrote. "I would even like to become a resident of the two-dimensional world." As of January 2010, he claimed to have more than 660,000 signatures and was still gathering more.

SHE'S DEAD. STILL.

In September 2008, a couple walking through a wooded area on the island of Honshu came across a grisly sight: a corpse wrapped in plastic. Dozens of investigators were brought in, the body was taken away, and, after several hours, forensic pathologists began to unwrap it. That's when they found out that it wasn't a body; it was an extremely lifelike silicone sex doll. Humiliated police officials vowed to catch whoever had pulled the prank, and news of the "sex-doll murder case" spread around the world. A few days later, a 60-year-old man came forward and confessed but said it wasn't a prank. He had bought the doll after his wife died years earlier, he told police, and had become very attached to it. He'd recently decided to get rid of it because he was going to live with one of his children. "He was confused about how to get rid of her," a police investigator told reporters. "He thought it would be cruel to cut her up into pieces and throw her out with the trash." The man, whom police did not identify, was charged with violating waste-management laws and was fined an undisclosed amount. Police said he was very sorry his doll was mistaken for a corpse.

THE DA VINCI TREASURE

The Asylum is a movie production company that makes blatant knockoffs of Hollywood blockbusters and usually releases them direct to video. Here are some of their familiar-sounding works that you may find at a video store near you (probably in the bargain bin).

The Day the Earth Stopped
(a rip-off of *The Day the Earth Stood Still*)

Sunday School Musical (*High School Musical*)

The Terminators (*Terminator: Salvation*)

AVH: Alien vs. Hunter (*AVP: Alien vs. Predator*)

Halloween Night (*Halloween*)

2012: Supernova (*2012*)

Transmorphers (*Transformers*)

The Da Vinci Treasure (*The Da Vinci Code*)

The Land that Time Forgot (*Land of the Lost*)

When a Killer Calls (*When a Stranger Calls*)

King of the Lost World (*King Kong*)

100 Million B.C. (*10,000 B.C.*)

Street Racer (*Speed Racer*)

Pirates of Treasure Island (*Pirates of the Caribbean*)

Monster (*Cloverfield*)

Snakes on a Train (*Snakes on a Plane*)

In Massachusetts, 1% of the construction costs of a prison must be spent on art.

SAVED BY SILICONE

When fake breasts become real heroes.

BUMPER BUMPERS. In Ruse, Bulgaria, a 24-year-old woman ran a red light at a busy intersection and slammed into a passing car. Although both cars were totaled, the woman escaped with minor injuries. How? According to police, "Her silicone breasts acted as airbags" (although she did require surgery to replace her implants, which ruptured in the crash.)

ROCKET DEFENSE. In 2006 a young Israeli woman was hit in the chest by shrapnel during a Hezbollah rocket attack near the Lebanese border. Her silicone implants absorbed the impact of the metal fragments and kept them from reaching her heart. "This is an extraordinary case," said her doctor. "She was saved from death."

BODY ARMOR. Jane Selma Soares of Rio de Janeiro, Brazil, was on her way home when she got caught in the crossfire of a shootout between police and a gang of drug dealers. She tried to duck out of sight, but a bullet caught her in the chest. Doctors later found the bullet…lodged in one of her breast implants. Soares, who suffered no serious injuries, eventually got new, larger implants. "I'm twice as happy," she declared. "First, because my prosthesis saved my life, and also because now I look even more beautiful!"

THE ONE THAT GOT AWAY. In 2003 Denise Leblanc and Mark Marzoni were deep-sea fishing off the coast of Panama when Marzoni hooked a 1,000-pound marlin. Marzoni was trying to reel in the fish as Leblanc, leaning over the side of the boat, filmed the catch. The marlin was nearly in the boat when it began thrashing—and suddenly impaled Leblanc with its sharp sword-like snout, spearing through her right arm, her right breast, and her side. The fish fell back into the water; Leblanc collapsed on the deck. Marzoni rushed to her aid and noticed that her right breast was…gone. Later, at the hospital, doctors made an astonishing discovery: The marlin's bill had shoved Leblanc's silicone implant through her ribcage and into her chest cavity, preventing the sharp snout from puncturing her lung and possibly killing her.

In the United States it's a federal crime to imitate Smokey Bear or Woodsy Owl.

GHOSTOLOGY 101

*Whether you believe in ghosts or not, isn't it fun to think that
a spirit might be hovering near you right now? Wait—
you're in the bathroom? Eww…well, maybe not.*

B OO!
Ghosts are as popular as ever—just look at hit television
shows such as *Medium* and *Ghost Whisperer*, countless
accounts of "real-life" hauntings on cable TV, and the steady
stream of scary movies from Hollywood. In nearly every U.S. city,
you can take a ghost tour or hire a team of "ghost hunters" to
investigate your attic. In fact, a 2007 *Associated Press* poll reported
that 34% of Americans believe in ghosts and 23% say they've
seen one. Are all these people crazy? Or are ghosts real? If so,
where's the evidence? We'll tell you everything you need to know
to hold your own in this spirited debate.

SOUL CALL

Any phenomenon that can't be neatly explained by science is
deemed *paranormal*. Those who study this field are called *parapsychologists*, but it's not something you can get a degree in at your
local university. Most "ghost hunters" don't consider themselves
parapsychologists, calling themselves *paranormal investigators*
instead. Here are a few of the supernatural things they look for.

• **Spirit:** From the Latin *spiritus* ("breath"), this is a blanket term
for any *discarnate being*, one that lacks a physical body. There are
many forms that a spirit can theoretically take on.

• **Ghost:** A person (or animal) who is no longer living, but exists
nonetheless, just not in the physical realm.

• **Entity:** Any disembodied consciousness that can be classified as
a ghost. The two terms are often used interchangeably, along with
phantasm, phantom, wraith, spook, sprite, and *specter.*

• **Apparition:** How a ghost appears visually. It can manifest in
many different forms, from a "full-bodied" apparition to a mist to
what are called "shadow people"—small, dark masses that take on
a loosely human form. (Interestingly, ghosts rarely appear as a
white sheet with two eyeholes.)

If all U.S. ships that serve as memorials were a separate navy, it would be the world's third largest.

- **Orb:** A self-illuminated ball of light that travels through the air with some kind of intent. There are several theories as to exactly what they are—many people think of them as simple spirit forms.

- **Poltergeist:** The German word for "noisy ghost," this phenomenon is believed to throw objects, bang on walls, and slam doors. Poltergeists are often believed to be connected to adolescent females (perhaps it's all the hormones).

- **Residual haunting:** If a person performed a specific act over and over during life—such as putting wood into a stove—it can leave a *psychic impression* that plays over and over, like a tape recording. In a residual haunting, the ghost doesn't realize it's dead; it just keeps performing its task obliviously. (Sometimes, in reports of ghosts walking through walls, the original blueprints of the building reveal that a door once stood there.)

- **Intelligent haunting:** If the ghost crosses in front of you and you say "Hello," and it stops and looks at you, that's an intelligent haunting—a dead person that interacts with you.

HOW TO BECOME A GHOST

In the 1970s, Dietrich Dörner, a German psychologist, introduced the "Psi-Theory," the idea that combinations of behaviors and emotions create "Psi energy," also called *psychic energy*, which Dörner claimed can exist separate from the body. This theory was later promoted by Loyd Auerbach, one of today's leading parapsychologists. He believes that after someone dies, their Psi energy can remain intact.

According to Auerbach, some causes of death are more conducive to keeping that energy intact: A sudden, violent end is one way. Another possibility is that people who die with nagging, unfinished business are more likely to "hold" that thought and spend the afterlife trying to finish it. Yet no matter what led to the death, a disembodied energy field is very faint by modern measuring devices. But it can theoretically last for years, even centuries.

WHY AREN'T GHOSTS NAKED?

According to parapsychologists, a ghost either consciously or unconsciously remembers what he or she looked like, and some choose how they will appear to the living. The theory goes that your Psi energy contains information about you, including how you look and the clothes you wear. Ghosts whose Psi energy is still intact after death probably hold on to some of that information.

But ghosts aren't necessarily shaped like humans. Here's what one ghost looked like, according to what Auerbach says the ghost actually *told* him:

> A deceased woman who was in constant communication with a young boy (and seen by others, as it happens) said that as far as she knew, she was a ball of energy, of consciousness, though she also said she really didn't know that "ball" was the right word, since she felt kind of formless. How she pictured herself was how others perceived her—she noted that she was more or less connecting mind-to-mind to the boy (and others), and projecting the idea of her form, clothing, and her voice to him.

HOW CAN GHOSTS MOVE OBJECTS?

Again, it's all about energy, say parapsychologists. Spirits gain strength by drawing energy from *electromagnetic fields* (EMFs), or concentrations of charged particles in the air. These can be either natural or man-made—emitted by, among other things, electrical appliances, copper wiring, and static in the air on a stormy night. Paranormal investigators have also discovered that reports of ghost activity are more abundant in areas that have high concentrations of limestone, copper, chalk, iron, and rushing water. Why? They act like batteries and create strong EMFs.

Ever heard of *cold spots*? Those are created when a spirit draws heat energy from the air. A room can be 65°F, except for one small area where the temperature is 30° colder. When a spirit obtains enough energy, it can manifest into an apparition, control the air around it, and even move objects, talk, sing, or make footsteps. There are even accounts of ghosts recreating smells like cigarette smoke, flowers, blood, and perfume.

PSEUDO OR SCIENCE?

All these ghostly theories, say skeptics, are just that—theoretical. What concerns skeptics the most is when parapsychologists, ghost hunters, psychics, and laypeople talk about ghosts as if they're real, even though they offer no scientific proof to back it up. One of the world's most famous skeptics, James Randi, is a former stage magician who once relied on illusions to entertain, so he knows what it takes to fool people. To prove his point, Randi formed a foundation that sponsors the "One Million Dollar Challenge." Paid for by donations from scientific and charitable trusts, the prize of $1 million will be awarded to anyone who can prove the existence of the paranormal (ESP or ghosts) in a laboratory setting. "Our $1 million is safe," maintains Randi. "Believers will insist on believing despite the evidence no matter how strong that is." He says that skeptics aren't necessarily out to prove that ghosts *don't* exist—their goal is to curb the rampant lack of critical thinking among the people who say they do.

Auerbach is one of Randi's strongest critics...and vice versa. According to Auerbach, no one has won the prize because there's no possible way of matching Randi's strict guidelines. Ghosts don't operate on cue, says Auerbach, and they don't follow people to labs (mostly).

OCCAM'S RAZOR

A 14th-century English theologian and philosopher named William of Ockham said that when you're trying to solve a mystery, you first have to "shave off" any unlikely assumptions. That leaves you with the simplest explanation—which is usually the correct one. As it relates to the paranormal, skeptics use what became known as "Occam's razor" to mean, "If you hear howling in the night, the simplest explanation is that it was the wind."

"Well, it cuts both ways," says Michael Schmicker, author of *Best Evidence—an Investigative Reporter's Three-Year Quest to Uncover the Best Scientific Evidence for ESP, Psychokinesis, and Ghosts.* "If a million people report a ghost, Occam's razor says that ghosts probably exist. Based on the evidence we have—ghost sightings, deathbed visions, near-death experiences, historical reports from various cultures and eras—Occam's razor says that consciousness *does* survive death." That said, skeptics cite numerous simple explanations for phenomena that believers attribute to ghosts:

• **Physiological:** A medical condition known as *phantom limb* afflicts amputees who can "feel" a missing appendage, proving that the brain is capable of creating a reality that does not exist in actual life. Joe Nickell, a senior research fellow for the Committee for Skeptical Inquiry, says that people create "false realities" all the

People who sense a "presence" in an empty room perceive it as the opposite sex 90% of the time.

time. For example, many who claim they've seen ghosts often report feeling paralyzed when they wake up and see the apparition in the middle of the night. "This is just sleep paralysis," he says. Also referred to as a "waking dream," this occurs when the body is asleep, which causes the paralysis, but the brain is teetering between sleep and consciousness.

• **Environmental:** Temperature and humidity fluctuations cause houses to settle and creak. High EMFs caused by faulty wiring can cause nausea and hallucinations. Mix in low-frequency sound waves, such as the buzz of a fluorescent light, and that can cause people to hear unusual things. The flickering lights themselves cause eye strain and fatigue. These factors, say skeptics, lead to most "sightings."

In a 2007 case in China, two brothers found a great bargain— a five-story house for $6,500, reduced from $34,000. Why? Strange, ghostly noises echoed through the home, scaring out the previous owners, and the ones before them, going back 10 years. The brothers traced the noises to a pipe and then to an under-ground stream. The "ghosts" turned out to be catfish splashing. The brothers sold the house for $133,000.

• **Psychological:** Either due to wishful thinking or for more nefar-ious reasons (such as TV ratings), most "hauntings" are fabricated by the witnesses themselves. Nickell concludes his article with, "I've investigated haunted houses, inns, theatres, graveyards, light-houses, castles, old jails, and even office buildings. And I've never once found a paranormal explanation."

CASE CLOSED...RIGHT?

But then a curious thing happens when you go to the comments section following Nickell's article, which ran on MSNBC's news site during Halloween 2009: You find post after post saying, "That's BS; me and my brother saw a ghost at the *same time* for 20 whole seconds!"—or, "Don't tell me I didn't watch my remote control fly across the room by itself!" And dozens more.

Despite what the skeptics say, ghost hunters aren't going to stop hunting for ghosts. For their story,
float on over to page 174.

Orcas (killer whales), when traveling in groups, breathe in unison.

THE WEEKLY WILD NEWS

Behold these bizarre animal tales that might seem like sensational tabloid stories…except they're all real.

SNAKE WITH FOOT KILLED WITH SHOE!

Suining, China – Dean Qiongxiu, a 66-year-old woman, was awakened late at night in September 2009 by a strange scratching sound. "I turned on the light and saw this monster working its way along the wall using his claw." The monster was a 16-inch snake…that had a tiny foot growing from its belly, complete with a claw. Dean whacked it to death with her shoe. Biologists were unable to determine why the snake had grown a foot.

STONED WALLABIES MAKE CROP CIRCLES!

Tasmania – "We have a problem with wallabies entering poppy fields, getting as high as a kite, and hopping around in circles," said Tasmania's Attorney-General Lara Giddings in 2009. The dope-loving, kangaroo-like marsupials are having an adverse effect on the country's opium crop, which is grown for use in legal morphine. In addition to the wallabies, deer and sheep are also getting high after ingesting the poppies—but unlike the wallabies, they only *walk* around in circles, which is less damaging than hopping.

GOAT BOY FRIGHTENS VILLAGERS, POLITICIAN!

Lower Gweru, Zimbabwe – In 2009 villagers were shocked when a goat gave birth to a…*thing* with the body of a goat but the head of a human baby. The newborn creature was so freakish that even dogs refused to get near it. The "Goat Boy" only lived for a few hours, but fearing that it was evil, the villagers burned the corpse beyond recognition. The province's governor, Minister Jason Machaya, believes the "abomination" was the result of an illicit affair between a man and a goat. "It is my first time to see such an evil thing," he said. "It is really embarrassing." Provincial Veterinary Officer Thomas Sibanda disagreed, stating that our two species are incapable of interbreeding. He theorized that the goat suffered from *hydrocephalus*, or water on the brain, which resulted in a huge, grotesque head.

The average American consumes 7 bottles of liquor, 12 bottles of wine, and 230 cans of beer a year.

LOITERING CROC ARRESTED, THROWN IN JAIL!

Gunbalanya, Australia – When a giant female crocodile wandered into this small Northern Territory town in 2009, "She just sat there next to a fence, trying to look innocent," said officer Adam Russell. He had no choice but to arrest her. "I wanted to jump on her Steve Irwin style, but the rangers wouldn't let me." Instead, they bound her jaws shut and hauled her off to the local jail, where she spent three days in a cell before being taken to a croc farm. "She got a bit cranky and started hissing when people came near," said Russell, "but otherwise she was a model prisoner."

MUTANT HYBRID-DOG THING BECOMES ROADKILL!

Turner, Maine – After 15 years of missing pets, sightings of glowing eyes, and mysterious shrieks in the night, in 2006 the reign of terror ended when the creature responsible was found dead on the side of a road. But what was it? "It was evil, evil-looking, like something out of a Stephen King story," said resident Michelle O'Donnell. "And it had a horrible stench I will never forget." The creature, described by some as a giant rodent-dog hybrid, has been blamed for killing (among many other things) a Rottweiler. Before wildlife officials could inspect the corpse, however, vultures had eaten most of it. No positive identification was ever made.

GAY PENGUIN GOES STRAIGHT FOR WIDOW NEXT DOOR!

San Francisco, California – Harry and Pepper were the most controversial pair of the 40 Magellanic penguins at the San Francisco Zoo. The two males paired off in 2003, causing a barrage of anti-gay protests. But once the furor died down, Harry and Pepper were given an abandoned egg to incubate. "Of all of the parents that year, they were the best," said zookeeper Anthony Brown. But then in July 2009, Harry left Pepper for Linda, whose mate had recently died. Brown called Linda "conniving," claiming she had lured Harry away. Whenever Pepper tried to visit his ex-husband, Linda aggressively chased Pepper away. The news of the breakup renewed the controversy: The Christian group OneNewsNow said it proved that "nature prefers heterosexual relationships." Outspoken gay-rights advocate Wayne Besen disagreed: "There is no 'ex-gay' sexual orientation. Harry is simply in denial. The penguin is living what I call the 'big lie.'"

Fuel for thought: About 1 in 6 pregnant women get a craving to chew on coal.

STOP TALKING

We're just going to let these folks' words speak for themselves.

"There are many dying children out there whose last wish is to meet me."
—**David Hasselhoff**

"I don't like any female comedians. I think of her as a producing machine that brings babies in the world."
—**Jerry Lewis**

"My notion of a wife at 40 is that a man should be able to change her, like a banknote, for two 20s."
—**Warren Beatty**

"Out getting a taco."
—**sportscaster Bob Griese, on the absence of NASCAR driver Juan Pablo Montoya**

"My music isn't just music—it's medicine."
—**Kanye West**

"I believe in white supremacy until the blacks are educated to a point of responsibility."
—**John Wayne**

"A woman's place is in the wrong."
—**James Thurber**

"I'm blacker than Barack Obama. I shined shoes. I grew up in a five-room apartment. My father had a little laundromat in a black community not far from where we lived."
—**Rod Blagojevich**

"I'll fight any man, any animal. If Jesus were here, I'd fight him, too."
—**Mike Tyson**

"The Romanians, they'll stick a knife in you as soon as look at you. There might be some good ones. Forgive me if there are any here, and hopefully that's a 'no' because I wouldn't get out of here."
—**English city councilor Robert Fraser**

"Boy, they were big on crematoriums, weren't they?"
—**George H.W. Bush, visiting Auschwitz**

"Old people should just die and know when it's time to move over and leave the future for the young."
—**Roseanne Barr**

STRANGE FOLK

*Just a few strange entries about strange people
who do strange things in this strange world.*

CARPET BAGGER

A 48-year-old man identified only as "Georgio T." goes to New York City bars and lies down on his stomach on the floor, because he likes it when people step on him. He even carries around a rug he can attach to his back, along with a sign that says "Step on Carpet." Georgio explains, "When we were kids, one friend wanted to be the doctor, another wanted to be the carpenter. I wanted to be the carpet."

THAT SUCKS

"Some people like baseball better than football," says Michigan teenager Kyle Krichbaum, "but I like vacuum cleaners better than anything." Kyle loves the sound, feel, and look of vacuum cleaners, as well as the act of vacuuming. Kyle's love of vacuum cleaners is purely platonic, he says, but he just can't get enough of vacuum cleaners. In fact, he has more than 200 vacuum cleaners...and vacuums his parents' house five times a day.

EEK!

A 37-year-old woman in Stockholm, Sweden, suffered from *musophobia*, an unreasonable fear of mice. Her 59-year-old ex-husband knew that, and wanted revenge after their bitter divorce—so he went to her apartment and pushed 19 mice through her mail slot. "She is now being cared for in a hospital," said police. The man was arrested on harassment and animal-cruelty charges (and has demanded that all 19 mice be returned to him).

STUCK ON YOU

Thomas Borkman was arrested in Cook, Australia, after he broke into a woman's apartment. The woman woke up to discover that Borkman had glued his face to the sole of her foot. It took surgeons three hours to separate foot from face. Police said that the act had "some sexual significance."

The city of Kobe, Japan, built a 60-foot statue of the cartoon robot Gigantor. Cost: $1.5 million U.S.

BEAT THE PRESS

You'd think that in this world of Internet searches and instant fact-checking, it would be hard to slip a fake story into the news stream. But actually, it's pretty easy.

THIS JUST IN! "VP guns for shootout with Hillary" **THE STORY:** In the early days of the 2008 presidential campaign, the *Boston Herald* published an odd news story: Vice President Dick Cheney had challenged presidential candidate Hillary Clinton to a hunting contest. According to the *Herald*, Cheney had issued the challenge during an appearance on NBC's *Meet the Press.* Then, the story went on, Clinton declined the offer, saying, "I fired a gun once, but I didn't like it, and I didn't recoil" (a joke referring to her husband's infamous "I smoked marijuana, but I didn't inhale" remark). The *Herald* story was picked up by Google News...and then by everyone else.

NEVER MIND: Apparently the editors at the *Herald* didn't bother to verify whether Cheney had recently appeared on *Meet the Press* (he hadn't). Nor did they notice that the writer listed as the original source was Andy Borowitz—a well-known comedian and satirist. Borowitz had posted the story on his blog as a joke, and was as surprised as anyone when he saw it had been picked up by the *Herald* as a real story. The *Herald's* publisher, Kevin Convey, admitted, "We were bamboozled."

THIS JUST IN! "Stunning photos of underwater North Pole" **THE STORY:** In August 2007, news sites around the globe ran a Reuters news-service story about how a crew of Russian deep-sea explorers had planted their flag on the seabed under the ice of the North Pole. The accompanying pictures showed the Russian submersible they'd used to find the pole.

NEVER MIND: No one in the dozens of news organizations that reran the Reuters story noticed that the photos were actually images from the movie *Titanic.* Who did notice? A 13-year-old boy from Finland, who contacted his local newspaper to inform them of the mistake. Reuters later apologized and claimed that they'd pulled the images from a Russian television broadcast that

---

showed how such an expedition *might* look. Reuters had incorrectly captioned the photos and sent them out to the world. The good news: A Russian submarine did actually find the underwater North Pole—just not the one in the photos.

THIS JUST IN! "Chinese rocket makes historic launch"

THE STORY: On September 25, 2008, China's official state-run news Web site, Xinhua.org, posted a story about the much-anticipated launch of the manned *Shenzhou 7* rocket—a mission that would feature China's first-ever space walk. The story described the launch in great detail: "The firm voice of the controller broke the silence of the whole ship. Now the target is captured 12 seconds ahead of the predicted time." The article concluded, "Warm clapping and excited cheering breaks the night sky, echoing across the silent Pacific Ocean."

NEVER MIND: Astute viewers noticed one mistake: The report was posted two days *before* the launch occurred. When pressed for an explanation, Xinhua.org blamed it on a "technical error."

THIS JUST IN! "United Airlines files for bankruptcy"

THE STORY: This headline flashed across the financial news site Bloomberg.com in September 2008. Almost immediately, United's stock began to plummet—from $12 per share down to $10, then to $8, to $3, eventually down to a penny—wiping out more than 99% of the stock's nearly $1 billion value. In short, the headline nearly put the already-struggling airline out of business.

NEVER MIND: The headline wasn't from that day; it was from a story that had run in 2002—six years earlier, when United *did* file for bankruptcy. (The company had since regained some of its financial footing.) The *New York Times* tried to piece together the chain of blunders: "An old *Chicago Tribune* article was posted on the website of the *South Florida Sun-Sentinel*. That article was picked up by a research firm, which then posted a link to it on a page on Bloomberg.com, which sent out a news alert." The timing couldn't have been worse. The country was in the grip of the 2008 economic crisis, and investors were jittery. When the goof was discovered, trading was temporarily halted. United's shares soon returned to their pre-panic price of $12.

55% of Americans believe that they have a guardian angel.

THIS JUST IN! "Photos from doomed airliner found in ocean"

THE STORY: On an evening news broadcast in June 2009, Bolivian television station PAT reported that it had obtained exclusive images of the final moments of Air France Flight 447, which had crashed into the Atlantic just days earlier on its way from Brazil to Paris, killing all 228 people on board. Taken from inside the main cabin, the photos show a passenger hurtling to his death through a gaping hole in the fuselage. The images, explained the newscaster, were recovered from a digital camera that was found among the floating wreckage. By tracing its serial number, PAT had determined that the camera belonged to a children's author named Paulo G. Muller.

NEVER MIND: As the story spread to news outlets all over the world, questions began flooding the station: "Why is it daytime in the photos, when the plane crashed at night?" "Who is Paulo G. Muller?" "Why does one woman in the photo look like Kate from *Lost*?" A brief investigation ensued, and the "photos" were indeed found to be two still shots from the ABC series *Lost* (about the survivors of a plane crash). It wasn't clear how the photos had made their way onto TV, but the station had unwittingly fallen victim to a hoax—and an old one. Three years earlier, after a midair collision between a Boeing 737 and a business jet over the Amazon, a Brazilian blogger named Carlos Cardoso had posted the pictures along with a story about how the camera's memory card had been found in the jungle. He'd made it all up, including the bit about the children's author (who didn't even exist). Cardoso did it to prove a point: "People don't apply enough skepticism when it comes to viewing things on the Internet."

*   *   *

HOW DO YOU SPELL "BANGKOK"?

The proper name of Thailand's capital city has many variations. This is believed to be the official one, coming in at 163 letters: Krungthepmahanakornamornratanakosinmahintarayutthayamahadilokphopnopparatrajathaniburiromudomrajaniwesmahasatharnamornphimarnavatarnsathitsakkattiyavisanukamprasit

---

Nothing special? Between 2000 and 2005, 1,022 American baby girls were named Unique.

THE WORLD'S GONE CRAZY 2000

Remember back on January 1, 2000, when a computer programming error turned the world into a backwoods wasteland of financial ruin?

WE'RE ALL GONNA DIE...EVENTUALLY!
In 1958 a computer programmer named Bob Bemer noticed a potentially catastrophic problem: The punch cards that were currently in use for programming only allotted two digits to represent the year, so it showed up as "58" rather than "1958." Bemer was concerned that in the year 2000, as the numbers rolled over from "99" to "00," computers either wouldn't know how to handle double zeros, or they'd interpret it as the year 1900...and erase all of the data because it "hadn't happened yet." Even after Bemer lobbied his fellow programmers, IBM, and the U.S. government, none of them seemed too concerned about it. Surely by the year 2000, they figured, computers would be so advanced that the two-digit system would be replaced, wouldn't it?

Not really. Saving space in long streams of computing code is important, so the two-digit system remained the standard for the next four decades. In fact, nobody really brought up the looming "millennium bug," "century date change," "faulty date logic," or "Y2K" (short for "year 2000") until the mid-1980s.

OPEN THE POD BAY DOORS, HAL

In his 1984 book *Computers in Crisis*, Jerome Murray foretold of a world that will come to a screeching halt. Because nearly every aspect of life was computer-controlled, Murray argued, all of those systems would shut down on January 1, 2000. Power grids would fail. Air navigation systems would crash, and so would airplanes. And all digital records—including the world's most sensitive financial information—would be deleted.

After that, each subsequent year that loomed closer to Y2K brought even more dire predictions and tips to survive. For example, *Y2K Family Survival Guide* was a popular home video hosted by Mr. Spock himself, sci-fi icon Leonard Nimoy. He warned:

"Elevators may stop, heat may vanish. Water delivery systems may not deliver water for cooking, drinking, and bathing." Nimoy also warned that hospitals would be nonoperational, pharmacies would be locked down and unable to distribute vital medications, and nuclear power plants could stop working...or worse. They could all suffer core meltdowns.

EVERYBODY PANIC!

The worldwide frenzy kicked in full force around mid-1998. Books such as *Time Bomb 2000* and *Deadline Y2K* flew off the shelves while news analysts worried that the world's governments would enact global martial law in order to stop the anarchy that was sure to commence when the computers all stopped working.

The United States Congress didn't want it to ever get to that point. "We're no longer at a place of asking whether or not there will be any power disruptions," said Sen. Chris Dodd, "but we are now forced to ask how severe the disruptions are going to be." So in late 1998, Congress passed the Year 2000 Information and Readiness Disclosure Act, which oversaw both the public and private sectors in getting all the computers to be compliant. Suddenly, millions of programmers got to work updating millions of computer systems. In the U.S. alone, more than $300 billion was spent to add in those precious two digits.

Meanwhile, the Clinton administration conducted preparation drills in 27 major cities for any "national-security special event," such as a terrorist attack or coup attempt. In fact, a CNN poll revealed that about two-thirds of Americans believed terrorists *would* attack the country on or around New Year's Eve.

As 1999 scrolled toward its inevitable end, canned foods were purchased by the caseload. Sales of guns, generators, and bottled water spiked. Insurance companies sold millions of "Y2K policies." All that was left to do was hope for the best...and be prepared for the worst.

THE END OF THE END OF THE WORLD

At the stroke of midnight on January 1, 2000, the world waited with bated breath to see what would happen. And as you no doubt remember, nothing much happened. The lights stayed on, planes didn't fall out of the sky, and bank records stayed intact.

What's interesting is that the countries that scrambled to be "Y2K compliant" (primarily the U.S. and Britain) endured about the same amount of glitches as the countries that did next to nothing to update their software, such as Italy and South Korea. And the glitches that did occur were relatively minor:

• Radiation monitoring equipment in Japan briefly failed, setting off an alarm at a nuclear power plant.

• A Japanese telecommunications carrier discovered a few date errors in its network, but services remained online and the problem was fixed in less than three hours.

• Bus ticketing machines stopped working in two Australian states.

• The IRS accidentally sent out a few tax bills for the year 1900.

• Ten percent of computerized cash registers in Greece printed receipts with the year 1900.

• A hydroelectric facility in Kazakhstan had to revert to manual operation for a few days.

• 150 slot machines in Delaware stopped working.

• The U.S. Naval Observatory, which runs the clock that keeps the nation's official time, didn't have problems. But its Web site did: A programming error resulted in the date being listed as January 1, 19100. The same thing happened to the Web site of France's weather service and on AT&T's site.

• A computer registering the first "millennium baby" born in Denmark incorrectly listed the baby as 100 years old.

IT WASN'T A COMPLETE WASTE OF TIME

The threat of the world plunging back into a new Dark Ages, and the hysteria that surrounded it, were over. But there was one positive result of what the *Wall Street Journal* called "the hoax of the century." New York City established redundant, secondary computer networks to ensure that subways, phones, and banks would run in case of a Y2K shutdown. These networks remained online, and during the terrorist attacks of September 11, 2001, lower Manhattan's computer systems—most notably, those belonging to the financial institutions—did not crash, thus preventing what could have been a worldwide financial collapse.

"HEY Y'ALL, WATCH THIS!"

Just a reminder: Think twice before showing off.

URINE TROUBLE NOW

On the way home from a party in April 2009, a 21-year-old Minnesota man needed to relieve himself, so he asked his friend, who was driving, to pull over on a bridge. While the man was on the ledge peeing, he kept pretending to lose his balance. "Oh, no, here I go!" he shouted. And then he fell for real...onto jagged rocks 30 feet below. He was seriously injured, but survived.

KIND OF?

To show off to his friends in September 2007, a man in Portland, Oregon, put his Eastern diamondback rattlesnake's head into his mouth...and it bit him. He barely survived. "It's actually kind of my own stupid fault," he said.

NOT MICHAEL PHELPS

During a summer 2009 flood in Chattanooga, Tennessee, a 46-year-old man was standing near a raging culvert of water. Wearing only a pair of shorts, he bet his friends $5 that he could swim across the culvert. No one took the bet. He jumped in anyway. His body was found five days later, a mile and a half away. "It was an ego thing," said his cousin.

COME ON BABY, LIGHT MY FIRE

In 2008 a 33-year-old Swedish man was at a party and wanted to prove to his girlfriend how tough he was. So he poured gasoline on his arm and lit it on fire. By the time paramedics arrived, the man had severe burns to his upper body and was in a state of shock. In addition to his injuries, he was cited for reckless endangerment. A befuddled police spokesman said, "Don't ask me what the point of the trick was supposed to be."

EYEBALL BLING

*We decked out Uncle John with all of these new, innovative
fashion accessories, and—well, he got a lot of funny
looks. (Try it on your favorite friend or relative.)*

EYE-CATCHING JEWELRY
You may have thought that there was jewelry for every possible body part: fingers, wrists, neck, toes, ankles, ears, lips,
bellybutton—but now you can wear jewelry on your eyeballs, too.
Dutch designer Eric Klarenbeek has come out with a line of contact lenses that have thin metal wires attached to the center of
the lenses. The wires hang down and can be adorned with the
jewels of your choice. So you can walk around with a short string
of diamonds hanging from each eyeball (or, if you're really chic,
just one). "People who have worn my eye jewelry are amazed at its
comfort," Klarenbeek says. "You can't feel the wire dangling, it
doesn't affect your sight, and the lens moves along gently with
your eyeball." Asked what would happen if someone were to tug
on the wire connected to a contact lens, Klarenbeek said he was
quite sure that it would not cause your eyeball to fall out. They
cost about $300 per lens.

LEFT-HANDED UNDERPANTS

When it comes to men's underwear, left-handers have always been
at a disadvantage. The vertical opening at the front of most briefs
and boxers, which allows men to do their business without dropping their drawers, is made with right-handed people in mind.
Watch a lefty try to take a simple tinkle while wearing right-handed underpants and you'll think he's been drinking, or perhaps he's
missing several fingers. British underwear company Hom has come
out with a new design—drawers with a horizontal rather than vertical opening, making it just as easy for a lefty to open as a righty.
"In our view," said one retailer, "this is a vital step toward equality
for left-handed men."

NICE CUP IN BRA

Ladies, if you've ever found yourself thinking, "I wish I had a bra that could be easily converted into a 1.5-meter putting green," wish no more. British lingerie maker Triumph has introduced the Nice Cup in Bra (it was made for the Japanese market). When it's worn, it's a functional, green, corsetlike bra. But when you get the urge to putt a few golf balls, just take the bra off, unroll it—and it becomes a putting green. The bra's cups become holes at the end of the green. It even has pockets for extra balls and tees, and if you sink a putt, a recorded voice says, "Nice shot!" But there's more—the Nice Cup in Bra also comes with a miniskirt printed with the words "Be quiet" that can be converted into a flag to hush the crowd while you're concentrating.

WINKING PANTS

Do you want to be able to wink at people behind you while you're walking down the street...without turning around? Well, thankfully, some enterprising clothes designers in Everett, Washington, have invented "Winkers," pants that have eyes painted on the butt, just under the crease, so that as you walk, the eyes seem to open and close. So you "wink" as you walk. Winkers cost between $140 and $160.

THE VENDING MACHINE SKIRT

Let's say you're walking down the sidewalk dressed in an ordinary skirt and—*Here come the bad guys! And they're chasing you! Run! Hide!* Too bad you weren't wearing this special piece of clothing: the Vending Machine Skirt, by Tokyo designer Aya Tsukioka. It looks like a normal skirt, but when you need to become invisible, it quickly unfolds into a large, rectangular piece of cloth that looks like a soda vending machine. Just hold it in front of you and hide behind it, the idea goes, and you'll blend into the scenery. "Vending machines are on every corner of Japanese streets, and we take it for granted," says Tsukiokais. "That's how I came up with the idea for this dress."

*   *   *

"Fashion is what you adopt when you don't know who you are."

—Quentin Crisp

PLANTS GONE CRAZY

The more we find out about plants, the more we fear them.

PLANTIMAL

The New Scientist reported in 2008 that biologist Mary Rumpho of the University of Maine discovered a species of sea slug that is an animal…and a plant. The primary thing that distinguishes plants from animals is that plants use *photosynthesis*—they convert sunlight into energy needed for survival, while animals have to eat plants or other animals to get energy. But *Elysia chlorotica*, an inch-long, leaf-shaped, gelatinous mollusk that lives in shallow ocean waters along the Atlantic coast, is an animal that does *both*. It eats algae—a plant—and then incorporates genes from the algae into its own DNA. Then it utilizes those genes to create chlorophyll, the pigment that plants use to perform photosynthesis. A baby sea slug, Rumpho found, eats algae for just the first two weeks of its life, and lives off sunlight for the remainder of its lifespan, making it the first multicellular animal-plant hybrid known to science.

RAT-IVORE

Researchers on the Philippine island of Palawan reported in August 2009 that they'd discovered a new—and gruesome—species of carnivorous plant. It's a type of "pitcher plant," a group of plants that grow deep, pitcher-shaped traps filled with sticky liquid. Insects are lured to the pitchers by sight or smell, fall into them, and become trapped in the liquid. Acidlike enzymes then slowly dissolve the captured bugs, and the plant absorbs nutrients from them. The plant on Palawan works the same, but its cone-shaped pitchers are huge—more than a foot deep and seven inches diameter at the opening, and they can trap and eat not only insects but even small mammals such as rats. "It is remarkable," lead researcher Stewart McPherson said, "that it remained undiscovered until the 21st century." The researchers named the rat-eating plant *Nepenthes attenboroughii*—a tribute to 83-year-old wildlife broadcaster Sir David Attenborough, who commented, "I'm absolutely flattered."

FABRICATED MEMOIRS

Coming next fall: The memoirs of Uncle John, *in which he describes his colorful past—training elephants in Antarctica, flying biplanes for the Secret Service, and negotiating a peace treaty between the Klingons and Crutons on Uranus. Who cares if it's not all true? It should make for great bathroom reading!*

MAKING IT UP AS YOU GO

Most successful memoirs are written by people who are already famous—that's why their books sell well—and while the stories might sometimes stretch the truth a bit, you can be reasonably certain that they're mostly accurate. But in recent years, a new type of book has infiltrated the publishing industry: totally made-up memoirs written by authors known to almost no one, who become famous only because their books become famous. Probably the best-known example is *A Million Little Pieces*, by James Frey. For years he tried to sell a story of drug abuse, crime, and redemption as a novel, but no publisher was interested in it. In 2003 he finally got publishing powerhouse Doubleday to release it—as a memoir—and it became a national sensation, selling millions of copies. Frey's rise and subsequent fall on *The Oprah Winfrey Show* is fairly well known, but there have been several other fake memoirs with far more fantastic claims than Frey's. Here are a few of the most outrageous "memoirists."

MEMOIR: *Honor Lost: Love and Death in Modern-Day Jordan*, by Norma Khouri (2003)

WHAT SHE WROTE: Khouri and her best friend Dalia owned a hair salon in Amman, Jordan, in the 1990s. After Dalia fell in love with a Christian soldier, she was stabbed to death by her Muslim father in an "honor killing." Khouri was forced to flee the country, first to Greece, then to Australia, and wrote her memoir in Internet cafés whenever she could. When *Honor Lost* became a bestseller in Australia, Khouri was subjected to threats against her life and had to go into hiding. The book quickly became an international success, and Khouri became a symbol of independence and courage for oppressed women throughout the Arab world.

At the same time? 17% of drivers pick their noses in the car, and 17% flirt with other drivers.

THE TRUTH: In July 2004, the *Sydney Morning Herald* exposed Khouri as a fake. She *was* born in Jordan—but her family moved away when she was three years old. She was raised in Chicago, where she lived for nearly 30 years. During the 1990s, Khouri and her American husband, John Toliopoulos, were reportedly involved in several shady real estate deals in Chicago, and in 1999, after being questioned by the FBI, they moved to Australia. She never owned a hair salon in Jordan, and there was no proof that "Dalia" ever existed. Khouri initially stood by the book, then in August 2004 admitted that most of it was made up. She defended it anyway, saying it was for a good cause. *Honor Lost* had sold half a million copies in 15 countries by the time the hoax was revealed.

MEMOIR: *The Blood Runs Like a River Through My Dreams*, by Nasdijj (2000)

WHAT HE WROTE: Nasdijj (pronounced NAS-de-gee) was born on a Navajo reservation to an alcoholic Indian mother who died young, and a white father who abused him. He eventually got married, had a daughter, then adopted a young boy who suffered from Fetal Alcohol Syndrome. At the age of six, the boy died in Nasdijj's arms. A section of the story was published in *Esquire* magazine in 1999, and the piece was nominated for a National Magazine Award. The full-length memoir followed, to wide critical acclaim, making the *New York Times* Notable Book list and winning the Salon.com Book Award. Nasdijj went on to write two more memoirs—both of them also critical successes.

THE TRUTH: In 2006 the alternative news magazine *LA Weekly* published a story, titled "Navahoax," that provided proof that Nasdijj was actually a white writer of gay erotica from East Lansing, Michigan, named Timothy Patrick Barrus. The entire story of Nasdijj the Navajo had been made up. Barrus lost a lucrative publishing contract and currently writes angry diatribes about the publishing industry on various Internet sites.

MEMOIR: *Love and Consequences*, by Margaret B. Jones (2008)

WHAT SHE WROTE: Half white and half American Indian, Jones was removed from her childhood home after being sexually abused by a relative. At the age of eight, she landed in a foster family in South Central, a predominantly African-American neighborhood in Los Angeles. There, she was raised by a black woman known as "Big Mom," whose grandchildren became Jones's foster brothers and sisters. By the time she was a young teenager, she had joined the "Bloods" street gang, started doing drugs and making crack cocaine, and witnessed one of her foster brothers gunned down in front of their house. Jones finally escaped that life, attended the University of Oregon, graduated with a degree in ethnic studies, and sold her fascinating story to Riverhead Books, a division of Penguin.

THE TRUTH: In February 2008, a week before its official release, *Love and Consequences* received a rave review in *The New York Times*. Alongside the review ran a photo of Jones. A woman named Cyndi Hoffman saw it and called the publisher...and said the story was all fake. How did she know? She was Jones's older sister. And the author's name wasn't Jones; it was Seltzer, and she grew up in an upper-middle-class home in Sherman Oaks, California (where she went to the same private school as the Olsen twins). The publisher questioned Jones/Seltzer, and she eventually admitted that the entire story was made up. She said she was doing a good deed. "I thought it was my opportunity," she tearfully told the *Times*, "to put a voice to people who people don't listen to." The 19,000 copies of the book that had already gone out to stores were recalled, and full refunds were given to people who had pre-ordered it. Seltzer has not been published since (we think).

MEMOIR: *Angel at the Fence*, by Herman Rosenblat (scheduled for publication in February 2009)

WHAT HE WROTE: During World War II, Rosenblat was interned at Buchenwald concentration camp in Germany. One day in 1944 a young girl named Roma approached him from outside the fence—and threw him an apple. She was Jewish, but was posing as Christian with the help of a family that lived nearby. For the next seven months, the girl came to the spot regularly to sneak the boy food. Years later, in 1957, while living in Brooklyn, New York, Rosenblat went on a blind date...and his date turned out to be Roma. They fell in love and got married. The story appeared in numerous magazines over the years.

THE TRUTH: Several Holocaust scholars and Buchenwald experts pointed out that the story couldn't be true. For starters, there was no way anyone, much less a child, could have freely approached the fence surrounding the camp. And the spot where Roma supposedly waited outside would have been right next to an SS barracks. Also, Roma was supposedly being hidden by a Christian family near the camp. If that had been true, it's unlikely that she would have left her hiding place...to stand outside of a concentration camp. The truth was that Rosenblat really did survive Buchenwald, and Roma really was hidden by a Christian family—200 miles from the camp; they never met in Germany. In late 2008, under pressure from the press and the publisher, Rosenblat admitted he made up the love story. "I wanted to bring happiness to people," he said. "My motivation was to make good in this world." The publication of *Angel at the Fence* was immediately cancelled.

Freyed again: Before the hoax was uncovered, the couple appeared on *The Oprah Winfrey Show* twice. Oprah called the book the "greatest love story ever told on this show."

MEMOIR: *Misha: A Mémoire of the Holocaust Years*, by Misha DeFonseca (1997)

WHAT SHE WROTE: When her parents were taken to Auschwitz by the Nazis in 1941, seven-year-old Misha left Brussels, Belgium, to search for them. Over the next four years, she traveled 1,900 miles, during which time she fought with resistance groups, wandered in and out of the Warsaw Ghetto, killed a Nazi soldier with a pocketknife, and, most amazingly, was fed and protected for a time by a pack of wolves. The book was first published in the U.S., didn't do well, but later became a bestseller in Europe. It even inspired an Italian opera and a French film.

THE TRUTH: Like *Angel at the Fence*, the book drew the suspicion of Holocaust historians from the start. In 2008, after an investigation by a Belgian newspaper, Misha DeFonseca finally confessed: Her name was Monique De Wael, and while her parents were in fact taken away by the Nazis, they were members of the Belgian Resistance—and not Jews, but Catholics. And she never went looking for them, but had spent the war years with her grandfather in Brussels. After admitting her deception, Defonseca said she had always "felt Jewish." And, she added, "The story in the book is mine. It is not the actual reality—it was my reality. I had been telling my story for years and believed it to be true."

THE HARSH REALITY OF REALITY SHOWS

First, we found out that pro wrestling was fake, and now they tell us that reality shows are way more scripted than we realized. Why? Because entertainment (and ratings) can't be left up to chance. Here are some behind-the-scenes stories.

PROJECT RUNWAY (Bravo, 2004–08; Lifetime, 2009–present)
Premise: In this show hosted by model Heidi Klum, aspiring fashion designers compete to create the best new clothing line.
Story: The judges send a contestant home at the end of each episode, but critics charge that it's not the least talented one who gets booted, but the least entertaining. The proof, they say, is in the closing credits, which contain a disclaimer that says that the final decisions are made by the producers—although during the show, the judges make it sound like it's their decision. "*Project Runway* has separated itself as the most shameless of all the reality shows in keeping around contestants who have no business being there just because they 'make good TV,'" said *Entertainment Weekly's* Dalton Ross.

Even some of the "real" moments are faked. One morning, Season 2 contestant Diana Eng woke up to find a camera staring her in the face. "They scared me so bad I jumped and screamed. They said that it wasn't good enough, so I had to pretend to wake up again."

AMERICAN IDOL (Fox, 2002–present)
Premise: Hoping to land a recording contract, amateur singers compete before a panel of judges. Viewers call in to vote for their favorite performer; whoever gets the fewest votes is off the show.
Story: After Season 8 contestant Ju'Not Joyner was voted off, he said of the show: "It's a fixed thing if I ever saw one"—referring to how the producers had labeled him a troublemaker after he called the show's contract a "slavetract." He also wouldn't let the show do a story on how he grew up in "the 'hood." Ju'Not said, "They

wanted me to put that out to the world and expose my personal business for ratings. I wouldn't do it."

HELL'S KITCHEN (Fox, 2005–present)

Premise: Aspiring chefs compete against each other in a working restaurant; one contestant is eliminated at the end of each episode. The winner—chosen by chef Gordon Ramsay—receives a coveted job as head chef at one of Ramsay's restaurants.

Story: Part of the premise is that the participants work long days and are cut off from the outside world, but many of the show's contestants have complained that they were treated like *prisoners.* "They locked me in a hotel room for four days," said Jen Yemola, a 2007 competitor. "They took all my books, my CDs, my phone, any newspapers. I was allowed to leave the room only with an escort. I couldn't talk to my family." The production crew are also under strict orders not to interact with them. Contestant Jessica Cabo said, "The only person I ever felt close to was the sound guy, because he was sticking a microphone up my shirt every day."

AMERICA'S NEXT TOP MODEL (CW, 2003–present)

Premise: In this show created by supermodel Tyra Banks (who's also the lead judge), young women compete for a modeling contract.

Story: The rules make it clear that the contestants must not have previous experience as a model in a national campaign, and they can't be friends of Banks. That's why viewers complained in 2007 after Saleisha Stowers, 21, won the crown over fan favorite Chantal Jones, 19. For one thing, Stowers appeared in a Wendy's commercial a year earlier (she says she was acting, not modeling). In addition, when she was 14, Stowers attended a "self-esteem camp" hosted by Tyra Banks. Then word got out that over the years, Stowers had modeled at several functions where Banks was present, including once on her talk show. Her rival, Jones, said, "I looked like an amateur because I am. Saleisha wasn't exactly an amateur."

Ever notice how reality-show contestants say, "I'm not here to make friends," and then later they all talk about how they've become such good friends? Turn to page 341 for more unreal reality stories.

SEXY *FINDING NEMO*

In recent years, it's become popular for college-age women to wear "sexy" Halloween costumes like naughty nurses and French maids. Here are a few more costumes, proving that not everything can be sexed up (although somebody's clearly trying).

• **Sexy Freddy Krueger.** What's sexier than a child killer back from the dead who haunts your dreams? This costume consists of Freddy's striped sweater, lengthened into a short dress, along with a glove in the shape of the character's signature knife-fingers.

• **Sexy Cab Driver.** Since cab drivers don't generally wear uniforms, this costume looks more like a "sexy cab": a short, low-cut yellow jumpsuit with black-and-white checkered sides.

• **Sexy Little Bo Beep.** A short blue-and-white dress. The weird part is that it comes with a matching costume for a small dog.

• **Sexy Elvira.** The cable-TV and beer-commercial spokesperson (played by Cassandra Peterson) already wears a low-cut dress with a slit up the side. The "Sexy Elvira" costume has an even more plunging neckline and a higher leg slit, if that's possible.

• **Sexy Finding Nemo.** How did they make a child-age, lost, mildly disabled (one bad fin) clownfish into a sexy outfit? With a short orange-and-white dress and matching stockings.

• **Sexy Dora the Explorer.** The cartoon character aimed at preschoolers is a preschooler herself, and she wears a purple shirt and orange shorts. This costume gives Dora a low-cut shirt and short skirt instead.

• **Sexy Super Mario Bros.** The Nintendo video game characters Mario and Luigi are chubby, middle-aged, mustachioed, stereotypically Italian guys who work as plumbers in Brooklyn. But they can be "sexy"…if you put short skirts on them.

• **Sexy Nun.** Short skirt, lots of cleavage, and a nun's habit. How sinful.

Surprise! 23% of all psychiatrists in the U.S. do business in the New York City metro area.

MOUNTAIN OF THE DEAD

More than 50 years ago, a group of experienced skiers met a gruesome end on a snowy mountain range. And to this day, no one knows for sure what happened to them.

INTREPID EXPLORERS

In January 1959, 23-year-old Igor Dyatlov led a group of 10 college students from the Ural Polytechnic Institute on a two-week cross-country ski trek across the northern Ural mountains of Russia (then the Soviet Union). To reach their destination, the eight men and two women first had to ski over a mountain pass known as Kholat Syakhl. In the language of the Mansi people native to the area, the name means "Mountain of the Dead." But as far as Dyatlov's team was concerned, that was just folklore.

Just three days into the trip, one of the members, Yuri Yudin, felt sick, so he left the group and returned home. The remaining nine continued on…and no one ever saw them alive again.

STORMY WEATHER

A few facts about the days leading up to the disappearance were pieced together from diaries and cameras that were later found at one of the expedition's campsites. On January 31, the group reached the base of the mountain and stored some equipment and food they would need on the way back. The next day, they started for the pass. But heavy snow caused whiteout conditions, and the group veered off course. Realizing their mistake, Dyatlov decided to make camp there on the slope and wait out the storm.

After that, all that's really known is that the group failed to report in as expected on February 12. Initially, this didn't cause much alarm; overland ski trips often run longer than expected. But as the days ticked by, family members became more and more concerned. On February 20, a rescue expedition of students and teachers was launched. The Russian army and police soon joined in, and on February 26, the first team reached the abandoned campsite on Kholat Syakhl.

A person from Sweden is more likely to know the size of the U.S. population than an American is.

ONE CRAZY NIGHT

When the film from one of the cameras was developed, the photographs showed the group of healthy young men and women posing for the camera, smiling, seemingly having a great time. But the scene the rescuers came upon showed a much different picture: One of the heavy canvas tents had been slashed through from the inside, as if the occupants were desperate to escape. Footprints led the searchers down the mountain to find two men, dressed only in their underwear, frozen to death. About a hundred yards away was Dyatlov himself, wearing only one shoe, also frozen to death. Additional searches eventually turned up two more frozen corpses away from their tent, both of whom were wearing each other's clothes. They all seemed to have no external wounds, and four bodies were still unaccounted for. They weren't found until May, in a nearby ravine.

When medical examiners couldn't find any injuries on the first five bodies, they ruled the cause of death as hypothermia. But of the four bodies found later, three had severe (but not life-threatening) injuries, one to the skull and two to the chest. And one of the women was missing her tongue, though it was unclear if it had been cut out or if she'd bitten it off herself. "In the absence of a guilty party," the final verdict stated, the members were deemed to have been killed by an "unknown compelling force." The inquest was officially closed; the files were packed away until 1993 when they were finally declassified. But the "official files" have only added to the mystery.

TIN-FOIL HATS: ON

As more evidence has come to light, three theories have been proposed to explain what happened on Kholat Syakhl, now called Dyatlov Pass.

• **Secret military tests:** Recent discoveries of scrap metal near Kholat Syakhl suggest that the Russians were using the area for secret military tests. Low levels of alpha radiation found on some of the victims' clothes suggest that the testing may have been nuclear. So perhaps the nine adventurers wandered into the middle of some kind of experiment. The Soviet government denied this, and the search team found no evidence of any type of explosion.

• **Alien attack:** Hikers about 30 miles south of the pass reported seeing orange spheres in the sky the night the expedition met its end. Similar sightings were recorded throughout February and March. During the open-casket funeral for four of the members who froze to death, their relatives noticed that the victims' hair had turned gray and there was a strange, orange cast to their skin. So perhaps the orange lights scared the first five out of their tents, where they died of exposure, and the four others who searched for them were then attacked by those same orange lights.

• **Avalanche:** Brian Dunning, author of *Skeptoid: Critical Analysis of Pop Phenomena,* looks for a more plausible explanation: "Sometime during the night, a loud noise, either from a nearby avalanche, a jet aircraft, or military ordnance, convinced at least five members of the group that an avalanche was bearing down on them. They burst out of the tent wearing whatever they happened to be sleeping in and ran." Then, says Dunning, they got lost trying to get back to the camp. And when the other four went to look for them, they got caught in a real avalanche—which might explain the internal injuries and the woman's missing tongue.

Dunning also points out that the radiation found on the clothes may have actually come from their camp lanterns, which contained a radioactive substance called thorium (the lanterns even had a radioactive symbol on them). So what about the orange skin and gray hair? "Their bodies had been exposed outdoors for weeks," said Dunning. "Of course they looked terrible."

CASE (NOT) CLOSED

Still, many lingering questions about the Dyatlov Pass Incident keep the conspiracy theories alive: Why did the searchers find so many sets of footprints? An avalanche would have covered them all up, along with the camp. And if it *was* a simple avalanche that killed the group, why would the Russian government try to cover it up? Why say the skiers were killed by an "unknown compelling force"? Nearly 30 years after the case was officially put to rest, the chief investigator, Lev Ivanov, made this statement: "I suspected at the time and am almost sure now that these bright flying spheres had a direct connection to the group's death." But just what were those spheres? Strange weapons, UFOs, or something else?

"If I could ask God just one question," said Yuri Yudin, the skier who had to turn back, "It would be, 'What really happened to my friends that night?'"

OWW! OWW!

Sometimes life slaps you upside the head…twice.

OWW! Ralph Needs, 80, of Groveport, Ohio, was hospitalized in 2009 after three robbers broke into his home, tied him up, and pistol-whipped him. They broke Needs's nose and stole his truck, computer, and credit cards.

OWW! OWW! Four days later, Needs's son was giving his dad a lesson in self-defense when he loaded up a 9mm pistol—and accidentally shot Needs in the hand. Needs was treated at a nearby (and familiar) hospital and released. His son was not charged with a crime.

OWW! A San Diego, California, Wells Fargo bank was robbed in September 2008. The robber escaped with an undisclosed amount of cash.

OWW! OWW! The same Wells Fargo bank was robbed—on the same day, three hours later—by another bank robber. An FBI spokesman said the robbers were, in order, "The Hard-Hat Bandit," known for wearing a yellow hard hat during his robberies, and "The Chatty Bandit," known for talking on a cell phone as he entered the banks he was about to rob. The two were not working together, the spokesman said. Both of the bandits were later arrested and sent to federal prison.

OWW! Hundreds of thousands of Brazilians lost their jobs during the recent economic crisis.

OWW! OWW! In July 2009, the Associated Press reported that people seeking information about their unemployment benefits on the Brazilian Labor Ministry's Web site were given passwords such as "bum" and "shameless." Labor Minister Carlos Lupi apologized, and blamed the prank on the private company that handles the Web site's security system.

OWW! Stephanie Martinez was working in the Pizza Patron restaurant in Denton, Texas, in July 2008 when a man in sunglass-

---

Brazilian soccer star Ramalho reportedly had to spend 3 days in bed after taking a suppository orally.

es and a bushy wig walked in, pointed a gun at her, and demanded money. She started getting cash out of the register—when fellow employee Rudy Sandoval jumped on the man and started punching him. In the melee, the robber's wig and glasses flew off.

OWW! OWW! When the wig and glasses flew off, Martinez recognized the robber: It was her father. "I dropped the money," Ms. Martinez said afterward. "I said, 'Don't hit him again! That's my dad!'" Her father ran out of the store and to a getaway car—in which, it turned out, Martinez's husband and mother were waiting. They were all in on the plot, though police later determined that Stephanie Martinez knew nothing about it. Her father, husband, and mother were captured and arrested.

OWW! In the middle of an October night in 2005, a mugger pulled a handgun on a man in Milwaukee, Wisconsin, and demanded money. The victim gave the mugger all the cash he had. A pickup truck, which police believe was the getaway car, then rushed up in reverse...and crashed into the robber and the victim. The driver of the truck then fled the scene, leaving the injured robber there.

OWW! OWW! OWW! OWW! OWW! The robber tried to get away with the cash by limping into the street...and was hit by a woman driving a Lexus. The woman in the Lexus backed up...and ran into him again. Them she backed up again...and ran into him one more time. After the third strike, the robber reached into his pocket for his gun...and shot himself in the leg. The woman ran into him again and drove off. Police showed up and arrested the robber, who was taken to the hospital with serious injuries. The victim was treated for minor injuries.

*　　*　　*

PAINFUL ACTIVISM

In 2008 Hollywood star and environmentalist Harrison Ford wanted to call attention to deforestation, so he had his chest hair waxed on live TV. "Every little bit of rainforest that gets ripped out," he cringed during the procedure, "it hurts!"

A Dutch company has devised technology to make lamps and other household items "float" in the air.

DON'T DO DRUGS. REALLY.

Or you might end up doing something very stupid. Like these people did.

- **In 2009** Jonathan James Sweat, 18, drove his SUV through the front window of the state attorney's office in Gainesville, Florida. When the police arrived, he told them they couldn't arrest him on DUI charges because he hadn't been drinking—he'd been smoking pot. He was arrested.

- **In 2008** an 18-year-old Seattle woman made an ATM deposit into her bank account. But she put the wrong envelope into the machine—instead of one filled with money, she accidentally "deposited" one that was full of methamphetamine. A bank employee found the meth the next morning. The woman was arrested.

- **A 40-year-old** Silverdale, Washington, man was pulled over for erratic driving in 2008. When he handed the officer his wallet, some white powder fell out of it. The man told the officer it was cocaine, but it was okay because he only used it when he was with prostitutes, and he'd been with one that evening. He was arrested.

- **Police raided** the house of a suspected drug dealer in Joliet, Illinois, in 2009 and found three marijuana plants in his back yard. The man's explanation: The plants were for his dog, who was learning to sniff out marijuana for law-enforcement officers. He was arrested. (The dog was not.)

- **A man** flagged down a police car on a Philadelphia street late one night in 2009 and told the officers that he'd lost his car... while he was trying to buy drugs. To compound the problem, his six-year-old stepson was in the car. The boy was found two hours later and taken to his mother. And though the man scored points for helping the police find his son, he was arrested.

- **A police** officer in Lebanon, Pennsylvania, was in a convenience store when he noticed something odd about 29-year-old Cesar Lopez. What caught his eye? Lopez had a baseball cap in his hand, and a small plastic bag of marijuana stuck to his forehead. He was arrested.

A strand of spider silk the width of a pencil could stop a Boeing 747 airplane in flight.

REAL FRANKENSTEINS

*Mary Shelley's fictional doctor who screamed "It's alive, it's alive!"
wasn't purely an imaginary figure. Lots of scientists over the
years have attempted to bring the dead back to life.*

JOHANN DIPPEL (1673–1734)

This theologian, alchemist, and natural-born troublemaker was born in the real Castle Frankenstein in Germany, and may have served as the inspiration for Mary Shelley's 1818 novel *Frankenstein*. He dabbled in many disciplines—and his religious views got him imprisoned for heresy. Why was he so controversial? Working in his lab, Dippel whipped up a concoction of human bones, blood, and bodily fluids that he called the "Elixir of Life"— the drinker, he claimed, would live forever. (He also discovered that his elixir, when combined with potassium carbonate, made a useful dye known today as Prussian blue.) There's no evidence that Dippel tried to stitch body parts together, but he was fond of putting legs, arms, heads, and torsos—both animal and human— into huge vats and boiling them down in the hope of, as he called it, "engendering life in the dead." According to some accounts, the resulting stench caused the townspeople to demand that he end the grotesque experiments or risk being expelled from the country. Dippel wouldn't give in, so he was exiled. He was rumored to have been later poisoned in Sweden.

LAZZARO SPALLANZANI (1729–1799)

Another possible inspiration for Shelley's mad doctor was this well-respected 18th-century Italian scientist, who decapitated snails to see if their heads would grow back and blinded bats to prove that they navigated by echolocation. While a professor at Pavia University, Spallanzani reported to the Royal Society in London that he had attained "resurrection after death" by sprinkling water on seemingly dead microbes. One of his contemporaries, the writer Voltaire, wrote, "When a man like him announces that he has brought the dead back to life, we have to believe him." But Voltaire was wrong—Spallanzani later realized the organisms were merely dehydrated, which led him to conduct further experiments proving that microbes could be killed by boiling (information that Louis Pasteur later put to great use). Italian researcher Paolo Mazzarello claims that Spallanzani was the inspiration for "Der Sandmann," a short story written in 1815 by E.T.A. Hoffman about a scientist who builds an artificial human. Written a year before Mary Shelley started *Frankenstein*, the story was a huge success in Europe and could well have planted the seed for Shelley's book.

GIOVANNI ALDINI (1762–1834)

At the turn of the 19th century, scientists first experimented with *galvanism*—using electrical currents to stimulate nerves and muscles. The pioneer was Luigi Galvani, who discovered that a dead frog's legs would kick when zapped with electricity. His nephew, Giovanni Aldini, took that work to a new level by galvanizing larger creatures. Huge crowds turned out to see the mad puppeteer manipulate the dead. According to a witness account:

> Aldini, after having cut off the head of a dog, makes the current of a strong battery go through it: the mere contact triggers terrible convulsions. The jaws open, the teeth chatter, the eyes roll in their sockets; and if reason did not stop the fired imagination, one would almost believe that the animal is suffering and alive again!

In 1803 Aldini released the book *An Account of the Late Improvements in Galvanism,* full of illustrations showing the results of his experiments in graphic detail. He was also the first person to apply the use of electrical impulses to treat the mentally ill—a procedure later known as electroshock therapy.

ANDREW URE (1778–1857)

This Scottish scientist was convinced that electrical stimulation of the *phrenic nerve*, a nerve that runs between the neck and the abdomen, could restore the dead to life. In 1818 he caused a sensation in Glasgow when he attempted to prove his theory by zapping the body of murderer John Clydesdale shortly after he was hanged. Although Ure was able to make the dead man appear to breathe and kick his legs, as well as open his eyes and make horrific faces, he was unable to resuscitate the corpse. However, the event is notable for what Ure suggested afterward: Successful resuscitation might have been achieved, he said, if the body had been shocked by two "moistened brass knobs" placed over the

---

phrenic nerve and diaphragm—an early description of what we now know as a defibrillator.

ROBERT E. CORNISH (1894–1963)

In 1932 this scientific wunderkind (he graduated from the University of California at age 18 and earned his Ph.D. by 22) became obsessed with the idea that he could bring the dead back to life, not be electricity but through the use of a teeter-totter, or seesaw. Inspired by the work of George Washington Crile on blood transfusion, Cornish believed that placing a recently deceased patient on a seesaw and moving him or her up and down rapidly, combined with an injection of epinephrine and oxygen, would get the blood circulating again. For over a year, he tried to revive victims of heart attack, drowning, and other sudden deaths with his seesaw therapy but had no success. Then, in 1934, Cornish was able to resurrect two dogs, Lazarus IV and V, for a short time (no word on the fates of Lazauruses I through III). He later played himself in the 1935 movie *Life Returns*, about a doctor who attempts to revive the dead.

VLADIMIR DEMIKHOV (1916–1998)

Russian physician Demikhov is credited with groundbreaking work in organ transplant surgery. However, his notoriety stems from some grotesque experiments with dogs. A surgeon in the Red Army in World War II, Demikhov honed his surgical technique while amputating the shattered limbs of wounded soldiers, skills he put to use later when he grafted the head of one dog onto the body of another. Demikhov made 20 of these two-headed creatures, none of which survived more than a month after surgery. His work was reported by *National Geographic* and *Time* magazine in the 1950s as part of a bizarre Cold War race between the United States and the U.S.S.R. to be the first to successfully transplant a human brain. So far, no one has been able to accomplish that feat.

But all of these men were nothing more than mad scientists from a bygone area. Right? Surely modern scientists don't try the same kinds of experiments...like creating part-human, part-animal creatures. Actually, they do. Turn to page 376 for "Manimals."

SITTIN' IN A TREE, PART I

*On December 10, 1997, Julia "Butterfly" Hill climbed to a platform
180 feet above the ground in a giant redwood tree she called "Luna."
She didn't come down for two years. Here's why she did it.*

THE GOOD

For 118 years, the Pacific Lumber Company logged the largest privately owned old-growth redwood grove in the United States, a stand of ancient trees up to 360 feet tall, 15 feet in diameter and up to 2,000 years old. P.L., as the locals in Scotia, California, called the company, began in 1863 with 6,000 acres of timberland. By the 1920s, the company had 65,000 acres and, with 1,500 employees, was the biggest employer in Humboldt County. By the time Stanwood Murphy became company president in 1931, the Save the Redwoods League of San Francisco was already very vocal about the need for preserving the ancient redwoods. Murphy listened and made a revolutionary change to his business: P.L. would no longer clear-cut its holdings (standard practice at the time), but would adopt a "selective-cut" system of logging. This meant that the company would cut no more than 70 percent of the mature trees in a stand, leaving enough younger trees to hold the soil and to seed a new generation. Murphy never allowed more trees to be cut than the forest could replace in a year.

Murphy and his heirs were hailed for their sustainable logging practices, as well as for their treatment of P.L. employees. The company provided the loggers affordable housing, health and life insurance, a pension plan, and, by the 1960s, scholarships for their children. According to Warren Murphy, the last Murphy to run Pacific Lumber Company, "We were the good guys. It was fun, it was easy—it was a great life."

THE BAD

In 1985 a Texas billionaire and corporate raider named Charles Hurwitz attempted a hostile takeover of the family-owned Pacific lumber. On September 27, the takeover became official: P.L. was now a subsidiary of Hurwitz's company, Maxxam Inc. of Texas... and life in Scotia changed forever.

THE UGLY

Maxxam Inc. now had a massive amount of acquisition debt: $800 million. New CEO Hurwitz decided to make some radical changes of his own. After announcing to P.L. employees his version of the Golden Rule—"He who owns the gold, rules"—he sold off the company assets, drained the $60 million pension fund and adopted a new logging policy: Clear-cut the redwoods as quickly as possible. Hurwitz made no secret of his plan to eliminate *all* of the ancient redwoods on P.L. property within 20 years. As the 1,000-year-old trees began to fall at an alarming rate, environmental groups protested. When they filed suits to stop the logging, Hurwitz responded by speeding up his operations, resorting to illegally clear-cutting hundreds of trees in an old-growth grove known as Owl Creek. He only had a permit for thinning the grove, and U.S. Fish and Wildlife Service officials maintained a presence there to ensure that Hurwitz stayed within the law. But the government agents only worked on weekdays, so Hurwitz's loggers went into the forest on weekends and holidays and took down as many trees as they could...as fast as they could.

TIMBER WARS

Environmental groups were up in arms. Earth First!, Save the Redwoods League (formed in 1918), the Bay Area Coalition for Headwaters, EPIC (the Environmental Protection Information Center), and the Sierra Club all joined forces. Thousands attended rallies in San Francisco and across Northern California. They staged sit-ins at the company's offices and marched through local timber towns protesting P.L.'s clear-cutting practices. But in the end, the demonstrations did little to slow the logging, so the protesters went to the groves and became activists. Some chained themselves to trees (hence the term "tree hugger"), others chained themselves to bulldozers; still others locked their arms together with steel bands to form human walls across access roads to stop the logging trucks.

In September 1987, they added a new tactic to their arsenal: two activists—code-named "Tarzan" and "Jane"—climbed a pair of redwoods that had been marked for destruction...and sat in them. If the loggers felled those trees, they could be charged with murder, so for the time being no one was going to cut them down. It was the first successful tree-sit.

Oldest driver to win a race at Daytona: Actor Paul Newman, in 1995. He was 75.

ENTER JULIA HILL

Ten years later, in October 1997, Julia Hill wandered into the Earth First! base camp in Stafford, California. The wide-eyed 23-year-old from Arkansas was anxious to do her bit to save the redwoods. In 1996 she'd nearly been killed by a drunk driver, and she spent most of the next 12 months in rehab. "As I recovered," she later wrote, "I realized my whole life was out of balance." A road trip out west brought her to the redwoods, where she'd had an almost religious experience while visiting a grove of the silent giants. "My spirit knew it had found what it was searching for," she said, and she resolved there and then to do whatever she could to save the trees. An activist who went by the name "Almond" sized her up, then said they needed someone to tree-sit "Luna," a 1,000-year-old redwood that Pacific Lumber had marked for felling with blue paint a few months earlier. So far the activists had prevented Luna's destruction by rotating tree-sitters in and out of it, but they'd run out of volunteers. Without hesitation, Hill said, "I'll do it."

MADAME BUTTERFLY

Over the next few days Hill got a crash course in the art of tree-sitting. Almond told her tree-sitters usually stayed up in the tree for three to seven days at a time, depending on their tolerance for cold, hunger, and threats from loggers. Volunteer ground crews hiked in food, water, and supplies, and packed out trash (including personal waste). Every rotation and every supply delivery required the ground team to sneak past P.L. security guards and Humboldt County deputies in the middle of the night. Almond advised Hill to take a "forest name" to protect her identity. Other tree sitters had names like Cedar, Geronimo, Blue, and Zydeco. What was hers going to be? Hill thought back to when she was seven and hiking in the Pennsylvania mountains. A butterfly had landed on her shoulder and stayed with her for hours. She chose "Butterfly."

Before she knew what was happening, Julia "Butterfly" Hill found herself standing at the base of the giant redwood, staring up. She'd never even climbed a rock before, much less a 200-foot tree. Now she was being strapped into a climbing harness and, after a quick lesson on how to tie knots, about to scale the equivalent of an 18-story building. She swallowed her fear and began to climb.

For the second part of Hill's story, go to page 261.

PIZZA HUH?

For years, China has been the world capital of pirated products. Shoppers there can browse through everything from stereos and clothes to office supplies and food—all cheap knockoffs of famous brands, with the names slightly changed. Here are a few of our favorite faux brands.

- Bucksstar Coffee (Starbucks)

- Cala-Cala (Coca-Cola)

- Chintendo Vii (Nintendo Wii)

- Skerpie (Sharpie)

- Sonia headphones (Sony)

- Penesamig (Panasonic)

- Hetachi TVs (Hitachi)

- Abercrombif & Titch (Abercrombie & Fitch)

- Georgi Amoni (Giorgio Armani)

- Cerono beer (Corona)

- Nire, Ekin, Mike, and IVIKE (all Nike)

- Cnoverse Ball Star (Converse All Star)

- Abcids and Odidoss (Adidas)

- Pantboy (*Playboy*)

- BYD cars (BMW)

- Fuma (Puma shoes. *Fuma* is Spanish for "smoke," so the Fuma logo is a puma leaping...with a lit cigar in its mouth.)

- Paradi (Prada)

- S&M's (M&M's)

- What Friends (Wheat Thins)

- Pizza Huh (Pizza Hut)

- PolyStation (PlayStation)

- Snooby (Snoopy merchandise)

- Sword of the Kings toys (*Lord of the Rings*)

- Ratman (Batman)

- Rock Hero: Jona Brothers (Guitar Hero: Jonas Brothers)

- iPoa (iPod)

- Unbelievable This Is Not Butter (I Can't Believe It's Not Butter!)

Odds are at least one molecule of every breath you breathe also passed through the lungs of Socrates.

SCAMMERS & SCAMMEES

*Your phone, your mailbox, your e-mail inbox, your television—tricksters
have more ways than ever to con you out of your money.*

MIXED MESSAGES

Old scams never die. Take Japan's *ore–ore sagi* (the "it's
me–it's me" scam). A crook calls a phone number, and if
the person who answers sounds elderly or vulnerable, he says, *"Ore,
ore!"* If the victim responds with: "Son, what's wrong? You sound
terrible!" the fraudster gives a sob story about how he was robbed
or in a car wreck, then asks for money. Today, the *ore-ore* has
migrated to cyberspace: A scammer hacks into someone's Facebook
account and sends out a plea for help to his or her contact list. It
happened to Jayne Schermann of Cape Girardeau, Missouri, in
August 2009. She received an urgent Facebook message from her
friend Grace, who said she'd been robbed at gunpoint in London
and couldn't make it home. Schermann wired $4,000 to "Grace."
Meanwhile, safe at home, the real Grace discovered that a hacker
was impersonating her on Facebook. She sent out warnings to her
friends, but it was too late for Schermann to get her money back.

HOW BUFFALO CAN YOU GO?

It's no fun being in debt, but at least no one threatens to send you
to prison...unless they're scamming you. In 2009 a young Maryland couple who had defaulted on a loan several years earlier started receiving threatening phone calls: "This is the sheriff's office. If
you want to stay out of prison, pay up your old debts now." But the
calls weren't from the police; they were from Final Claims Asset
Locators, a Buffalo, New York, company owned by Tobias Boyland, a career criminal who'd spent 13 years in prison for armed
robbery and drug dealing. Posing as cops or debt collectors, Boyland's employees would phone people at random and tell them
that they were investigating an old debt. They'd mention a fake
bank, tell the victim the amount of the "debt," and would offer to
settle at a lower rate if the customer would pay up immediately. In
June 2009, Boyland received a visit from a *real* cop and was arrested.
According to New York's Attorney General Andrew Cuomo,
"Boyland's lies and intimidation caused many innocent people to

---

pay money they didn't owe just to stop the terrifying calls." If convicted, Boyland and 12 of his associates face lengthy prison terms.

DOUBLE...OR NOTHING

In 2009 two con men swindled three Australian businesses out of a total of $143,000 by convincing them that they could duplicate banknotes. After establishing a friendship with the victims, the scammers would place a $100 bill between two sheets of a "special material" and then pour a "special liquid" over it. When the sheets were opened, presto—there were *two* $100 bills inside instead of one. (Actually, they used simple sleight-of-hand tricks to sneak in a second bill.) The amazed victims gave the men thousands in cash, which the fraudsters took for "processing," promising to double it. They returned later with a foil-wrapped package, insisting that it shouldn't be opened for 24 hours while the chemicals finished the duplicating process. When the victims opened the package, there was only blank paper inside. Investigators haven't caught the pair yet, but they've determined that the "special liquid" consists of hair spray, bleach, and baby powder.

WHAT A DRAGASANI

In 2009 a movie enthusiast in Oregon placed a bid on eBay for a rare Marx Brothers movie poster. Someone else outbid him, but soon after, he received an e-mail saying that he could get the same poster at a much lower price through another source. The bidder smelled a rat, did some checking, and found that this was a long-standing scam that originated in the small town of Dragasani, Romania. Fraudsters there (mostly young men with formidable computer skills) have set up thousands of bogus online auctions for everything from memorabilia to electronics to MiG fighter jets, and the "winning" bidders are instructed to pay through unrecoverable methods like Western Union. In 2008 Dragasani's mayor, Gheorghe Iordache, bragged to London's *Sunday Times* that the fraudsters have brought a lot of money to the poverty-stricken town. "I've heard about local guys who have BMWs, Mercedes, Porsches—and they don't even work!" The mayor said that the scammers even put Dragasani's town hall up for auction. And where do most of their "buyers" come from? "They're mainly Americans because they're on the Internet most often and they're naïve."

THE CRAZY BIZARRE FILM FESTIVAL

If you want to watch a really weird movie, we've searched through our vast video library to find these nine.

BRAZIL (1985) Comedy
Premise: Terry Gilliam's vision of a futuristic bureaucracy run amok follows low-level civil servant Sam Lowry (Jonathan Pryce), who gets caught up in intrigue while trying to fix a mistake that sends an innocent man named Buttle to his death while the real terrorist, Tuttle (Robert De Niro), goes free.

Why it's crazy: "Lacking unity or coherence," wrote film critic Emanuel Levy, "the text is largely composed of outlandish sequences and special effects…to paint a chaotic, nasty universe, defined by inventive settings and some indelible images."

THE MACHINIST (2004) Thriller
Premise: Trevor Reznik (Christian Bale) is spurned by co-workers after he's involved in a workplace accident that results in a man losing an arm. Reznik blames the incident on the new guy—an employee that nobody else seems to have seen.

Why it's crazy: Trevor barely eats and hasn't slept for two years. Watch him descend into madness in this ultimate example of method acting. Bale (who portrayed Batman the following year) nearly starved himself to lose more than 60 pounds for the role.

NORTHFORK (2003) Drama
Premise: Set in 1955, this visually stunning film follows the few remaining residents of Northfork, Montana—a town about to be submerged by a new dam. A priest (Nick Nolte) stays behind to take care of a sick orphan, Irwin (Duel Farnes).

Why it's crazy: Irwin believes he's a lost angel who has fallen to Earth and had his wings amputated by humans. Other angels visit him. Look for Anthony Edwards as an eccentric angel named Happy, and Daryl Hannah as another named Flower Hercules.

There is a type of bird called a *butwink.*

Kent Turner of Film-Forward.com says, "This droll, surrealistic fantasy is like a gentler David Lynch hallucination."

ERASERHEAD (1977) Horror

Premise: The plot—largely left up to interpretation—revolves around a couple's challenges raising a horrifically deformed baby.

Why it's crazy: Disturbing imagery abounds in director David Lynch's first feature film. Critics have called this cult classic both "baffling" and "a masterpiece."

HEAD (1968) Musical

Premise: After their successful TV show ended, the Monkees (Peter Tork, Davy Jones, Micky Dolenz, and Michael Nesmith) released this take on politics, hippies, and pop culture.

Why it's crazy: Hyped by the studio as "the most extraordinary adventure, western, comedy, love story, mystery, drama, musical, documentary satire ever made," the film has a plot that's almost impossible to follow. Just enjoy the strange vignettes, bizarre visuals, and great music. *Head* was cowritten and produced by Jack Nicholson.

FREDDY GOT FINGERED (2001) Comedy

Premise: Starring, cowritten, and directed by comedian Tom Green, this loosely plotted film stars Green as Gordy, an unemployed cartoonist who still lives at home and tries to frame his father (Rip Torn) by saying he…did something to Gordy's younger brother, Freddy.

Why it's crazy: As bizarre as it is offensive, the film had to be edited down to avoid an NC-17 rating—and it's hard to imagine what Green cut out. Roger Ebert gave it a rare "zero stars" review but later said, "The thing is, I still remember *Freddy Got Fingered*. I refer to it sometimes as a milestone. And for all its sins, it was at least an ambitious movie, a go-for-broke attempt to accomplish something."

MEMENTO (2000) Mystery

Premise: Directed by Christopher Nolan, *Memento* stars Guy Pearce as Leonard, a man who suffers from *anterograde amnesia:*

When brain-damaged patients give bizarre answers to questions, they are said to be *confabulating.*

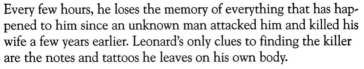

Every few hours, he loses the memory of everything that has happened to him since an unknown man attacked him and killed his wife a few years earlier. Leonard's only clues to finding the killer are the notes and tattoos he leaves on his own body.

Why it's crazy: The film begins at the end, and all of the scenes take place in reverse order. As eFilm critic Scott Weinberg wrote, "It's a joyously twisted Rubik's Cube of a movie."

AFTER HOURS (1985) Comedy

Premise: Martin Scorsese's film about one night in New York City follows Paul Hackett (Griffin Dunne) as he embarks on a quest to find a woman he met in a restaurant (Rosanna Arquette).

Why it's crazy: "Darkly comedic and delightfully manic," wrote *Entertainment Today*'s Brent Simon, "This is a fresh, funny look at one man's downward mental and emotional slide into an evening of unmitigated SoHo hell."

SYNECDOCHE, NEW YORK (2008) Drama

Premise: A playwright named Caden (Phillip Seymour Hoffman) writes a play about his life and, through the course of the film, creates a city-size set in a Manhattan warehouse.

Why it's crazy: This movie within a play within a movie within the lead character's mind(?) is difficult to explain. Most critics who praised it agreed that one viewing isn't enough to truly appreciate screenwriter Charlie Kaufman's (*Being John Malkovich*) directorial debut. It gets especially crazy when actors are brought in to play Caden and his friends and family; the actors soon take over the lives of the people they are playing...or something like that. (Uncle John really needs to watch it again.)

*　　*　　*

MOVIE-STAR CONFESSION

"It was always very strange when I was young and would meet someone who genuinely seemed to be afraid of me. They couldn't separate me from the monster I became in a movie. You wouldn't believe how often people ask me to make my head spin around."

—**Linda Blair, star of *The Exorcist***

Celeb phobia: Cameron Diaz is grossed out by doorknobs. She won't touch them with her bare hands.

THE TOURIST OF DEATH

Here's a recipe for an Internet phenomenon: Begin with a major disaster, create an improbable image that cuts to the core of the disaster, and then distribute the image to a stunned and gullible public.

INBOX HORROR

Were you one of the millions of people who were e-mailed this photograph in the weeks after the terrorist attacks of September 11, 2001? A young man wearing a black ski coat and knit cap is standing on the observation deck of the World Trade Center with Manhattan in the background. Behind him, a jet airliner is flying straight for the building, just seconds away from crashing into the floors below. The date stamp on the bottom right corner: "9-11-01."

By telling two conflicting stories—the blissfully ignorant tourist, and the hijacked plane that was about to take his life—the image perfectly captured the sense of security and complacency that Americans felt before the terrorists shattered it and "changed everything." The caption on the photo drove home the point even more:

This picture was from a camera found in the wreckage of the WTC, developed by the FBI for evidence and released on the net today. The guy still has no name and is missing. Makes you see things from a very different position. Please share this and find any way you can to help Americans not to be victims in the future of such cowardly attacks.

WAIT A SECOND

The photo was convincing enough at first...until people took a closer look at it. Why was the tourist wearing a coat and hat when the attack took place on a warm summer morning? Why was he on the observation deck a half-hour before it opened? Why was the plane in the photo coming from the north, when it actually approached from the south? Oh, and why was it the *wrong kind of plane*? But those inconsistencies didn't slow it down. According to columnist J. Scott Wilson: "In one day, I received no less than 150 copies of it from various readers, friends, and acquaintances. Despite the numerous impossibilities present in the photo, folks just seemed to accept it at face value."

But not everyone. Many wanted to know: Who was this guy? Who manipulated the photo? And why?

But before any answers were found, the image took on a life of its own all over the Internet. Several Web sites sprang up, such as *TouristOfDeath.com* and *TheTouristGuy.com*, featuring shots of "Waldo" (as he came to be known) showing up in other photos of historic disasters. There he was, posing in front of the *Hindenburg* as it went down in flames! And then in Tokyo, while Godzilla laid waste to the city! And there he was back on the World Trade Center, but now, instead of a plane, he's about to be done in by the Stay Puft Marshmallow Man from *Ghostbusters!*

WHODUNIT?

All the hype and spin-offs only added to the mystery of who this man in the photo really was. Over the next few weeks, commentators and pundits alike blamed everyone from bored students at MIT, to a "true-blooded American" attempting to stir up patriotism, to Osama Bin Laden sympathizers who wanted to gloat. And then, in early November, a 41-year-old Brazilian businessman named José Roberto Penteado sent an e-mail to *Wired News*: "I believe that some friends planted my face onto that body." He said he'd never even been to New York and couldn't explain why someone would do it, but the guy in the photo looked just like him.

Penteado became an instant celebrity. He appeared on several Brazilian talk shows and was featured in news stories all over the world. People approached him on the street and asked for his autograph, and Volkswagen's Brazilian subsidiary offered to buy the rights to the image from him and put it in a series of TV commercials. Suddenly, Penteado stood to profit…for doing absolutely nothing at all.

There was one problem, though: Although he resembled the Tourist of Death, why didn't he have the original photo that his head was lifted from? And why was his jaw wider than the Tourist of Death's? And, when people really scrutinized it, Penteado's face appeared to have a different shape altogether.

Meanwhile, halfway around the world in Hungary, a group of friends knew for certain that Penteado was a fake, because they knew who the *real* fake was.

EXPOSED

Back in November 1997, a 21-year-old man named Peter Guzli from Budapest, Hungary, had taken a vacation to New York City. While sightseeing, his buddy snapped a few shots of him on top of the WTC. Nearly four years later, shortly after the attacks occurred, Guzli found himself drawn to that picture folder. On a lark, he searched online and found an image of a plane (which was actually sitting on a tarmac in Houston, Texas, when the photo was taken) and then used Photoshop to cut the plane out of the picture and superimpose it over the background of his vacation shot. He added the fake time stamp and sent it to a few friends as a joke...never expecting that one of them would send it to *his* friends, who then sent it to *their* friends, and so on, and so on.

The more famous his doctored image became, the less Guzli wanted anything to do with it. He knew that a lot of shell-shocked Americans would take offense at his attempt at dark humor. But then, when Penteado's fame began to spread, Guzli's friends urged him to come forward and claim the money for the VW commercial himself. Guzli refused, so his friends decided to do it for him. Two months after the picture first went viral, images with and without the plane were posted onto a Hungarian news site. From there, the mainstream press got hold of the pictures, and the Tourist of Death finally had a name.

STAYING OUT OF DANGER

When Guzli was pressed for an explanation, he admitted that he "didn't have sleepless nights" over the incident, "but I certainly didn't want people to point their fingers at me on the street. I don't think this thing has to do with empathy or the lack of it. The people I intended it for all said they had a great laugh. That's all." When asked if he planned to profit from his fame, Guzli said he'd think about it. But after Volkswagen withdrew their offer (apparently realizing how tacky it would be to profit from such a horrific event), Guzli happily went back to anonymity.

But that picture—recently named by several publications as one of the most powerful images of the 2000s—will live on in infamy, along with its hundreds of silly variations.

The Iraq Tourism Board recently sent delegates to London. Goal: To market Iraq as a vacation spot.

ABNORMAL ACTIVISTS

*Most protests are pretty dull: A group of people march
somewhere, hold up signs, and yell things, and maybe the
police come. We set out to find demonstrators who have
a little more pizzazz—ones crazy enough to squirt
a cop with milk straight from the cow.*

PINK DAWN
The Problem: For seven years, a two-story-tall pink flamingo
(made of chicken wire and pink bedsheets) attached to an
outside wall above the Cafe Hon in Baltimore, Maryland, was a
local attraction. But in October 2009, cafe owner Denise Whiting
was surprised to get a notice from the city saying that she would be
charged an annual fee of $800 because she didn't have a permit for
the large outdoor display. Whiting was furious: "It really has become
a hallmark of Baltimore." Instead of paying the fee, Whiting
removed the flamingo. Citizens and business owners were outraged
that the city would crack down so hard on such a favorite local
landmark. Then DJs at a local radio station, 98 Rock, got an idea.

The Protest: On the rainy morning of October 27, workers arriving at City Hall were greeted by hundreds of fake pink flamingos
sticking up out of the lawn "in silent protest."

Did It Work? With a crowd gathering outside, Mayor Sheila
Dixon went out to the flamingo field and talked to Whiting. The
mayor agreed to reduce the fee to $400 and promised to promote
local businesses with new signs on the freeway. Whiting paid the
fee and, a few weeks later, built a new giant flamingo—this time
made of fiberglass. Said Mayor Dixon: "I hope that Flamingogate
will now be behind us."

A DROP IN THE BUCKET

The Problem: European dairy farmers' operating costs have been
steadily rising in recent years. But with supplies up and demand
down, they've had to sell their dairy products at lower prices. For
years farmers have been pressing the European Union Farm Commission to set minimum prices, but their requests have been
repeatedly denied.

Danish farmers track and monitor their cows using CowDetect radio frequency tags.

The Protest: In October 2009, more than 2,500 farmers drove their tractors to EU headquarters in Brussels, Belgium, and dumped millions of gallons of milk and thousands of pounds of eggs and manure into the streets. Armored police arrived and formed a riot line to push the protesters back. During the struggle, one angry farmer grabbed one of his cows' udders, pointed a teat at the police, squeezed, and sprayed milk at them (it traveled an impressive 15 feet). The cops blocked the milk with their riot shields, but the cow broke free from the farmer's grasp and chased a bystander down the sidewalk. It took the efforts of several farmers and police officers to apprehend the cow. Meanwhile, the protest continued.

Did It Work? So far, no. The EU Farm Commission insists that it can't control how much foodsellers charge. Expect more milk protests in the future.

600 CHEEKS AGREE

The Problem: In summer 2009, citizens in the Canadian town of Sarnia, on the shore of Lake Huron, were outraged to see, day after day, a large, wing-shaped balloon floating 1,000 feet above the lake. The balloon, which was monitored by a U.S. defense contractor, carried a surveillance camera capable of reading the name of a boat from nine miles away. According to the U.S. Department of Homeland Security, it was only there to monitor shipping traffic. Sarnia's citizens, including the mayor, complained to the Canadian government that it was an invasion of their privacy. "The U.S. has no right to spy on us!" said one local. But there was little the Canadian government could do because, technically, the balloon was hovering over U.S. waters.

The Protest: An estimated 300 Sarnians decided to make a statement that their government couldn't: They marched down to the waterfront, dropped their pants, and mooned the balloon.

Did It Work? The mooning turned out to be a moot point, since the balloon wasn't even in the sky that day (it had been knocked down by a storm a week earlier). But protesters agreed that baring their behinds was a "symbolic measure." And after the balloon was repaired, it was relocated...to the skies above Afghanistan.

Better not to think about it? *Lasagna* comes from the Latin word for "chamber pot."

THE BUILDING BLOCKS OF CHANGE

The Problem: In 2006 the German power company E.ON announced plans to build a coal-fired power plant in the English town of Kingsnorth. Despite charges that the plant would "emit more greenhouse gases than the entire country of Ghana," construction crews got to work, with a planned completion date of 2012. As part of a public-relations campaign, E.ON built a small-scale Lego replica of the plant in the Legoland theme park in Windsor, England. Right near the Lego Big Ben and Lego Westminster Abbey, the Lego model of the power plant stood four feet high, and its giant smokestack even emitted steam.

The Protests: On July 8, 2008, museum attendees were surprised to see six tiny Lego protesters "climbing" the smokestack, followed by the unrolling of a banner from the top of the power plant that read "Stop Climate Change." Tiny Lego police dotted the scene around the smokestack, along with a Lego police helicopter.

The museum wasn't the only place activists infiltrated that day; all over the U.K., thousands of people gathered to protest against the power company and the government. Naked environmentalists (real people) scaled the walls of E.ON's corporate offices, a group blockaded a biofuel depot in Essex, and dozens of activists lay down in a pool of oil in front of the Royal Bank of Scotland to stage a "die-in."

Did It Work? Maybe. A year later, E.ON announced that the power plant would be delayed until 2016. It wasn't due to the protests, said a company spokesman, but because "electricity demand has fallen during the global recession."

SLAVES TO FASHION

The Problem: Sir Phillip Green is one of England's richest men, thanks to TopShop, his successful chain of retail clothing stores. According to a 2007 article in London's *Times Online*, "Factories owned by Green, worth nearly £5 billion, employ hundreds of Sri Lankan, Indian, and Bangladeshi workers in Mauritius, where they labor for up to 12 hours a day, six days a week." Reportedly, the workers were paid only a few cents per day.

The Protest: On December 5, 2008, dozens of activists wearing Santa Claus suits marched to the front of TopShop's flagship store in London. There, they treated holiday shoppers to "A TopShop

Christmas Carol," a skit that parodied the Dickens classic, with Green as Scrooge. The real Green tried to have the protest disrupted, but the police let the show continue. After the play, the Santas, carrying heavy sacks and signs reading "End Slave Labor," marched to TopShop's corporate headquarters and dumped the contents of the sacks—thousands of signatures from people urging Green to treat his workforce more fairly.

Did It Work? Not really. Green claimed that he would "address the matter," but he has repeatedly refused to join the Ethical Trading Initiative, an "an alliance of companies, trade unions, and voluntary organizations working in partnership to improve the lives of workers across the globe."

EAT YOUR HEART OUT

The Problem: In 2009 the European Union imposed a ban on importing most Canadian seal products on the grounds that Inuit hunters, who provided the raw material, were "inhumanely killing seals." The Inuits claimed that they'd been humanely—and sustainably—killing seals for thousands of years. Joining in the debate was Michaëlle Jean, who served as Canada's Governor General, a largely ceremonial position appointed by Britain's Queen Elizabeth II. Many wondered whether she would side with Europe or with Canada.

The Protest: Jean made a surprise appearance at an Inuit community festival in Rankin Inlet, Nunavut. With cameras rolling, "Her Excellency" brandished a traditional Inuit *ulu* blade, crouched over a freshly killed seal, and began to skin it. Then she pulled out a chunk of the seal's heart, held it up for all to see…and took a bite out of it. "It tastes like sushi," she said.

Did It Work? The European Union upheld the ban. When asked to comment about whether Jean's gesture had helped or hurt the Inuits' cause, an EU spokesperson said it was "too bizarre to acknowledge."

*　　*　　*

"Though a good deal is too strange to be believed, nothing is too strange to have happened."
　　　　　　　　　　　　　　　　—**Thomas Hardy**

STAIRWAY TO WEIRD

*There's a lady who's weird / all that glitters is weird /
and she's weirding a stairway / to weirrrrrd…*

STAIRS: A woman in Queensland, Australia, called police in August 2009: An angry cow had climbed the stairs to her front door and was attempting to get into her house. Police went to the woman's home and made the cow mooove along.

STAIRS: Naeema Screven of New York City was hurrying to get to her subway train in 2008 when she ran *down* an "up" staircase. A transit cop stopped her, pepper-sprayed her, put her in handcuffs, arrested her, and took her to jail. Screven sued the city for $3 million. The "Down the Up Staircase Case" is still pending.

STAIRS: An Italian man was headed to his 40th high school reunion in the city of Trieste when his car's satellite navigation system told him to make a right turn. He did—right down a staircase. The car bounced down two flights of steps before finally coming to a halt. A special tow truck had to be brought in to pull the car back up to the road, and, 90 minutes later, the man finally made it to his reunion (with a really funny story to tell).

STAIRS: In 2009 an exercise promotion team sponsored by Volkswagen installed pressure sensors—to produce musical notes—on a staircase next to the escalator in a subway station in Stockholm, Sweden. They also painted the steps black and white to make them look like piano keys. Result: the number of people who used the musical stairs rather than the escalator increased by 66 percent. (And the number of "chopsticks" related homicides increased by 400 percent. Kidding.)

STAIRS: Chinese media reported in 2006 that an elderly couple was discovered living in a cave in a mountain range in south-central China. They'd lived there in almost complete seclusion for more than 50 years. The husband had carved a staircase into the mountainside, the story said, to make it easier for his wife to get up and down the mountain. There are more than 6,000 steps in it. It had taken him decades to construct.

Annual cost of untreated mental illness in the United States: more than $100 billion.

CLERGY GONE WILD

Five priests, two pastors, a nun, and a rabbi all walk into a Bathroom Reader article...and bring shame to their respective faiths.

HEY, BIG SPENDER

Whenever Reverend Gregory Malia walks into one of his favorite New York strip clubs, the waitresses and dancers all flock to him. Why? "He's a great tipper," said one of the dancers. The Episcopal priest at St. James Parish drives all the way from Wilkes-Barre, Pennsylvania, and lavishly spends the money he makes from running a pharmacy dedicated to blood disorders. He once bought a $35,000 bottle of wine and left a $17,000 tip. "I work hard. I make good money. How I spend it is my business."

NAUGHTY HABITS

Father Antonio Rungi (of the Passionist order) announced the "Miss Sister 2008" online beauty pageant in the hopes of enticing more women to join the church. Nuns would post photos wearing their habits, along with "vital statistics" about their spirituality and social awareness. "We are not going to parade nuns in bathing suits," Rungi explained. "But being ugly is not a requirement for becoming a nun. External beauty is gift from God, and we mustn't hide it." (The Vatican would have nun of it and shut the pageant down before it began.)

MR. POPULARITY

Students at the University of Illinois got more than spiritual guidance from Father Christopher Layden; he also sold them cocaine. After cops found three grams of the drug in his office in 2008, he was arrested for dealing, but stayed out of court by pleading guilty to possession. The Diocese of Peoria suspended Father Layden, despite reports that he's a "very popular priest."

EM-BEELZEBUB-MENT

Parishioners at St. Vincent Ferrer Church in West Palm Beach, Florida, were shocked when auditors reported that $8.7 million was missing from the church's account. They were even more

---

According to one poll, 1 in 20 British kids thinks Adolf Hitler was a German soccer manager.

shocked to learn that Fathers John Skehan and Francis Guinan were skimming donations to buy gambling trips, rare coins, a condo in Florida, and a pub in Ireland. Skehan was sentenced to 14 months in prison; Guinan got four years. Judge Krista Marx called their crimes "unmitigated greed and unmitigated gall."

THE PARTYIN' RABBI

Rabbi Baruch Chalomish told police he'd rented an apartment in Manchester, England, so he could "relax and have a party." However, his parties caught the attention of the cops, who raided the apartment and arrested Chalomish for dealing cocaine and hiring prostitutes. At his 2009 trial, Chalomish told the jury he was a just a wealthy guy who liked to assist people less fortunate than himself, and he only used cocaine when he couldn't sleep. (He later admitted to spending $1,600 a week on the drug.) The rabbi was cleared of distribution charges but found guilty of possession.

REVEREND JOHN

LifePrint Church's Rev. John Kameron Erbele, of Burnsville, Minnesota, "looks nothing like a traditional pastor," wrote the *Missoula Independent*. "He has pierced ears, a long, blond, shaggy mop, and is only seen wearing a tie if someone's getting married or buried." Erbele's flock adored him, which is why they were crushed when he was one of 16 men lured to a hotel room to pay for sex in a 2009 police sting. Erbele pleaded guilty and was sentenced to probation and "John School," an educational program for men who solicit prostitutes. At last report, LifePrint Church officials hadn't decided whether to allow him back on the pulpit.

UNHOLY TRINITY

Father Carmelo Mantarro, a 70-year-old priest from Roccalumera, Italy, was having an affair with a married woman, but his biggest mistake was getting caught in bed with her by Sister Silvia Gomes De Sousa, a 39-year-old nun with whom Father Mantarro was *also* having an affair. De Sousa went into a fit of rage: She set fire to his house and then threatened him with a machete. In court, she explained that she "just flipped" because "we had been together four years and I had even had two abortions because of him." Sister De Sousa was released on bond. Whatever became of Father Mantarro wasn't released to the press.

63-year-old Capuchin monk Cesare Bonizzi spreads the gospel by singing in a heavy-metal band.

THE END IS NIGH

*"Nigh" means "near," and when we're talking about the end of
planet Earth, nigh can be anywhere from this evening to millions
of years from now. Doomsayers have been predicting the
imminent end of the world for centuries. Here are
a few of the more interesting predictions.*

A PARTIAL HISTORY OF THE LAST DAYS

The book of Revelation, the final book of the New Testament, is the source of many doomsday predictions. The book, attributed to John the Apostle and written toward the end of the first century, has been interpreted wildly throughout its history. It was almost left out of the biblical canon when fourth-century bishops feared it was too susceptible to misinterpretation and abuse. (Thomas Jefferson called it "the ravings of a maniac.") Its vivid imagery, including the Beast (and its corresponding number, 666), the Four Horsemen of the Apocalypse (Conquest, War, Famine, and Death), and the Second Coming of Christ, have provided a bounty for doomsayers ever since.

• An early doomsday sect known as the "Lotharingian computists" deduced that the world would end on Friday, March 25, 970 (the same day as Good Friday). When the world didn't end that day, they said the end would come in the year 1000—a millennium from the birth of Christ. When that date passed as well, it was revised to 1033, the anniversary of the Crucifixion.

• A 1184 English document called the "Letter of Toledo" said the end would occur on September 23, 1186. The Archbishop of Canterbury took it so seriously that he ordered a three-day fast in advance of Judgement Day. The date came and went without incident, but the letter continued on—true believers kept passing it around, adjusting the date as each successive prediction proved incorrect. The practice continued for centuries.

• By adding 666 to the year of the inception of Islam (618), Pope Innocent III calculated that the Second Coming would occur in 1284.

• In the 1490s, Dominican friar Girolamo Savonarola became the

---

A rare species of tree snail is named *Crikey steveirwini* in honor of "Crocodile Hunter" Steve Irwin.

leader of Florence, Italy. Believing the end was near, Savonarola sent boys door to door to collect items associated with sin—mirrors, cosmetics, perfumes, poetry, paintings—which he burned in his infamous "Bonfire of the Vanities." When Judgement Day didn't come in 1498, Savonarola was overthrown, excommunicated, tortured on the rack, and finally hanged.

• In 1814 Joanna Southcott convinced her followers that she was pregnant with a second "Christ-child," who would be born on Christmas Day that year—despite the fact she was in her sixties. Christmas came and Southcott failed to give birth, but she did die that day, so her followers carried on. More than a century later, in 1927, they presented a sealed box to the Bishop of Grantham that, they said, contained an important message from the late prophetess. Inside was a worthless lottery ticket.

• Joseph Smith, founder of the Mormon Church, predicted in 1835 that Jesus would return within 56 years, by 1891.

• Jehovah's Witnesses have set the date for Armageddon no less than seven times—1914, 1918, 1920, 1925, 1941, 1975, and 1994. They are not currently making predictions.

• Hal Lindsay, author of the bestselling 1970 book *The Late, Great Planet Earth*, used Revelation to calculate that the end would come in 1988 (the founding of Israel in 1948 + a biblical generation of 40 years). He later revised it to 2007 (Israel's 1967 land acquisition + 40 years). When that prediction failed as well, he revised the definition of a biblical generation to be 60 to 80 years rather than 40. He now puts the End at 2047.

• As the year 2000 approached, Armageddon Books, "the world's largest Bible prophesy bookstore," predicted…huge sales: "We're about to enter what should be the most opportune time ever for marketing items related to the end times," they told investors. "We expect sales to rise sharply in the coming months. Sales for the first quarter of 1999 were up nearly 400% over the same period in 1998." That prediction, at least, came true.

Y2K AND BEYOND
The year 2000 inspired a slew of end-of-the-world predictions from a disparate group of modern prophets.

- **Edgar Cayce.** The spiritual founder of the modern New Age movement predicted that the north and south poles would "flop" that year, causing apocalyptic floods and earthquakes.

- **Michael Drosnin**, former *Wall Street Journal* reporter. In his bestselling book, *The Bible Code*, Drosnin used computer analysis of the Torah to conclude that World War III would begin at the turn of the new millennium…or maybe in 2006.

- **Yisrayl Hawkins**, a former Texas cop and rockabilly singer. He told his followers in the House of Yahweh that nuclear weapons would "block out the sun" on October 13, 2000. He later revised the date to September 12, 2006. And then in June 2007, he said that 80% of humans would be dead from a nuclear war by October 13 of that year. When that didn't happen, Hawkins adjusted the date again—to June 12, 2008, the same year he was charged with bigamy for allegedly having 30 wives. The charges were dropped. Hawkins currently has no pending predictions.

- **Prince Charles.** In July 2009, the heir to the British throne said that we humans had just 96 months (6.4 years) to change our ways or face economic and environmental doom. Charles claimed that unfettered consumerism was contributing to "irretrievable climate and ecosystem collapse, and all that goes with it. The age of convenience is over." The prince, who has been criticized for his own carbon footprint (he owns several homes and travels extensively) didn't say how he came up with the 96-month figure.

SIX MINUTES TO MIDNIGHT

In 1947 former Manhattan Project physicists working on "The Bulletin of the Atomic Scientists" created the Doomsday Clock. It's updated every few years to represent how close they think we are to nuclear war, or "midnight." That first year, they set the clock at 11:53 p.m.—7 minutes to midnight. In 1953 it got as close as 2 minutes to midnight because of an increase in the number of thermonuclear tests conducted by the United States and the Soviet Union. A series of test-ban treaties and improved relations between the major nuclear powers pushed the clock all the way back to 11:43 p.m. in 1991. But as more countries have either acquired nuclear weapons (India and Pakistan) or announced nuclear ambitions (North Korea and Iran), the clock has ticked steadily forward. In January 2010, the scientists set the Doomsday Clock to 11:54 p.m.

HIGH NOON

Two other scientists say the end is coming not at midnight, but at high noon. That's the end of *world* itself. However, the end of all life on Earth will occur much sooner—at 5:00 a.m....and it's already 4:30. Fortunately, say astrophysicist Donald Brownlee and paleontologist Peter Ward in their book *The Life and Death of Planet Earth*, each hour lasts a billion years—so we still have 500 million years, give or take. Calculating Earth's total life span at 12 billion years (and starting their clock at midnight), they say that life can be sustained for only one billion of those years—and we're already halfway through that period. The best-case scenario is that Earth will hang around long enough to be consumed by an expanding sun. On the other hand, they warn, we could be pummeled by an asteroid or taken out by a nearby exploding star any second now. Not very comforting, but then, said Brownee, "Mother Nature wasn't designed to make us happy."

*   *   *

OOPS!...HE DID IT AGAIN

In September 2007 Chris Crocker, 19, from eastern Tennessee, achieved Internet fame for his tearful YouTube rant urging the press to stop making fun of Britney Spears after she performed poorly at the MTV Music Video Awards. More that 29 million viewed the video. Two years later, Spears was caught lip-synching on her 2009 Circus tour, once again receiving a drubbing in the press. But Crocker, then 21, announced (in dramatic fashion) that he wouldn't be defending her this time. In a follow-up video, he screamed at Spears and tore her poster off his wall. "A lot of people may call me a traitor," he cried, "but I never got a phone call, not a thank you, not nothing from Britney's team! Not a single, solitary anything! Not even a lousy fruit basket!"

TURKEY TIME

The crazy things we do for a taste of turkey.

ONLINE TURKEY. Have you ever been to a fancy restaurant where you got to pick out the exact lobster you wanted to eat? In 2009 a large English farm called Farm, Park & Wild introduced an online service where, via a webcam, customers can spy on turkeys as they plump up each day. When it comes time to order a bird for Christmas dinner, customers can select which turkey they've had their eye on.

"WILD" TURKEY. Do you love turkey but wish it could get you drunk too? In the fall of 2009, Paul Hurley, owner of O'Casey's, a New York City tavern, began serving turkey infused with vodka. For three days, Hurley soaks each bird in a blend of strong, fruit-flavored vodka. The turkey is then cooked and served with gravy (which also has a lot of vodka in it).

TURKEY SODA. Nearly every year, Jones Soda, makers of organic soda pop, releases a set of strangely flavored sodas for the holiday season. Past offerings have included Ham, Turkey and Gravy, Latkes, Smoked Salmon Paté, Brussels Sprouts with Prosciutto, Broccoli Casserole, Wild Herb Stuffing, Sweet Potato, Green Pea, Dinner Roll, and Antacid. In 2009 Jones introduced Tofurkey-flavored soda, which tastes like the tofu-based imitation turkey product…which, most consumers agree, doesn't really taste like turkey in the first place. But Tofurkey soda does taste like "real" Tofurkey, Jones promises.

TOO MUCH TURKEY. You may have heard of *turducken*—a chicken stuffed inside of a duck, which is then stuffed inside of a turkey. A company called Heal Farm has gone way past the three-bird level to create the 12 Bird True Love Roast—a Christmas treat of 12 birds, all stuffed inside each other (each layer represents one of the 12 days of Christmas). The dish is made up of a turkey, stuffed with meat from a goose, chicken, pheasant, partridge, squab, quail, poussin fowl, guinea fowl, and three kinds of duck. The 12 Bird True Love Roast weighs 55 pounds, can feed up to 125 people, and costs $1,039.

IT'S A GROSS JOB...

...but somebody's got to do it (we guess).

HAZARDOUS MATERIALS DIVER. Who does the Environmental Protection Agency call when they find leaky barrels of toxic waste at the bottom of a lake? Who does the municipal dump call when the pumping system under the garbage sludge needs to be repaired? They call in a HAZMAT diver—a scuba diver with specialized training...and an extra-thick wetsuit.

HOT-ZONE SUPERINTENDENT. When there's an outbreak of a lethal, airborne disease with no known cure, scientists travel to the site of the epidemic to isolate and study the pathogen inside a mobile laboratory. And then they need somebody to keep the equipment running, ensure that doors and windows are airtight, change pathogen-loaded air filters, and keep the lab clean. The "hot-zone superintendent," who spends a large percentage of his or her time getting into and out of protective clothing, is actually exposed to more deadly pathogens than the scientists studying them are.

BIOLOGY SUPPLY PREPARER. Remember those frogs you dissected in junior high? Somebody had the job of killing and preserving them. At companies like Ward's Natural Science in New York, workers process insects, pigeons, and frogs that are later sent to biology classes. The company buys them from breeders, euthanizes them, and preserves them in embalming fluid before they're packed into 55-gallon drums of formaldehyde.

FERTILITY CRYOBIOLOGISTS are employed by sperm banks and fertility clinics to process "donations." They first conduct an analysis of donated semen under a microscope to determine sperm count, then place it in a centrifuge, which separates the sperm from the other seminal fluids. They then add preservatives and freeze the sperm. Advances in this technology have helped infertile women bear children and have even led to HIV-positive parents being able to conceive healthy babies.

Street sign stolen more than 350 times in Eugene, Oregon: High Street.

I FOUND A _____
IN MY _____

If you were thinking "fly in my soup" or "$10 bill in my glove compartment," think a little weirder.

I FOUND A...naked "friend of President Obama"

IN MY...shower

HUH? Two children went into their house in Crestview, Florida, in November 2009 and heard someone taking a shower. They thought it was just their father...until a strange, naked man walked out of the bathroom. The naked man said that "President Obama let him in the house" and told them to go away. The kids ran next door and called the police. When officers arrived, Donald Leon May, 48, was still in the house, although by then he'd wrapped a towel around himself. He was arrested on charges of felony burglary and petty theft. (And it turned out that he was not a friend of President Obama.)

I FOUND A...cat

IN MY...new couch

HUH? Vickie Mendenhall of Spokane, Washington, bought a used couch from a thrift store for $27 in March 2009. Then the noises began: For several days, she heard strange sounds in the house, but couldn't figure out where they were coming from. Finally, Mendenhall's boyfriend was sitting on the couch one day watching television when he felt something underneath him. He lifted the couch up—and found a cat stuck inside it. The cat was in bad shape, so Mendenhall took it to the animal shelter where she worked and began nursing it back to health. She contacted the thrift store, but they had no record of who had donated it. So she put notices in a few local papers—and soon Bob Killion, also of Spokane, contacted her. He'd donated the couch to the store on February 19, he said, and his nine-year-old cat, Callie, had disappeared around the same time. Callie had survived being stuck in the couch for an amazing 18 days. Killion was shocked—and very happy to have his cat back.

In 2009 Italian cops pulled over a car and found 1,700 small animals crammed into the trunk.

I FOUND A…liquored-up mail carrier
ON MY…kitchen floor, eating my noodles
HUH? Marie O'Kelly, 95, of Marion, Iowa, was watching television in her home one day in November 2009 when she heard a noise in the kitchen. She thought her daughter had come to see her, but when nobody came into the living room, she went to check—and found a woman in a mail carrier's uniform sitting on her kitchen floor. The woman was obviously drunk, and she was eating leftover noodles from O'Kelly's refrigerator—with her hands. "I said, 'What are you doing here?' and she didn't answer me," O'Kelly told a local newspaper. "She just kept eating those noodles." O'Kelly called police, and 46-year-old Kristine A. Pflughaupt, a 17-year employee of the U.S. Postal Service—who was on the job at the time of the incident—was arrested for public intoxication. Pflughaupt was placed on unpaid leave and an investigation was ordered.

I FOUND A…gecko
IN MY…chicken egg
HUH? One evening in May 2008, Peter Beaumont of Darwin, Australia, was making eggs for dinner. "I was cracking the eggs into a pan when I noticed one of them was all cloudy," he said. "I looked at the shell and saw a tiny dead gecko." Beaumont, who is a doctor and the president of the Australian Medical Association, said the egg was intact before he cracked it, so the gecko could not have entered it from outside. How did it get in there? Beaumont has a theory: He thinks the tiny lizard crawled up inside a chicken's butt, possibly to feed on an embryo. Then it died and ended up being trapped inside a forming egg. Beaumont believes it was the first reported case of a gecko entering a chicken's butt to look for food. And, even more strange, the discovery might lead to a medical breakthrough: It may explain how salmonella bacteria enter chicken eggs, something that is not well understood. (Beaumont thinks that geckos may carry the germs to eggs via chicken butts.) The theory is now being studied by scientists.

*　　*　　*

"Everything is funny as long as it is happening to somebody else."
—Will Rogers

Women get songs stuck in their heads longer than men do, and are more likely to be irritated by them.

THE MAYOR WITH TWO NAMES

Here's a strange story about a mayor who was well liked by the citizens of his small town. But they didn't know about his bizarre, secret past.

MEET DON LAROSE

In the mid-1970s, Don LaRose was a happily married man with two young daughters. A respected pastor in the town of Maine, New York, he often gave sermons warning against the evils of Satan. Then, in 1975, he suddenly vanished. Three months later, Minnesota police picked up a homeless man who said his name was Bruce Kent Williamson—but he couldn't remember much other than that. After he was checked into a mental hospital in Chicago, his memory started to come back. He said he thought his name was also Don LaRose and that he'd been abducted by "Satanists" who were "determined to expunge every last bit of righteousness" from him. He said they brainwashed him with shock treatments until he believed he was a totally different person. "In truth," he said, "I'm not sure who I am." Staff were able to locate his family and send word that he was safe.

LaRose's wife went to Chicago and brought her weary husband home. Though his memory was still cloudy, he tried to pick up the pieces of his former life. In 1977 the LaRose family moved to Hammond, Indiana, and Don resumed his duties as a Baptist minister. At first, life was good. But underneath, he was a terrorized man. LaRose told local police that his Satanist abductors had caught up with him again and were threatening to make his life a "living hell if he didn't stop blaspheming Satan." The police didn't believe him. Then, in 1980, Don LaRose disappeared again.

MEET KEN WILLIAMS

A few months later, a man in his early 40s named Ken Williams arrived in northwest Arkansas. While Don LaRose had been a clean-shaven man with glasses, Ken Williams had a graying beard, bushy eyebrows, and no glasses. That was all the disguise he needed —for the next 27 years, LaRose lived as Ken Williams. After

remarrying in 1986, he was once again a respected family man...
but the guilt of leaving his first family haunted him. "What I had
done weighed heavily on my heart and mind from the first day I
rode out of Hammond," he later wrote. "What happened in 1980,
whether it was right or wrong, I did because I was under threat
for the safety of my family. If I'd stayed, there'd be bodies in a
grave." In 21 years of marriage, he didn't even tell his wife about
his former life. Williams was appointed mayor of Centerton,
Arkansas, in 2001 after the town's previous mayor resigned. He
was reelected twice.

THE JIG IS UP

Williams might have continued living with his secret if he hadn't
been so preoccupied with his former life. In March 2007, he created the Web site *DonLaRose.com*, which chronicled his former
self's mysterious disappearance. One of LaRose's nephews found
the site on the Internet and shared it with his family; they were
amazed at how detailed it was. And then they saw the name of the
site's creator: Bruce Kent Williams. It was so similar to "Bruce
Kent Williamson" that they knew they'd finally found him. Not
only was he not dead, not homeless, and not in a mental institution, but there he was—the *mayor* of a town. Rather than call the
police, they called the *Benton County Daily Record*—and the story
shocked Centerton's 5,500 citizens. At first, Williams denied it,
but soon admitted to the accusations and resigned. His second
wife, Pat, asked, "Who are you—Don LaRose or Ken Williams?"
He replied, "I'm a little of both, I guess."

A TALE OF TWO FAMILIES

Pat Williams supported her husband: "I love him. I'll stand by
him. We're in it for the duration." And many people in Centerton
felt the same way. Said one citizen: "I can verify the fact that
Mayor Ken Williams was always unbiased, fair in his decisions,
and wise beyond his years. An honest gentleman."

But with Don LaRose's family, it was a different story. His first
wife, who had since remarried and still lived in Indiana, refused
to speak to the press about the ordeal. So did his two adult
daughters. His father, 97-year-old Adam LaRose, did take questions from his hospice, and explained that he'd never gotten over

the sting of being abandoned by his son: "I would love to see him again. That would be my day." LaRose has since met with some of his family, including his father. However, LaRose's 22-year-old grandson, Tony Hofstra, is skeptical: "I don't know if he's crazy or if he's lying to everybody about this Satanic attack and all these threats. I don't know if he just didn't want to pay child support and disappeared."

In August 2008, police determined that Williams had committed a crime, and he was brought up on felony forgery charges. He pleaded guilty and was sentenced to five years' probation and 100 hours of community service. "I just wanted to put the experience behind me," he said.

STILL PREACHING

Today, he runs two Web sites. The first, *KenWilliamsMinistries.com*, makes no mention of Don LaRose. His other site, *DonLaRose.com*, contains an eight-chapter book that Williams calls his "amazing story of survival." Is it true? No one—perhaps not even Williams himself—knows for sure (he's said that some of the details of his ordeal are still murky). Either way, it's a chilling read:

> I also have a recurring dream which is always the same, but with some variations. In each dream I am either tied to, or strapped to, a wooden chair, an arm chair or a recliner. In each dream the electrodes are attached to my head and I am begging them not to do it. And in each dream, when the switch is thrown, I scream as loudly as I possibly can because of the excruciating pain.

LINGERING QUESTIONS

• Where did he get the name Ken Williams? From a teenager who was killed in a car accident in 1958. Authorities aren't sure how LaRose was able to acquire his Social Security Number.

• Were there ever any "Satanists"? Police have found no evidence of their existence outside of Williams's stories—and even those are sketchy. Shortly after his secret came out, he wrote on his Web site, "Since my unveiling on Wednesday, I have revised this report to delete portions of the story designed to keep people from following my trail." But now that the story has been told in media outlets all over the world, who knows if the Satanists will ever catch up to LaRose/Williams, or if they existed in the first place.

CELEBRITY FLIP-OUTS

You may have heard Christian Bale's profanity-laced tirade on the set of Terminator: Salvation. You may have seen rapper Kanye West interrupting Taylor Swift's acceptance speech at the 2009 VMAs (not to mention Mel Gibson's and Michael Richards's racially fueled blow-ups). Here are some other stars who lost it.

CRAZY LOVE

In 2009 former Hole singer Courtney Love was at a party in New York City when she had to go to the bathroom. Unfortunately for a partygoer named Sebastian Karnaby, he accidentally walked in on Love while she was sitting on the toilet with her skirt down around her ankles. Karnaby quickly turned and left, but Love got up, pulled up her skirt, and chased after him, repeatedly screaming, "I'm gonna get you f***ing thrown out!" She then jumped on his back and tried to drag him over to the security guards, claiming it was he who attacked her. They believed him…and asked Love to leave. "She was like a possessed woman," Karnaby said afterward. "I never wanted to see Courtney Love on the toilet. It wasn't a pretty sight."

MESSAGE FROM HELL

In 2007 Alec Baldwin and Kim Basinger, once one of Hollywood's golden couples, were divorced and battling for the custody of their 11-year-old daughter, Ireland. A court had granted Baldwin a pre-arranged phone call with Ireland, but she didn't answer. He was told to leave a message at the beep, and boy, did he ever: "I'm tired of playing this game with you. You have insulted me for the last time! You don't have the brains or the decency as a human being. I don't give a damn that you're 11 years old or that your mother is a thoughtless pain in the ass who doesn't care about what you do!" Baldwin ended by calling his daughter a "rude, thoughtless little pig." The tape was leaked to the press and played all over the news, prompting an explanation from the actor: "I have been driven to the edge by parental alienation for many years now. You have to go through this to understand." Baldwin later revealed that he contemplated suicide after the tirade but didn't do it because Basinger might have considered his death a "victory."

LINE DANCE

In the semifinals of the 2009 U.S. Open tennis tournament, Serena Williams, ranked #2 in the world, was two points away from losing the match. Williams served, but the line judge—a small woman sitting to the side of the court in a chair—ruled that Williams's foot had touched the line (a call that's rarely made, especially at the end of a tournament). That cost her one point. Williams—known for her fierce but reserved demeanor—went ballistic on the judge, yelling, "I swear to God, I'm going to take this f***ing ball and shove it down your f***ing throat!" The umpire docked Williams another point for the outburst...and that cost her the tournament.

I HATE H***ABEES

While filming a scene for the 2004 movie *I Heart Huckabees*, actress Lily Tomlin was on the set, sitting behind a desk and taking orders from director David O. Russell, who kept changing her lines and the way she was sitting. "For Christ's sake," Tomlin finally said, "Let's just take it one f***ing line at a time instead of changing everything—do it this way, do it a different way." Outraged, Russell started yelling and ran up to the desk and swept all of the props onto the floor. "Okay, bitch!" said Russell. "I'm not here to be f***ing yelled at. I worked on this f***ing movie for three f***ing years, and I don't need for some f***ing **** to yell at me in front of the f***ing crew! I'm trying to f***ing help you, bitch! Go f*** yourself!" Then Russell kicked a waste basket into a wall. Tomlin's co-star, Dustin Hoffman, fled the set. Tomlin remained in her chair and calmly said, "You go f*** yourself. Go f*** your whole movie." Russell left the set and could be heard yelling all the way down the hall. He soon returned and yelled at Tomlin some more. Then the crew left the set, putting an end to the day's filming. After the movie was released (to so-so reviews), both Tomlin and Russell tried to downplay their fight. Tomlin even claimed it raised the energy level of the production. "I'd rather work with someone who's human and available and raw and open."

*   *   *

"Is it weird in here, or is it just me?"

—Steven Wright

To demonstrate flaws in the patent system, in 2001 an Australian lawyer patented the wheel.

ZERO TOLERANCE

With so much crime in the world, some states and businesses have adopted "zero-tolerance" policies. But sometimes they go a little too far.

WHOPPER, JR.

Kaylin Frederich went into a Burger King in Sunset Hills, Missouri, with two relatives in August 2009. After the family had ordered their food and started eating, an employee told them that they had to leave—because Kaylin wasn't wearing shoes, a violation of the restaurant's "no shoes, no shirt, no service" policy. What was unusual about that? Kaylin was six months old at the time and was being carried by her mother because she wasn't old enough to walk. Her mother, Jennifer Frederich, alerted the media, prompting a quick apology from Burger King.

GRANDMA METH-HEAD

Many states restrict or ban the sale of cold medicines that contain the ingredient pseudoephedrine because it can be used to make crystal methamphetamine. In Indiana, you can buy only a certain amount of pseudoephedrine-based medicines in a seven-day period (and you have to fill out a form). But 70-year-old Sally Harpold didn't know that. One day in 2009, she bought a box of Zyrtec for her husband (who had allergies), and a few days later she bought her adult daughter some Mucinex-D for a cold. That was over the drug limit, so Harpold was arrested for intent to manufacture crystal meth. The charges were later dropped.

AN UNARMED MAN WALKS INTO A BANK

Steve Valdez of Tampa, Florida, went to a Bank of America in September 2009 to cash a check from his wife, but the bank refused. Why? Because B of A required a thumbprint as a form of identification, and Valdez could not provide one; he has two prosthetic arms. Even after presenting two forms of identification, he was denied and told by the manager to either come back with his wife or open an account. Bank of America later apologized to Valdez.

TASTELESS TOYS

*Maybe it's just us, but there are a few things you just shouldn't
have to do to a toy—like shave it, or breast-feed it.*

SHARP TOY. In 2007 the toy company Zizzle introduced
Jack Sparrow's Spinning Dagger, a tie-in with the *Pirates of
the Caribbean* movies. The toy, for kids "ages five and up,"
consists of a plastic dagger attached to a wristband. With a flick of
the wrist, the child can spin the dagger from a "concealed" position to one where it's ready to stab—or at least ready to poke
somebody's eye out. Parents' groups protested that the clearly dangerous toy lacked any kind of warning label.

HOMELESS TOY. Mattel's American Girl dolls are one of the
most popular toy lines of the 2000s. Each doll represents a different era and has her own storyline: "Julie Albright" is a girl from
San Francisco in the 1970s; "Kit Kitteridge" is from the '30s. And
then there's a modern girl, "Gwen Thompson," whose deadbeat
dad walked out on the family, leaving her to be raised by her single mom...in a car. Cost: $95.

THIRSTY TOY. Dolls that cry, eat, drink, poop, pee, and talk
are old news. But Spanish toy company Berjuan went for a new
level of realism: breast-feeding. Bebé Gloton ("Gluttonous Baby")
includes a special shirt that girls (target age: 8 to 10) put on. Bebé
Gloton then latches on to a nipple on the shirt and makes sucking
sounds. It's available only in Spain.

ADULT TOY. Obviously, Mattel couldn't make a magic broomstick that actually flies. But their Nimbus 2000 (modeled on
Harry Potter's flying broomstick) should have been fine for kids
playing make-believe, who would just put the foot-long toy
between their legs and run around, pretending they were flying.
The problem was that Mattel installed a battery that made the
broomstick "simulate movement"...by vibrating. To recap: That's
a foot-long toy meant to be stuck between the legs that *vibrates*.
The product was quickly discontinued.

Scorpions can survive being frozen solid for as long as three weeks.

HAIRY TOY. You Can Shave the Baby, a doll available only in Japan, is a baby with some unfortunate hair growth. Topped with a huge helmet of orange hair, the baby also sports hair "suspenders," hairy ankles, and a nest of orange pubic hair that's so overgrown that it looks like a diaper. Kids are supposed to have "fun" giving the baby a much-needed shave. (No word on whether the hair ever grows back.)

GROSS TOY. The *placenta* is the organ that develops inside a woman's uterus during pregnancy which nourishes the growing fetus. After childbirth it's expelled, and normally it's disposed of. But British designer Alex Green turns placentas into teddy bears. The skin of the five-inch tall toy is a placenta that's been treated until it turns into a soft leather, then stuffed with brown rice. "Of course, a lot of people feel it's grotesque," said Green.

UNSETTLING TOY. The German company Playmobil makes hundreds of different miniature play sets depicting everyday life, jobs, and fantasies, from suburban living rooms to hospitals to pirate ships. One of their weirder ones is the HAZMAT Disposal set. It consists of two action figures dressed head to toe in protective suits and helmets, along with large industrial vacuums, some "WARNING" signs…and a leaking plastic drum of toxic waste.

SEXY TOY. Introduced in the U.K. in 2006, the Peekaboo Pole Dance was a collapsible, child-size stripper pole. It came complete with a CD of "stripping music," a lacy garter, and a wad of play money. It was banned almost immediately.

*　　　*　　　*

ACTUAL WEB SITES DEDICATED TO HATING STUFF

- ihatecilantro.com
- ihatestarbucks.com
- ihatetomcruise.com
- ihatebankofamerica.com
- ihatemycurls.com
- ihateclowns.com
- ihatepickles.com
- ihatehighschoolmusical.com
- ihatethebeatles.com
- ihatedentists.com

EXPLODING HEAD SYNDROME

Here's a look at some of the more unusual mental conditions we've come across lately. (Uncle John has complained about having Exploding Head Syndrome more than once. The doctor says it's all in his head.)

The Cotard Delusion. In this condition, the sufferer perceives that he or she is dead, nonexistent, rotting away, or missing internal organs. The condition may be the result of a disconnect between two different parts of the brain: the part that recognizes faces and the part that responds emotionally to such recognition. When sufferers look at their reflection in the mirror and feel no emotional response or sense of self, the theory goes, they interpret this to mean that they are dead. The delusion is believed to be similar to one called the Capgras Delusion, in which the sufferer believes a loved one has been replaced by an identical-looking imposter.

Mirrored Self-Misidentification. This is another self-perception disorder. When you look in the mirror, do you see yourself looking back at you? If so, you can check this mental illness off your "What's wrong with me?" list. People suffering from Mirrored Self-Misidentification believe they see someone else staring back at them. In severe cases, the sufferer may even believe that the "other" person is following them around. Like the Cotard Delusion, Capgras Delusion, Reduplicative Paramnesia (see next page), and similar disorders, Mirrored Self-Misidentification is often experienced as a *monothematic delusion*—it's the only delusion the person suffers from. They perceive the world normally...except for the person in the mirror who keeps following them around.

Exploding Head Syndrome. This condition causes the sufferer to "hear" a loud noise going off as they drop off to sleep, or when they wake up in the middle of the night. To the sufferer, the sound—which has been described as similar to a firecracker going off, a gun being fired, or an electrical short circuit—seems to be coming from inside his or her own head. While Exploding Head

Syndrome can be quite startling—some sufferers believe they are having a stroke or hearing actual gunfire—the condition is usually painless and always harmless. And since the sound is imagined, not real, it doesn't damage hearing. The cause is unknown.

Reduplicative Paramnesia. This delusion makes the sufferer believe that he or she is in a location that's the exact duplicate of another. Patients may also think that they have been moved from the original location to the duplicate site. The condition is often associated with strokes, hemorrhaging, and other injuries to the front or right side of the brain. People being treated for such an injury may believe that they have been moved from one hospital to an identical one in a different city, and that the attending physicians and nurses work in both facilities.

Allochiria. Touch your left arm with your right hand. Did you perceive the sensation on your left arm? If you suffered from Allochiria, you would have perceived the touch on your *right* arm. That's the sensory form of the disorder, which was named after the Greek term for "other hand." Allochiria also comes in an auditory form, in which the sufferer believes that sounds he or she hears are coming from the opposite direction of where they actually originated. There's also a visual form, where patients perceive objects that are to their left as being toward their right, and vice versa. When asked to make a drawing of a scene in front of them, some sufferers will draw a mirror image of what's actually there. The condition is often associated with damage to the right parietal lobe of the brain.

*　　*　　*

TERMINATOR 4: GROUNDHOG DAY

In 2009 the animal-rights group PETA urged Punxsutawney Phil's keepers to replace the famous groundhog with a robot groundhog. PETA charged that Phil is cruelly kept in a cage all year and then subjected to bright lights and big crowds every February 2nd in Punxsutawney, Pennsylvania, where he "predicts" how much longer winter will last. The groundhog's keepers scoffed at the idea: "He's treated better than the average child in Pennsylvania."

In Iowa it's against the law for one-armed piano players to charge for their performances.

DO IT YOURSELF

If you ever find yourself in need of a handheld weapon that shines a bright light into the eyes of your enemies and makes them puke—and you can't find one at the local hardware store—this article is for you.

LOCKED AND LOADED

Background: Bruce Simpson is a consultant to companies that manufacture jet engines and the publisher of a popular technology Web site in Auckland, New Zealand. In 2003 he started writing about how easy it would be for a terrorist to build a cruise missile—one that can hit a target that's hundreds or even thousands of miles away—from inexpensive parts bought over the Internet. When Simpson felt that this information wasn't receiving enough attention from authorities, he decided to teach them a lesson.

Do It Yourself: Simpson started building a cruise missile in his garage. He tracked his progress via video, which he posted on his Web site. This time there was no shortage of attention—the project made headlines all over the world. Simpson claims that while he was building the missile, he got offers from buyers in Iran, Pakistan, and China to purchase the technology. In December 2003, when the missile was nearly complete, the New Zealand government ordered him to stop working on the project. Simpson said he had no plans to build more cruise missiles, but that he thought he'd "made his point." He added that he'd given the missile to a friend "for safekeeping."

Cost to Build: About $5,000.

OFF THE DEEP END

Background: In 2007 Tao Xiangli, a 34-year-old electronics-store employee in Beijing, China, decided that he wanted to build a submarine.

Do It Yourself: On September 3, 2009, Tao, who has only a fifth-grade education, led a group of reporters to a reservoir outside of Beijing—and showed them his homemade submarine. The 20-foot-long submersible was made out of five oil drums connected end to end, with an entrance/exit turret, complete with a proper hatch on top, made from a partial drum rising from the submarine's rear. The sub is powered by two electric motors connected to two propellers. A pressurized air system lets water in and forces it out of the bottom of the sub, allowing it to dive or rise to the surface, and it even has a periscope made from a digital camera. "I made it bit by bit," Tao told the reporters, "purely out of my imagination." To prove that it worked, he jumped into the sub, shut the hatch, and disappeared under the reservoir's surface. Four and a half minutes later, the sub resurfaced, the hatch popped open, and out came Tao, flashing the "V for victory" sign. What are his plans for the sub? "I made it not for a patent," he said, "but so that a talent scout can discover me."

Cost to Build: About $4,400.

SAY CHEESE, WORLD

Background: In 2009 Justin Lee and Oliver Yeh, students at the Massachusetts Institute of Technology, decided to build a camera-equipped airship that could reach a high enough altitude to take photos of the Earth like spaceships do—showing the curvature of the planet, the thin layer of atmosphere, and the blackness of space above.

Do It Yourself: Lee and Yeh hooked up a styrofoam beer cooler to a helium weather balloon. Inside the cooler was a $30 digital camera (with the lens sticking out), set to take photos every five seconds. They also stuffed the cooler with a couple of Coleman disposable hand warmers to keep the camera batteries from freezing in the high altitude. And they added a GPS-equipped cell phone so that they could (hopefully) find the cooler when it fell back to Earth. On September 2, 2009, at 11:45 a.m., Lee and Yeh launched their camera. Five hours later, it was cruising at an altitude of 93,000 feet—almost 18 miles—when the balloon popped. The cooler fell for 40 minutes before it landed. The GPS system worked, and the duo found the cooler about 20 miles from the launch site. Soon after, their spectacular photos of the planet were shown on news programs all over the world. (If you want to see the photos and learn how to build your own space camera, do an Internet search for "Project Icarus.")

Cost to Build: About $150.

BRIGHT LIGHTS, BIG CHUNKS

Background: In 2007 Intelligent Optical Systems, a company in Torrance, California, was awarded an $800,000 contract by the Department of Homeland Security to develop an "LED Incapacitator," or, as the company called it, a "Dazzler." What's that? It's a nonlethal weapon that looks like a flashlight and emits rapidly changing wavelengths of very bright light, causing whoever it's pointed at to experience headaches, nausea, and even vomiting. That same year, an electronics geek named "Lady Ada" attended a conference where she saw a demonstration of the Dazzler.

Do It Yourself: When Lady Ada got home, she did some research, found the patent for the Dazzler technology, figured out how it worked, and decided to make one herself. And she was pretty sure she could do it for less than $800,000. She could, and she did. We can't explain how it works—it involves a lot of resistors and circuit boards and ohms and amps—but we can tell you that all of the complicated electronics in the "Bedazzler," as Lady Ada calls it, are housed in an extra-large $40 flashlight from Sears. And, as she informs her readers: "This project does indeed cause nausea, dizziness, headache, flashblindness, eye pain and (occasional) vomiting. So don't use it on your friends or pets."

Cost to Build: About $250.

*　　*　　*

THA WRLDZ GON TXTY

A California teenager named Crystal Wiski bragged to Sacramento's KCRA News that she sent and received nearly a third of a million text messages in April 2009 (303,398, to be exact). Crystal's mom (who has an unlimited texting plan) told the news station that her daughter was still able to work 40 hours per week at her job and maintain straight A's. An amazing feat, considering Crystal must have had to send and receive an average of 420 texts every hour of every day for the entire month. (No word on the length or brevity of the texts. We're guessing a lot consisted of "lol" and "thx bff!") Her explanation: "I'm popular. I can't help it."

In Hong Kong, a wife may legally kill her adulterous husband (but only with her bare hands).

HAPPY NOTHING DAY!

And other weird—but real—"holidays."

Jan. 3: Remember You Die Day

Jan. 16: Nothing Day

Feb. 4: Liberace Day

Feb. 11: Pro Sports Wives Day

Feb. 13: Blame Someone Else Day

Feb. 28: International Sword Swallowers Day

Mar. 3: What If Cats and Dogs Had Opposable Thumbs? Day

Mar. 14: International Fanny Pack Day

Mar. 21: Corn Dog Day

Mar. 24: National Chocolate Covered Raisins Day *and* American Diabetes Association Alert Day

Apr. 11: Baby Massage Day

Apr. 19: National Hanging Out Day

Apr. 26: Hug an Australian Day

May 13: Root Canal Appreciation Day

May 25: Nerd Pride Day

June 22: Stupid Guy Think Day

June 26: Ugly Dog Day

July 2: I Forgot Day

July 13: Gruntled Workers Day

July 31: National Talk in an Elevator Day

Aug. 10: S'mores Day

Aug. 28: Crackers Over the Keyboard Day

Sept. 15: Felt Hat Day

Sept. 22: Hobbit Day

Sept. 24: Punctuation Day

Oct. 1: Fire Pup Day

Oct. 14: International Top Spinning Day

Oct. 30: International Bandanna Day

Nov. 2: Cookie Monster Day

Nov. 15: National Bundt Pan Day

Nov. 19: Have a Bad Day Day

Nov. 30: Stay Home Because You're Well Day

Dec. 26: National Whiners Day

Frozen Dead Guy Days and The Emma Crawford Coffin Race are both unofficial Colorado holidays.

THE GREAT BEYOND

Three strange stories about death.

A DEAD RINGER. Ademir Jorge Goncalves shocked his loved ones when he showed up, very much alive, to his own funeral in 2009. The 59-year-old Brazilian bricklayer had spent a night drinking with friends at a truck stop—and didn't know he was "dead" until his funeral had already begun. During the night, he'd been misidentified as the victim of a car crash. And, in keeping with Brazilian tradition, the body was buried the next day. "People are afraid to look for very long when they identify bodies," police explained regarding the badly disfigured corpse. A niece added: "My two uncles and I had doubts about the identification. But my aunt and four of Ademir's friends said it was him." The crash victim was later correctly identified and buried by his own family.

AT LEAST THEY NEVER ARGUE. When Le Van's wife died in 2003, the 55-year-old Vietnamese man was so heartbroken that he took to sleeping on her grave. After a year and a half, he decided to dig a tunnel so he could get closer to her. But that still wasn't close enough, so Van dug up his wife's desiccated corpse, filled it out with clay to make her look more lifelike, and put her in his bed so he could sleep beside her. Five years later, she was still there, and both Van and his son hugged her every night before going to sleep. Local authorities found out about the morbid arrangement and told Van to rebury her, citing sanitation laws. Sadly, he agreed. "I'm not like normal people," admitted Van.

'TIL DEATH DO US PART. James and Lolie Brackin had been happily married for 59 years. On the morning of December 12, 2009, they were sitting together in their Florida nursing home watching television when Lolie matter-of-factly told an aide, "I'm going to die today." The aide returned to her a short while later and found that Lolie had stopped breathing. Moments later, James, 79, also died of natural causes. "They didn't like to go anywhere alone," their daughter said.

GHOSTOLOGY, PART II

*Now that you've read the ghostology primer on page 97, you
may want to start seeking out your own spirit activity...or at
least figure out why your car keys keep showing up in
places where you know you didn't leave them.*

WHO YA GONNA CALL?

Ghost hunters can be divided into two main types:
those who try to obtain evidence of a haunting, and
those who try to disprove claims by looking for real-world explanations for why, say, footsteps are heard in the attic. If the investigators can't find a rational explanation, then they say a place
"may" be haunted. If you've ever seen *Ghost Hunters* on the SyFy
Network, then those words are familiar—it's the methodology of
the lead investigators, Grant Wilson and Jason Hawes, founders of
The Atlantic Paranormal Society (TAPS). Though not scientists,
they attempt to take a scientific approach to investigating. But
because so little is known about the "other side," Hawes admits,
"there are really no experts in this field."

According to ghost hunters, the first hurdle that the serious
investigator must overcome is his or her own imagination. As
humans, if our eyes don't receive a complete picture, our brain
will attempt to fill in the rest, usually with something already
familiar. This is sometimes called *matrixing*. It's for this reason that
paranormal investigators have come to rely on an array of electronic gizmos that act as objective observers and recorders. But
there's a catch: One of the main tenets of the scientific method is
that in order for a hypothesis to be proven, the results must be
reproducible in a controlled setting. With a haunting, that's virtually impossible. "Sometimes ghosts appear; sometimes they don't,"
says Hawes. That one caveat alone will keep any scientist who
values his or her reputation from stating that the existence of
ghosts has ever been "proven." That's why, instead of proof, ghost
hunters look for "evidence."

THE GHOST HUNTER'S ARSENAL

So if you have an extra few thousand dollars lying around, here's some of what you'll need in order to gather evidence of a ghost's existence in such a way that no scientist or skeptic could ever deny your claim. That, by the way, is the "Holy Grail" among paranormal investigators…and it hasn't happened yet.

• **Digital video recorder (DVR):** Because paranormal activity is most often witnessed between 1:00 and 3:00 a.m., when the lights are off, investigators use an infrared camera with a night-vision setting. The more DVRs, the better, because apparitions usually appear for a second or two, and moving objects are difficult to document with a still camera. If there's a room you think is active, just place the camera on a tripod and let it record all night.

• **Digital still camera:** Ghost hunters will take hundreds of photographs of a location and scrutinize every one for anomalies, mysterious shadows, mist, apparitions, and orbs. (More on this on the next page.)

• **Digital audio recorder:** Investigators use recorders to try to capture *voice phenomena*. There are three kinds: *direct voice phenomenon*, when a ghost speaks loud enough to be heard by the naked ear (such as "Get out!"); *radio voice phenomenon*, when it uses TV or radio static to amplify its voice, also referred to as *white noise*; and *electronic voice phenomenon* (EVP), when a recorder picks up ghostly voices that are so faint that our own ears can't hear them. "Is there anyone here that would like speak with us?" asks the investigator. When he reviews the audio later, there just may be an answer.

• **Electromagnetic field detector:** This device, most commonly used by electricians to find live circuit boxes inside walls, is used by paranormal investigators to find EMFs—or pockets of free-floating energy—that may be the result of an entity.

• **Thermal imaging camera:** By drawing energy from a room, spirits can make the air colder or warmer. Sometimes they even leave heat signatures, which these cameras can record.

• **Proton packs** are wearable particle accelerators that, when fired, create a charged proton stream which can be used to snare a negatively charged ectoplasmic entity (a ghost) and then safely contain it. (Just kidding—that's what they used in *Ghostbusters*.)

ELECTROMAGNETIC FRAUD DETECTORS

In his article "The Shady Science of Ghost Hunting," Benjamin

Radford, managing editor of the *Skeptical Inquirer*, writes, "The uncomfortable reality that ghost hunters carefully avoid—the elephant in the tiny, haunted room—is of course that no one has ever shown that any of their equipment actually detects ghosts. If a device could, then by definition, ghosts would be proven to exist." Wilson and Hawes share this concern, and are frustrated by all the inexperienced investigators who chalk up anything they "capture" as a "ghost." These erroneous reports are called *false positives*. Here are the most common examples.

• **Orbs:** As we told you earlier, orbs are flying balls of light that are believed to be basic spirit forms. About 99% of orb photos and video can be dismissed as lens flare, a spot on the lens, dust, or an insect. (When an illuminated piece of dust or a bug is close to the lens, it can appear in the photograph or video as a round ball of light.) Other common causes are using a flash or shooting toward the sun, a streetlight, or any other light source. There are also countless photos posted online that show a "vortex"—a strange, white stream of fuzzy light crossing the frame. Skeptics have another name for this phenomenon: "camera strap."

• **Mist:** Most digital camera technology (both still and video) is not yet advanced enough to create a clear image of a dark scene. So the computerized sensor will fill in incomplete areas of the frame with pixilation. This can look like mist—one of the forms a ghost can theoretically take on—and often gets reported as such.

• **Electronic voice phenomena (EVPs):** "Matrixing" is very common with auditory stimuli, especially when aided by the power of suggestion (such as hearing satanic messages when you play "Stairway to Heaven" backward). When an investigator is listening to hours of static or a hissy recording of an empty room, it's easy to mistake a random warble for a "voice." But sometimes the tape picks up discernable voices. Sound waves can travel in odd paths, and the voices of people walking nearby, even outside the building, may have been discerned by the recorder, but not by the investigators' ears at the time. As a result, nearly all EVPs can be explained.

But like orbs and mist, reports of EVPs are all over the Internet and TV shows—and they make the skeptics' skin crawl because they're so easily disproved. This makes it even more difficult for

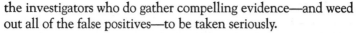

the investigators who do gather compelling evidence—and weed out all of the false positives—to be taken seriously.

"Like most ghost hunters," writes Radford, "Wilson and Hawes claim to be skeptics but are very credulous and seem to have no real understanding of scientific methods or real investigation. Audiences don't seem to wonder why these 'expert' ghost hunters always fail: Even after more than 10 years of research, they still have yet to prove that ghosts exist."

SO WHERE IS THE EVIDENCE?

Wilson and Hawes (and their defenders) claim that there *are* several pieces of evidence gathered by TAPS that can't be easily explained away. Though most episodes end with the team telling the business or homeowner that their place isn't haunted, occasionally the evidence seems fairly conclusive that it *is*. Two examples:

• In one episode, the team placed two video cameras in a hallway—one an infrared camera, which records only heat signatures, and the other a regular camera. During the analysis, they looked at the footage from both cameras, and at the exact same time, the thermal camera recorded a human-shaped figure moving down the hall…while the regular camera recorded an empty hallway.

• In a home purportedly haunted by victims who were murdered by the Manson Family in the late 1960s, the team used a type of EMF detector to ask a spirit to light up the apparatus and answer yes-or-no questions. The spirit did so repeatedly, and verified that it was Sharon Tate, one of Manson's victims.

The obvious problem is that there will always be accusations— leveled at either the investigators or the producers of *Ghost Hunters*—that they manufacture evidence for better ratings. They all deny it, but the "elephant" that Radford speaks of remains in the tiny, haunted room. (Whether *you* believe or not, check out one of the scariest ghost stories we've ever heard on page 297.)

*   *   *

"As for ghosts, there is scarcely any other matter upon which our thoughts and feelings have changed so little since early times."

—Sigmund Freud

The 3 U.S. states with the most ghost sightings: California, Virginia, and Pennsylvania.

POLITICS AS (UN)USUAL

The most popular politicians are often the ones who seem like they're
"one of us"—ordinary people. But just like us ordinary people,
they sometimes make some very weird decisions.

GETTING A LEG UP

Hajnal Ban, a city councilor in Logan City, Australia, always felt that at 5'0" she wasn't taken seriously, either as a lawyer or as a politician. So in 2001, she went to an orthopedic clinic in Russia and paid $40,000 to have her legs broken in four places. Then, over the course of nine months, surgeons stretched Ban's legs by a millimeter or so every day. After nearly a year of excruciating pain in a foreign hospital, Ban returned to her city council position…three inches taller.

SMOKING SECTION FOR ONE

In Australia, it's illegal for people under the age of 18 to smoke. But officials at the Department of Education of the Capital Territory (the district that includes the capital city of Canberra) have allowed a 16-year-old student at Stromlo High School not only to legally smoke, but to take cigarette breaks during her classes. The ruling was based on a doctor's recommendation that the student is "so clinically addicted to nicotine" that she can't function without constantly consuming it—and that *not* smoking would make her schoolwork suffer.

HOW STEREOTYPICAL

In 2006 Bonilyn Wilbanks-Free was the town manager (similar to a mayor) of Golden Beach, Florida, when she referred to one of her assistants as "Mammy." The assistant, whose name is actually Barbara Tarasenko, is African American, and Wilbanks-Free, who is white, was evidently referring to an old racial stereotype of smiling, motherly, African-American maid characters. Tarasenko, visibly offended, wasn't any happier when Wilbanks-Free tried to soften her first comment by saying, "You know how much I love Aunt Jemima." A month later, Wilbanks-Free resigned her position.

It is still technically against the law for a woman to wear pants in Paris.

DOWN-HOME COOKIN'

In 2008 a heated presidential campaign and a press hungry for human-interest stories was the perfect recipe for…well, "Recipegate." Presidential candidate John McCain and his wife Cindy—heiress to a multimillion-dollar beer distribution company—were often criticized by their opponents as being out of touch with ordinary Americans. To counter that image, the McCain campaign began posting "Cindy's McCain Family Recipes" on its Web site. One problem: The folksy recipes were lifted word for word from the Food Network Website—a fact that a New York attorney discovered when she went searching online for a tuna recipe. After news outlets got hold of the story, the McCain campaign quickly deleted the recipes and blamed the "error" on a low-level staffer, who was later "disciplined."

A POLITICALLY CORRECT IDEA

In 2008 the Tunbridge Wells Borough Council in Kent, England, issued a ban on the term "brainstorming" because the term—which means coming up with ideas at a meeting—might be considered offensive to epileptics, whose seizures have been described by doctors as a "storm of the brain." Instead, the council recommended the terms "thought sharing" and "blue-sky thinking."

WANDERING COMRADE

In 1995 the Russian presidential delegation made an official state visit to Washington, D.C. The Clinton administration put the party up in Blair House, where visiting dignitaries often stay. But in the middle of the night, Secret Service agents found a man standing in the middle of Pennsylvania Avenue in his underwear, extremely drunk and trying to hail a cab so he could go get a pizza. The agents returned the man to Blair House after they determined his identity: Russian President Boris Yeltsin.

*　　*　　*

"The radical invents the views. When he has worn them out, the conservative adopts them."

—**Mark Twain**

Connecticut state representatives were caught playing solitare on their laptops during a 2009 budget mtg.

MONKEY SEE, MONKEY DO

After Uncle John saw the movie The Matrix, *he was so inspired that he tried to run up the theater wall. He fell down. But he fared much better than these people…who also tried to copy something they saw on a screen.*

MONKEY SEE: Joe Brumfield of Covington, Louisiana, watched an episode of *CSI: Crime Scene Investigation* in which a car thief soaked a vehicle in gasoline and set it on fire so it couldn't be traced back to him.

MONKEY DO: Brumfield stole a car and then tried the tactic. But as he was dousing the car, he splashed gas on his hands and arms. And then he lit the car on fire…along with himself. He tried to call 911, but couldn't hold onto the (stolen) phone with his flaming hands. Brumfield ran to a nearby hospital, where he was treated for second-degree burns. Doctors alerted police, who were nice enough to wait until Brumfield was released to book him for auto theft. "Car thieves should not play with matches," said officer Jack West.

MONKEY SEE: In 2009 Darenell Jones had a lot to drink at a wedding in Farmington, New Mexico. Afterward, he and some friends went to a hotel room to watch Ultimate Fighting Championship's *UFC Fight Night* on TV.

MONKEY DO: The friends decided to recreate some of the Ultimate Fighting moves…but there's a reason why UFC matches aren't held in third-story hotel rooms. During the "fight," Jones was thrown against a plate-glass window, which gave way, and he fell out—breaking through the glass and falling 20 feet to the sidewalk below. Paramedics tried to save him, but were unable to. According to police, "It was horseplay, basically."

MONKEY SEE: According to amateur filmmaker Mark Twitchell's Facebook profile, "Mark has way too much in common with Dexter Morgan." Who's Dexter Morgan? He's the fictional lead character on the television show *Dexter*, about a crime-scene investigator (Michael C. Hall) who moonlights as a vigilante who traps and murders rapists and serial killers.

There are more captive tigers in Texas than there are wild tigers in India.

MONKEY DO: In November 2008, Twitchell, of Edmonton, Alberta, turned one of *Dexter's* plots into a real-life nightmare. After he answered an online personal ad, pretending to be a young woman, Twitchell lured 38-year-old Johnny Altinger to his house. Except Altinger wasn't a serial killer; he was just a man looking for a date. His body was never found, but police identified enough evidence in Twitchell's garage—including a script to a "show" that detailed his evil plot—to charge him with first-degree murder.

MONKEY SEE: In the 1999 movie *Fight Club*, Tyler Durden (Brad Pitt) runs an underground club where men have bloody fistfights with each other. They also belong to "Project Mayhem," a terrorist cell that blows up symbols of corporate America, including, in one scene, a Starbucks coffee shop. The film has garnered a huge cult following, and one of the biggest fans was 17-year-old Kyle Shaw, who maintained that he actually wanted to *be* Tyler Durden.

MONKEY DO: In 2009 Shaw started his own fight club in New York City, but fighting his fellow teenagers wasn't enough. So, following the model of Project Mayhem, Shaw built a crude home-made bomb and set it off in front of a Starbucks in the middle of the night, destroying an outdoor bench. Ignoring the first rule of Fight Club, which is that you do not talk about Fight Club, Shaw bragged about it to his friends, one of whom tipped off the police. (Coincidentally, the jail that Shaw went to had its own version of a fight club, called "The Program." While he was on a pay phone, a much larger inmate walked up and hit Shaw in the face, giving him a black eye for his appearance in court the next day.)

* * *

DEADLY IRONY

In December 2009, police in North Fort Meyers, Florida, responded to a call about a man lying on the tracks of the Seminole Gulf Railway. When police found him, he'd been run over by the train. They have no idea why the man was lying on the tracks, and at press time they had no leads about his identity. All they could initially determine was the cause of death: He'd been struck and killed by the "Murder Mystery Dinner Train."

NASA lingo: Mishaps in space exploration are referred to as the works of the "galactic ghoul."

MONKEYS INVADE TEXAS!

How did a bunch of Asian snow monkeys come face to face with a Major League Baseball legend? If you can't picture it, don't worry—neither could we. Here's the story.

SURROUNDED

Baseball Hall of Fame pitcher Nolan Ryan worked out of some serious jams during his 30-year career. But nothing he faced on the mound was quite as unnerving as what he saw near Dilley, a small town in south Texas, in 1996. "There were thousands of them," Ryan recalls in his signature Texas drawl. "It's kind of like one of these things you see in Africa—they were all over the truck." The invaders were two-foot-tall Asian snow monkeys, known for their thick brown fur, long pink faces, and penetrating stare. Dozens of them were peering into the truck, examining Ryan, while hundreds more crowded around. But Ryan wasn't just a casual observer; he was acting in an official capacity as the Texas-appointed "Snow Monkey Ambassador." How in the world did he get there?

THE ARRIVAL

The story started in 1972, when encroaching urban development outside of Kyoto, Japan, forced a troop of snow monkeys, also known as Japanese macaques (*Macaca fuscata*), out of their natural habitat in the mountainous region of Honshu Island. Temperatures there can drop well below freezing, making the snow monkeys, the northernmost-dwelling nonhuman primate in the world, well adapted to cold weather. And on Honshu, 150 of them began to terrorize a Kyoto suburb, stealing from gardens, farms, and food markets.

Local wildlife experts decided that the only solution was to relocate the entire troop of 150. But to where? After a long search, officials found what they were looking for: the South Texas Primate Observatory, near Dilley. The monkeys were trapped, caged, and flown across the Pacific by the American National Guard in the first large-scale primate relocation of its kind. After they arrived in Texas, a few monkeys died in the

After he was almost killed by a minivan in 1999, author Stephen King...

much warmer climate, but the survivors soon adapted, foraging for mesquite beans and cactus fruit on the arid South Texas land. The population was kept secured on the ranch by an electric fence, and for 20 years the animals thrived, with their population reaching about 600.

SOCIAL DISORDER

But by 1995, the snow monkeys were in trouble. Primate researcher Lou Griffin had been the primary person responsible for bringing the animals to the region, and the land set aside for the monkeys was on her husband's family ranch. But when Griffin's marriage failed, her ex-husband's family partitioned the ranch and the 180-acre parcel where the monkeys lived went into foreclosure. The facilities fell into disrepair, and the electric fence failed. Even worse, the primates were suffering from overpopulation, and several small groups of males had instinctively wandered off the ranch looking for other snow monkey troops to join. Result: Just as they had done in Kyoto, the monkeys infiltrated nearby farms and neighborhoods.

They became a "nuisance," damaging trees, knocking over garbage cans, raiding kitchens, and frightening people. And thanks to a 1994 U.S. Fish & Wildlife Service ruling that declared the monkeys an "exotic unprotected species," they did not fall under the protection of the Endangered Species Act. In other words, they were fair game for hunters. Although concerned locals and animal-rights advocates managed to keep most hunters at bay, on the final day of the 1995–96 hunting season, tragedy struck. Four monkeys discovered a trap of deer corn set by hunters, who shot and killed three of the primates—including two nursing females—and blew an arm off of the fourth one.

That was it, local residents decided. Something had to be done about these monkeys.

SEND IN FOR RELIEF

At a heated public hearing later that spring, citizens argued that the monkeys should have been granted protected status because they were privately owned. It was the same situation, they said, as when cattle roamed away from their land; it's against the law to shoot them simply for leaving their owner's property. Although the citizens were technically correct, the Texas Parks & Wildlife Commission (TPWC) hadn't been quick enough to enforce the rule and, as a result, three monkeys were dead. Now the TPWC had a public-relations disaster to clean up, so they brought out the biggest gun they had: 48-year-old Nolan Ryan, native Texan and popular sports hero, who was serving on the TPWC at the request of the governor. Ryan was crowned "Snow Monkey Ambassador."

So, what does a Snow Monkey Ambassador do? Ryan had no idea. But one of the first things he was asked to do was to take a ride out to Dilley with a wildlife expert to see the monkeys for himself. They weren't hard to find; they mobbed the truck and peered in curiously at the two passengers. "I was in there with the lady," Ryan later told interviewers, "and she said, 'Let's get out.' I said, 'I ain't getting out!'"

A KISS BEFORE FIGHTING

Ryan reluctantly agreed, and slowly climbed out of the truck. A snow monkey leapt from the roof onto his shoulder, and Ryan became "petrified wood." But the monkey didn't bite; it had other ideas. The wildlife expert had brought along Hershey's Kisses, which the monkeys were far more interested in than anything else. "You give them Hershey's Kisses, and they sit there and they very neatly open it," Ryan explained, "and about the time they get it unpeeled, another one will come over and knock them down and pick it up and eat it."

Ryan wasn't the only celebrity involved with the snow monkey cause. Las Vegas showman Wayne Newton was also enlisted and put on a benefit concert in San Antonio to raise money for the monkeys. Newton's work, Ryan's high-profile "ambassadorship," and a 1997 *National Geographic* documentary helped raise the funds necessary to repurchase the sanctuary land, rebuild the facilities, and round up the monkeys.

Since then, the troop's population has been curbed via birth control, and the ranch is now called the Born Free USA Primate Sanctuary. Along with the snow monkeys, the sanctuary offers a home to primates rescued from circuses and abusers. Nolan Ryan has retired from his post as Snow Monkey Ambassador but still loves to tell the story of his strange encounter.

What's *ichthyoallyeinotoxism*? LSD-like hallucinations brought on by eating certain tropical fish.

BANANAS!

Bananas—they're sweet and kid-friendly…and seem to be in the news a lot more than they ought to be.

MONKEY GOT YOUR GUN?

Seventeen-year-old John Szwalla walked into a Winston-Salem, North Carolina, convenience store in May 2009, showed owner Bobby Ray Mabe that he had something under his shirt, and demanded money. Mabe could see that the object under Szwalla's shirt was a banana, so he, along with a customer, jumped on the robber, beat him up, and restrained him while they waited for the police. Szwalla managed to eat the banana before officers arrived at the scene, but he was arrested and charged with attempted armed robbery anyway. (Police took photographs of the banana peel as evidence.)

FILL 'ER UP

Have you always wanted to eat a banana that had a thin ribbon of something else running down the inside of it? You're in luck: Someone in Argentina has invented the "Destapa Banana: The First Banana Refiller in the World." Just attach the device to the tip of a banana and push down on the plunger, and it extracts a thin core from inside the banana. Then simply fill the middle of the banana with jelly, liquid chocolate, melted ice cream, jalapeño sauce, fish oil—whatever you like—and peel and eat.

YELLOW JUICE

Have you ever wondered why banana juice has never caught on like orange or cranberry juice? It's because bananas are so high in starch that their liquid can't be extracted by traditional juicing methods. But scientists at the Bhabha Atomic Research Centre in Mumbai, India, have recently patented a new banana-juicing process that results in a sweet, nutritious juice that contains no added water or sugar, requires only a dash of citric acid for preservation, and has a shelf life of about three months. The scientists hope the new juice will help get kids off sugary, "unnatural" sodas and make lots of money for banana-rich India.

ARTISTIC A-PEEL

LondonBananas.com has nothing but photographs of banana peels that have been discarded at various locations around London: in dumpsters, in alleys, and at entrances to famous landmarks like the Underground. According to the site's photographer, S. Astrid Bin, "On average, I see about five skins a day, and my one-day record is 22. I don't go looking for them."

SHOWER POWER

In 2008 scientists at the University of Agricultural Sciences in Bangalore, India, convinced the owners of a one-acre banana plantation to try an experimental new fertilizer. Its secret ingredient: human urine. Thousands of gallons of pee were collected at local schools and hospitals, and 150 banana plants were given doses of the fertilizer every day. Result: The bananas that had been treated with urine bore fruit two to three weeks earlier than bananas that hadn't, and their bunches weighed an average of five pounds more.

PEELY-CRAWLIES

If you ever find yourself on a crab-fishing boat, don't take along any bananas. Why? They're considered bad luck on crab boats, and if you're found with one, tradition has it that the captain will turn around, go back to the dock, and throw the banana—and you— off the boat. No one's sure how the superstition started, but it's believed to date back to the 1700s and the Caribbean banana trade. Bananas come from tropical regions that also were home to many poisonous spiders—and it was very bad luck to be trapped on a boat with a bunch of those. The superstition is still common today.

CUT TO THE CHASE

In April 2008, eleven high-school seniors in Zion, Illinois, were suspended for seven days after taking part in a "vicious and dangerous" prank. What did they do that was so heinous? Ten of them put on banana costumes, while the eleventh donned a gorilla costume—and the gorilla chased the bananas through the school's hallways. Most of their fellow students thought it was funny, and said the punishment was ridiculous. "What's funnier than a gorilla chasing bananas through a school?" asked Andrew Leinonen, the gorilla mastermind of the prank. "Nothing."

Veterinarians can now detect fraudulent udder-beautifying schemes used on county fair show cows.

SURVEY SAYS...

*We took a poll, and 72 percent of BRI employees
thought there were too many polls out there.*

• The winner in a 2009 British poll for "Best Celebrity Mom":
Britney Spears—who, only two years earlier, briefly lost custody of
her children after a mental breakdown and had to undergo
parental counseling.

• In 1995 two University of Wisconsin researchers published in
the *Journal of Clinical Psychiatry* perhaps the most exhaustive
research ever conducted on nosepicking. Their polling found that
66 percent of people pick their noses "to relieve discomfort or
itchiness," while only 2 percent did so "for entertainment." Most
common finger used: the index finger (65 percent).

• In a recent poll, 35 percent of parents admitted that that they
play video games when their kids aren't home.

• A European pollster asked 15,000 women from 20 European
countries to rate European men on their lovemaking habits. German men were ranked as the worst lovers because they were "too
smelly." Second worst: the English, who were "lazy" lovers. (The
best: Spanish men.)

• A 2010 *New York Times*/CBS News poll found that 70 percent
of Americans support "gay men and women" openly serving in
the military. In the same poll, however, only 60 percent of
respondents said they support "homosexuals" serving openly in
the military.

• In 2009 *Travel and Leisure* magazine asked 60,000 Americans to
rate 30 cities in various categories. The city with the "least physically attractive" citizens: Philadelphia. It also ranked near the bottom on cleanliness, friendliness, and safety.

• According to a 2006 *Washington Post* poll, 79 percent of Americans believe they are "above average" in appearance, 86 percent
feel they are "above average" in intelligence, and 94 percent
believe they are "above average" in honesty.

In 2006 Dong Changsheng of China pulled a 3,300-lb. car 32 feet...using his lower eyelids.

BOTOX YOUR ARMPITS

*Cosmetic surgeons can do some amazing things to you these days.
Here are a few real procedures you can try if you have a
little defect—and a lot of money lying around.*

• Have you always wanted to look like an elf, or Mr. Spock? Consider **ear-pointing** surgery. A small slice at the top of the ear is cut out and the two sides of the incision are stitched together, creating a pointy ear. It's considered such a minor procedure that most doctors farm it out to tattoo artists and ear-piercers.

• As humans age, more things deteriorate than just our physical appearance—even our voices age, growing drier, scratchier, and quieter with time. A **voice lift** reverses all that. An incision is made into the throat and the vocal cords are strengthened with either a synthetic implant, the patient's own fat, or ground-up tissue from medical cadavers.

• Do you have an "innie" belly button, but would rather have an "outie," or vice versa? There's a surgery for that. Technically called **umbilicoplasty**, this procedure involves a surgeon manipulating the fat and skin in the belly button to make it protrude more or recede into the belly, whichever you prefer.

• Botox treatment, an injection of the botulinum toxin, causes mild, temporary paralysis and smoothing of whatever tissue it's injected into, making it popular for erasing facial lines. Now there are **Botox armpit treatments**, which use the same technology to halt underarm perspiration for three to six months. The treatment can also be performed on overly sweaty feet.

• The **weight-loss tongue patch** is an increasingly popular procedure in California cosmetic-surgery clinics. A stamp-size plastic mesh patch is sewn onto the top of the tongue. Every time the patient eats solid food, the patch digs into the tongue, causing excruciating pain. Result: The patient switches to a liquid diet, which hastens weight loss. (The patch is removed after the target weight is reached.)

6EQUJ5

It's the stereotypical sci-fi movie scene: The nerdy astronomer is sitting in a poorly lit room, searching through data for some kind of evidence that we're not alone in the universe. Suddenly, among all of the bleeps and blips and printouts, something strange catches his attention... something that looks like nothing he's ever seen before.

THE "WOW!" SIGNAL

That scene played out in real life on the morning of August 19, 1977. Jerry Ehman, an astronomer working at the "Big Ear" radio telescope on the outskirts of Delaware, Ohio, was going over the results of the telescope's most recent survey of the night sky. His computer had spewed out pages and pages of numbers representing everything the telescope had detected. As Ehman was scanning the records from the night of August 15, a series of six numbers and letters stopped him in his tracks: "6EQUJ5." What did they mean? In the language of radio telescopes, they represented an unusually strong burst of radio waves that originated in the constellation Sagittarius. Unable to explain what might have caused the reading, Ehman simply circled that part of the computer printout. Next to it, he wrote: "Wow!"

It was only later, as astronomers began to eliminate all other possibilities, that many became convinced that the "Wow!" signal was something more than a flash in space. Perhaps *much* more.

ALL EARS

The hunt for extraterrestrial life was already well under way before that night in 1977, and it's still going strong today, led largely by a nonprofit organization called SETI (the Search for Extraterrestrial Intelligence). SETI's mission is to sanely conduct the search for "little green men"—a pursuit that some detractors claim is insane. SETI's astronomers are generally skeptical of UFO sightings; most think it's improbable that aliens have already visited Earth. SETI maintains that the universe is a very big place, so if we're going to find life on other worlds, we'll probably have to use powerful radio telescopes that can detect signals from a faraway, inhabited planet.

A Brazilian company created a Doggie Love sex doll for "lonely" pets.

Here's how the thinking goes: If you were a member of an alien race living on a planet across the galaxy, and you pointed a regular optical telescope at our solar system, it would look like any other medium-sized star. However, if you pointed a *radio* telescope in our direction, it would be immediately apparent that one of the planets had life on it. Why? Because our radio and television signals escape our atmosphere every day and fly off into space. Theoretically, aliens could be watching *Desperate Housewives* right now.

SETI has access to some of the most powerful radio telescopes in the world—and in 1977, the Big Ear was one of the biggest. But it was designed to be largely automated (astronomers have better things to do than listen to radio static all day), recording the results of its observations on rolls of printer paper. And what Big Ear detected that day was a very intense radio signal. It had no way of converting that signal into sound or images; the only information it had was that small group of numbers and letters.

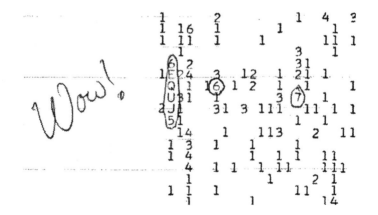

OFF THE CHARTS

Looking at Ehman's printout above, the numbers represent the "brightness," or strength, of a signal that the radio telescope picks up—with 1 standing for a "dim" signal and 9 standing for a very "bright" one. In the unlikely event that the signal detected is stronger than a 9, the printout uses letters, with "A" being brighter than 9 and "Z" being the brightest possible source the observatory could record. So a signal that went as high as "U" naturally caught Ehman's attention. In the 35 years that the Big Ear was in operation, this was the only time it detected a radio signal that powerful.

It wasn't just the power of the signal that caught Ehman's attention; it was the way it rose and fell over the three minutes it was detected. The Big Ear was a massive telescope and couldn't turn the way a normal telescope could to follow the stars across the sky; it could only sit there as stars came and went past its field of vision. So, given the Earth's rotational speed, it could observe any point in the sky for only a few minutes as that point passed overhead. Any signal it detected would be expected to show up faintly, rise to its highest point, and then fall back down again. This is precisely what the "Wow!" signal did: It rose from 6 to E to U and back down to 5 again in exactly three minutes. This was a strong, steady signal.

THEORIES ABOUND

Because no known object in the night sky should be emitting a radio signal that strong, astronomers crunching the data came up with several perfectly normal (and a few abnormal) explanations:

• **Terrestrial sources:** It's possible that an ordinary local signal, like a television or radio broadcast, somehow got detected by the sensitive antennas of the Big Ear. Scientists consider this explanation unlikely; it's illegal to broadcast radio waves of the strength detected—and even if someone did break the law, the direction of the signal made it almost certain that the source was in space.

• **"Extraterrestrial terrestrial" sources:** Some piece of radio transmission from the Earth may have hit a reflective surface in space (a satellite, a piece of space junk, or a meteor) that bounced the signal back to the Big Ear. The odds of this happening are…well, astronomical, but some skeptics are more comfortable with this explanation than some of the alternatives.

• **Scintillation:** Light from space *scintillates* as it moves through our atmosphere. This is a fancy way of saying it gets brighter and dimmer. (It's what makes stars appear to twinkle.) Radio waves do something similar, and the Big Ear telescope may have detected an unusually powerful scintillation of a weak radio source in space—a quasar, for instance.

• **Defective antenna:** It's also possible that the Big Ear was just malfunctioning. Radio telescopes are large, complicated machines, and any number of things can go wrong. But the Big Ear's performance on that night has been checked and rechecked, and no problem has ever been found.

• **Something new:** Since no known object in the universe emits such strong radio waves, and no (legal) device on Earth is even capable of it, it's possible that the signal came from some *unknown* object in deep space—perhaps some undiscovered kind of star...or something even stranger.

E.T. PHONE EARTH

Obviously, the most exciting theory is that the "Wow!" signal is a bona fide message from another world. But this explanation has problems of its own—namely, why haven't they called back? The region of the night sky that the signal came from has been surveyed more than 50 times since 1970, by telescopes many times more powerful than the Big Ear. To date, there has been only radio silence from that patch of Sagittarius.

But that silence has done nothing to stop the speculation. Perhaps, some astronomers theorize, the signal comes in pulses, once every few hours or so, and we've simply missed it. Or it may sweep across the sky like the beam from a lighthouse. Or maybe it was a one-time thing, a brief transmission, or one that we caught only the tail end of. The SETI scientists can't state outright that the signal was created by intelligent beings on a distant planet. However, they do admit that most of the other possibilities have been all but ruled out. "Either the 'Wow!' signal was an intercepted transmission from another civilization, or it's a previously undiscovered astrophysical phenomenon," said Dr. Paul Shuch of SETI. "Either possibility is mind-boggling."

STILL SEARCHING

The Big Ear radio telescope is no more—it was torn down in 1998 to make room for a golf course, and its astronomers have moved on to other projects. But the questions raised by the "Wow!" signal haven't disappeared. Meanwhile, astronomers still sit in small rooms, poring over mountains of data, hoping to be the one who detects that tiny blip that will alter the course of human history.

Found on the handle of a hammer: "Caution: Do not use this hammer to strike any solid object."

WHAT'S IN *YOUR* PANTS?

*We're betting that whoever invented pants
never saw these stories coming.*

W**hat's in *Her* Pants:** A bat
Story: Anna Buchan, 19, of Aberdeen, Scotland, was
being driven to work by her mother one morning in
July 2008 when she suddenly let out a scream—something was
crawling up her thigh, *inside* her pant leg. Buchan hurriedly pulled
down her pants and saw what it was: a small bat. She managed to
grab the animal and, once she arrived at work, put it in a box.
Wildlife officials advised her to release it after nightfall. "It's so
cute and small," Buchan said, after she regained her composure.
"I'll be sorry to see it go."

What's in *His* Pants: A ferret
Story: In October 2009, a teenager walked out of a Pet Supermarket store in Jacksonville Beach, Florida, and confronted 38-year-old Rodney Bolton. Why? The boy had just seen Bolton stuff a
ferret down his pants inside the store. Bolton denied it, but when
the teen wouldn't leave him alone, he pulled the ferret out of his
pants and thrust it into the kid's face—and it bit him. Police
arrived a short time later and arrested Bolton. He was charged
with robbery and battery with a "special weapon"—the ferret. The
brave teenager was treated on the scene and released.

What's in *His* Pants: Wieners
Story: Police in the town of Innisfail, Australia, were called to a
supermarket in October 2009 because a man had been seen leaving the store after shoplifting several items. Police found the 38-year-old suspect in the parking lot—with several sausages stuffed
into his pants. According to reports, the sausages "were recovered
but were not returned for sale in the store."

What's in *His* Pants: Pigeons
Story: Customs officers at the airport in Melbourne, Australia,
became suspicious when they found two small eggs in the pocket

of a man traveling from Dubai. They told him they'd have to search him, asked him to take his pants off—and found two live pigeons taped to his thighs. The unidentified 23-year-old was arrested for trying to smuggle live animals and faces up to 10 years in prison.

What's in *His* Pants: A scar
Story: David Walker, 28, of Dinnington, England, was in a pub one night in March 2004 with his "lifelong friend," Stuart Simpson. After drinking approximately 15 beers, the two friends got into an argument: It was Simpson's turn to buy a round, but he didn't buy one. So Walker got angry, left the pub, went home, shoved a sawed-off shotgun down his pants, walked back to the bar, and, on the way there, shot himself in a *very* delicate place. While he was still recovering from emergency surgery, Walker was sentenced to five years in prison for illegal possession of a firearm. He says he has no memory of the incident whatsoever.

What's in *Her* Pants: "Trees"
Story: In January 2008, police in Palm City, Florida, pulled over a car driven by 24-year-old Theresa Linette Rochester. According to the police report, officers "observed a large bulge in the groin area of Rochester that resembled a male penis." Pretty sure that Theresa didn't have a penis in there, one of the officers asked her what the bulge was. "She stated it was 'trees,'" the report said—a street name for marijuana. A subsequent search found that she had about an ounce of the drug in plastic bags in her pants. Rochester was arrested for drug possession.

What's in *His* Pants: Fire
Story: Kenneth Ray Brooks walked into the Centura Bank in Orlando, Florida, in September 2006, demanded cash, got it, shoved it down his pants, and quickly left the building. A few minutes later, police patrolling the area noticed a man walking down the street with smoke pouring from his pants. It was Brooks—a dye pack hidden in the bills had exploded and somehow lit his pants on fire. Brooks was arrested and, according to officers, "walked very, very slowly to a waiting ambulance."

Female buffalo on California's Catalina Island receive regular birth-control injections.

GOING THROUGH THE MOTIONS

A "motion" is a request made by an attorney during a court case, asking the judge for permission to make some type of change to the case. But, according to the BRI's legal expert, some motions are anything but ordinary.

MOTION: Delay the start of the trial because it conflicts with a college-football game.

ARGUMENTS: In a 2008 insurance case in Louisiana, the trial was scheduled to begin on January 7—the day of the national college football championship game between the hometown Louisiana State University Tigers and the Ohio State Buckeyes. The defendants' lawyer, Stephen Babcock, argued, "In addition to the opportunity to be the BCS National Champions, this game also represents LSU's chance to even their win-to-loss ratio with Ohio State. All opposing counsel are self-professed LSU fans, and consequently, have no objection." Babcock even pointed out in a footnote that all the lawyers associated with the case were veteran members of a Tigers fan club called the "Tiger Pimp Nation."

RULING: The judge was apparently a part of Tiger Pimp Nation as well. The motion was granted.

MOTION: Delay the trial because deer season will interfere with jury selection.

ARGUMENTS: In 2006 Bobby Junior Cox of Lonoke County, Arkansas, faced a number of serious charges in a highly publicized case. *Voir dire*, or jury selection, was scheduled to begin on November 8—three days before the state's six-week-long deer-hunting season began. Cox's lawyer argued that every defendant is entitled to a jury that represents a cross-section of his local community, and getting such a jury might be difficult. Because local residents often scheduled their vacation time during hunting season, many prospective jurors would want to be excused from serving.

RULING: The trial judge agreed with Hall's arguments, and the motion to reschedule voir dire was granted.

MOTION: The opposing lawyers should have lunch together.

ARGUMENTS: In a case involving a medical group in 2006, the plaintiff's attorney, David Selden, thought that a friendly chat over lunch would be the best way to resolve some pretrial disputes with the opposing attorney. He even offered to pay, but his opponent, Dow Ostlund, didn't respond. Selden finally filed a motion asking the court to compel Ostlund to have lunch with him. Ostlund eventually told the judge that he "would love to have lunch at Ruth's Chris Steak House"—a restaurant that isn't open for lunch. Selden objected to Ostlund's choice, but said he would find a way to oblige—if Ostlund paid for his own meal.

RULING: The judge granted Selden's request, and suggested 11 "fine restaurants within easy driving distance of both counsel's offices," ordered that the two meet for lunch no later than August 18, and even specified how the tab was to be paid, right down to the 20% tip. Ostlund probably realized after oral arguments what the judge would decide. Ostlund and Selden eventually sat down over a catered lunch…at Selden's office.

MOTION: Delay the trial because the lawyer's dog just had puppies (and a massive storm is about to hit).

ARGUMENTS: In a 2006 Florida case, the defendant's attorney made a motion to have a hearing involving some findings the court had made. On July 13, 2006, the court ordered the plaintiff's lawyers to submit their response to the motion by September 6. But by late August, Tropical Storm Ernesto was bearing down on southern Florida. On August 28, the plaintiff's lawyers, Stanley and Susan Rosenblatt, moved for an extension of time to file their response. The Rosenblatts' reason: With the storm coming, they and their staff would need the next few days to get through the storm, leaving them with little or no time to complete the work needed to respond to the motion. Finally, Susan Rosenblatt added, "In addition to the normal preparations for her family and office, undersigned counsel has seven puppies (born to her King Charles Cavalier) that are dependent upon her, and additional preparations for them are needed for the possible hurricane."

RULING: The court granted the motion, and the puppies weathered the storm.

THE OBJECT OF MY AFFECTION IS AN OBJECT

Uncle John really loves his favorite toilet (he calls it "Commodius Rex"). But now that he's read about these people, he's careful to tell us that he doesn't love it that way.

BACKGROUND
Psychology textbooks are filled with cases of strange obsessions. There are people who can't stop thinking about shoes, or food, or perhaps a...uh...close relative. But people classified as *objectum-sexual* are literally "in love" with inanimate objects. The term was coined in the 1970s by a German woman named Eija-Riitta Berliner-Mauer, who was—and still is—"married" to the Berlin Wall. "OS" people have deep emotional—and often physical—relationships with their...things. According to *Bizarre* magazine:

> Look hard enough, and you'll discover an Internet populated by tales of love affairs with objects. Joachim A., for example, confesses to his affair with a Hammond organ that began when he was 12. He's now in a steady relationship with a steam locomotive. Psychology student Bill R. tells of his sexual obsession with his iBook (he defines it as a homosexual relationship, as he regards his laptop as male), and Doro B. talks about falling for a metal processing machine she encountered at her work.

Here are a few more matches made in...well, we're not exactly *where* they're made, but here they are.

ERIKA ♥ THE EIFFEL TOWER

Erika La Tour Eiffel is in love with—you guessed it—that big tower in Paris. It's not her first OS relationship, though. She's also a world-champion archer and credits her success to her ex-"beau"—Lance, her bow. Setting her sights on bigger and better things, the 37-year-old San Francisco woman now claims to be the wife of the Eiffel Tower. The two were married in 2007. Like most OS people, Eiffel believes in the concept of *animism*, the theory that everything has a soul—and, in turn, a personality. But the relationship is not easy, since her "husband" is solidly attached to the ground 5,500 miles away. Eiffel visits when she can but admits, "There is a

---

Nuts: The female marine Bobbit worm bites off the male's genitalia and feeds it to her young.

huge problem with being in love with a public object. The issue of intimacy—or rather lack of it—is forever present." To deal with these and other issues, Eiffel runs a Web site where OS people from around the world share their stories.

AMY ♥ 1001 NACHTS

"I love him as much as women love their husbands and know we'll be together forever," says Amy Wolfe, a church organist from Pennsylvania. The "him" she's referring to is an 80-foot roller coaster called 1001 Nachts, located at the Knoebels Amusement Park in the Pocono Mountains, 80 miles from her home. After a 10-year courtship, they were married in 2009. Wolfe claims that their relationship is both "sexual and mental." Like Eiffel, Wolfe must deal with being in a long-distance relationship. To cope, she has posters of 1001 Nachts on her ceiling and carries around some nuts and bolts that she picked up from the ground underneath the roller coaster.

EDWARD ♥ VANILLA

"Vanilla" is a Volkswagen Beetle that has stolen Edward Smith's heart. Smith is part of a subculture of OS known as *mechanophiles*, people who are in love with vehicles. "I'm a romantic," says the 57-year-old Washington man. "I write poetry about cars. I sing to them and talk to them just like a girlfriend." But that doesn't mean Smith is loyal. Another feature of OS "relationships" is that they're often not monogamous. Smith claims to have had, er…physical relations with more than 1,000 cars in his life, as well as several aircraft, including the helicopter that was used in the 1980s television show *Airwolf*. But Vanilla is his current main squeeze. (He previously had a five-year relationship with another VW Beetle named "Victoria.") What does Smith look for in a potential lover? He's not sure; it just has to "speak" to him. "There have been certain cars that just attracted me, and I would wait until nighttime, creep up to them, and just hug and kiss them."

NISAN ♥ NEMUTAN

Nisan is a balding, heavyset 37-year-old Japanese man. Nemutan is a large, stuffed pillow printed with a picture of Nemu, a bikini-clad character from an X-rated version of the popular video game

---

Designer Lauren McCarthy invented the Happiness Hat. It stabs you in the head if you stop smiling.

De Capo. The two first met at a Tokyo comic book convention in 2006. They became friends at first but then started spending more and more time together. Nisan took Nemutan on drives, they posed for photos together, they played at playgrounds, and they even dined together at restaurants. After three years, the couple is still inseparable. And now they're famous, since their story was told in a 2009 *New York Times* article about "2-D lovers," a growing subculture of *Otaku*—the obsessive Japanese fandom related to *anime*, *manga*, and video games. It's uncertain how many people are 2-D lovers—they're usually productive members of society—but they care *very* deeply about these characters. "Of course she's my girlfriend," says Nisan. "I have real feelings for her. People are probably wondering what psychiatric ward I escaped from. I would think the same thing if I saw me."

OBJECTIFYING SCIENCE

As outlandish as these "love affairs" might sound, psychologists have studied them at length and have come up with a few theories on why these people become so attached to their objects.

• They're fetishists. Fetishism, a well-documented psychological phenomenon, involves being turned on sexually by objects or body parts—say, leather clothing, or feet. But OS people maintain that their relationships are more focused on love than on sex.

• Some research suggests that there may be a link between OS and a form of autism called Asperger's syndrome, which results in the sufferer having difficulty interacting with other people. But many in the OS community are very social and don't fit the typical Asperger's profile.

• Many OS people suffered from a past severe emotional and/or physical trauma and are unable to form a loving bond with another human out of fear. Put simply, they may prefer to be in a relationship where the other partner can't abuse or leave them.

• Some theorize that OS may be just another form of sexual orientation, albeit a very rare one. Just like hetero- and homosexuality, objectum-sexuality often manifests at the onset of puberty.

Erika La Tour Eiffel can't really explain it. She calls the feelings she has for objects "innate." As her Web site says, "We are not looking for a cure, but more comprehension into our make-up as an emerging part of society."

NEWSPAPER CORREKSHUNS

Every once in a while, a newspaper makes a mistake. What are we saying? They make mistakes all the time. Luckily, most papers have a policy of issuing a correction. And some, like these from the very recent past, are hilerious.

Anchorage Daily News: "There was an error in the Dear Abby column that was published on Monday. In the fifth paragraph, the second sentence stated that Charlie's hiccups were cured temporarily through the use of carbon monoxide. It should have read carbon dioxide."

The Guardian (U.K.): "In our entry on Garrison Keillor's *Lake Wobegon Days*, we referred to *A Prairie Ho Companion*; we meant *A Prairie Home Companion*."

The Sun (U.K.): "In my column on August 22, I suggested that Sharon Osbourne was an unemployed, drug-addled, unfit mum with a litter of feral kids. This was not intended to be taken literally. I fully accept she is none of these things and sincerely apologise to Sharon and her family for my unacceptable comments. Sorry, Sharon…"

The Amherst Citizen (Nova Scotia): "A Nov. 9 story about Nova Scotia's black minority was accompanied by an inaccurate photograph caption. The photo, said to depict run-down houses around Dartmouth, was actually of a pig farm. *The Citizen* apologizes for the error."

The Sentinel-Review (Woodstock, Ontario): "In an article in Monday's newspaper, there may have been a misperception about why a Woodstock man is going to Afghanistan on a voluntary mission. Kevin DeClark is going to Afghanistan to gain life experience to become a police officer when he returns, not to 'shoot guns and blow things up.' *The Sentinel-Review* apologizes for any embarrassment this may have caused."

Denver Daily News: "We would like to offer a sincere

apology for a typo in Wednesday's Town Talk regarding New Jersey's proposal to ban smoking in automobiles. It was not the author's intention to call New Jersey 'Jew Jersey.'"

The Sunday Paper (Atlanta, Georgia): "An earlier version of this story incorrectly described Buffington's special support hose as 'mercury-lined.' The hose are mercury-gauged, meaning that barometric mercury is used to measure the compression of the hose. They are not mercury-lined, which would, of course, make them poisonous."

Us Weekly: "In our feature 'Why She Left Him,' the woman identified in the photograph as former adult-film star Ginger Lynn Allen is neither Ms. Allen nor an adult-film actress. *Us* regrets the error."

The Sun (U.K.): "In an article published on *The Sun*'s website on January 27 under the headline 'Gollum joker killed in live rail horror,' we incorrectly stated that Julian Brooker, 23, of Brighton, was blown 15 feet into the air after accidentally touching a live railway line. His parents have asked us to make clear

that he was not turned into a fireball, was not obsessed with the number 23, and didn't go drinking on that date every month. Julian's mother did not say, during or after the inquest, that her son often got on all fours creeping around their house, pretending to be Gollum from the J.R.R. Tolkien novels. We apologise for the distress this has caused Julian's family and friends."

Portland (Maine) Press Herald: "A story on Wednesday about foraging for edible mushrooms contained a photo of *amanita muscaria*, which is a poisonous and hallucinogenic mushroom. It was a copyeditor's error."

The Guardian: "We misspelled the word 'misspelled' twice, as 'mispelled,' in the Corrections and clarifications column on September 26, page 30."

Iowa State Daily: "In Friday's issue, the article 'Decorate your dorm on the cheap' inaccurately described furniture purchased at Goodwill and Salvation Army stores as being 'complete with that old-urine smell.' The *Daily* retracts its false statement and deeply regrets the error."

MOONSTRUCK

Is our moon to blame for this crazy world?

LUNAR-TICS

The idea of someone being "moonstruck"—driven insane by the influence of the moon—dates back to the ancient Greeks and Romans. In fact, the word "lunatic" derives from Luna, the Roman goddess of the moon. The Greek physician Hippocrates (460–370 B.C.) observed the moon's effect on the tides, and concluded that the moon must exert some influence over the brain's "moistness" and cause madness. This belief persisted through the Middle Ages: People refused to sleep where moonbeams might strike them, and werewolves were said to wreak havoc during the full moon.

STATISTICAL ANOMALIES

To this day, it is a common belief that weird things happen when the moon is full, a phenomenon sometimes called "the Transylvanian effect." Police officers and emergency room workers attest that crime, accidents, and suicides all increase on full moons. Nevertheless, rigorous statistical analysis has shown that there is little correlation between human behavior and the phases of the moon. More than 35 major studies have been conducted on lunar cycle influence. The findings: There are no significant increases in ER visits, births, or crime.

OVER THE MOON

Still, it will probably take more than statistics to convince people that the moon doesn't effect us in some way. As Hippocrates noted, the moon's gravitational force affects the tides, and the human body is composed largely of water. And there is evidence of lunar influence in the length of menstrual cycles and the circadian rhythms that govern sleep.

But Michael Shermer, editor of *Skeptic* magazine, has this simple explanation for why we *think* full moons cause weirdness. "We don't remember the unusual things that happen on all the other times, because we're not looking for them." Or perhaps a brightly lit night is simply conducive to mischief.

THE CHEMTRAILS CONSPIRACY

What's crazier? That some people actually believe the United States government is purposely spraying caustic chemicals into the air? Or that those people have evidence to back up their claims?

THE UNFRIENDLY SKIES
In May 2000, an anonymous letter started making the rounds on the Internet. Here's an excerpt:

I work for an airline in upper management levels. I will not say which airline. I wish I could document everything, but to do so would result in possible physical harm to me. Airline companies in America have been participating in something called "Project Cloverleaf" for a few years now. They told us that the government was going to pay our airline, along with others, to release special chemicals from commercial aircraft. When asked what the chemicals were, they told us that information was given on a need-to-know basis and we weren't cleared for it. They told us the chemicals were harmless, but the program was of such importance that it needed to be done at any cost. The public doesn't need to know what's going on, but that this program is in their best interests.

The writer went on to say that Project Cloverleaf made use of a "Powder Contrail Generation Apparatus," which was attached to the planes.

By the time the letter appeared, discussion of "chemtrails" had already become a fixture on late night talk radio shows, in alternative magazines, and online. Dozens of conspiracy Web sites reported (and still report) that, far from being harmless, chemtrails are something to be very afraid of. But what are they?

LINE UP

If you look up when a jet plane passes overhead, you'll often see a white plume that looks like a chalk mark in the sky. That's called a *contrail*, short for "condensation trail." A contrail forms when water vapor around the exhaust from a jet plane flying above 30,000 feet freezes. Sometimes, though, planes leave behind trails that are thicker, longer, and longer-lasting. These, according to

---

An *Ad Age* magazine study says America is so diverse now that "average Americans" don't exist.

conspiracy theorists, are "chemical trails," or *chemtrails*. Here's how they say you can tell the difference:

✓ Contrails are visible about one wingspan's distance behind a jet plane. Chemtrails are directly behind a plane, with no gap between the plane and the trail.

✓ Contrails form straight lines. Chemtrails crisscross the sky in zigzag patterns that often form a large grid.

✓ Contrails last for moments and then dissipate. Chemtrails last for hours and leave behind a hazy stain in the sky.

Contrails are basically just water vapor—an incidental by-product of regular aircraft. But chemtrails, say the conspiracies, contain a mixture of pesticides and heavy metals, such as barium and aluminum. They're dispensed by either passenger jets or unmarked planes that fly repeatedly over the same area, at lower-than-normal altitudes. Once in the sky, chemtrails are supposedly heated by super-powerful radar or microwaves, creating chemical fibers known as "angel hair" that fall to the ground in a toxic mist.

COUGH, COUGH

So why are these dastardly doses of death being dumped on us? There are several theories.

Population control: It's a part of the Illuminati's "New World Order Depopulation Agenda," the aim of which is to kill off masses of undesirable people, or at least render them sterile so they can't multiply. (This is occurring in North America and Western Europe—but not China because that nation, according to the theory, "is being groomed by the NWO to replace the United States as the leading nation of the world, both economically and militarily."

Urban unrest: Some conspiracy theorists claim that spraying chemtrails over low-income inner-city neighborhoods has resulted in increased outbreaks of violence and crime, causing unrest in the cities, which will eventually lead to chaos. (No word on what kind of outcome that chaos is supposed to lead to.)

Weapons testing: The military is using chemtrails to test out various forms of biological warfare…and U.S. citizens are the guinea pigs.

Weather control: Imagine one country threatening another country with, "Surrender—or you won't see any rain for 20 years!" Chemtrails may be the means to achieve this.

Environmental aid: Another theory is far less grim. Chemtrails were designed to stop global warming by increasing what's called "global dimming." Believers point to physicist Dr. Edward Teller, known as the "Father of the Hydrogen Bomb" and also the father of the "Star Wars" missile defense program. In 1997 Teller wrote in the *Wall Street Journal* that the same chemicals used in topical sunscreen could be used to block the harmful atmospheric rays that cause global warming and that passenger jets are perfectly suited to disperse them into the atmosphere. Interestingly, chemtrails started appearing in much greater numbers shortly after Teller's article was published.

HAARP ATTACK

At the heart of the chemtrails controversy is the U.S. Air Force project HAARP (High Frequency Active Aural Research Project) in Alaska. According to its Web site, HAARP is an unclassified research project that studies the ionosphere and radio science. Conspiracy theorists, however, say this is a ruse. They claim the *classified* mission of HAARP is to establish a massive radar grid that combines electromagnetic waves with chemtrails in order to spread the chemicals across the world's atmosphere, giving the American military-industrial complex control over everything from the weather, to enhanced surveillance, to mind control.

To back up their claims, they exhibit a 1996 research study published by the USAF called "Weather as a Force Multiplier: Owning the Weather in 2025." The unclassified report was produced by students, faculty, and scientists from academic branches of the Air Force. They were challenged to imagine a set of fictional scenarios set 30 years in the future and what possible responses the military might have. These scenarios describe using weather modification to achieve "battlespace dominance" by enhancing precipitation (making rain), inducing drought, generating cloud cover, and disrupting satellite communications and radar.

THE RAINMAKERS

Government control of the weather is not a new concept. During World War II, attempts were made to combine chemical agents with cloud seeding, and during the Vietnam War covert cloud-seeding operations tried to make enough rain to muddy jungle trails and hinder the movements of enemy soldiers. These operations were exposed in the late 1960s, and by the early 1970s the U.S. Senate called for an international treaty against weather manipulation. They got one: the United Nations Convention on the Prohibition of Any Hostile Use of Environmental Modification Technique, which was ratified by the U.S. and 30 other nations, and entered into effect in 1978.

DEATH RAY 2000!

But just because something is illegal, does that mean the government won't do it? Carolyn Williams Palit, a Texas woman in her 50s, believes that not only is the government continuing to spread chemicals in the atmosphere, but that they're actually weapons:

> It involves the combination of chemtrails for creating an atmosphere that will support electromagnetic waves, ground-based electromagnetic field oscillators called "gyrotrons," and ionospheric heaters. They spray barium powders and let it photoionize from the ultraviolet light of the sun. Then they make an aluminum-plasma generated by "zapping" the metal cations that are in the spray with either electromagnetics from HAARP, the gyrotron system on the ground [the Ground Wave Emergency Network], or space-based lasers. The barium makes the aluminum-plasma more particulate dense. This means they can make a denser plasma than they normally could from just ionizing the atmosphere or the air. More density [more particles] means that these particles are colliding into each other and will become more charged. What they are ultimately trying to do up there is create charged-particle, plasma beam weapons.

Palit believes we are victims of "state-sponsored torture" and that Congress is knowingly using American tax dollars to fund it.

THE OFFICIAL RESPONSE

In response to Palit, her many followers, and all the other conspiracy theorists, NASA, the USAF, the EPA, and the NOAA (National Oceanic and Atmospheric Administration) have all released rebuttals, explaining that chemtrails are nothing more than really big contrails, caused by various atmospheric, weather, and air traffic conditions.

In their "Aircraft Contrails Factsheet," the agencies explained the difference between short-lived contrails and persistent contrails—the ones most likely to be mistaken for chemtrails. The photographs in the pamphlet show the crisscrossing patterns and grids that chemtrail believers so often point to as proof that the lines are not contrails. In 2005 the USAF released their own "Contrails Facts," a long, exhaustive document that goes into infinite detail about contrails, and debunks chemtrails, calling them a "hoax."

Unfortunately, the Air Force didn't do themselves any favors by using the word "hoax"; that just stoked the conspiratorial fires, as people started picking apart every word in the Air Force's explanation as proof of just the opposite. "The latest line of attack would earn approval from George Orwell himself," wrote one Web site. "Chemtrails are now counted by our children in staged 'educational' events. These events serve the purpose of indoctrination into an Orwellian world that declares the operations to be 'normal.' It is a world in which there is no need to question this authority."

PROTECT YOURSELF

So if you believe the government, then you have nothing to worry about. But if you *don't* believe the government, is there anything you can do? One option is to construct your own "Chembuster"— a device that will "absorb bad energy and release good energy." To build one (you can find directions online), combine aluminum shavings, magnets, crystals, and copper pipes with epoxy or polyester resin in a large bucket. Use a dowsing rod to find a good spot to place your bucket, apply "psychic insights," and voilà, the chemtrails will no longer affect you because the Chembuster is "transmuting the atmospheric orgone energy envelope from a polarity that allows chemtrails to persist, to another orgone polarity, which will cause chemtrails to disperse."

There. Now you can breathe easy!

*   *   *

"I was walking home one night and a guy hammering on a roof called me a paranoid little weirdo...in morse code."

—**Emo Phillips**

Worldwide, 56 near misses between planes and UFOs have been reported. (No accidents...so far.)

I CAN EXPLAIN!

Sometimes people come up with ingenious
excuses for the crazy things they do.
And then there are these people.

Accused: Marco Fella of Callington, Cornwall, England
Busted: Fella was arrested in November 2008 after he bit his girlfriend's finger and hit her in the head with a dog toy.
I Can Explain! Fella said the attack came about because he hadn't had enough Mars candy bars. He claims he's a sugar addict and normally eats about 10 candy bars per day. He also told police that the attack happened after he asked his girlfriend to put on a thong, and she put on "large pants" instead. Fella was ordered to attend an anger management course.

Accused: Jessica Vasquez, 19, of Indianapolis, Indiana
Busted: Vasquez was arrested in May 2008 in a road-rage case, during which she passed a car being driven by 81-year-old Evelyn Page, slammed on her brakes, and stopped. Then she ran back to Page's car, punched her in the face, pulled her from her car, and threw her to the ground, fracturing the elderly woman's legs in 14 places.
I Can Explain! Vasquez said it was self-defense. Page, she told police, had first endangered her by driving too slowly, forcing Vasquez to drive past her and slam on her brakes. And why did she assault her? Because, according to Vasquez, the 81-year-old threatened to "beat her up." Vasquez pleaded guilty to aggravated battery and was sentenced to 20 years in prison. "I felt sorry for her," Page said. "She's not a lady."

Accused: Lorena Alvarez of Lake Worth, Florida
Busted: One evening in April 2009, Alvarez was driving around Lake Worth looking for her boyfriend, who had not come home after work. She spotted him sitting in his pickup truck in the parking lot of a convenience store, drove into the lot—and smashed her car into his truck. Then she backed up and did it

---

Average amount spent by Americans on clothes each year: $1,881. On books: $118.

again. She rammed the pickup several more times before police finally arrived.

I Can Explain! Alvarez told police that she was only trying to protect other motorists because her boyfriend was about to drive drunk. The police didn't believe her, and she was arrested on charges of aggravated battery with a deadly weapon and two counts of child endangerment—because her two sons, aged one and seven, were in her car at the time.

Accused: James Yates, 47, of Columbus, Ohio
Busted: Yates was arrested in February 2006 at England's Manchester Airport for public drunkenness. What's worse, he was a pilot, and was headed to his scheduled American Airlines flight to Chicago with 181 passengers onboard. Yates's blood alcohol level was almost eight times over the maximum allowed for pilots. He was charged with "carrying out an activity ancillary to an aviation function while over the drink limit."

I Can Explain! Yates admitted in court that he had done some drinking the night before the incident and was still drunk in the morning only because he'd unknowingly consumed a third of a bottle of whiskey…in his sleep. He said that he often did strange things while sleeping, and he was headed to the plane not to fly it, but to tell the flight captain that he was too drunk to fly. His excused worked for the jury, however—they acquitted him. He was suspended from his job, but American Airlines said that they might hire him back. (No word on whether they did.)

Accused: Peter Ivan Dunne
Busted: Dunne was awaiting trial for sex offenses in Ireland in 2003 when he fled the country. He was convicted *in absentia* but was arrested several years later in England. In July 2009, he went before the High Court in London to explain his actions and try to persuade them not to extradite him to Ireland.

I Can Explain! Dunne said that he had fled Ireland only because he was afraid that he'd have to eat onions in prison. He's allergic to them—especially the red variety, he told the judges—and insisted there was a "a real risk, or near certainty" that he would die from onion poisoning if they sent him home. He also said that he had converted to Judaism, and that his past experiences in an

Irish prison made him certain that not only would he be fed non-kosher meals (with onions, presumably), he would also be mocked for his religion. Sending him back, he argued, would therefore be a violation of the European Convention on Human Rights. The judges disagreed, and Dunne was sent back to Ireland, where he's currently awaiting sentencing.

Accused: Alexander Kabelis, 31, of Boulder, Colorado

Busted: Kabelis was arrested in May 2009 for slashing the tires on almost 50 cars and trucks—nine of them police and sheriff's vehicles.

I Can Explain! Kabelis told police that he had several reasons for slashing the tires, including being mad at his mother, losing his driver's license years earlier, having to wear braces as a child, and being poisoned by radiation from the nearby Rocky Flats nuclear facility. Strangely, none of those excuses worked, and police charged him with criminal mischief and carrying a concealed weapon.

Accused: Thousands of television owners in the United Kingdom

Busted: Owning a TV requires a license in the U.K., at an annual cost of £142.50, or about $225. More than a quarter-million people are fined annually for having unlicensed TVs.

I Can Explain! Every year, the office of TV Licensing publishes a list of the most original excuses used by people who were fined. Some of our favorites:

• "My husband has just spent £3,000 on this massive flat-screen digital TV, so we can't possibly afford a license."

• "My dog, not me, watches it to keep him company while I'm at work."

• "I couldn't make my last payment because my baby vomited on my shoulder and I didn't want to go to the shop smelling of sick because the guy I fancy works there."

• "I have not been making payments because a baby magpie flew in to my house and I have had to stay in to feed it."

• "The subtitles on my TV are set to French, so I'm not paying a U.K. tax for something I can't read."

Ew! The U.S. Army has recently developed a dried meal that can be safely rehydrated with urine.

RU OK, U.K.?

*We've hit just about everybody else, so here are a few
jabs at our friends in the United Kingdom.*

BAD WELSHMEN

In October 2009, a group of six martial-arts experts donating their time to a charity took turns carrying a 31-year-old wheelchair-bound man up Mount Snowden, the highest peak in Wales. (It's 3,560 feet high.) They were following the easiest but longest route to the peak, and about halfway up, they got tired... and left the man sitting in his wheelchair beside the path as they continued up the mountain without him. What's worse, when they returned hours later, they told the man that they were too tired to carry him back down the mountain and left him again. They notified someone when they reached the bottom, and a team of rescuers reached the man a few hours later. "The poor bloke was sitting there in his wheelchair for quite a while," said climber Dave Morrell, who witnessed the rescue. "He was getting very cold." The man was treated for mild exposure and released. Ian Henderson, a member of the rescue team, called the martial artists "cheeky."

SMILE—YOU'RE ON DUMBA** CAMERA

In January 2010, staff at an Asda clothing store in a shopping mall in Warrington, England, found a small camera in a light fixture inside one of the ladies' changing rooms. They called police, officers checked the camera...and found two very clear pictures of the man who had put it there: He'd inadvertently taken two shots of himself while he was setting up the camera. Police released the images to the public, and a few days later, a 44-year-old man (unnamed in press reports) was arrested on voyeurism charges.

BRAKE-ING UP IS HARD TO DO

In June 2009, Haylie Hocking of the city of Bristol went online to find a male stripper for her "hen's night," or bachelorette party. She and a friend were looking at a stripper Web site when she spotted one man who looked familiar: It was Jason Brake—her fiancé. It turned out that Brake was not only living a secret life as a stripper, but he'd also appeared in several adult films. Hocking, who had already chosen her bridesmaids, booked a horse-drawn carriage, and bought a $1,200 dress, immediately called off the wedding. "I am sorry and did not want to hurt her," said Brake. "I still love Haylie and would have stopped doing porn if she had asked me to." He also said that in the future he'd be telling prospective mates up front about his career.

YOU'RE DEAD TO ME!

A few days before Valentine's Day in 2009, 24-year-old Benjamin Barton, a student at Southampton General Hospital, told a hospital guard there that he needed to get into the morgue because he'd left some work there. The guard told him he'd have to come back the next day, so Barton went to a store, bought an axe, and returned that night to smash his way into the morgue. For the next 90 minutes, he went through confidential computer records… and several of the corpse drawers as well. What was he looking for? A fellow student named Amy Ogden—whom he had a terrible crush on (unrequited; Ogden had a boyfriend). Barton hadn't seen Ogden at the school for days and, for reasons known only to himself, became convinced that she was dead. She wasn't: She was visiting her family in another city. Police were able to track down the lovesick Barton through information he left with the guard, and he later pleaded guilty to criminal damage and was fined £1,000 ($1,600 US).

ROGER THAT

Annette Edwards of Worcester, England, is a world-renowned rabbit breeder, best known for owning the world's largest rabbit—a 49-pounder named Alice. But Edwards has another interesting hobby: Over the last few years, the 56-year-old woman has spent nearly $15,000 on plastic surgery procedures to make herself look like Jessica Rabbit, the voluptuous co-star of *Who Framed Roger Rabbit?* "My love of rabbits made me decide to go for the operations and make the big change," she said. "I've had a breast uplift, a brow lift, chin implants, and botox injections." She also likes to pose for the cameras in a shiny, tight, red dress slit up to her hips and a pair of long, purple gloves—just like the costume worn by Jessica Rabbit in the film. The U.K.'s *Mail Online* noted that the look "is bound to be a hit among members of the other sex."

In Louisiana, it is illegal to shoot a teller with a water pistol while committing a bank robbery.

MARRYIN' COUSINS

There are a lot of fish in the sea, but what if your fish is your first cousin, or your first cousin once removed? You can get married, depending on what state you live in. (By the way, a first cousin once removed means that you and your cousin are from different generations.)

• First cousins and first cousins once removed can marry with no restrictions in Alabama, Alaska, California, Colorado, Connecticut, Florida, Georgia, Hawaii, Maryland, Massachusetts, New Jersey, New Mexico, New York, Rhode Island, South Carolina, Tennessee, Vermont, and Virginia.

• First cousins once removed, but not first cousins of the same generation, may marry in Arkansas, Delaware, Idaho, Iowa, Michigan, Missouri, Montana, New Hampshire, North Dakota, Pennsylvania, South Dakota, and Texas.

• Marriage between first cousins of any type is illegal in Kentucky, Nevada, and Ohio.

• If first cousins get married in a state that allows cousin marriages, the marriage will still be valid if they move to Kansas, Nebraska, Oklahoma, Washington, or Wyoming. (But they can't get married in those states.)

• First cousins in which one of the parties was adopted may marry in Louisiana, Mississippi, Oregon, and West Virginia.

• In Minnesota, cousins can marry if they are a member of one of the state's four indigenous Native American tribes that traditionally allow the practice: Okijbwe, Sioux, Chippewa, or Dakota.

• First cousins wishing to marry in Maine have to pass a genetic test to ensure that their children won't have birth defects.

• If two brothers marry two sisters, the resulting children from each of those marriages are called *double first cousins*, and they may not marry each other in North Carolina.

• Many states just try to avoid the issue of cousins having children together by imposing age restrictions. In Arizona and Indiana, first cousins over age 65 can marry; in Wisconsin and Utah, it's 55; and in Illinois, it's set at age 50.

Singer Sting believes in ghosts. He claims one visited him in his bedroom.

ODD EATS

These top chefs create some crazy dishes.

FISH WRAP. Chef Homaro Cantu serves sushi that includes no fish and has almost no calories...because it's made out of paper. Invented in his Chicago restaurant, the paper is made with soy and cornstarch and then run through a printer that imprints it with photos of fish, rice, and seaweed—all in vegetable-based ink. Result: edible, three-dimensional sushi paper crafts. Cantu's plans for the future include using helium and superconductors to make levitating food.

MASH-UPS. At one of the world's finest restaurants—Fat Duck, located near London—head chef Heston Blumenthal practices *molecular gastronomy*, which combines chemistry and various scientific processes such as flash-freezing and crystallizing food with nitrous oxide, or turning alcohol into vapor. Some of his bizarre new dishes: sardine-flavored sorbet, bacon-and-egg ice cream, and chocolate infused with leather, oak, and tobacco aromas.

FOAMING AT THE MOUTH. Ferran Adria, head chef at El Bulli in northeastern Spain, also dabbles in molecular gastronomy. His most famous achievement is *food foam*. In order to enhance or concentrate a flavor, Adria condenses the ingredients down to an airy foam that melts in your mouth. Using a special bottle charged with nitrous oxide cartridges (similar to a whipped cream container), Adria has concocted such culinary treats as espresso foam, mushroom foam, and beef foam.

AN UPLIFTING MEAL. For the Gastronomy 2009 avant-garde food festival in Bogotá, Colombia, two students from the Quindio culinary school made a dessert out of Viagra. Their passion fruit pudding (garnished with whipped cream and chocolate and served in a parfait glass) featured a dissolved pill for erectile dysfunction. Co-creator Juan Sebastian Gomez said the idea was to "reinvent Viagra as an aphrodisiac." (What was it before?)

Some Japanese restaurants practice *nyotaimori*: serving food on human bodies (usually naked).

ODD JOBS

At the BRI, our job is to search for crazy stories and put them in a book (with a two-headed duck on the cover) that will be read in the bathroom. In comparison to these professions, our job is quite normal.

MOURNING CLOWN. An Irish company called Dead Happy Ireland sends out their "mourning clowns" to wakes and funerals. The clowns make balloon animals, squirt water out of their corsages, stumble toward the open casket as if they're going to fall in, and fart at inappropriate times. Says founder John Brady, "I've been to so many funerals, and they're always so sad. Wouldn't it be nice to have something funny happen?" Cost: 150 Euros (about $220).

DOG POOP PICKER-UPPER. This used to be a job exclusively for neighborhood teenagers who needed to earn a little money, but today dog-pile removal is big business. For example, Poop Patrol in San Diego has a fleet of trucks and workers use specialized "extraction tools." Their motto: "Always on doody."

GROSS STUNT PRODUCER. Thinking up new and detestable ways to make reality-show contestants (and viewers) cringe, these people create and sample eyeball soups, maggot slushies, and other foul "food." "If I can't keep it down," said *Fear Factor* production assistant Josh Silberman, "then perhaps it's not edible."

GUMBUSTER. When there's something strange stuck to the sole of your shoe, who ya gonna call? Gumbusters! Equipped with a contraption similar to a rug cleaner, Gumbusters will superheat the sticky goo so it can be easily washed and vacuumed off the floor or sidewalk. They're in great demand in most major cities (except in Singapore, where chewing gum is illegal).

LA-Z-BOY CHAIR TESTER. This job is not quite as easy as it sounds. "You can work up quite a sweat after the first hour or two," says Mike Pixly, who rocks back and forth up to 2,800 times per shift at the La-Z-Boy factory in Monroe, Michigan. Though he only earns $6 per hour, this "motivated self-starter" (as his

---

In 2009 a woman who was bitten on the buttocks by a police dog sued the dog. (She lost.)

boss calls him) appreciates the great workout for his calves and abdominal muscles.

MILITARY ROLE-PLAYER. Defense contractors are looking for a few good actors to take part in elaborate war games that help soldiers train for upcoming missions. These days, the casting calls are primarily for actors who look, or better yet speak, Arabic to play Middle Eastern villagers and combatants. The job entails running around shooting guns loaded with blanks, negotiating with soldiers, and playing dead.

CHICKEN SEXER. These skilled hatchery workers must separate baby chicks by gender—females will become egg layers; males are saved for later consumption or breeding purposes, or are disposed of. How do the sexers determine gender? Sometimes by the appearance of the feathers, but most often by squeezing the chick until its anal vent opens up—a little bump means it's a male.

MEDICAL MARIJUANA TESTER. Using a grant from the National Institutes of Health, the University of Iowa pays people $620 to be subjects of a 60-hour study. Basically, the subjects smoke marijuana joints while researchers monitor their brain function in an effort to help determine whether marijuana can be used medicinally, or if it does little more than give users the munchies.

CONDOM TESTER. Durex in Australia recruits men of all sizes to try their products and give feedback on comfort and durability. While it's not a paying job, testers receive $60 worth of Durex products, and one lucky guy wins a $1,000 bonus. (And for the ladies, there's also a job called "tampon tester.")

LAUGHTER THERAPIST. Has modern life become so bleak that we need specialists to teach us how to laugh? Yes, according to "joyologist" (and clinical psychologist) Steven Wilson, who helps his patients reconnect with the "joyful, zestful, exuberant laughter we all had as babies." A good belly laugh, Wilson says, can lead to a stronger immune system, less stress, and a slower aging process (except for the wrinkles that form on your cheeks from all that laughing).

RIP: REST IN PLASTIC

This story has everything a great Bathroom Reader *article
should: death, a mad scientist, an eccentric celebrity,
and polymerized semisolid body parts.*

THE ANTI-FRANKENSTEIN

Some call what Professor Gunther von Hagens does with dead bodies ghoulish and degrading. Not helping his image is his trademark outfit—a pressed black suit and a black fedora (the kind of hat Freddy Krueger wears). But the 65-year-old German anatomist dismisses his critics: "In all human history, the human body was always exploited for disgusting feelings. I'm doing the opposite. I break with the tradition of Frankenstein."

Von Hagens is the founder of Body Worlds, a touring exhibition that has attracted more than 29 million visitors since 1995. The show utilizes *plastination*—a process von Hagens invented and patented in the late 1970s—that preserves dead bodies and organs for display and study. The process combines his two favorite childhood activities: building model airplanes and learning anatomy from the doctors at a hospital where he spent a lot of time because he was a hemophiliac.

Plastination involves removing the liquid (water and fats) from a corpse and replacing it with reactive polymers (plastics) so that the body will become semisolid and won't decay. Once completed, the mostly skinless figures (with muscles, organs, and bones showing) are set in various poses. A typical Body Worlds exhibit may feature skinned cadavers sitting around a table playing poker (one is handing another a card with his foot in a parody of the *Dogs Playing Poker* painting). Or you may see an anatomically correct couple performing a gymnastics routine, or a corpse riding a skateboard, or a plastinated rider on a plastinated horse. "Plastinates show the beauty of our body interior," says von Hagens.

JUST PLAIN SICK

"It's pornography of the dead human body," says Catholic philosopher Thomas Hibbs of Baylor University. "The problem with death in our culture is not that we have taboos about it, but that we lack a rich language for articulating the experience and its meaning. It's hard to see how Body Worlds will help solve that problem."

Dr. Hibbs is one of many theologians offended by von Hagens's works. Britain's Bishop of Manchester has repeatedly referred to von Hagens as a "body snatcher" and claims that the donation of bodies for plastination has resulted in fewer organs being donated for transplant. Ethics questions have dogged Body Worlds from the beginning, including accusations that von Hagens steals his cadavers from prisons and insane asylums in China and former Soviet countries. Von Hagens responds: "What I certainly *never* use for public exhibitions are unclaimed bodies, prisoners, bodies from mental institutions, and executed prisoners." All of his cadavers, he says, are from willing North American and European donors (a claim that was verified by a California ethics commission investigation in 2004).

MASTER OF CEREMONIES

Von Hagens revels in the controversy. He agrees that people don't really know how to discuss death, and his aim is to take the awkwardness out of it. For example, in 2002 the professor performed the first public autopsy in the U.K. in 170 years. Despite being threatened with arrest, von Hagens went ahead with the gruesome show. Police, along with 500 spectators, jammed into a London theater to watch him cut into a recently deceased 72-year-old man. Audience members gasped as von Hagens sawed through the cadaver's skull with a hacksaw and then again when he reached into the body's torso and pulled out handfuls of organs, declaring, "I have liberated the lungs and heart!" Though the smell was reported to have offended some viewers, the autopsy went off without a hitch, and von Hagens managed to avoid arrest. He was eventually exonerated of any crime, and the autopsy "show" was later broadcast on Channel Four Television.

Riding high on his fame, von Hagens once offered to plastinate Pope John Paul II, who died shortly afterward. The request was denied, but then von Hagens set his sights on an even bigger fish.

THE KING OF PLOP

Someone claiming to be an associate of Michael Jackson contacted

---

von Hagens in March 2009 and told him that the eccentric pop star was fascinated by his body-preserving technology. "He's definitely up for undergoing the plastination procedure when the time comes," the representative told him. So von Hagens scheduled a Body Worlds exhibit to coincide with Jackson's summer 2009 shows in London and made this offer: "I could give Michael the gift of physical immortality—he has already achieved this with his music. As a plastinate, he could continue to have his body shaped and changed as he did when he was alive."

A few months later, of course, Jackson died amid a firestorm of scandal. Von Hagens acknowledged in a press release that the person who contacted him may not have been a spokesperson for the performer after all. "Without a signed body donation form by Michael Jackson himself or by all of his family members, I will not become active." But then he made an impassioned plea: "I can offer the family of Michael Jackson a whole-body plastination free of charge. The pose would be a dancing one, to be determined by the family in detail." There was no response from the Jacksons. Or was there?

DISAPPEARING ACT

Mystery still surrounds Michael Jackson's interment at Forest Lawn Memorial Park in Los Angeles. The funeral, which took place more than two months after Jackson's death, was shrouded in secrecy and attended by only a few of his close friends and family in a "non-public" area of the cemetery. Forest Lawn officials have since offered this warning to would-be visitors: "Fans who believe they can find Jackson's above-ground crypt in the expanses of the Great Mausoleum should rethink that," noting the tight security including several surveillance cameras. All the secrecy is probably due to the family's wish for privacy and their concern that a public gravesite would be mobbed by well-wishers or damaged by vandals.

But, some have theorized, maybe the King of Pop isn't interred at Forest Lawn at all. Maybe he's been plastinated in some laboratory to one day appear in the biggest Body Worlds exhibit of all.

But even if Jackson doesn't show, there are another 9,000 living people lined up to be plastinated…including the good doctor himself.

…"My Boyfriend's Arm." Another company offers the Lap Pillow, shaped like a woman's lap.

WE'RE DOOMED!

Here's some happy news to brighten up your day. Kidding!

SHAKY SCI-FI

In December 2009, geologist Markus Haering was put on trial in Switzerland—for causing earthquakes. In 2006 and 2007, Haering was the leader of a team working with Swiss authorities in the city of Basel on the "Deep Heat" project, the first experiment designed to generate electricity by boiling water on naturally heated rocks three miles below Earth's surface. But the city of Basel lies on an active geological fault line, and, according to geologists, the drilling and pressurized cold water caused a series of earthquakes in the city, one of them reaching 3.4 on the Richter scale—and causing millions of dollars' worth of damage. Haering faced up to five years in prison for "intentionally" causing the earthquakes, a charge Haering called ridiculous. He was found not guilty a few weeks later, but his company had to pay for the damage.

Creepy Bonus: Scientists think that humans may have actually caused several earthquakes in recent decades. One study on the May 2008 quake that hit Yingxiu, China, killing more than 80,000 people, said that the tremors may have been caused by fluctuations in the amount of water contained by nearby Zipingpu Dam. The dam was built less than 600 yards from a fault line, and geologists believe that filling the reservoir behind the dam probably caused—and then intensified—the Yingxiu quake.

SUNSHINE ON MY...YIKES!

In May 2009, a home in the Seattle suburb of Bellevue was severely damaged by a fire. Fire officials investigated and couldn't find a cause initially. But after further inspection, they said that the only plausible explanation was that the fire was caused by sunlight and water. Sunlight, they said, had been hitting a glass dog bowl filled with water—which had acted like a magnifying glass and had ignited something, probably dry leaves, on the house's wooden deck. "It's very unusual," said Lt. Eric Keenan of the Bellevue Fire Department, "but it's not unheard of."

81% of men think that they're above-average drivers. Only 67% of women do.

Creepy Bonus: Later in 2009, biophysicist Gabor Horvath at Eotvos University in Budapest, Hungary, reported that he had concluded studies on this very phenomenon and found that sunlight magnified through drops of water on leaves, either from rain or dew, could cause leaves or grass to ignite…and could start forest fires.

HERE COME THE MUTANTS

Plum Island, a tiny, government-owned facility off Long Island, New York, has long been a controversial site: Since 1954 the U.S. government has conducted tests on animal diseases—and carried out biological warfare testing—on the island, and an unknown number of vaccines and disease pathogens are still being stored there. In January 2010, a security guard came across what was described as the "mutated" corpse of a white male about six feet tall with a large build…and unnaturally long fingers. Government officials said they would be performing an autopsy on the body…but don't expect to hear much more from the secretive lab anytime soon.

Creepy Bonus: Plum Island is the place where Clarice Starling (Jodie Foster) offers to let Hannibal Lector (Anthony Hopkins) vacation if he helps her catch a serial killer in the *The Silence of the Lambs.*

OOPS

On March 6, 2006, an employee at Nuclear Fuel Services (NFS) in Erwin, Tennessee, a private facility that supplies nuclear fuel to the U.S. Navy, noticed a yellow substance oozing under a door and into a hallway. It turned out to be a liquid form of highly enriched uranium—the kind used in nuclear power plants and, if it's *very* highly enriched, in nuclear weapons. Nine gallons of it had leaked from a transfer pipe and onto the floor, where it came within four feet of falling down a narrow elevator shaft. In a puddle, highly enriched uranium is actually not that dangerous. But if enough of it is allowed to collect and form a spherical shape, which might have happened if it had fallen down the elevator shaft, it can attain "critical mass," meaning that a nuclear chain reaction could have begun—the kind that fuels a nuclear power plant. The spill was contained and cleaned up, but the accident

---

Potato beetle larvae protect themselves from being eaten by covering their bodies in poison poop.

was severe enough that the plant was closed for the next seven months.

Creepy Bonus: That accident occurred in March 2006, but the Nuclear Regulatory Commission (NRC), which oversees all activity related to U.S. nuclear energy projects, didn't tell the public until April 2007. And it was only discovered then because the NRC casually mentioned a uranium leak—without saying where it had happened—in their annual report to Congress.

JUST BEAUTIFUL

In the last few years, demand for the antiwrinkle beauty aid Botox has grown so much that there is now a thriving black market for it—and that makes terrorists happy. The active ingredient in Botox is botulinum toxin, a protein produced by the *Clostridium botulinum* bacteria. It is one of the most toxic substances known to exist: A single gram of the stuff, properly dispersed, could kill thousands of people. In Botox, the toxin is used only in extremely small amounts; it would be virtually useless to a terrorist in that form. But the problem is that because of the black market, there may be a factory somewhere in the world—or perhaps dozens of them—producing unregulated botulinum toxin. Illicit buyers may also be able to get the toxin from legitimate sources and then use it for deadly purposes. In either case, thanks to the worldwide demand for Botox, botulinum toxin is out there, available to the highest bidder—and that means that it may become, or already has become, available to terrorists.

Creepy Bonus: A strain of bacteria that produces one type of botulinum toxin occurs naturally in spores on the bottoms of lakes and ponds. Under the right conditions, usually after hot summers when water levels drop drastically, the spores can multiply rapidly and produce dangerous levels of the toxin. This botulinum toxin is one of the leading causes of death in waterfowl, especially wild ducks, in the world. A single outbreak can kill more than a million birds in a matter of months. And because outbreaks are linked to warmer temperatures, more and more of them are being reported around the world...and more are expected in the future.

COPS GONE CRAZY

We respect the police for keeping us somewhat safe in this crazy world. But as these stories prove, cops are only human.

A RE Wii HAVING FUN YET?

In September 2009, narcotics investigators in Polk County, Florida, searched the home of a known drug trafficker. While removing weapons, drugs, and stolen goods, several officers passed the time by taking part in a video bowling tournament on the suspect's Wii video-game system. The cops competed fiercely, stopping their search when their turn came up. Little did they know their activities were being recorded by a wireless security camera that the drug dealer had set up to watch for intruders. A local TV station got hold of the footage and aired clips of the cops giving each other high-fives and distracting their fellow bowlers with lewd gestures. "Obviously, this is not the kind of behavior we condone," Lakeland Police Chief Roger Boatner said. The impromptu tournament might even jeopardize the case against the career criminal, whose lawyer called the search improper. "Investigations are not for entertainment," he said.

BETWEEN A GUN AND A HARD PLACE

MRI machines are huge, complex magnets; even the tiniest metal object can severely damage one. In 2009 Joy Smith, an off-duty deputy from Jacksonville, Florida, took her mother to get an MRI... and forgot that she was still carrying her police-issue Glock handgun. Smith walked into the MRI room and her gun was pulled from its holster; she tried to hang onto it, but her hand became stuck between the pistol and the machine—which made a horrible nose before shutting off. Smith sustained only minor injuries. The MRI center didn't fare as well: Between repairs to the machine and a day's lost revenue, the cost to the center topped $150,000.

GUILT BY ASSOCIATION

In September 2009, Dutch police officers raided a farm near Wageningen University in the Netherlands and destroyed an entire crop of what they called "some 47,000 illicit cannabis

---

In 2001 Kyle Connor was called for and dismissed from jury duty for the second time. (He's only 8.)

plants" with a street value of $6.45 million. However, according to university officials who cried foul, the plants were *not* psychotropic marijuana—which is illegal to grow—but hemp-fiber plants— which are perfectly legal to grow, and for which they had a permit. The plants had been part of a multiyear study to test hemp as a sustainable source of fiber. The project has been postponed while the school attempts to recoup the costs from the police department. "The street value from a drug point of view," said a disappointed university official, "is less than zero."

TAKE A BITE OUT OF A CRIMEFIGHTER

Two employees of the Police Officer Standards and Training Council in Meriden, Connecticut, had, according to reports, a "spirited" relationship—analyst Rochelle Wyler and training coordinator Francis "Woody" Woodruff, a former police chief, regularly taunted and insulted each other. One day in April 2009, Woodruff jokingly referred to Wyler as a "clerk." She responded, "Whatever, Woody. Bite me." So Woodruff grabbed her left arm and bit her, leaving tooth marks and a bruise. Woodruff claimed he was just "horsing around," but Wyler reported the incident, and Woodruff was arrested and charged with assault.

SNOWBALLISTICS

One snowy afternoon in December 2009, about 200 office workers took part in a snowball fight on 14th Street in Washington, D.C. Everyone was having a good time…until someone threw a snowball at a Hummer SUV driving down the road. The Hummer slid to a halt; a large, imposing man got out. "Who threw that damn snowball?" he shouted. When no one answered, the man pulled out a pistol, sending people running for cover. A few tense moments later, a uniformed police officer arrived and ordered the man to drop his weapon. That's when the gunman identified himself as Detective Mike Baylor. With the danger passed, the crowd started chanting: "You don't bring a gun to a snowball fight." At first, the D.C. police department denied that the detective, a 28-year veteran, pulled out his gun. But the incident was caught on several cell phone cameras and soon made the rounds on YouTube…and then the local news. D.C. police chief Cathy Lanier called Baylor's actions "totally inappropriate." He was placed on desk duty.

THE MOOLATTE

And other questionable, perhaps racist,
marketing decisions.

DELICIOUSLY OFFENSIVE
In 2004 Dairy Queen wanted a share of the hundreds of
millions of dollars Starbucks was making with its blended,
frozen Frappuccino coffee drinks. So Dairy Queen came out with
its own version: coffee mixed with chocolate, ice cream, and milk.
To market the drink's combination of milk and coffee, they called
it the MooLatte. An outcry went up almost immediately: The
name of the product, which combined a brown thing with a white
thing, was far too similar to an outdated, offensive word for a person of mixed black and white heritage: *mulatto*. Dairy Queen
denied that there's any connection, and the MooLatte is still on
the menu.

OFFBEAT
The German company TrekStor had some success with their
MP3 player, the i.Beat. But in 2007, they released a new version
of the device with a smooth black finish and an unfortunate
name: the "i.Beat Blaxx." After a firestorm of criticism, the company renamed it "TrekStor Blaxx."

TASTELESS COOKIE
In 1996 Mattel contracted with Nabisco to make an Oreo-cookie-
themed Barbie doll. The toy came dressed in blue-and-white
clothing printed with little pictures of Oreos. At first, Mattel
received a few complaints that the toy promoted junk food, but
the protest letters flooded in after they released an African-American version of the doll. Mattel apparently wasn't aware that "oreo"
was a racial epithet leveled by black people at other black people
who were accused of acting "too white"—like an Oreo cookie,
black on the outside, but white on the inside. Mattel quickly took
the toy off the market, and today African-American Oreo Barbies
are a collector's item.

Americans watch more than 250 billion hours of TV a year—more than 28 million years' worth.

LOONEY WORD ORIGINS

More histories behind some of the euphemisms we use to describe those who are wired differently. (Part I is on page 40.)

BONKERS
The original meaning, from the early 20th century, was "slightly drunk." It was most likely coined by British sailors, who used the term "bonk" to describe a blow to the head. Following that logic, a drunk person would act as if he'd been hit on the head—"bonkers." It wasn't until the end of World War II, however, that the word took on its "crazy" connotation.

WACKY
Related to "bonkers," "wacky" comes from "whacky," late 1800s British slang for "crazy"—also from the notion of being whacked on the head a few too many times. Today, "bonkers," "wacky," and "wacko" refer to one who appears "humorously crazy," and unlike most "crazy" words, are often terms of endearment.

SCREWBALL
This term predates baseball, first appearing in the game of cricket for a "ball bowled with 'screw' or spin." By the 1920s, "screwball" was being used to describe a baseball pitch that breaks from left to right when thrown by a right-handed pitcher, the opposite of the more conventional "slider." The term entered the American lexicon as slang meaning "an eccentric person" in 1933 and went on to define a genre of films—"screwball comedies"—during the '30s and '40s. The word later morphed into the phrases "a few loose screws" and "his head's not screwed on tight," culminating in the modern term, "screwy."

LOON
It's not short for "lunatic," nor does it come from the bird known for its eerie, haunting calls. The "crazy" definition of loon actually comes from the Dutch word *loen*, which referred to a stupid person. In fact, Shakespeare's reference to a "whey-faced loon" in *Macbeth* predates the name of the bird in the English language.

Lawsuits filed by California inmates cost the state's taxpayers more than $33 million per year.

People who act out in an outrageous manner or who believe wild conspiracy theories are most often called "loons" or "loony."

CUCKOO

As a name for a bird (based on the sound of its "coo-coo" call), this word dates back to A.D. 1240. By the 16th century, it was being used to refer to a stupid person, perhaps because the bird's song is so simple and repetitive. The slang sense of cuckoo as "crazy" didn't show up until later, after the invention of cuckoo clocks; one possibility was that listening to a cuckoo clock's chime could drive you insane. By the 1950s, "cuckoo" in its "crazy" sense had been shortened to "kook" and "kooky."

MAD

This may be the earliest English word used to describe insanity. First appearing sometime between A.D. 1000 and 1300, it comes from the Old English *gemædde*, "beside oneself with excitement." Much later, "mad" was also used to mean "beside oneself with anger." The "crazy" connotation spawned a few other phrases:

• **Madcap.** The "cap" in this word is an obsolete term meaning "head." So a madcap was a "crazy head." When it originated in the 16th century, it was a serious reference to a maniac, but today it's usually used in phrases like a "zany, madcap adventure."

• **Mad as a hatter:** In the 19th century, the process that hatmakers used to turn beaver or rabbit fur into felt hats involved toxic mercury nitrate. Years of breathing these fumes poisoned many hatmakers—leaving them with slurred speech, twitching, and other erratic behaviors. Although hatmaking is now safe, the phrase remains popular thanks to the Mad Hatter in Lewis Carroll's 1865 *Alice's Adventures in Wonderland*.

• **Mad as a March hare:** In England, certain hares only mate in March, and males of the species leap about wildly to attract a female's attention. The phrase dates back to the 1520s, and also made its way into *Alice's Adventures in Wonderland*.

• **M.A.D. (Mutual Assured Destruction):** In the 1960s, the U.S. and the U.S.S.R. each had enough nuclear weapons to easily obliterate each other. And each had sworn to retaliate if attacked. So *more* weapons meant *less* of chance of nuclear war. This mad paradox got the world (somewhat) safely through the Cold War.

Who's mad now? In 1952 *Time* magazine dismissed *Mad* magazine as "short-lived, satirical pulp."

"THAT'S AWFUL!" AWARDS

Because we believe that some people deserve to be publicly recognized for their especially bad behavior.

Winner: Owners and staff at a day-care center in Maywood, Illinois

Background: Police were called to the day care after receiving a tip about illegal activities going on there.

That's Awful! The day care had been doubling as a dogfighting facility. When police raided the home, they found 10 kids being cared for, as well as nine badly injured and malnourished dogs, splattered blood, syringes, and equipment used to train fighting dogs. Four people were arrested on felony dogfighting charges. The wife of one of the arrested men ran the day care, and was reportedly not involved in the dogfighting.

Winner: 37-year-old Jackie Denise Knott of Albertville, Alabama

Background: In October 2009, someone called the police on Knott, who was driving her minivan down the road with a large cardboard box on the roof.

That's Awful! Knott's 13-year-old daughter was inside the box. Knott told police that the box was too big to fit in the van, and that her daughter was inside it to make sure it didn't blow away. She said it was safe—because she had secured the box to the car with a coat hanger. Police arrested Knott on child-endangerment charges. Her daughter came to her defense, saying it was her own idea to get in the box, and that her mother was "an awesome mom."

Winner: A 19-year-old man in Philadelphia

Background: A woman in a Philadelphia suburb looked out her window in September 2009 and saw a cat that someone had left in her yard.

That's Awful! The cat was wrapped, from tail to neck, in duct tape. The woman quickly got the cat to the local Humane Socie-

---

As much as 10% of the U.S. national income can be attributed to organized crime.

ty, where they managed to remove all of the tape, freeing the very affectionate—and dehydrated—young female cat underneath. The Pennsylvania Society for the Prevention of Cruelty to Animals (PSPCA) offered a $2,000 reward for information leading to the arrest of the person who taped up the cat. One week later, a 19-year-old man, whom a PSPCA spokesman described as "very remorseful," came forward and admitted that he'd done it. He was arrested on animal-cruelty charges. More than 100 people applied to adopt the kitty—her real owners were never located—and she quickly found a home. Her new name: Sticky.

Winner: Robert Stark Higgins of Stuart, Florida
Background: A local homeowner called police in 2009 to report that Higgins was in his backyard.
That's Awful! Higgins was in the man's swimming pool…and was covered in feces. He grabbed a towel and ran away, but police dogs tracked him down easily. Higgins was charged with several offenses, and told police that he had been drinking. (No word on whether the homeowner planned to *ever* swim in the pool again.)

Winner: Kathy White of Marquette, Michigan
Background: In January 2009, White and her husband were in their living room playing their Nintendo Wii bowling game that they had just gotten for Christmas. White took a swing with one of the game's remote controls just as her five-month-old miniature Sheltie puppy, Ozzy, jumped in the air.
That's Awful! The swinging remote in White's hand hit the dog's head…and killed him. A frantic White called her neighbor, who ran over and checked the dog's heart; there was no pulse.
That's Great! The neighbor blew into Ozzy's snout several times—and the puppy woke up. He was rushed to a vet and, after a couple of weeks, was as good as new. (But he's no longer allowed in the room when the couple are playing with the Wii.)

*   *   *

"Cynical realism is the intelligent man's best excuse for doing nothing in an intolerable situation." —**Aldous Huxley**

Common Wii injuries: Black eyes (hitting bystanders), hand injuries (hitting things) & tennis elbow.

PROBLEM SOLVED!

You know the saying "Necessity is the mother of invention"?
Well, some people's "necessities" may be on the nutty
side—but they still make for cool inventions.

PROBLEM: Spiders that get stuck in the bathtub.
INVENTOR: Edward Thomas Patrick Doughney of Harrold,
England

STORY: We don't know when it happened, but we're pretty sure that at some point, Doughney walked into his bathroom and found a spider in the bottom of the bathtub...dead. The bug had climbed into the tub during the night and couldn't get out because of the slippery tub walls. Mr. Doughney is the sensitive type, and he felt terrible that, by virtue of owning a bathtub, he'd killed a spider.

PROBLEM SOLVED! To save spiders who may, in the future, unwittingly wander into bathtubs, in 1994 Doughney invented the "Incy Wincy Spider Liberator"—otherwise known as a "Spider ladder provided with means for attachment to an item of sanitary ware, European Patent Application Office 2,272,154." The Incy Wincy is a long, thin, ladderlike device made of flexible latex. Using a suction cup, you attach the top of the ladder to the inside of the tub, near the rim, and let the rest of it hang down into the tub. So a spider that becomes trapped in the tub and roams around searching for a way out will find the Incy Wincy Spider Liberator and be able to climb its way to safety. (And Mr. Doughney will be able to sleep at night.)

PROBLEM: Answering the call of nature while hiking...if you're female.
INVENTOR: Moon Zijp of the Netherlands
STORY: Zijp was traveling through the jungles of Indonesia and discovered that, as a woman, she often found it inconvenient and uncomfortable to take a pee. And she sometimes had to walk deep into the jungle to find a place that provided enough privacy to squat down.

PROBLEM SOLVED! Zijp invented the "P-Mate"—a disposable device that allows women to stand up and pee like men. It's ideal, Zijp says, for use outdoors or in dirty public toilets. The P-Mate is made from thin, hygienically produced cardboard, and when popped open it becomes, basically, an eight-inch-long funnel. From the P-Mate Web site: "Simply pop open the P-Mate, move your clothing aside, and place the cupped opening against your body. Relax and pee!" (And if that's not clear enough, check the Internet for the interview Zijp did on Dutch television, during which she demonstrated how to pee like a man in front of millions of viewers.) The product is now available in many countries around the world. Cost: $4.95 for a pack of five.

PROBLEM: Too many domestic squabbles get "settled" with a kitchen knife.
INVENTOR: John Cornock, an industrial designer in the U.K.
STORY: In 2005 John's wife, Liz, read an article by a team of British doctors about the dangers of the common pointed kitchen knife—which is used in nearly half of all fatal stabbings in the U.K. The doctors called for a ban on such knives.
PROBLEM SOLVED! Cornock set to work, and in 2009 he announced the arrival of his "New Point" line of "anti-stab" kitchen knives. They look like regular knives, but the tips, instead of being pointed, are rounded and have a dull edge. This, Cornock says, prevents the knives from being used to stab people. "There can never be a totally safe knife, but the idea is you can't inflict a fatal wound," said Cornock. "Nobody could just grab one out of the kitchen drawer and kill someone." (Unless they used it to slit someone's throat.)

PROBLEM: Fear. Sheer, unadulterated fear.
INVENTOR: Jeffrey L. Walling, Virginia Beach, Virginia
STORY: Are you afraid that terrorists and kidnappers are going to come to your house while you're sleeping, burst into your bedroom, and do horrible things to you and your pets?
PROBLEM SOLVED! Figuring that at least a few people were that afraid, Jeffrey Walling invented the "Quantum Sleeper" (United States Patent 7,137,881) in 2006. What is it? A bullet-

proof, biological-weapons-proof, terrorist-proof, kidnapper-proof, and a whole bunch of other stuff-proof…bed. It looks like a giant coffin when it's closed up, but there's a lot more to it than that. Just a few of the Quantum Sleeper's features:

- 1.25" polycarbonate bulletproof plating/shielding
- Biochemical-filtering ventilation system
- Motion sensors
- One-way windows so you can see out from the closed-up bed—but the bad guys can't see in.
- A built-in cell phone, shortwave radio, and CB radio
- A microwave, refrigerator, CD player, and DVD player
- A toilet

If you've got a five-alarm case of paranoia—and a whole lot of money—the Quantum Sleeper may be just what you need for a good night's sleep. Cost: $160,000.

*　　*　　*

FAMOUS FOR 15 SECONDS

Adessa Eskridge, 27, was departing her plane at Los Angeles International Airport in 2008 when six police officers approached her at the gate. One of them told her, "Keep your sunglasses on. You're going to help us with something." Before she knew it, Eskridge was being escorted through baggage claim. A group of paparazzi ran up and started photographing, filming, and asking her questions: "Jamie-Lynn, how was your trip?" "Jamie-Lynn, any boyfriend rumors?" A cop told Eskridge, "Don't say anything, just keep your head down." When they finally got her to safety, the police thanked Eskridge for posing as a decoy for Jamie Lynn Spears (Britney's younger sister) who was also arriving in L.A. that day. Eskridge was furious. She demanded to be compensated $100,000 for the ruse, which led to photos and video of her—not Spears—all over the Internet. LAX officials refused, so at last report, Eskridge is suing the airport for $2 million. Said her lawyer: "The police did not want to subject Ms. Spears to the pushing, shoving, humiliation, and possible physical injury that come with the paparazzi, but instead decided that Ms. Eskridge was not important enough to give the same protections to."

Vocabulary booster: A person with great energy and vitality is a *spizerinctum*.

MAGICAL MOUNTAIN

*People believe a lot of strange things. One of the strangest happens to
be about a place 50 miles south of the BRI's headquarters: picturesque
Mt. Shasta in northern California. It's known for its hiking, skiing…
and the invisible people who live inside the mountain.*

SACRED SPOT

Towering 14,179 feet above sea level, Mt. Shasta's snow-
capped peak has been surrounded by mystery and legend
since indigenous people first encountered it thousands of years
ago. And ever since white settlers arrived in the area in the mid-
1800s, the mountain—as well as the nearby town by the same
name—has been the scene of some very weird sightings, including
UFOs and mystical creatures roaming around the mountain's
slopes. In fact, Shasta City was one of the first centers of the
"New Age" movement in the United States. It's still home to hundreds of energy readers, spiritualists, psychics, and alien-seekers.

Shasta's New Age movement can be traced back to 1886,
when 18-year-old Frederick Oliver, from the nearby town of
Yreka, first visited the mountain and fell into a trance. Under the
control of "other forces," Oliver wrote *A Dweller on Two Planets*.
And to thousands of people, the book—still in print today—is not
science fiction, but the source material for their belief system.

THE LEMURIANS

Dweller tells the history of Mt. Shasta, which Oliver claimed was
channeled directly to his mind by an immortal creature named
Phylos, whose race, the Lemurians, once lived on a Pacific Ocean
continent called Mu. Like Atlantis, Mu was a "lost continent"
that modern scientists say never existed.

Lemurians, Oliver wrote, talk to each other telepathically in a
language called Solara Maruvia, but Phylos spoke English to Oliver (curiously, with an English accent). Oliver described the
Lemurians as physically stunning—seven feet tall with long, flow-
ing hair and lean, graceful bodies. They wore white robes lined
with sacred stones, and jewel-encrusted sandals. Technologically
advanced even by today's standards, the ancient Lemurians devel-

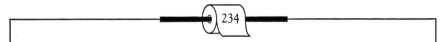

oped water generators, antigravity machines, high-speed trains, and devices comparable to cellular phones and televisions.

But for all their expertise, the Lemurians could not prevent the cataclysmic earthquake they knew was coming. One night about 12,000 years ago, Mu began shaking and sinking into the sea. But the 25,000 Lemurians were ready—they all boarded tall ships bound for the uninhabited land of what is now northern California. Once there, their engineers hollowed out Mt. Shasta and constructed a subterranean city called Telos. According to Oliver/Phylos, they chose that particular mountain because it's "the earthly incarnation of the Great Central Sun, the source of all physical and spiritual energy in the universe." And so, for twelve millennia, the Lemurians have lived peacefully inside the mountain.

BEAM ME UP

Floating in the sky directly above Mt. Shasta, Oliver went on, is yet another Lemurian city: "The Crystal City of the Seven Rays." It's visible only to the most tuned-in human psychics, who describe it as a huge, floating, purple pyramid, the point of which extends into space. From within the Crystal City, the Lemurians operate interplanetary, interdimensional spaceships called the "Silver Fleet" (which would seem to explain all of the UFO sightings near Mt. Shasta). The Lemurians represent our galaxy in the intergalactic "Confederation of Planets."

Good luck actually seeing a Lemurian yourself, or one of their spaceships, or their Giant Purple Pyramid City. Few people have. That's because the Lemurians merely exist on a "vibrational level" to which humans are not physically attuned (in other words, they're invisible). Thankfully, there are dozens of books out there about the mountain's inhabitants and its spiritual energy, all of them based on Oliver's…er, Phylos's *A Dweller on Two Planets*.

DAYS OF FUTURE PASSED

But time may be short for the city of Telos: The mountain the Lemurians moved into is actually a dormant volcano, which the United States Geological Survey warns may erupt again in the next 200 years. So if you happen to live in another area on Earth that contains a massive pocket of spiritual energy, you may soon be getting some beautiful, seven-foot-tall, invisible neighbors.

There are more Walmarts in the United States than there are colleges.

BIG NEWS

*The growing pains of modern society as it awkwardly
adapts to an expanding obesity problem.*

• In 2009 Colorado's Rocky Mountain Health Plans (RMHP)
refused to cover Alex Lange because he had a pre-existing condition:
obesity. Alex's parents were furious. Why? "He's only four months
old," said his father, Bernie, to reporters. "He's breast-feeding. We
can't put him on the Atkins diet or on a treadmill." Amidst all
the negative press ("RMHP Denies Healthy but Big Baby!"), the
company explained that it had a relatively new process of deter-
mining which babies are most "insurable"—and at 17 pounds,
Alex didn't make that list. RMHP has since changed its policy to
insure any healthy baby regardless of weight. The Langes' "happy
little chunky monkey" is now covered.

• In 2006 Lincoln University in Pennsylvania instituted a new
graduation requirement: a three-credit "Fitness for Life" class. But
the only students required to take it are the ones who are certified
as clinically obese. Lincoln student and school newspaper editor
Tiana Lawson, who, according to the rules, had to take the course,
wrote, "I came here to get an education, which is something I
have been doing quite well, despite the fact that I have a slightly
high body mass index." The head of Lincoln's physical education
department defended the Fitness for Life requirement (which consists of Tae Bo, aerobic dance, and water aerobics): "We as educa-
tors must tell students when certain factors are going to hinder
them from achieving and maximizing life goals." So far, about 600
students have had to take Fitness for Life.

• The Topeka, Kansas, branch of American Medical Response,
one of the biggest ambulance companies in the United States,
began charging extra in 2009 for "larger" patients. Now, if you're
picked up by an AMR ambulance and weigh more than 350
pounds, you'll be billed for a $543 surcharge. AMR claims that
they respond to so many calls from overweight people experienc-
ing medical emergencies that they've had to spend thousands of
dollars on winches, hoists, and extra-large, reinforced cots.

MIXED NUTS

Here's an odd collection of unrelated—but very odd—news and information that we discovered in a pile of peanut shells and candy wrappers under someone's (Jay's) desk as we were finishing up this book. (You might want to wear gloves.)

LOUD NIGHT

The maker of Great Britain's most successful snoring remedy, Helps Stop Snoring, made a public call for recordings of heavy snorers in 2009. They then assembled the snore recordings into a snore-version of the Christmas song "Silent Night," and put it up on their Web site. They called it the world's first "snorechestra." (Everyone who sent in their snores was given a year's supply of anti-snoring products.)

THAT LYIN' SHIRT

Brad Gellert, 32, of Apollo Beach, Florida, was arrested in March 2009. In his mug shot, Gellert can be seen wearing a T-shirt that reads "I [Heart] My Marriage." Gellert had been arrested for trying to choke his wife during an argument.

A WORLD OF LOVERS, PART 1

Are you the kind of person who likes to kiss and tell? Well, if you do, go to *JustMadeLove.com*—and tell the world about it. The site, which uses the Google Maps program, allows you to zoom into your exact location and enter your information, and it shows up as a marker on a map on the *JustMadeLove.com* site. You can even leave a comment about how "it" went. A sample, from Greenland: "*böyle bişi yokk doymuyor istiyor en son kanattımm onu pes etti yarım saat sonra bı daha ıstıyor hep ısıyor.*" (We hope that's not dirty.)

A WORLD OF LOVERS, PART 2

Lloyd's Pharmacy in England launched the "Sex Degrees of Separation" online calculator in 2009—which allows you to figure out how many *indirect* sexual encounters you've had in your life. You enter your age, how many *direct* partners you've had, and how old each partner was, and the calculator estimates how many direct encounters each of your direct encounters has had, which is the number of your indirect encounters. The pharmacy launched the program as an educational tool on the subject of sexually transmitted diseases.

DELICA-TUSSLE
Police were called to a supermarket in Aachen, Germany, in December 2009 to break up a three-way fight between a 74-year-old man, a 35-year-old woman, and her 24-year-old brother. The elderly man was beating the younger man over the head with a salami; the woman was trying to stab the older man with a wedge of Parmesan cheese. Police broke up the tasty melee, and all three food fighters were arrested.

MOUNTAINS OF CONTROVERSY
Officials in Foshan City, Guangdong, China, approved the installation of a new sculpture in a city park in 2009: a statue of a girl whose tiny body is about eight inches tall, with a pair of enormous breasts—about 16 feet wide, 16 feet high, and 20 feet long. Local parents were outraged. "The park used to be a great place for families," one mother said, "but now what attracts my son the most is the huge breasts. I have tried to educate him with some scientific knowledge, but all he thinks when he sees the statue are smutty thoughts." A park spokesman said the sculpture would remain in the park anyway. (He added that someone had vandalized the piece one night…by trying to put an enormous bra on it.)

*　　*　　*

IRONIC APPAREL
Imitating the "Livestrong" cancer-awareness bracelet program, in 2004 Bristish students were given blue "Beat Bullying" bracelets in an attempt to end schoolyard violence. However, because famous athletes and musicians were sporting the bracelets as part of the campaign, they became collectors' items (eBay sellers could get up to $30 apiece for them). Result: Bullies beat kids up in order to steal their "Beat Bullying" bracelets.

PHOTOSHOPPED

Retouching photographs is nothing new, but thanks to graphics programs such as Adobe Photoshop, it's become hard to tell what's real and what some graphic designer created on a screen—unless they did a really bad job. Here are a few extreme examples of "digital manipulation."

THE IMAGE: The official 2006 campaign Web site of New Orleans mayoral candidate Kimberly Williamson Butler featured a photo of her standing in the city's famous French Quarter.

THE TRUTH: When close observers noticed some Mickey Mouse garbage cans in the photo, the campaign was forced to admit that they'd superimposed a photo of Butler onto a background image of Disneyland's "New Orleans Square." Butler's campaign designer deleted the garbage cans, but that didn't end the mocking from the press. So they took the same image of Butler and superimposed it over a photo of the real New Orleans. (She lost the election.)

THE IMAGE: The cover of the March 2005 issue of *Newsweek* magazine featured Martha Stewart emerging from between two curtains. The headline: "Martha's Last Laugh—After Prison, She's Thinner, Wealthier & Ready for Prime Time."

THE TRUTH: Stewart's head was digitally added to a thin model's body. The only acknowledgment that it was fake came in the credits on page 3: "Cover: Photo illustration by Michael Elins; head shot by Marc Bryan-Brown." After the magazine received a great deal of criticism, *Newsweek's* assistant managing editor, Lynne Staley, said that they didn't mean to "misrepresent the news" but had no choice because the issue was put together before Stewart was actually released from prison. "Anybody who knows the story and is familiar with Martha's current situation would know this particular picture was a photo illustration," she said.

THE IMAGE: In September 2009, a Ralph Lauren ad featuring

23-year-old supermodel Filippa Hamilton was created for a campaign in Japan. Although it's no shock that fashion-model shots are manipulated (the skin is smoothed, the waist is drawn inward, the bust is drawn…bustward), Hamilton looked like a freak of nature in the ad.

THE TRUTH: Hamilton's photo was altered so much that her waist was narrower than her head and her arms looked like string beans. (Google it—it really is quite disturbing.) As soon as the ads appeared, women's groups cited it as perhaps the most outrageous example of the fashion industry creating an unnatural—and unhealthy—image for girls and women to try to achieve. The controversy took another turn when Hamilton appeared on the *Today* show to claim that the company had actually fired her for being "too fat" and for not being able to fit into the sample clothes that she had to wear. Ralph Lauren execs denied it, but they did admit to going too far with Photoshop: "We have learned that we are responsible for the poor imaging and retouching that resulted in a very distorted image of a woman's body."

THE IMAGE: "Come have fun in Toronto and celebrate our diversity!" That was the message that the city's summer 2009 "Fun Guide" was supposed to send with its cover photo of a mixed-race family leaning into the camera, arm in arm, all smiling. The mom and two kids appeared to be Hispanic, and the dad was African Canadian.

THE TRUTH: Earlier that year, the City of Toronto had issued an order that all of its official publications had to reflect the ethnic diversity of the area. But instead of finding a photo of a multicultural family, the designers found a picture of a black man on a stock-photo Web site and then Photoshopped it into a picture of a mother with two kids. The result is obviously a fake—the man is lit differently, his head is too small, and it looks as if someone cut his head out with scissors and pasted it on top of the original photograph. Kevin Sack, Toronto's director of communications, defended the picture: "The policy doesn't say 'no Photoshop,' the policy says 'show diversity.' And that's of course what we try and do. Nothing wrong with that. You won't find a more inclusive organization than us."

FRANKEN-FOOD

Not everything that goes into our food is mentioned on the label.
Food manufacturers pay millions to keep their products from being
regulated, leading to some strange practices. Franken-food
is a science fact…and it's what's for dinner.

THE NATIONAL FOODBALL LEAGUE

Food production is a high-stakes game with many players: corporations, farmers, consumer safety groups, scientists, doctors, the government, and, of course, consumers. Each group has its own agenda and its own game plan. We've tried to sort through it all to bring you clear, unbiased information, but there doesn't seem to be a single study result out there that hasn't been disputed by *somebody*. Hopefully the players who say these food products are perfectly safe are correct—and the ones who say we're all going to turn into hairy mutants and die gruesome, horrible deaths are wrong. Here's a look at what's in your food…and who doesn't want you to know about it.

FEELING A BIT HORMONAL

Hormones—chemicals naturally produced by the body—have several important duties, including regulating reproductive functions. In humans, the imbalance of even a single hormone can lead to a host of problems, including obesity, depression, and even cancer. Yet injecting growth hormones into cattle (to make them gain weight faster and require less feed) has become standard practice for the U.S. beef and dairy industries: More than 80% of American cattle are injected with them. In addition to synthetic hormones used to increase milk production, six other naturally occurring hormones have been approved for use in beef by the U.S. Food and Drug Administration (FDA): zeranol, estradiol, melengestrol acetate, trenbolone acetate, progesterone, and testosterone.

But after extensive research and testing, the European Commission (the European Union's executive body) concluded that "no acceptable daily intake could be established for any of these hormones" and connected them to an increased risk of severe hormonal imbalance as well as various types of cancer. Two of these hormones, estradiol and zeranol, are also linked to poor develop-

---

Hallmark makes cards for 105 different types of family relationships.

ment in children. It's now illegal for European farmers to inject their cattle with hormones, but the FDA says they're safe and doesn't require hormone-treated foods to carry any labeling.

ATTACK OF THE KILLER TOMATOES

Chances are, you eat genetically modified, or "GM," foods every day. Over 105 million acres of GM crops are grown in America—mostly corn, soy, wheat, and canola—common ingredients in nearly every packaged food from corn flakes to soup to fish sticks.

To produce a genetically modified plant, the desired DNA is placed in a carrier, often a virus like E. coli, and implanted in the host plant's cells. Subsequent generations of the plant then carry the genetic mutation. Most GM crops have been modified to withstand larger amounts of pesticides, or to make the plants last longer and resist damage. One example: "fishberries." A gene from a species of Arctic codfish that creates an antifreeze protein was infused into the genetic code of strawberries in order to make them more frost-tolerant. Proponents of GM argue that inter-species crossbreeding is simply the next step in plant development.

And because they're technically "living crops" and not additives, GM foods aren't required to undergo safety testing before being put on the market. So what could possibly go wrong?

• In 1992 Murray Lumpkin, M.D., then director of the FDA's Division of Anti-infective Drug Products, warned that DNA doesn't always break down in the stomach. Some of it can be absorbed by gut bacteria, which could then become resistant to antibiotics or mutate in unexpected ways. The University of Georgia's Dr. Sharad Phatak says, "When you insert a foreign gene, you are changing the whole metabolic process. Will any one gene kick off a whole slew of changes? We don't know for sure."

• Combining genes may lead to new allergic reactions. In 1992 an eight-year-old girl with a seafood allergy reportedly died after eating fishberries. And in 1996 production of a GM soybean containing Brazil nut genes was halted after it was found to cause allergic reactions.

The first, and so far only, safety evaluation of a GM crop was commissioned in the early 1990s by Calgene (now owned by Monsanto, one of the world's largest agricultural biotechnology companies) for their FLAVR SAVR™ tomato. Though the test was never peer-reviewed, Calgene's report to the FDA concluded that there were no significant toxic effects...even though several test rats died within a few weeks of eating the GM tomatoes. And no studies were done on their intestines, even though 7 out of 20 rats developed stomach lesions. In humans, this could cause life-threatening hemorrhages or worse.

SEND IN THE THE CLONES

Workers at agricultural supplier J.R. Simplot Company noticed that one of their cows was eating the same amount of food as the other cows but was gaining 8 pounds a day (as opposed to the average 3.5-pound daily weight gain). So Simplot cloned the cow. Now they have *eight* identical cows that all gain 8 pounds a day. That's a big benefit of animal cloning: It can take the guesswork out of farming, leading to higher yields and higher profits.

But the downside: Animal cloning is a new and unproven technology that may have severe safety implications. Even Ian Wilmut, the lead scientist who cloned Dolly the sheep in 1996, warns against eating cloned animals. He says that defects in clones are common, and even a small imbalance in a clone could lead to hidden food safety problems. And the technology is so new that there have been few studies on the risks of eating cloned food.

Nevertheless, in January 2008, the FDA ruled that the meat and milk from cloned livestock are safe for human consumption, despite pressure from Congress to delay the FDA's decision until additional safety studies could be conducted. (They never were.) What's more, the FDA does not require labeling, so consumers have no way of knowing whether these products are on their supermarket shelves.

BEAM ME UP

Food irradiation is a process that uses high-energy gamma rays, electron beams, or X-rays (about seven million times more powerful than a medical X-ray) to kill hidden bacteria and insects during food production. So what's wrong with that? Critics argue that the process allows food handlers to be sloppy with sanitation, knowing that the food is going to be irradiated later. Besides that, irradiation can do some strange things to food.

Meat, fruits, and vegetables that are irradiated can, at the very least, lose some of their vitamin content. And the rays that kill harmful bacteria also kill beneficial bacteria and enzymes. But of even more concern to scientists at the International Institute of Concern for Public Health are the "unique radiolytic byproducts" of irradiation—substances that can cause gene mutations. And while it won't make your food radioactive, irradiation can form toxic chemicals such as benzene and formaldehyde, both suspected of causing cancer and birth defects.

Just as with other controversial food-related issues, some scientists say irradiation is perfectly safe. The FDA maintains that irradiation is an "effective way of combating food-borne illness." Their findings, however, are based on studies done in the 1950s. Consumer safety groups continue to lobby for new tests, but U.S. food regulations currently allow the irradiation of wheat, white potatoes, spices, dry vegetable seasonings, fresh eggs, fresh produce, and meat and poultry. Wholly irradiated foods must be labeled "irradiated" or "treated with radiation" and display the radura symbol (a flower inside a green circle). But no special labeling is required on manufactured products that contain irradiated ingredients, and the FDA is considering a new rule that would allow some irradiated foods to be marketed with no labeling at all.

FOOD FOR THOUGHT

Americans have the largest, cheapest food supply in the world. And much of the bounty has come from advances in food science, including genetic engineering and cloning. Americans also have one of the lowest rates of food-borne illnesses, thanks in part to irradiation. So should we just relax and chow down? Maybe, or maybe we need more long-term, large-scale testing. And maybe we should know what we're eating. Award-winning microbiologist Dr. John Fagan advocates the labeling of all newly introduced foods. "Without labeling," he says, "it will be very difficult for scientists to trace the source of new illness caused by modified foods." In the meantime, there is a large-scale study of the long-term health effects of modified foods— it's happening right now, and we are the test subjects.

*   *   *

"Scientists tell us that the fastest animal on Earth, with a top speed of 120 ft/sec, is a cow that has been dropped out of a helicopter."

—Dave Barry

Getting your tongue pierced can sometimes lead to *endocarditis*—inflammation of the heart valves.

NOT-SO-GOOD VIBRATIONS

Why does Earth hum? Because it doesn't know the words.

WHAT'S THE BUZZ?

Bob and Leona Ehrfurth of Green Bay, Wisconsin, have a problem: Their house hums. Or sometimes it's more of a rumble. "It's like there's a semitruck parked right outside with the engine running," said Leona. "It doesn't matter if the windows are open or closed, you still hear it," added Bob. "We could move, but why should we have to? We didn't cause it."

The question is: What did?

SOUND REASONING

• Local authorities haven't been able to find the cause. But one possibility is that it's a phenomenon simply called "the Hum"—the background noise that our planet makes. Instances of the Hum have been reported all over the world as a persistent low-frequency noise that sounds like an idling truck. Individual Hums are so localized they're often given a specific geographical name—for instance, the "Bristol Hum" or the "Taos Hum."

• Some speculate that those who report these Hums are simply suffering from a condition called *tinnitus*, where the patient hears sound in the ear, typically ringing, that has no outside source.

• A second possibility: *spontaneous otoacoustic emissions*, or noises that human ears generate all on their own. Most people never notice them, but a small segment of the population does.

• A third possibility is that people are hearing the effects of ocean waves colliding. When waves with similar frequencies traveling in opposite directions collide with each other, they create a pressure wave that carries all the way down to the seafloor. All of those pressure waves pounding the seabed generate a frequency of their own that may be audible on land.

But the true cause of the Hum—and the noise in the Ehrfurths' house—remains a mystery.

How's the fish? The Maldives Hilton recently opened the world's first underwater restaurant.

THE CURSE OF CRISTIANO

Take the world's highest-paid soccer player and the world's most famous hotel heiress. Add a witch and a sorcerer, and what do you have? A story tailor-made for The World's Gone Crazy.

SOCCERY

European soccer fans take their sport *very* seriously. So sports tabloids and Internet sites were flooded with lurid headlines in 2009 when 25-year-old Cristiano Ronaldo, superstar of the fabled team Real Madrid, was sidelined by an injury that refused to heal—and the injury was blamed on a witch. And, as an added bonus, professional celebrity Paris Hilton had managed to work her way into the story.

OCCULT OF PERSONALITY

It began on September 25, 2009, when an anonymous letter showed up in the clubhouse of Real Madrid. It read:

> This is not personal. I have nothing against this great club. I am a professional and someone has paid very well for me using my powers. I have been hired to make Cristiano Ronaldo suffer a serious injury. I can't promise it will be serious but he'll certainly be out of action—more than playing!

The letter went on to claim that the curse was already working; it was responsible for breaking Ronaldo's recent scoring streak. The story was picked up by the tabloids, and everyone got a chuckle out of it...until five days later, when Ronaldo was fouled in a game and went down hard. The diagnosis: "ankle traumatism and Grade-1 ligament sprain." Bad news.

The letter writer was soon discovered to be a Portuguese "occult practitioner" named Pepe the Witch. And this wasn't his first tangle with Real Madrid. Since 2003 he's cursed the club several times, targeting such megastars as David Beckham and Sergio Ramos. Not surprisingly, Pepe also likes to play the media: When asked why he cursed Ronaldo, he cryptically explained he was given 15,000 euros by a "jilted lover" who was

---

a "non-European and a very wealthy heiress from a well-known family."

Celebrity-watchers knew that this could only be Paris Hilton. Also known for her media savvy, Hilton let the story simmer for a while before hinting to *Life & Style Magazine* that she may have hired Pepe. Why? She'd had a failed relationship with Ronaldo in June 2009 after meeting him at a Los Angeles nightclub, where, according to reports, the two "lip-wrestled all night and ran up a $20,000 bar tab." The subsequent fling was short, and, according to inside sources, Ronaldo dumped her. "I can't stand it when someone is mean," Hilton later complained. "I want a man anyway, not someone who runs about like a little girl."

When Pepe was asked to remove the curse, he refused, assuring fans that he would do "everything possible to prevent Cristiano Ronaldo from continuing his career in football." To make sure, Pepe constructed a voodoo doll of Ronaldo and said he would stab it in the spine "over and over" and wouldn't stop even if "Ronaldo's crying mother" knelt before him.

LIMPING ALONG

Although the incident made for some titillating headlines, few people actually took Pepe's "curse" seriously. But after a few weeks passed by, Ronaldo was still in pain. He persevered and kept playing, but then reinjured the ankle in a game on October 10th. Through early November, he was unable to play or train with the team. His doctor was baffled; the ankle should have been healing, but it wasn't. Ronaldo was sent to a specialist in the Netherlands, who couldn't figure it out either. Now some people started seriously wondering: Was the curse real?

To be on the safe side, "a person very close to Ronaldo" (his mother, according to some rumors) decided to get some help—and hired the "Sorcerer of Fafe," a 46-year-old Portuguese man named Fernando Nogueira, who claimed he could cast a spell to disarm Pepe's curse and heal the injured ankle. "I have lit candles next to a picture of Cristiano to put the matter to an end," said Fafe.

Did it work? By late November, Ronaldo's ankle had healed and he'd returned to the team, where—for a time, anyway—he could get back to the business of being one of the world's most famous soccer players.

The red part of a turkey's head is called the *snotter*.

DISTRACTED DRIVERS

Are you driving your vehicle down the road right now?
Then don't forget to look up and check traffic every now
and then while you read these fascinating stories.

CLEAN GETAWAY

When police noticed water pouring out of the cab of a truck traveling down a road in China in June 2009, they assumed the truck had mechanical problems and pulled it over. Instead of a leaky radiator, the officers found the driver naked and soaking wet from having just taken a shower—behind the wheel. He explained that his air conditioner had broken, and his wife (in the passenger seat) helped him rig up a "sprinkler kettle system" to keep him cool, complete with a bicycle wheel suspended above him to accommodate a shower curtain. To keep the dashboard dry, his wife held a sheet of plastic over it. The man was cited for reckless driving.

DANCIN' FOOL

Romanian police are searching for a truck driver who posted a video on the Internet of himself dancing: He claps his hands, stands up in his seat, and then jumps *out of* his seat, mugging for the camera with his hand either barely on or not on the steering wheel, while his truck is speeding down the highway. So far, police have been unable to locate the man.

CAP'N CRUNCHED

Concerned drivers in Needham, Massachusetts, called to notify police that a vehicle was driving erratically, crossing double yellow lines, and tailgating other cars. When police caught up to the driver they found him eating a bowl of cereal with milk. His excuse for the reckless driving: "I was hungry."

NIT-PICKING

In Canada, talking on a cell phone while driving can get you a $500 fine under the "Distracted Driving" laws. But according to Ontario's transportation minister, Jim Bradley, the law doesn't go far enough. "There are many other activities occurring during driving that are just as dangerous, if not more so. The other day I was almost side-swiped by a man who was completely distracted while picking his nose. And I don't mean just a nose scratch—he was in up to his knuckle." Bradley proposed raising the fine to $850. A rival politician, Randy Hillier, scoffed at the idea: "What's next? No eating broccoli with dinner due to the possibility of passing gas into the atmosphere thereby increasing global warming?"

BUS DRIVER MANIAC

In San Antonio, Texas, in 2008, onboard security cameras recorded a bus driver reaching into his shirt pocket, getting his phone, starting to text...and then slamming into a stopped car, causing a massive pileup. The bus was carrying disabled passengers. There were no serious injuries, but the driver was fired.

IF ANYONE SHOULD KNOW BETTER...

In 2009 Amanda Meyer, a police officer in Jacksonville, Florida, was driving her cruiser when she glanced down at her dashboard-mounted computer. When she looked up, there was a tanker truck stopped at a railroad crossing. She swerved...but not in time to avoid the 40-mph collision. Thankfully, the gas tanker was empty, but Meyer, who suffered minor injuries, was cited for reckless driving and fined $149.

IT'S SNOT FAIR

Michael Mancini was stopped in traffic in the town of Prestwick, Ayrshire, Scotland, in 2010. He took out a tissue and blew his nose. A moment later, a policeman signaled for the 39-year-old furniture restorer to pull over into a nearby parking lot. But it wasn't just any policemen—it was Officer "Shiny Buttons" (his real name is Stuart Gray), known for his strict adherence to the letter of the law. Officer Buttons witnessed the nose-blowing incident and cited Mancini for distracted driving, which carries a fine of £60 ($93). "You've got to be kidding," said Mancini. "My van wasn't even moving!" Officer Buttons wasn't kidding. Mancini appealed to police department officials to drop the charges, but they refused, so he had to pay the fine and his license was suspended. "What is the world coming to?" he complained to reporters.

IMPULSE BUYS FOR THE RICH & FAMOUS

Poor people are starving and the middle class is a dying breed. Meanwhile, the world's wealthiest continue to live in the lap of luxury while they lap up ludicrously luxurious stuff like this.

BOTTLED WATER. "Image is everything," says Kevin G. Boyd, the Hollywood producer who created "Bling H_2O" spring water. The frosted-glass bottle comes decorated with handcrafted Swarovski crystals and filled with water "bottled at the source in Dandridge, Tennessee." Like a fine wine, it must be uncorked to drink. Cost: $38 per bottle.

FLIP-FLOPS. Created in 2004 by Brazilian jewelry designer H. Stern, a "regular" pair of these sandals—encrusted with gems or made of crocodile skin—will run you a few thousand dollars. The top-of-the-line model comes adorned with diamonds and more than 1,500 feathers made of gold. Cost: $17,000.

SUNGLASSES. Billed as the "world's most expensive sunglasses," these shades are sold as a high-end luxury accessory by the Italian company Dolce & Gabbana. Features: "A sexy gold rim, and the lenses are a soothing brown in color." (It also has adjustable nose pads.) Cost: $383,609.

JEANS. Design houses Earnest Sewn and Van Cleef & Arpels collaborated to create a limited run of Alhambra Designer Jeans featuring Van Cleef's signature Alhambras (four-lobed cross icons based on Moorish architecture). "The stretch denim is finished with a white mother-of-pearl and yellow gold Alhambra button, miniature Alhambra rivets, and a 14-inch Alhambra chain that attaches to a hand-crafted leather wallet." Cost: $11,300.

POOL CUE. This cue is called "The Intimidator," but not just because of its price tag. Sold by McDermott Handcrafter Cues, the pool stick features four "bladed wings" on the handle... making it look like a Klingon Bat'leth sword. (So if you're losing the game, you can simply disembowel your opponent.) Cost: $150,000.

NAIL POLISH: Four companies, including *Allure* magazine, collaborated to come up with "I Do"—a nail polish containing powdered platinum. The first batch, which came in a platinum bottle, cost $55,000. Now it's sold in glass bottles for a mere $250.

A PAIR OF GUITAR PICKS. Sold by Australian company Starpics, these two picks are made from a piece of the four-billion-year-old Gibeon meteorite (chunks of which were discovered in 1836 strewn over a 70-mile-wide area of Namibia, Africa). For the nonmusical, there are also Gibeon meteorite rings, pocket knives, and pens. Cost: $4,764.

PIZZA. The "Louis XIII" gourmet pizza takes three days to prepare, but famed chef Renato Viola of Alerno, Italy, will travel to your house to bake it for you. Toppings include three types of caviar, two types of lobster, and hand-picked pink Australian salt. The final touch: It's misted with cognac. Cost: $12,000.

ICE CREAM SUNDAE. Created especially for the 50th anniversary of the Serendipity 3 Café in New York City, the Golden Opulence Sundae includes five scoops of Tahitian ice cream rolled in edible gold leaf, gold-painted truffles, marzipan cherries, and sweetened caviar, all of which is topped by a gilded sugar flower. Cost: $1,000.

TOILET. If you win the lottery, you could be reading this on your new Toto Neorest. Features: hands-free flushing, a lid that automatically opens and closes, a remote control to set the seat temperature—and for emergencies, a powerful "Cyclone® flush" setting. Cost: $5,000.

BURIAL PLOT. Even if you can't take it with you, at least you can rest easy at the most posh spot in Southern California's Santa Barbara Cemetery. This plot boasts a spectacular view of the Pacific Ocean and has room for two. Cost: $83,000.

A WORD FROM THE ODD ANIMAL SEX DEPT.

It turns out that there's a lot more to the birds and bees than pretty wings and cute mating dances. There's also stabbing, exploding...and a little murder.

CUPID'S SLIMY ARROWS

All land snails are *hermaphrodites*—they have both male and female sexual organs, all of which are located on their necks. Before they mate, they engage in a courting period that lasts from a few minutes to several hours, during which the snails touch their "feet" together, caress each other's appendages, and even "kiss" each other's lips. Then the snails engage in copulation, when each transfers sperm to the other. (The sperm is stored in special sacs and used later.) After the courtship phase and just before the moment of sexual engagement, some snail species attempt to violently pierce each other's sex organs with what scientists call "love darts"—thin barbs of calcium, about a quarter-inch in length, that are produced near the sex organs. This piercing can continue for several rounds of mating, during which new calcium darts continuously form. A 2006 study determined what the love darts are for: Snails that are successfully speared by the darts are able to store twice as much sperm as snails that aren't. It turns out that nearly all of the sperm received during mating is digested and killed by enzymes before it can be used for fertilization. The study found that love darts carry a chemical that impedes production of the enzymes, allowing more sperm to make it to the storage sacs. So snail couples that are more successful at piercing each other have a better chance of producing young.

SKYROCKETS IN FLIGHT

In the world of honeybees, male bees, known as drones, have one main purpose: sex. When they're only a few weeks old, drones leave their hives and gather in "drone congregation areas," or DCAs, with drones from several other bee colonies. DCA's hover

---

A Pew Research poll reported that 32% of teenagers have been victims of cyber-bullying.

30 to 150 feet in the air and sometimes span 100 yards or more, with the drones hanging out like randy teenage boys waiting for girls to come by. The girls—virgin queen bees who have been sheltered in the hive and fed a diet of royal jelly—leave the hive on "mating flights" when they're just one to two weeks old. Instinctively, they fly into DCAs, and the young drones give chase. Between 10 and 30 will mate with a single queen in flight, a spectacle that has rarely been witnessed. During the midair mating, the genitals of a drone rupture—biologists describe them as "exploding"—which throws the drone off the queen, leaving his sex organs inside her. Then he dies. The queen flies off to establish a new colony, where she will use the sperm from her explosive mates for the rest of her life (up to three years). Drones that aren't able to find a virgin queen to mate with go back to their hive, where they are so useless that they have to be fed by female workers. When autumn comes, they're kicked out and eventually starve to death.

Extra: Want to know how to tell if a bee is a drone? Look at the eyes: A drone's are huge—twice as large as those of a worker or queen. Bee experts say drones need the enhanced vision to find the queen during in-flight mating.

LOVE POTION

Male giraffes spend a lot of their time roaming around their home ranges searching for females who are ready to mate. When a female's in the mood, she rubs her neck on the male's neck and flanks. The next move is the male's: He walks behind her and nudges her butt with his nose. This induces her to urinate and, in an activity that's been witnessed for centuries but never fully understood, the male takes a big mouthful of the urine. A 2006 study finally confirmed why the males do it: A male giraffe can tell by the hormone content in the female's urine exactly where she is in her reproductive cycle. And he'll try to mate with her only if she's in her peak "fertile window," which occurs every two weeks and lasts just two days. If she isn't in that window, it isn't worth the considerable energy it takes to attempt to mate with her. If she is, the male will follow her around, often for many hours, necking with her and generally bothering her until, if she deems him a suitable mate, she finally stops walking. This indicates to the male that he can mate with her. Once he's mounted, the rest is over in less than a minute.

BOYGIRL

If you're ever in Africa or Asia and you come across a hyena with a large penis, you'll probably think it's a male. But there's a good chance you'd be wrong. While still nursing, all hyena pups receive a large dose of the male hormone *androgen* via their mothers' milk. This makes the pups more aggressive, a helpful trait in the hard-scrabble life of a hyena pack. But it also has side effects for the females: The hormone produces a *pseudopenis*, a growth that's several inches long. The difficult part comes when it's time for mating: A male has to be able to insert his own *actual* penis into the female's pseudopenis—a tricky business—and only the most persistent and patient males are able to do it. Even more bizarre: The hyena birth canal is located in the pseudopenis, meaning that the females also give birth to their babies through it.

THAT'S NO LUMP

The anglerfish lives deep in the world's oceans and is known for having a long growth that protrudes from the top of its head and ends with a fleshy blob. The blob acts as bait that anglerfish use to "angle" for their food—other fish. But for many years, scientists couldn't solve a mystery: why the only anglerfish that were ever caught were females. Then someone noticed strange, fleshy growths on the females' bodies. Further study finally determined what the lumps were: male anglerfish, which are much smaller than females (in some species, $\frac{1}{30}$ of their size), and are born without a functioning digestive system. Upon hatching, the first thing a male does is hunt down a female and bite into her side, back, or belly. Enzymes released from the male's mouth dissolve the female's flesh, and he eventually fuses onto her. Their blood-streams merge, and for the rest of his life, the male lives off of the female like a parasite. Over time, his organs, teeth, bones, and eyes all disappear. All that remains are his testes. When the female is ready to mate, she releases eggs, and what remains of the male releases sperm to fertilize them. Bonus: A large female will often play host to several males, and will live the rest of her life with their manly lumps on her body.

THE BLIND PAINTER

Ever seen Esref Armagan's paintings? Neither has he.

THE MIND'S EYE

If you looked at Turkish painter Esref Armagan's portraits of trees, skies, a fish playing a cello, or even former U.S. President Bill Clinton, you would never guess that the painter was born without eyes—meaning he's not simply blind, he *has no eyes*.

Born in Istanbul in 1953, Armagan grew up in an impoverished family and never went to school. But for as long as he can remember, he loved to draw, and he's developed his talent over the years. So how does he create his paintings?

• First, Armagan learns as much as he can about his subject. He touches it (if possible), reads up on it, asks his friends to describe the colors and the shading, and, in some cases, he draws a rough portrait of the subject.

• Then, with a picture firmly in place in his imagination, he draws a raised "map" of the subject on a piece of paper using a Braille stylus, a type of pen with a sharp point used for etching.

• When Armagan is ready to begin painting, he uses the fingers of his left hand to "read" the map, and dips the fingers of his right into quick-drying oil-based paints that are always arranged in the same order on his palette. Throughout the process, he keeps one hand on the map and one hand on the canvas until he knows the piece is complete. On some paintings, he forgoes the 3-D map altogether and just paints from "memory."

Armagan's works have garnered praise in galleries across Europe and in New York, and not just because they were painted by a blind person, but because they're actually *good*. (According to many art critics, he's better at some techniques, including using perspective, than most sighted painters.) "No one can call me blind," he says. "I can see more with my fingers than sighted people can see with their eyes."

BRAIN POWER

Art critics aren't the only ones interested in Armagan's unique talents; neuroscientists are studying his visual cortex, the part of

---

In 2008 a Canadian man wedged his head in a sewer while trying to retrieve his wallet and died.

the brain that makes sense of the information streaming in from the eyes. Why study Armagan's visual cortex when he can't see? Because of a phenomenon known as *neural plasticity*—the brain's ability to adapt to its own unique limitations.

For example, when a sighted person tries to remember the image of something he's already seen, he uses his visual cortex, but to a lesser degree than when he's actually looking at something. Scans of Armagan's brain, however, reveal that when he paints, his visual cortex is extremely active. If you were to put a scan of a sighted person who is *looking* at an object next to a scan of Armagan's brain while he's *painting* an object, they would look very similar. Only a trained neuroscientist would be able to spot the clues signaling that Armagan never actually looked at the image.

LOOKING INTO THE FUTURE

According to Professor John M. Kennedy, a cognitive psychologist from the University of Toronto at Scarborough: "Mr. Armagan is an important figure in the history of picture-making, and in the history of knowledge. His work is remarkable. I was struck by the drawings he has made as much as by his work with paint. He has demonstrated for the first time that a blind person can develop on his or her own pictorial skills the equal of most depictions by the sighted. This has not happened before in the history of picture-making."

Kennedy is one of several neuroscientists who believe that their studies of Armagan will change what we know about how sight works, and may one day be used to help blind people learn to "see" the world just as well as Armagan does.

*   *   *

WORST APP EVER

There are thousands of "apps" for Apple's iPhone, but none drew more complaints than the "Baby Shaker": a video game in which the player shakes the iPhone until a virtual baby stops crying (then two red X's appear over its eyes). The app was only available for download for two days in 2009 before Apple removed it. The company explained that it should have been rejected before it was added, but someone must have "missed it." Alex Talbot, the app's designer, admitted, "Yes, the Baby Shaker was a bad idea."

YOU'RE SUING ME FOR *WHAT*?

Please don't sue us, no matter how much pain and suffering
you may endure while reading about the crazy reasons
people come up with to sue each other.

BERRY, BERRY ODD

After eating Cap'n Crunch Crunch Berries for four years, in 2009 Janine Sugawara of California finally came to the realization that there aren't any real berries in Crunch Berries. So she sued the cereal manufacturer for false advertising. The case was quickly dismissed: "This Court is not aware of, nor has Plaintiff alleged the existence of, any actual fruit referred to as a 'crunchberry.'" The judge also noted that the same attorneys lost a previous lawsuit complaining that Froot Loops didn't contain real fruit.

THAT'S A LOT OF ZEROS

Dalton Chisolm was bouncing checks. And he didn't know why. Angry, he called Bank of America to get answers. Not satisfied by their "insufficient funds" excuse, Chisolm sued B of A for "1,784 billion, trillion dollars"—more than the entire world's gross domestic product of $60 trillion. Sylvain Cappell, a math professor at New York University, said, "If he thinks Bank of America has branches on every planet in the cosmos, then it might start to make some sense." The case was dismissed.

FALLEN FROM GRACE

Shin Lim Kim was injured in 2008 while serving as a "catcher" at the Portland Onnuri Church in Beaverton, Oregon. What does a catcher do? He or she stands behind a parishioner who is about to be touched by a pastor, and catches the parishioner if they fall to the floor in a fit of religious ecstasy (or, as it's called, is "slain in the spirit"). Kim, a small woman, was asked to catch Hyun Joo Yoon, a larger woman who, according to Kim's lawyer, "began flailing, falling on, and injuring the plaintiff." Kim claimed that no one warned her of the dangers of catching a person or provided her with any training. She also argued that Yoon was negligent for failing to control her body once the pastor laid his hands on her. According to the lawsuit, Kim suffered a painful injury to her spine that made her "sick, sore, nervous, and distressed." She's suing both the church and Yoon for $125,000.

OY VEY!

In her routines, comedian Sunda Croonquist often talks about her mixed heritage: Her mother's African American, her father's Swedish, she was raised Catholic, and she married into a Jewish family. "I'm a black woman with a Jewish mother-in-law," goes one of her jokes. "The only thing we have in common is that we don't want to get our hair wet!" Not laughing: Croonquist's Jewish mother-in-law, Ruth Zafrin. In 2009 she sued the comedian for "spreading false, defamatory, and racist lies." Croonquist agreed to stop telling mother-in-law jokes and to take any information pertaining to her family off her Web site, but she refused to pay monetary damages. The case is still pending.

WHICH PART OF THE NAME DIDN'T HE GET?

In 2005 Anthony Beninati was attending the Burning Man festival in Nevada, a weeklong event that features a lot of stuff getting burned (see page 422). One night, Beninati walked too close to a bonfire, fell down, and burned his hand. He sued Burning Man organizers for not warning him that he might get burned (even though he'd attended the festival twice before). In his deposition, Beninati admitted that he knew "fire is dangerous and causes burns." Case dismissed.

THAT'S COLD-BLOODED

In 2000 a lawyer named Linda Ross sued a California phone company, GTE, for $100,000 because they mistakenly put her Yellow Pages listing under the category "Reptiles." (Ross's phone number had once belonged to a business called the Reptile Show, but GTE failed to update its records when she acquired the number.) Ross claimed that the listing caused her public humiliation: She received dozens of prank calls; people hissed at her when she walked by them; Jay Leno even made fun of her on *The Tonight Show*. There were no follow-up news reports about the lawsuit, so we're guessing it was sssssettled out of court.

According to British researchers, terrorists and extremists almost never buy life insurance.

WHAT COMES AFTER WEIRD?

Is there a word for something that's so weird that the word "weird" can't begin to describe it? If so, please use it for these stories.

THERE'S A SUIT IN MY BUCKET

In October 2009, Alicja Tomankiewicz of Mikowice, Poland, sued her neighbor Waldemar Wilk...for kicking and damaging a $4.50 plastic bucket that she kept in her front yard. The case went to court, where Wilk pleaded not guilty. He even brought a video to the courtroom showing footage of Tomankiewicz using the bucket and argued that it proved that since the bucket wasn't damaged, he couldn't have kicked it. The judge said Wilk couldn't prove that the video had been taken *after* he had allegedly kicked the bucket, and the footage was therefore inadmissible as evidence. Then the judge ordered that an expert be brought in to determine whether kicking a bucket could actually damage it. It could, the expert testified, and Wilk was found guilty. He appealed the case, and after 18 months of litigation, the lawsuit was dropped.

TAKE IT ALL OFF

A police officer in Tiffin, Ohio, pulled over Jaime Aguirre, 42, in November 2009 for a traffic violation, and smelled marijuana coming from his car. A subsequent search of the vehicle instead turned up hundreds of X-rays of women's torsos. Aguirre was a technician at a medical imaging center, and he'd allegedly taken the images, illegally, from his office. Why? He was using them for sexual-gratification purposes, police said. Aguirre was arrested on several charges and held in lieu of $250,000 bail. "This," said Police Chief David Blough, "is one of the strangest things I've ever seen."

MYSTERY BY THE FOOT

On August 20, 2007, a 12-year-old girl found a running shoe on Jedediah Island, off the coast of British Columbia, Canada. She looked inside the shoe and saw a sock. She looked inside the

---

A recent poll shows that 67% of Americans believe Democrats are better lovers than Republicans.

sock—and found a human foot. Medical examiners later identified it as belonging to a man and said that it didn't appear to have been severed, but seemed to have detached due to decomposition underwater, possibly from the body of a drowning victim. Six days later, a couple on nearby Gabriola Island found another running shoe...with a sock inside it...with a human foot in it. It, too, was from a male. In February 2008, a third foot—again, complete with shoe and sock—was found on nearby Valdes Island. This one was also a man's. In May a fourth foot was found on Kirkland Island, this time belonging to a woman. A fifth foot found the following month on Westham Island was confirmed to be from the same person as the foot found in February. August brought another foot in a sock and running shoe, and so did November—this one a match to the foot found in May. In July 2009, police announced that they had determined the identity of the person associated with the first foot, a man who had suffered from depression and may have committed suicide. In October 2009, an *eighth* human foot was found in British Columbia. The case has been called one of the most bizarre in Canadian history, and no explanation for the mystery feet has been found.

MOOVING VIOLATION

Police in Tonowanda, New York, were called to a water-treatment facility late one night in October 2009. The caller said that a man in a cow suit had stopped by the plant, buzzed the intercom, asked for directions, and then run away. Police came out to investigate and found Jeffrey S. Barber of Hamburg, New York, near the plant. He was still wearing the cow suit, which was soaking wet, and he appeared to be intoxicated. When asked what had happened, Barber told officers he was driving home from a Halloween party, and his GPS device had told him to take a right turn. He turned down a street called Aqua Lane—and drove off the dock at the end of the street, straight into the Niagara River. He smashed out a window, "like I saw how to do on TV," he said, and swam to safety. Then he walked to the water-treatment plant to ask for directions—still wearing his cow suit—thinking it was the University of Buffalo. Barber was found to have a blood-alcohol content of 0.20, far over the limit for driving, and was arrested. Police recovered his car from the river the next day, with three beer bottles, four whiskey bottles...and one fake cow head inside.

DISTURBING PSAs

Do we need TV to tell us how to behave? Well, it worked with "Only YOU can prevent forest fires," "Every litter bit hurts," and dozens of other public-service TV ad campaigns. But how far should an ad go to make a point, even with the best intentions? Perhaps these folks went a bit too far.

SAFETY FIRST! In 2007 the Canadian Workplace Safety and Insurance Board produced a series of public-service announcements to warn of workplace hazards. Here's a sample of what TV viewers saw.

• A young female chef says to the camera, "I'm on the fast track to becoming head chef, and I'm supposed to be getting married next week. But I won't, because I'm about to have a terrible accident." Suddenly, she slips, falls, spills a huge cauldron of hot oil all over herself, and screams in gurgling agony as her face literally melts.

• Warehouse manager: "Get that skid." Forklift driver: "Okay." Bad move. The forklift drives up to a shelving unit and the shelves collapse, burying the driver in a crushing mountain of steel pipes. With pipes protruding from his bleeding torso, the driver delivers a monologue about the importance of managerial oversight.

DON'T SMOKE! This Australian announcement starts with a close-up of a cancer-ridden mouth. The camera pulls back to reveal a woman who says, "Smoking causes mouth cancer. If it didn't, I wouldn't need radiotherapy and chemotherapy." She then refers to the quit-smoking number that's printed on every pack of cigarettes before the camera zooms back in to linger on her chipped, yellow, rotten teeth, her mouth sores, and her oozing, bloody gums.

TEXTING AND DRIVING DON'T MIX! This PSA from England begins with three teenage girls in a car, talking and laughing. The driver starts texting...she crosses the center line and smashes into another car, and then another car smashes into them, shattering windows and sending girls flying. The camera pans over the blood-covered bodies; the driver screams in terror. As onlookers and rescue workers try to help, a little girl in one of the other wrecked cars is crying, "Mummy, Daddy, wake up! Mummy, Daddy, wake up!" (Mummy and Daddy don't wake up.)

Canadian Gilbert Nelles says a beam from a UFO made him into a reincarnation of Elvis Presley.

SITTIN' IN A TREE, PART II

When we left Julia "Butterfly" Hill (page 132), she was just beginning her two-year stint on a platform near the top of a 1,000-year-old redwood tree called "Luna" to save it from being felled by loggers.

NEITHER RAIN NOR SNOW...
Winter had already begun to settle in on the forest when Julia Hill climbed Luna on December 10, 1997. Her cold-weather gear consisted of a T-shirt, a thermal shirt, one pair of thermal pants, a wool sweater, a pair of wool pants, and a light-weight sleeping bag. Hats were a challenge; they kept getting blown away by the constant wind. Gusts of 70 mph tossed the platform around like a boat on a rough sea, shredded its tarp roof, and howled so loudly that she couldn't think. It rained continuously, and storms would last for days. Lightning struck so close that the platform shook, the sky lit up like a neon sign, and Hill's hair stood on end. She endured only one snowstorm that winter, but the chronic cold, combined with being constantly wet, gave her frostbite. At one point she broke a toe, but her feet were so numb she never knew it until she saw the toe turn from white to blue to black. The pain was excruciating. She took duct tape, cardboard, and toilet paper from her "medical" kit and wrapped it around her toe to form a makeshift cast, but from that time forward, her feet were in constant pain.

THE GROUND WAR
While Hill was struggling to survive the rain and cold, loggers from Pacific Lumber—whose livelihoods depended on cutting down trees—kept up a constant campaign of harassment. They hacked off the baby sucker trees growing out of Luna's trunk, each blow of the ax shaking Julia's perch. They felled nearby trees so that they crashed through Luna's outer branches, nearly shattering Hill's 4' x 7' platform. To keep her from sleeping, the loggers trained floodlights on her and blew bugles and air horns all night long. They hired a helicopter the size of a passenger plane to buzz the platform, creating 300-mph updrafts that nearly sucked her and a visiting reporter out of the tree. They tried to starve her out by preventing her support team from bringing food and supplies.

Some Internet "safe browsing" filters block access to chicken-breast recipes.

And they hired "Climber Dan," a former logger who specialized in taking activists out of trees by force. Climber Dan ended up cutting a traverse line connecting Luna to a nearby tree while "Almond," who was helping Julia tree-sit for the first few months, was on it. Almond would have plummeted 100 feet to the ground if a branch hadn't broken his fall.

RECORD BREAKER

Hill never intended to stay up in Luna for more than a few weeks. "But two weeks turned into three," she wrote later, "and after three, I thought, 'I'm so close to a month I might as well stay.'" During those first few weeks, she shared her perch with other tree-sitters, but one by one the others came down, unable to stand the cramped, uncomfortable platform any longer. Hill, however, found herself becoming more and more attached to life in the treetops. She actually began to think of Luna and herself as one entity.

Nevertheless, at 71 days she'd had her fill and was ready to quit. The cold weather and the shaking she'd endured during storms had taken their toll, and she was near her breaking point. Then a visiting journalist named Erik Slomanson put a provocative idea in her head. "You know, if you want to do this right," he said, "you've got to stay to the 100-day mark because the world record is 90 days, and Americans love record-breaking."

The challenge of breaking the record gave her the impetus to go on. Plus, the efforts of the loggers to intimidate her out of the tree completely backfired. "I didn't ask anyone's permission to stay in Luna; I just did it," she said. "Ironically, their opposition just encouraged me to continue on." Added to that was her fear that the moment she came down, Pacific Lumber would immediately cut down her tree. That had been the company's pattern with other tree-sitters. "There's no way I'm letting this incredible tree fall," Julia told her support team. "I'm not going to do it. As long as I have the ability to keep this tree standing, I'm staying up here."

LIFE IN A TREE

Weathering storms was one thing; dealing with harassment was another. But what about the mundane tasks of everyday life? For instance, how did she...

After realizing that its initials had become crude Internet slang...

- **Get supplies?** The ground crew gave Hill a pager and established codes to let her know they were coming, when they were nearby, and when to drop a duffel bag attached to a rope. Once the crew stuffed the bag with supplies, she would haul it back up. When the company security guards surrounded the tree to keep the crew from getting to Hill, her crew found ways to outwit them. Once 19 activists danced around the tree, yelling, "23! 23!"—the code for her to drop her duffel bag. All of them held supply sacks, but only some of bags actually had supplies. While the guards repeatedly tackled activists with decoy sacks, one of the activists managed to clip the real bag onto the rope.

- **Get water?** She rigged the tarps sheltering her platform to collect rainwater, which she used for washing, cleaning, and personal hygiene.

- **Cook?** Hill used a single-burner camp stove fueled by propane. She made couscous, oatmeal, farina, and instant soup, and combined them with dried fruit, nuts, fresh vegetables, and spices.

- **Bathe?** She took sponge baths. She heated water on her camp stove, stripped from the waist down, scrubbed for two minutes, dried off quickly, and put her clothes back on. Then she repeated the process from the waist up. Temperature, water, and fuel rations didn't allow for rinsing. She rarely washed her hair; it used too much water, and she was afraid a wet head would make her sick.

- **Go to the bathroom (the #1 question on all Bathroom Readers' minds)?** At first she used a funnel with a hose over the side of the platform to urinate. When the wind kept ripping the hose away, she changed to a funnel and a jar, which she emptied over the side. By the time the urine fell 180 feet to the ground, the wind had turned it to a fine mist and spread it over a wide area. (Because Luna was in a rain forest, the acidity of the urine did not burn leaves or plants, which it would have done in a dry forest.) For solid waste, Hill used a bucket lined with a heavy-duty trash bag. The bag was stashed in a hole in Luna's trunk that had been formed by lightning years before, and was packed out with the other garbage.

- **Sleep?** Hill slept under a tarp in a three-season sleeping bag the first year. The second year, she was given a winter sleeping bag and a bivouac, a tent-like shelter that wrapped around the bag.

- **See at night?** Candles were her primary source of light after dark. She also had a headlamp, but that required precious batteries, so she rarely used it.

- **Communicate with the outside world?** At first, Hill only talked by yelling down to her crew when they came with supplies every few days. Later she was given a radio phone powered by solar panels connected to two motorcycle batteries, an emergency cell phone, a hand-cranked radio, a tape recorder, a digital camera, a video camera, walkie-talkies, and a pager.

- **Keep from going crazy?** Hill had roommates at first, other activists who stayed for days or weeks at a time. After they dropped out, she had visitors—journalists, fellow activists, and, on a few occasions, celebrities, including Grateful Dead drummer Mickey Hart, actor Woody Harrelson, and singer Bonnie Raitt. But most of the time, she was alone. She immersed herself in books, educating herself about forestry and environmental issues. She listened to radio shows and talked to experts about slope erosion, watershed analysis, and timber-harvest plans. She spent hours reading about a variety of topics, from sustainable logging and northern California history to Charles Hurwitz's financial dealings. In the end, Hill's treetop studies earned her an honorary doctorate in humanities from the New College of California.

THE END IS NEAR

After she broke the 100-day tree-sitting mark, Julia "Butterfly" Hill suddenly became a public figure on a national level, bringing tremendous visibility and sympathy to her cause. Money began to pour into the environmental groups filing suits against the Pacific Lumber. Not only was the company hemorrhaging money trying to defend itself in court, it was losing the public-relations battle as well: Political figures from Senator Dianne Feinstein all the way to President Clinton joined the chorus criticizing Pacific Lumber.

A year into Hill's sit, the California State Legislature passed a bill to protect the tree but not the grove. "Even with the new protections," Hill told a reporter. "Luna and the slope she stands on will be destroyed under the Headwaters Forest Agreement and Habitat Conservation Plan, along with hundreds of other steep, unstable slopes and thousands of acres of virgin and residual old growth. The government once again has turned its back on the local residents and the endangered species that it is required to protect."

During Hill's second year, Pacific Lumber began to offer its own concessions. P.L. representative John Campbell regularly talked with Julia from the bottom of the tree, attempting to negotiate a settlement. But he wouldn't guarantee that Luna's grove would be spared after Hill came down, so there she remained. "My bottom line is protection in perpetuity for Luna, and a substantial buffer zone around her to protect her fragile ecosystem."

Finally, on December 18, 1999, Pacific Lumber/Maxxam Inc. signed a preservation agreement and deed of covenant to protect the giant redwood and a 20-foot buffer zone around the tree. After 738 days, Hill had won her battle. She climbed down Luna, and her feet touched soil for the first time in more than two years.

STILL STANDING

Today Luna remains protected, at the center of a grove stretching 200 feet in every direction. Because of its isolation deep in the forest, the grove isn't really a tourist destination. However, members of a nonprofit group called Sanctuary Forest regularly visit to ensure that the promises made by the company are being kept. As for Pacific Lumber, the firm filed for bankruptcy, Hurwitz and Maxxam Inc. pulled out, and in 2008 a new company—whose majority shareholder is the clothing chain The Gap—was created with a corporate mission to log using sustainable forestry practices.

Hill became a motivational speaker and wrote a book about her adventure. She also co-founded a nonprofit group that trains small groups to work toward social change. At last report, Hollywood is making a feature film about her two-year adventure.

But at her core, Julia "Butterfly" Hill will always be an activist. "When you see someone in a tree trying to protect it," she said, "every level of our society has failed." In 2002 she joined a protest outside of Occidental Petroleum's offices in Ecuador to stop construction of an oil pipeline through the Amazon rain forest. "The little gringos have been arrested," said Ecuadorian President Gustavo Noboa, "including the old cockatoo who climbs trees."

LOUD NOISES!!!

The world's so damn loud we can't even hear ourselves complain!

BACKGROUND
The 20th century was by far the loudest hundred years in human history. Since the Industrial Age took full swing in the late 1800s, life has become louder and louder. Very little has been done to curb noise pollution, despite overwhelming evidence that prolonged exposure to excessive auditory stimuli adversely affects learning abilities, concentration, and stress levels in humans and even in wildlife. Without any real support from state or federal governments, some local municipalities have come up with their own noise-violation procedures. Some examples:

RECORD TIME

In *Uncle John's Endlessly Engrossing Bathroom Reader*, we reported about Paul Sacco, a Colorado judge who sentenced teen noise violators to a few hours of listening to Barry Manilow music. In 2009 Sacco expanded his catalog of music-as-punishment to include the *Barney* theme song and an hour-long marathon of the Styx song "Come Sail Away" as sung by *South Park's* Eric Cartman. The tactic may be catching on. When a Miami Beach driver was caught blasting 50 Cent in his Jaguar at 5:00 a.m., Judge Jeffrey Swartz sentenced him to two hours of the Verdi opera *La Traviata*. (Reportedly, it turned the offender into an opera fan.)

TRAIN IN VAIN

There are very few problems dire enough to make citizens *volunteer* to pay a tax increase to get them fixed, but that's exactly what happened in a neighborhood of Vancouver, Washington. Residents got tired of the loud train whistles that blew every time a locomotive came through. "You can't even talk on the phone," said one local. So they asked the city government to erect barriers to keep cars off the tracks when the trains are coming—thereby eliminating the need for the whistles. Officials said no; they didn't have the $1 million it would cost. "Fine," said the residents, "Then *we'll* pay for it. Raise our property taxes. That whistle is driving us crazy."

The Japanese have a theory that beauty is imperfect and changeable. It's called *wabi-sabi*.

GOING CUCKOO

The residents of a Phoenix, Arizona, neighborhood complained to city officials about the bells of Cathedral of Christ the King Church. They chimed on the hour, every hour, every day, every week. "It makes us feel like captives in our own homes," said one citizen. Officials finally put an end to the siege: They took the church's bishop, Rick Painter, to court, where he was sentenced to probation. From now on, if the church bells ring on any day but Sunday, the church will be fined and the bishop will go to jail.

WITCHY WOMAN

It wasn't the bonfire in her yard that prompted Brenna Barney's neighbors in Waukesha, Wisconsin, to call the cops—it was her incessant chanting. Barney is a practicing Wiccan, and she was performing elaborate rituals "in celebration of the New Moon." When the police arrived, Barney fought back (which led to a resisting-arrest charge), arguing that they were violating her religious rights. The cops disagreed. So did her neighbor, Vicki Denova, who defended the 911 call: "To be honest, your choice is your choice as long as you're not affecting other people."

REVENGE OF THE NOISE-MAKERS

In the middle of the night in May 2009, Marsha Coleman of Salem, Oregon, couldn't sleep because of the loud party going on next door. So she went over and asked the neighbors to *please* keep it down. Bad move: After she got back home, some of the drunken revelers showed up on her porch and banged repeatedly on her door. Frightened, she called 911. A deputy rushed to Coleman's house and was in the middle of taking her statement when they heard another series of loud knocks on the door. Then they heard a slurring voice yell, "This is the Marion County Sheriff!" The deputy opened the door and found one of the partiers, 32-year-old David Bueno, whose party ended right there, as he was arrested for impersonating an officer and disturbing the peace.

For more people and machines driving us crazy with their incessant noise, cover your ears and head over to page 409.

TEEEEEEEETH!

Stories about those little, white, hard things that grow in your head.

W**HAT'S IN YOUR WALLET?**
In March 2009, a customer at a Walmart in Falmouth, Massachusetts, was looking at a wallet he was thinking of buying when he unzipped one of its pockets—and found 10 human teeth inside it. Since there was no blood on any of the teeth, police could not use DNA testing to identify who they belonged to. A Walmart spokeswoman said it was an "isolated incident."

PULLING STRINGS
A young girl had a loose baby tooth, so her parents tied a string around it…and attached it to a remote-controlled car. Mom then sent the car flying cross the living room and—pop!—out came the tooth. The parents filmed the event and put it YouTube. It has since been viewed more than 270,000 times. (The little girl, it should be said, was unharmed and seemed to get a kick out of the whole thing.)

WE'RE PRETTY SURE IT WORKED
In September 2009, Darrel Vandervort of Lakehurst, New Jersey, was arrested after he pulled several of his teeth out with a pair of pliers—and sprayed blood around a female friend's apartment. Police said Vandervort was trying to frighten the woman.

PEARLY WHITES
Are you bored with your boring old jewelry? Of course you are! And that's why you should get some new pieces from Australian jewelry designer Polly van der Glas, who makes rings, pendants, and necklaces—decorated with human teeth. "I have been collecting hair, teeth, and fingernails for years," she says. "They line the shelves of my apartment in beautiful jars." Prices go up to about $690 (U.S.) for a sterling-silver ring…with four large teeth sticking out if it.

PCs infected with software that allows hackers to control them remotely are called "zombie computers."

MIGHTY MOUTH

Japanese researchers announced in 2009 that they had successfully implanted the jaws of several mice with "tooth seeds," which
later grew into mature, healthy teeth. The seeds were made up of
cell tissue programmed with genetic instructions for growing
teeth, and, the researchers said, the discovery could one day lead
to growing replacement teeth, and perhaps even organs, in
humans.

HOT CAPS

Seattle resident Shane Carlson was arrested in January 2010 and
charged with several break-ins of cars, homes and dental offices.
Carlson had been stealing old teeth from the offices, police said,
and selling the gold fillings and caps he pried from them, netting
up to $10,000 per robbery. The thefts had been going on for
months, and police were only able to identify Carlson when someone found a bagful of teeth—roots and all—on a Seattle sidewalk,
and forensic investigators found Carlson's fingerprints on several
of them.

SINKER BALL

Security guards at New York's Citi Field were called to a restroom
during a May 2009 baseball game between the New York Mets
and Atlanta Braves...because a woman had gotten her arm stuck
in a toilet. One of her gold teeth had fallen in, she said, and she'd
tried to retrieve it. It took several hours to get the woman
unstuck—and she never found her gold tooth. (The Mets also
lost, 8–7.)

WHILE YOU WERE SLEEPING

Elizabeth Smith of Florence, South Carolina, went to a dental
clinic in 2006 to have a single cracked tooth repaired—but
when she came out of the anesthesia, she found that *all sixteen*
of her upper teeth had been removed. The clinic then tried to
cover up their error by changing Smith's medical records,
according to the ensuing lawsuit. In 2009 a jury finally ruled in
Smith's favor and awarded her $2 million in damages. She plans
to use the money on restorative surgery as soon as possible, her
lawyer said.

Q: What is *digital emunction?* A: It's a fancy way of saying "picking your nose."

HELP WANTED: IN HELL

Think the Emancipation Proclamation ended slavery? Think again.

POSITION: Tomato picker, in the town of Immokalee, Florida, regarded as the "tomato capital of America." **Perks:** Room and board (sort of).

Job Description: Working 10 to 12 hours a day picking tomatoes. Work very fast for 10 hours and you can make about $50 a day.

Meals: You get two meals a day—eggs, beans, rice, tortillas, and sometimes some meat. That'll cost you $50 a week.

Lodging: Home is the back of a box truck in a garbage-strewn backyard. You have to share it with a couple of other people. There's no toilet, so you'll do your business in a bucket in the corner of the truck. The room costs you $20 a week. The "shower" is a hose in the yard. (Cold water only.) Each shower you take costs $5.

Days Off: You don't get days off. If you don't go to work, even if you're sick, you'll be beaten. If you try to run away, you'll be beaten and locked in the truck, or chained to a pole in the yard.

Getting Paid: Some weeks you'll receive some of your pay, sometimes you won't get anything. And remember, everything costs money—the room, the showers, the meals, and more—so within a few months you may actually *owe the boss money.* Seriously. If you work for years, you may end up owing *tens of thousands of dollars.* You will actually be worse off than a slave.

TRUE STORY: The conditions described above were the actual conditions endured by 12 Mexican and Guatemalan men for two and a half years. They were all offered work by the Navarettes, a family in Immokalee, with promises of room and board and riches, and ended up living in squalor and earning nothing but debts. In 2007 they finally escaped, and six members of the Navarette family were arrested. Brothers Geovanni and Cesar Navarette received the stiffest sentences, each getting 12 years in prison. The worst part of the story: Authorities believe that there may be thousands of people living in similar conditions in south Florida. (And they may have picked the tomatoes that are sitting in your refrigerator right now.)

"The world breaks everyone, and afterward, some are strong at the broken places." —Hemingway

SHOW ME THE STUPID

Okay, then. Read the stuff below.

Subject: Two unidentified thieves in Melbourne, Australia
Background: In October 2008, the thieves looked in through the window of an empty model home and saw a large plasma-screen television.

Show Me the Stupid: The thieves smashed through the home's front door—and discovered that the television was made of cardboard. Like the home, it was a model, only for display. Police said the intruders took out their frustration…by messing up a bed (which was real).

Subject: Jorge Espinal, 44, of Ft. Worth, Texas
Background: Espinal got an itch on his back late one night in May 2008.

Show Me the Stupid: He grabbed the first thing handy to scratch it with—a revolver—and shot himself in the back. Espinal was treated at a hospital and released.

Subject: Michael Sampson, 41, of Salina, Kansas
Background: Sampson was on trial in a Salina courtroom in November 2009.

Show Me the Stupid: During the trial, the judge saw Sampson sitting at the defense table holding his thumb and fingers in the shape of a gun—and "firing" the imaginary gun at witnesses for the prosecution. He also made throat-slashing gestures. Sampson was charged with four counts of making a criminal threat and one count of aggravated intimidation of a witness.

Bonus Stupid: Sampson was in court on charges of driving on a suspended driver's license and littering. He was found guilty of the suspended-license charge, but his sentence worked out to only 10 days in jail, and he was acquitted of littering. His courtroom threats, however, mean that he now faces several years in prison.

Subject: Joseph Whittenton, of Jacksonville, Florida

The AlterG antigravity treadmill lets you run while being lifted by air pressure. Price: $25,000.

Background: In May 2008, someone broke into a Hungry Howie's pizza shop and stole an undisclosed amount of cash. Police watched surveillance video, and arrested Jacksonville resident Joseph Whittenton a short time later.

Show Me the Stupid: How were police able to identify and arrest Whittenton so quickly? Because he worked at Hungry Howie's Pizza...and was still wearing his uniform when he carried out the robbery. He was jailed on burglary charges.

Subject: A man in Northern Territory, Australia

Background: Constable Wayne Burnett of the Northern Territory Police pulled over a vehicle on a highway south of the town of Alice Springs in 2008.

Show Me the Stupid: The driver had a case of beer sitting in one of the car's seats—with a seat belt around it—and a small child sitting on the floor, unrestrained. "This is the first time I've seen beer take priority over a child," said the constable. The driver was fined $750 ($710 U.S.).

*   *   *

HE MUST REALLY *HATE* PANDAS

There are fewer than 2,000 endangered giant pandas left in the wild. In 2009 Chris Packham, an English naturalist and author, came up with a controversial plan to deal with them: "It's time to give up on the cute and cuddly panda and let them go, because we just can't afford it." Packham argued that precious conservation dollars could be used more effectively to save other, more resilient endangered species. He pointed out that pandas, which used to be carnivores, have adapted poorly to a bamboo diet ever since they were pushed from their lowland forest homes due to development. Plus, pandas are slow to reproduce and...aren't really the most intelligent of the large mammals.

Not surprisingly, the backlash from Packham's fellow conservationists was harsh (people called him all sorts of names that we can't reprint here). "Boy, I really upturned the apple cart," he said. "I'm sorry I upset people. I don't hate pandas, I love cuddly animals. I love *all* animals!"

THE WORMS CRAWL IN

Patient: "Doctor! Doctor! I've got an autoimmune disease!"
Doctor: "Take 2,500 parasites and call me in a month."

THE PROBLEM

Humans are too clean. That's the theory that some scientists have come up with to explain why autoimmune conditions such as Crohn's disease, ulcerative colitis, multiple sclerosis, and asthma have reached epidemic proportions in the modern world. When bacteria were linked in the 19th century to devastating infectious diseases such as cholera and diphtheria, better hygiene and improved sanitation helped keep them in check. But over the last 60 years, a strange new trend toward chronic inflammatory diseases has cropped up in industrialized nations. And it's getting worse.

THE SOLUTION

The "hygiene hypothesis," formulated in 1989 by British doctor David P. Strachan, claims that lack of exposure to infectious agents in our childhood years has made modern humans susceptible to allergies and a whole host of other ailments later in life. Strachan's theory focuses on the need to expose humans to "good bugs" to strengthen the immune system. Since then, several scientists who have built upon the theory have suggested it be renamed the "old friends hypothesis." Just who are these "old friends"? They're certain parasitic worms and other helpful organisms that have co-existed with humans throughout our history.

Recent studies show that people in third-world countries—who are constantly exposed to dirty water, decaying vegetation, and unsanitary living conditions—rarely develop the autoimmune and chronic inflammatory diseases that plague more-developed countries. In effect, our obsessively hygienic life may have eliminated the "old friends" that once regulated our immune system, leaving us vulnerable to a host of diseases. It took millions of years for this

---

The "Cry Translator" iPhone app identifies 5 baby cries: hungry, sleepy, annoyed, stressed & bored.

synergistic relationship to develop, and less than a century to break it apart.

WIGGLE ROOM

Some researchers are now testing patients with *helminthic therapy*, which reintroduces these old friends to the immune system. In one study, doctors have their patients deliberately infest themselves with parasitic worms. Once inside, the tiny worms wriggle around and kick the immune system into high gear, supposedly strengthening its ability to fight disease. So far, say researchers, the results have been remarkable, leading some doctors to believe that worm therapy may benefit sufferers of arthritis, fibromyalgia, heart disease, atherosclerosis, eczema, irritable bowel syndrome, lupus, autism, migraine, and even psychiatric disorders.

But after a century of being told that parasites are bad for us, people are naturally apprehensive when a doctor places a cup full of tiny, slithering red worms in front of them and tells them to drink up. It took researchers at Nottingham University more than three years to recruit 52 candidates for their worm study. In contrast, it took them only *one day* to recruit 1,500 people for a trial to assess whether flavonoids, found naturally in chocolate, may ward off heart disease. (The researchers might get more test subjects if they were to dip the worms in chocolate sauce.)

The U.S. Food and Drug Administration has yet to approve the therapy, so it may take some time—and a bit of "retraining"—before helminthic therapy worms its way into a doctor's office near you.

*   *   *

THE CADILLAC OF ARMORED CARS

Looking for a luxury armored car? Consider the Russian-made Dartz Prombron Red Diamond Edition SUV. Features: A grenade-proof V-8 engine, diamond-encrusted dashboard gauges, three-inch-thick bulletproof windows, and a tungsten exhaust system. They'll even throw in three bottles of Russo-Baltique, the world's most expensive vodka. Most luxurious of all, the seats are upholstered in whale-penis leather. (Those in the know say it's one of the softest materials on Earth.) Cost: $1.5 million.

Insurance: *DENIED!*

*Do U.S. health insurance companies enjoy
finding any odd reason to not cover you?*

CLAIMANT: Peggy Robertson, 39, of Centennial, Colorado, was covered by her husband's health plan...until he changed jobs in 2007. The family's new carrier was Golden Rule, a subsidiary of UnitedHealth Group (the largest insurance company in the United States).

DENIED! Golden Rule deemed Robertson an "unacceptable risk" because her second child was born by cesarean section. According to Golden Rule, that increased the odds that she'd need to have a cesarean again, and they didn't want to pay for it. The only condition under which they *would* cover her: If she agreed to be sterilized. "It makes no sense," said Robertson. "I'm in perfect health." U.S. Senator Barbara Mikulski (D–MD), speaking on her behalf, called Golden Rule's policy "morally repugnant."

OUTCOME: Robinson didn't want to become sterile, so she opted out of the coverage.

CLAIMANTS: The Scaglione family of Lake of the Pines, California, applied for group family medical coverage in 2009.

DENIED! According to Blue Shield's records, the mother, Valerie, suffered from a skin disease called rosacea. "I've never had that a day in my life," she said. Blue Shield also claimed that one of her daughters, Samantha, once had bronchitis. That wasn't true, either. Valerie figured it was a "glitch in the system" and asked Blue Shield to adjust their records. The company refused and, according to Valierie, wouldn't say why.

OUTCOME: All five Scagliones—none of whom have any chronic illnesses—now collectively pay more than $2,000 per month for coverage. "That's way more than our mortgage," says Valerie. Anthony Wright, director of a consumer-advocacy group, said the Scagliones' ordeal isn't unusual: "We've seen people who have been denied health insurance for things as minor as heartburn. It's getting to the point where living is a preexisting condition."

Tree-climbing kangaroos can jump to the ground from the height of a five-story building.

CLAIMANT: One night in early 2008, a 45-year-old woman was at a bar in Fort Lauderdale, Florida, when a man that she had met there gave her a "knockout drug." She awoke the next day fearing she may have been sexually assaulted. As a precaution, her doctor prescribed an anti-AIDS drug. A few months later, the woman applied for health coverage with a new provider.

DENIED! Upon seeing her medical records, the insurer assumed she had a preexisting condition—AIDS—and refused coverage.

OUTCOME: She was told she could reapply in four years, once it was clear that she was AIDS-free. Today she wonders whether she should have taken the medication in the first place: "I'm going to be penalized my whole life because of this."

CLAIMANT: Six-year-old Madison Leuchtmann of Franklin County, Missouri, was born without ear canals. In November 2009, the kindergartner was about to outgrow a headband device that gave her very rudimentary hearing. Madison's doctor said she needed permanent devices implanted inside her ears before she turned seven, or she may never be able to hear again. Cost of the implants: $20,000.

DENIED! Cigna HealthCare refused to pay for the implants, claiming, "Hearing-assisted devices are not medically necessary."

OUTCOME: The Leuchtmanns are continuing to appeal the decision. As Madison's doctor fumed, "This is obviously medically necessary. You have a child who has no ear canals!"

CLAIMANT: Jody Neal-Post, 52, applied for insurance with a new carrier. On the application form, she admitted that she'd previously received counseling and medical treatment, including a Valium prescription, to help cope with the emotional fallout from being abused by her ex-husband.

DENIED! Because of the counseling and treatment, the company ruled her too high a risk for them to insure. "I was just flabbergasted," she said.

OUTCOME: Neal-Post happened to live in New Mexico, one of the few states with strict laws prohibiting insurers from denying coverage because of past domestic abuse. Neal-Post also happened to be an attorney, and she filed an official complaint with New Mexico's Public Regulatory Commission. She got her coverage.

CLAIMANT: In 2007 Nataline Sarkisyan was 17 years old and suffering from leukemia. She received a bone-marrow transplant from her brother, but there were complications and her organs began to shut down. Doctors told her parents that she needed a liver transplant—soon—or she would die. Her doctors approved the request to put Nataline on a waiting list for a liver, pending her health insurer's approval.

DENIED! After several days of deliberating, Cigna refused to cover the cost of the transplant because it was "outside the scope of the plan's coverage" and Nataline had "little chance of surviving the procedure." Her doctors appealed, claiming she had a 65-percent chance. Cigna still refused. Nine days after the initial request, Nataline's family—along with 120 members of the California Nurses Association—protested at Cigna's Glendale offices.

OUTCOME: While the demonstrators shouted outside, Cigna agreed to make a "one-time exception" and cover the costly procedure. But it was too late—before the operation began, Nataline died. Her family is currently embroiled in a legal battle against Cigna.

CLAIMANT: Rosalinda Miran-Ramirez woke up one night in 2009 to discover that her nightgown was covered with blood—because she was bleeding from her left nipple! Her husband rushed her to the emergency room, where doctors discovered a tumor and performed a biopsy. Thankfully, the tumor was benign.

DENIED! Blue Shield of California refused to pay the $2,791 emergency-room charges. The company insisted that Miran-Ramirez's decision to go to the emergency room was "not reasonable" because her bleeding breast did not constitute a "real emergency."

OUTCOME: Miran-Ramirez contacted a local television station, KPIX-TV in San Francisco, and told her story on the six o'clock news. "I am not a clinical person," she said, "but if your breast is bleeding, for me that's an emergency." Amid all of the negative press, Blue Shield "reassessed the claim"...and covered the ER visit.

MISS LANDMINE

...and other nontraditional beauty pageants around the world.

Pageant: Miss Klingon Empire
Details: Held at the annual Dragon*Con science-fiction convention, this contest features women competing in costume as ridge-browed, long-haired members of the warrior alien race from *Star Trek*. Talent is also a factor—the 2009 winner sang Blondie's "One Way or Another" while thrusting a sword at an imaginary foe.

Pageant: Miss Atom
Details: Sponsored by the Russian nuclear power industry as a public-relations campaign to make nuclear power look more attractive, this annual pageant recognizes the most beautiful woman of the year...who also works in a Russian nuclear power plant. The 2009 winner, Yekaterina Bulgakova of the Institute of Research for Atomic Reactors, won an all-expenses-paid trip to Cuba.

Pageant: Miss Landmine Angola
Details: During Angola's decades-long civil war, millions of land mines were planted around the countryside, and thousands of innocent people have lost limbs by stepping on them. This pageant was created by an artist to bring attention to the plight of land-mine amputees—who are also the contestants—and to teach them to feel good about themselves despite their physical imperfections. Nevertheless, first prize is a prosthetic limb.

Pageant: Miss Navajo Nation
Details: This pageant's concept isn't that unusual, but the talent portion is something you won't see on the Miss America broadcast. In proving their "Tribal Skills," each contestant has to butcher a sheep. Scoring is based on cleanliness and efficiency.

Pageant: Miss Plastic Hungary
Details: In 2009 Miss California USA, Carrie Prejean, dealt with allegations that the Miss USA organization paid for her to get

breast implants. But in the Miss Plastic Hungary pageant, contestants are *required* to have had some sort of feature-enhancing cosmetic surgery—mere Botox injections aren't enough. Bonus: The winner's plastic surgeon also gets an award.

Pageant: Miss International Queen
Details: Don't let the name fool you—this isn't for natural-born women; it's for transvestites and transsexuals. Held each year in Thailand (where there is a large population of both, though contestants fly in from all over the world), it offers a top prize of $10,000.

Pageant: Ms. Senior Sweetheart
Details: Beauty pageants aren't just for young women; this one is for ladies age 58 and over. Segments include an interview, a talent portion, and an evening gown competition. It began in 1978 as a fundraiser for a Lions Club in Fall River, Massachusetts, but was so popular that it became a national competition just a year later.

Pageant: Ms. Downhome
Details: A tongue-in-cheek competition for Canadian women, this pageant judges contestants on their "Canadian" skills. Events include baiting a hook, and dancing to fiddle music while holding an open bottle of beer in each hand. There's also a swimsuit segment, in which each competitor has to carry a fish while wearing a bikini.

Pageant: Zombie Beauty Contest
Details: Female attendees of Comicon, a Phoenix pop-culture convention, dress up in zombie costumes and ghoulish makeup—and ball gowns—to compete for the title. Clever costumes score high points, so contestants are judged on beauty as well as *braaaaaaaaaains.*

Pageant: Miss Drumsticks
Details: Held since the 1940s as part of the Turkey Trot Festival in Yellville, Arkansas, this pageant judges women solely on their legs. To make the judging more impartial, most contestants wear turkey masks over their faces.

Online dating site AshleyMadison.com uses the tagline "Life is short. Have an affair!"

TRY, TRY AGAIN

These folks prove that perseverance doesn't always end in success.

• **Cha Sa-soon,** a South Korean woman, took a written driving test nearly every day for more than four years...and failed each time. Finally, in November 2009, after 950 tries and $4,200 in fees, the 68-year-old woman achieved the minimum passing score of 60 percent. Everyone at the motor-vehicles office cheered. But unfortunately for Cha, she still needs to pass the *driving* part of the exam.

• **Vincent J. Howard,** a former parking-meter attendant in the Detroit suburb of Mount Clemens, pleaded guilty in May 2005 to stealing $120,000 from meters—one coin at a time, over the course of 23 years. Police raided Howard's home and found several thousand dollars' worth of coins, another $500 in his car, and $2,000 in the city-owned car he drove on his rounds. In addition to losing his job, Howard was ordered to repay all of the stolen money within two years.

• **For 30 years,** British college professor Norman Sherry worked tirelessly on a three-volume biography, *The Life of Graham Greene,* about the globe-trotting English writer who died in 1991. Over the years, Sherry subjected himself to dangers and tropical diseases like dysentery and gangrene while tracking Greene's footsteps. But by the time he finally released the last volume of the 906-page book in 2004, he'd already been upstaged by the writer's longtime mistress, Yvonne Cloetta, who had just published *her* biography of Greene. To make matters worse, Sherry's final volume was panned by critics (the *Guardian* said it was "badly written, full of lazy assumptions and statements of the crashingly obvious"). Sherry lamented, "I almost destroyed myself writing this book. Now that I'm finished, my life has been taken from me."

• **In 2010 the Society** for Research of Paranormal Science forced a German fortune-tellers' society to admit that nearly all of the 140 predictions its members had made for 2009 turned out to be wrong, including the assassination of Barack Obama and terrorist attacks in Frankfurt and Berlin. The one prediction they got right: the death of Michael Jackson. (That one had been on the "permanent prediction" list for years, so, in this case, persistence did pay off.)

THE RIGHT TO LIE

As kids, we all learned that lying is wrong. We heard it from our parents, family members, teachers, and clergy. Turns out that doesn't apply to giant corporations and TV networks.

THE INVESTIGATORS

In November 1996, investigative journalists Jane Akre and her husband, Steve Wilson, were hired by the Fox affiliate in Tampa, Florida, WTVT-Fox 13, to produce a series of news stories called "The Investigators." Fox 13 put together a big promo campaign for the series, with the tagline "Uncovering the truth. Getting results. Protecting you."

The first idea that Akre came up with was an exposé of rGBH, the recombinant bovine growth hormone sold under the brand name Posilac. A synthesized protein that farmers inject into dairy cows to increase milk production by up to 25%, Posilac was developed by Monsanto, the world's largest agricultural biotechnology corporation, in 1994. That same year—despite opposition from consumer groups, dairy farmers, scientists, and the Cancer Prevention Coalition—the FDA approved it for public consumption.

FAIR AND BALANCED

Even though Monsanto touted Posilac as "the single-most tested new product in history," Akre and Wilson did some digging and found that the only study the FDA conducted was a 90-day test using 30 rats. According to its own rules, the FDA cannot state that a product doesn't cause cancer in humans unless it has undergone a two-year study using hundreds of rats. Not only that, but the FDA ignored the results of an extensive Canadian study that concluded: "Posilac did not comply with safety requirements; it could be absorbed by the body, and therefore, did have implications for human health"—among them, potential early puberty in girls and higher risks of breast and colon cancer.

Akre and Wilson knew they were on to something *really* big when Florida dairy farmers and grocers admitted to them that they used and sold Posilac because Monsanto had threatened to sue them if they didn't. Just how far did this company's influence go?

The reporters brought their findings to Fox 13 general manager David Boylan, who—at first—was thrilled with the scoop. The station aired promos that asked viewers, "What's in *your* milk?"

WE DECIDE. YOU REPORT.

About a week before the story was set to air in February 1997, Boylan called Akre and Wilson into his office. He told them that Fox's lawyers, using information provided by Monsanto, had some "edits" for the story to make it more Posilac-friendly. Akre and Wilson refused to change a single word. Boylan told them it wasn't a request—Roger Ailes, president of Fox News, had actually been warned in a letter from Monsanto's law team that "if this story runs in Florida, there will be dire consequences for Fox News." What consequences? Monsanto was responsible for a major chunk of advertising on the 22 local stations that Fox owned; Fox stood to lose a major sponsor. Wilson pleaded with Boylan, "But this is news! This is stuff people need to know!"

"We'll tell you what the news is," replied Boylan.

THE STAND-OFF

Akre and Wilson reluctantly agreed to delay the story until May and work with Monsanto to produce something that both the station and the company would approve. But every draft they submitted was returned to them with numerous changes, such as replacing the word "cancer" with "human health implications."

"No fewer than six air-dates were set and canceled," said Wilson. "In all my years as a print, radio, and television reporter, I've never seen anything like it." After several months, it was obvious to Akre and Wilson that Fox had no intention of running the story; they were just stonewalling until the reporters either conceded to the lawyers' edits…or just quit. Neither side would budge.

Finally, Akre and Wilson issued an ultimatum to Boylan: If they weren't allowed to tell *their* story, they'd report Fox to the FCC for violating the Communications Act of 1934, which bars programmers from "broadcasting false signals." Fox offered the investigators a deal instead: Accept $200,000 to walk away from their jobs, and sign an agreement that would prohibit them from ever talking about Monsanto to anyone else, ever again. Akre and Wilson turned down the offer. In December 1997, they were fired.

TWEEEEEEET!

The following April, the journalists held a press conference to announce that they were suing Fox News for wrongful termination under Florida's whistle-blower law, which states that an employee cannot be terminated for reporting illegal activities of his employer. "This isn't about being fired for no cause," said Wilson. "This is about being fired because we refused to put on the air something we knew to be false and misleading. We were given those instructions after some very high-level lobbying by Monsanto and also, we believe, by Florida's dairy and grocery industries."

After several delays, the case finally went before a jury in 2000. Acting as his own lawyer, Wilson called several high-profile witnesses—including consumer advocate Ralph Nader and newsman Walter Cronkite, who testified that Fox's actions were a "violation of every principle of good journalism." Even more damaging, however, were the admissions by Fox's own team that there was nothing in the original version of the story that was false.

Fox's lawyers countered that the station had given Akre and Wilson every opportunity to tell their side of the story, but only if they gave Monsanto's side as well. In the end, said Fox, the investigators were fired because "in the view of the station's management, the reporters were not willing to be objective in the story nor accept editorial oversight and news counsel."

ON THE AIR

Meanwhile, Fox 13 had hired a new investigative reporter and run a "toned-down" version of the Posilac story—one that had been pre-approved by Monsanto. In response, Akre and Wilson set up a Web site and released the full text of their original story, along with updates on the case.

As the trial wore on, it looked bad for Fox. An announcement from six Canadian government scientists disclosed, according to Wilson, that they had been under political pressure to approve Posilac, and that the FDA had "misreported" their findings. But it was neither celebrity witnesses, scientists, nor Fox's admissions that ultimately swayed the jury. It was Jane Akre's testimony:

> As a mother, I know this is important information about a basic food I've been giving my child every day. As a journalist, I know it is a story that millions of Floridians have a right to know. We were

fired for standing up for the truth. Solely as a matter of conscience, we will not aid and abet their effort to cover this up any longer. Every parent and every consumer has the right to know what they're pouring on their children's morning cereal.

THE VERDICT

Fox lost. The jury ruled that Akre had been "wrongfully fired" and awarded her $425,000. (Interestingly, the jury concluded that Wilson was not similarly wronged by Fox. He thinks it's because he may have come off as "overbearing" during the trial.)

But Fox wouldn't admit defeat. The network appealed the verdict, utilizing a legal loophole as their defense: "The FCC's policy against the intentional falsification of the news—which the FCC has called its 'news distortion policy'—does not qualify as the required 'law, rule, or regulation.'" In other words, Fox's lawyers claimed that Akre did not deserve whistle-blower status because, technically, Fox hadn't broken the law; they just violated a "policy." Fox's lawyers also noted that there are no written rules against distorting news in the media and argued that, because of this, the First Amendment actually allows broadcasters to "deliberately distort news reports on public airwaves" if they so choose. Basically, Fox claimed they had a constitutionally guaranteed right to lie.

In February 2003, the Florida Second District Court of Appeals ruled in a 2-to-1 decision that Akre's settlement be overturned; Fox didn't owe her a penny. Shortly after, Fox countersued both journalists for $1.7 million to recoup legal fees and court costs. In the end, Wilson was ordered to pay Fox 13 $156,000.

WHERE ARE THEY NOW?

Today, Jane Akre is the editor-in-chief of InjuryBoard.com, a consumer-protection group. Steve Wilson is an investigative journalist in Detroit, Michigan. And he's still making waves and making enemies: In 2008 he reported that Detroit's embattled mayor, Kwame Kilpatrick, violated terms of his bond by traveling to Canada without giving prior notice, and Kilpatrick was sent to jail.

And what about Posilac? Because of the potential health risks to both humans and cows, by 2000 the synthesized protein was banned in several countries—including Japan, Australia, Canada, and most of Europe. But it's still legal in the United States.

SEBASTIAN CABOT SINGS!

...and some other albums that you probably don't need to hear to know that they weren't such a good idea.

Joe Pesci, *Vincent LaGuardia Gambini Sings Just for You*
In 1992 Pesci starred as the Italian-American lawyer Vincent LaGuardia Gambini in *My Cousin Vinny*. More than six years later, he released an album in character as Gambini, a stereotypical New York Italian, singing old standards such as "What a Wonderful World" and "I Can't Give You Anything but Love," all littered with expletives. While some listeners hailed it as a comedic success, the timing of the marketing campaign was off— so much time had passed since the movie came out that the album fell flat. Bad reviews didn't help, either; one critic described it as "a mound of failed songs and lame jokes."

Scarlett Johansson, *Anywhere I Lay My Head*
Many young actresses (Lindsay Lohan, Hilary Duff) have released pop albums, but Johansson (*Lost in Translation, Girl With a Pearl Earring*) did something different—an album of songs written by the gravelly voiced, world-weary songwriter Tom Waits. Despite a good supporting cast (a guest spot by David Bowie and production by critically acclaimed musician Dave Sitek), the album tanked— perhaps because audiences couldn't relate to a glamorous, 22-year-old millionaire singing lines like "Give a man gin, give a man cards / give an inch he takes a yard / and I rue the day that I stepped off this train."

Eddie Murphy, *Love's Alright*
Murphy recorded three albums of pop/soul music, including one in 1985 that featured his sole hit, "Party All the Time." But, to his fans' disappointment, none of his music had any trace of the humor or edginess that made Murphy a star comedian and actor. On his 1993 album, *Love's Alright* (his last to date), he lined up a dozen celebrity cameos from megastars like Garth Brooks,

---

Study finding: 25% of people suffer from paranoid thoughts brought on by media sensationalism.

Michael Jackson, and Paul McCartney for the opening track, "Yeah." Any witty lyrics here? Not really—over a psychedelic backing track, Murphy and his famous friends take turns saying or singing "yeah."

Robert Mitchum, *Calypso Is Like So...*

In 1956 and '57, Harry Belafonte almost single-handedly ushered in a calypso-music craze in the U.S. with his two smash-hit albums, *Belafonte* and *Calypso*. Of all people to cash in on the fad, perhaps the least likely was the stone-faced, tough-guy movie star Robert Mitchum (*The Night of the Hunter, Thunder Road*). While filming a movie in Trinidad in 1957, Mitchum fell in love with the music. His album, *Calypso Is Like So...*, is a fairly authentic attempt, too, with steel drums and horns. But Mitchum couldn't quite pull it off—even though he was a good enough vocalist to sing his own parts in several musicals, his voice wasn't up to the challenge. And more embarrassing, if not a little racist, was the fact that he adopted an "island" dialect, singing "dis" and "dem" for "this" and "them."

Rachael Ray, *Too Cool for School Mixtape for Kids*

A hip tape of TV chef and talk-show host Rachael Ray singing for kids? Actually, no—Ray doesn't sing or play an instrument on this 2006 album, none of the songs have anything to do with school, and it's not even a tape, it's a CD. The album is just a Ray-approved collection of pop songs that kids would theoretically like, such as Janis Joplin's "Mercedes Benz" and Harry Nilsson's "Coconut"—which also happens to be one of the few songs that have anything to do with food.

Sebastian Cabot, *Sebastian Cabot, Actor / Bob Dylan, Poet*

Cabot was the hefty British character actor best known for playing Mr. French on the '60s sitcom *Family Affair*. With his clipped, upper-crust accent and impeccable diction, his delivery is pretty much the opposite of Bob Dylan's braying mumble. That made this 1967 album an especially odd choice, with Cabot half-singing, half-speaking the songs and poems of Dylan, who, at the time, was one of the hottest acts in music.

Singapore is the only country where adult children are legally responsible for supporting their parents.

URBAN LEGENDS

Urban legends make this crazy world go 'round.

THE LEGEND: Kentucky Fried Chicken founder Harland Sanders (1890–1980) was a vehement racist and a member of the Ku Klux Klan. When he died, he bequeathed a large portion of his fortune and a percentage of KFC's future profits to the KKK.

HOW IT SPREAD: It's unclear who started the rumor or why, but KFC is one of many companies that have fought off urban legends of secret racism. (There's one about Tommy Hilfiger being disgusted that black people wear his clothes, and another that says that Microsoft's Word thesaurus contains hidden bigoted messages.) Sanders, whose image on KFC buckets was designed to resemble a 19th-century Southerner, was a natural target.

THE TRUTH: Sanders never made any public comments regarding race, and he wasn't a member of the KKK, which by the mid-20th century was no longer the large, influential organization it once was. Further, Sanders sold the Kentucky Fried Chicken company in 1964, long before he died in 1980. Not only did he not donate a sum to the KKK, but since he no longer owned the company, he was in no position to divert its profits.

THE LEGEND: Members of Alcoholics Anonymous can trade in their "sobriety chips"—medallions given out to celebrate a week, month, or year of alcohol-free living—for free drinks at any bar.

HOW IT SPREAD: This legend has been around since at least the late 1940s, when the chips were first handed out at AA meetings. While nobody knows where it started, its spread reflects the misconception that alcoholism is merely a choice, and that alcoholics in recovery will backslide given the smallest opportunity to do so—like a free drink.

THE TRUTH: A sobriety chip is a token and reminder to AA members to stay the course of sobriety, and that's all. Bars do not accept them as currency.

Fully loaded: The back seat of the Lexus LS 600h offers a built-in electric shiatsu massager.

THE LEGEND: To permanently archive its vast library of audio recordings (speeches, historical events, classic American music), the Library of Congress is transferring everything to 78s—a record format that hasn't been widely used since the 1940s. When considering its storage options, the LOC was concerned that 50 years from now there may be no way to read electronic data, whereas 78s can be listened to with a simple mechanical device. And while electronic recordings can be erased by a stray magnet, 78s are durable enough to last for centuries.

HOW IT SPREAD: This rumor got its start as a fake news story on National Public Radio's *All Things Considered* on April Fool's Day 2003. Apparently, a few people didn't get the joke.

THE TRUTH: Astute listeners quickly noticed that something was off. Since one side of a 78 can hold only about three minutes of sound, and the Library of Congress has millions of recordings, that would take a *lot* of 78s—and several decades' worth of work—and long songs and speeches would have to be split over several discs. As the faux news story pointed out, "Experts estimate that the archiving project will catch up with recordings made before 2003 by April 1, 2089."

THE LEGEND: Pop singer Lady Gaga was one of the hottest new musicians in 2009. While she had two #1 hits, she was perhaps more famous for her elaborate videos and stage show, and for wearing garish costumes, influenced by drag queens and the gay club scene, both on- and offstage. At one concert, she shocked audiences when she opened up her undergarments…and exposed male genitalia. So not only is she influenced by drag queens…she *is* a drag queen. Lady Gaga is a man.

HOW IT SPREAD: The moment in question did happen, but it was a stage stunt—with a prosthetic, albeit a very real-looking one. A subsequent interview with singer Christina Aguilera helped spread the rumor: When a reporter asked Aguilera (who bears a resemblance to Lady Gaga) what she thought of Gaga, Aguilera said, "I don't know who that is. Isn't she a man?"

THE TRUTH: Lady Gaga's real name is Stefani Germanotta… and she's a woman (we're pretty sure).

ANIMALS FIGHT BACK!

*If the world were less crazy, humans and animals might live
harmoniously in some Disneyesque existence with lots of
tra-la-las and Mr. Bluebirds on our shoulders and
whatnot. But no—it's a deer-eat-kid world.*

ROUGHING THE PASSER

In October 2009, seven-year-old Brandon Hiles was playing football with his friend, nine-year-old Wyatt Pugh, when an errant pass sent the ball into the woods in their Wintersville, Ohio, neighborhood. Brandon ventured into the underbrush to retrieve the ball...and found himself face to face with "Devil Deer," a large white-tailed buck known around the neighborhood for its aggressiveness. Devil Deer charged, and Brandon tried to run but was lifted up from behind and thrown to the ground. The deer started stomping on Brandon with its powerful hooves before Wyatt came to the rescue, brandishing a big stick. "I was swinging it like I had a sword in my hand," he later bragged. After Wyatt whacked it several times, Devil Deer ran off. Brandon was bruised but otherwise okay.

BEARPLANE

In 2009 a bush pilot in Alaska landed his 1958 Piper Cub in a remote area for a day of fishing. When he returned to the plane that evening, it had been practically dismantled: Parts of the hull were torn off, three tires were flat, and the tail section had been ripped open. The pilot knew immediately that this was the work of a bear—it was looking for food in the cargo hold, which smelled fishy from a previous trip. Unfazed, the man radioed another pilot, who flew over and dropped three tires and three rolls of duct tape. The man put his plane back together and flew home (and cleaned it thoroughly).

WE DON'T NEED NO STINKIN' BADGERS

For two days in 2003, the rural community of Evesham, England, was under siege by a rampaging badger. One of its victims was retired BBC producer Michael Fitzgerald, who was attacked by the animal in his garage. "To hear your husband screaming in such pain," said his wife, "it was like a horror movie." Even police officers were no match for the badger, which reportedly weighed 30 pounds—it chased after them, forcing them to take refuge in their patrol car. Authorities called in Michael Weaver, chairman of the Worcestershire Badger Society. "In 24 years of work with badgers," he said, "I've never heard of anything like this." Weaver eventually trapped the animal under a crate, but not before it bit four more people, including two men who were heading home from a pub and a woman walking her dog. And, to make the story even more bizarre, the townspeople soon found that the badger was an escapee—named Boris—from a nearby wildlife center. Because the animal had lost its fear of humans, it had to be euthanized. "The real tragedy about Boris," lamented Weaver, "is that it shows that people shouldn't try to tame wildlife or treat them as pets, because they are not."

THAT'S NOT THE KOOL-AID MAN

Dozens of students at a Russellville, Alabama, elementary school were sitting in the cafeteria enjoying their lunch when all of a sudden a deer crashed through a plate-glass window and started running around the room. As kids screamed and ran away, cafeteria attendants used tables and chairs to corral the confused doe and then shooed her outside with a broom. Worried that the deer might have been rabid, the school's principal ordered a massive cleanup: "We Cloroxed everything—tables, walls, floors, sidewalks—you name it, we Cloroxed it." No evidence of rabies was found.

THE HAIRY EYEBALL

After a man went to a hospital in Leeds, England, complaining of red, watery eyes, doctors discovered "hair-like projections" stuck in the cornea of one of his eyes. How did they get there? Three weeks earlier, the man was cleaning the tank of his pet Chilean Rose tarantula when the spider blasted him in the face with a mist of "barbed hairs," which tarantulas use as protection against predators. The doctors issued a warning: "We suggest that tarantula keepers be advised to wear eye protection when handling these animals."

Some NY parents pay $1,000 or more on "coaches" who help their kids pass kindergarten tests.

I MAY HAVE OVERREACTED

Maybe. Just a little.

LEAP YEAR

A 35-year-old woman in Wuhan, China, climbed to the roof of her seven-story apartment building in January 2010 and threatened to jump. After trying to talk her down for several hours, police finally had to distract the woman, grab her, and pull her to safety. Why was she so distraught? Her husband had left for work, she explained to her rescuers...without wishing her a happy birthday. (After police contacted the husband, he promised to throw her a lavish party that evening.)

YOU GIVE ME FEVER

On New Year's Eve 2006, more than 100 firemen, EMTs, police officers, and other emergency personnel responded to a call to the family home of Richard Berger in Carmel, New York. Reason for the call: Someone had broken a medical thermometer and spilled a tiny amount of mercury inside the house. Afraid to touch the mercury and not knowing what else to do, the Bergers called 9-1-1. The spill was "contained" by an emergency cleanup crew...in full HAZMAT gear. To nobody's amazement, there were no injuries.

NOW I *HATE* ALEX

In 2007 Shelby Sendelbach, a sixth-grader at Mayde Creek Junior High in Katy, Texas, confessed to writing "I love Alex" on the wall of the school gym. Shelby was called to the principal's office, questioned by a police officer, read her rights, and charged with a "level 4 infraction"—the same level applied for gun possession and making terrorist threats. (Only Level 5—for sexual assault and murder—is worse.) And she was sent to a special "disciplinary" school for four months. Officials said they were just following the rules.

Nike employees call themselves "Ekins" (Nike spelled backward), and many have "swoosh" tattoos.

EARTH'S GONE CRAZY

First the world goes crazy—then Earth does, too. We're doomed!

A NEW OCEAN?
In 2005 several earthquakes and a volcanic eruption struck an area known as the Afar Depression in northern Ethiopia. Just days later, geologists discovered a crack in the earth near the volcano. It began to grow, and it's still growing today— it's now more than 35 miles long, 25 feet wide, and, in some places, 130 feet deep. Geologists tell us that the quakes, eruption, and crack were all caused by the well-known phenomenon of plate tectonics; two of the Earth's continental plates, which meet under the region, are drifting away from each other. That's also the same process that formed the oceans—and, according to scientists, we are witnessing the beginning stages of the formation of a new sea. But it's happening much faster than anyone ever thought possible. "The ferocity of what we saw during this episode stunned everyone," says Cindy Ebinger of University of Rochester. The crack, she says, will eventually become enormous, and will fill with water from the nearby Red Sea, cutting off the nations of Djibouti, Eritrea, and part of Ethiopia from the African continent and turning the region into an island. (It will take a few million years, geologists say…but they could be wrong.)

LINES IN THE SAND
Among human populations, there are natural boundaries—mountain ranges or rivers, for example—and political boundaries, which are arbitrary lines drawn on a map, but are unrelated to physical barriers. But a 2009 study at the University of Haifa in Israel found that political boundaries sometimes affect not just people, but also animals. Along the southern section of the Israel-Jordan border, the boundary was drawn over desert. It's virtually the same on each side, but the Jordanian desert boasts a higher variety of reptile species. And UH scientists also found that Israeli gerbils behave differently—to be exact, they appear to be far more cautious—than Jordanian gerbils. Studies conducted in Europe had similar findings. For instance, many of the red deer who live near

the border between Germany and the Czech Republic will not cross from one country into the other. Reason: During the Cold War, an electric fence separated the countries. The fence was torn down in 1989, and even though the deer living there now weren't even alive 20 years ago, the memory of the boundary has been passed down through the generations.

EXTREME MAKEOVER: BEACH EDITION

Sometime during the night of July 2, 2009, a 1,000-foot-long section of beach below Bluff Point, near Homer, Alaska, rose about 20 feet. What was once a long, flat expanse of sand and gravel suddenly turned into a much higher, boulder-strewn beach. Geologists studied the strange event and finally determined that the bluff, which rises about 460 feet above the beach, had "slumped," meaning that a large section of its face had slid downward. The massive amount of moving earth drove itself under and into the beach, squeezing and contracting the surface and forcing it upward. The newly risen beach is a geological treasure trove that may offer valuable information about similar processes that have occurred on coastlines around the world. And, added Alaskan geologist Bretwood Higman, "It's good to have a reminder that the Earth is alive."

RETURN OF THE BLOB

Giant blobs of bubbling, gelatinous mucus have been spotted—and are growing, in some cases, to several miles wide—on the surface of the Mediterranean and Adriatic Seas south of Europe. Technically, they're called *marine mucilage*, and scientists have been aware of them since 1729. But only in the last few years have the mucus blobs become a problem, possibly due to rising sea temperatures. A mucilage begins as a cluster of microscopic sea creatures, some living and some dead, that becomes a home and feeding ground for other, larger creatures. The trouble with mucilages, according to researchers at the Polytechnic University of Marche in Italy, is that they become gigantic breeding grounds for bacteria and viruses, including *E. coli*, that could potentially threaten fish, other sea life, and, presumably, anyone who eats them. The largest blobs can also become heavy enough to sink to the ocean floor and smother even more sea life.

THE HOLE THING

On October 18, 1984, Rick and Pete Timm were rounding up cows on a remote patch of their farm near Grand Coulee, Washington, when they came across a strange sight: a hole in the ground about seven by ten feet wide and two feet deep. It had a flat bottom and straight vertical walls—as though it had been cut out by a cookie cutter, one geologist later said. Even stranger: The Timms found an intact piece of earth about seven by ten feet by two feet deep—the same size and shape as the hole—about 75 feet away. It had obviously come from the hole they'd found, but there was no sign that it had been dragged or rolled, and no tracks from any machinery that might have been used to extract and move it. It was, they said, as if a chunk of earth had been scooped up, carried through the air, and set down. The Timms called a geologist, who couldn't figure it out—so he called in *more* geologists, none of whom could come up with any plausible explanation for the hole. A similar event occurred three years later in Norway. No explanation for the "cookie-cutter hole" phenomenon has ever been discovered. But, naturally, many people around the Timms' farm speculate that it was the work of aliens.

*　　*　　*

POPULAR PIZZA TOPPINGS AROUND THE WORLD

Brazil: peas and slices of hard-boiled eggs

Germany: asparagus spears and eggs, sunny-side up

Sweden: bananas

Japan: squid, maple syrup, ketchup, and *mayo jaga,* a mixture of mayonnaise and potatoes

Russia: the traditional Russian mixture of *mockba,* which consists of sardines, tuna, salmon, mackerel, and onions

Costa Rica: coconut

Quebec: apples and sultanas (yellow raisins)

Scotland: corn

GOOGLE SUGGESTS...

Have you ever typed something into the Internet search engine Google, only to have it complete your sentence and offer you a list of things you may—or may not—be looking for? That's called the "Google Suggests" function, and its suggestions are based on what people search for most often. Based on these recent actual examples, people are searching for some pretty strange things.

You enter: **"WHERE IS."** Google suggests...
- where is **Chuck Norris**
- where is **Lady Gaga from**
- where is **the Geico Gecko from**
- where is **your appendix**
- where is **my refund**
- where is **Dubai**
- where is **my mind**

You enter: **"IS IT POSSIBLE."** Google suggests...
- is it possible **to curve a bullet**
- is it possible **to get pregnant without intercourse**
- is it possible **to sneeze with your eyes open**
- is it possible **to lick your elbow**
- is it possible **to have purple eyes**

You enter: **"DO Z"** Google suggests...
- do **zombies exist**
- do **zombies poop**
- do **zebras make noise**
- do **zoo hair parlor**

You enter: **"UNCLE JIM"** Google suggests...
- uncle jim's **worm farm**
- uncle jim's **worms**
- uncle jimmy's **dirty basement**
- uncle jimmy's **licky things**

Google's unofficial company motto: **"Don't be evil."**

You enter: "MY PARA" Google suggests...
- my paradise lyrics
- my parakeet is scared of me
- my pyramid
- my parakeet is puffed up
- my paranoid next door neighbor
- my parasites

You enter: "POOPY" Google suggests...
- poopy time fun shapes
- poopyjoe
- poopy savanna il
- poopy's bar and grill
- poopy diaper
- poopy face tomato nose

You enter: "IS IT TRUE THAT" Google suggests...
- is it true that Miley Cyrus is pregnant
- is it true that Lady Gaga is a man
- is it true that when you sneeze someone is talking about you
- is it true that Lil Wayne died
- is it true that everyone has a twin

You enter: "DOES YOUR TONGUE" Google suggests...
- does your tongue grow back
- does your tongue have hair
- does your tongue need healing
- does your tongue piercing hurt
- does your tongue have bones

You enter: "TOM CRUISE IS" Google suggests...
- Tom Cruise is nuts
- Tom Cruise is short
- Tom Cruise is a midget
- Tom Cruise is an idiot
- Tom Cruise is dead

Britain's National Health Service granted a prescription for Viagra to a convicted sex offender.

THE HAUNTING, PART I

We scoured the annals of paranormal investigations to find real proof of ghostly activity. There wasn't any...until we found this bizarre case. You know how, during a horror movie, you always think, "Don't go in the attic"? Here's why.

FROM BAD TO WORSE

In November 1988, 26-year-old Jackie Hernandez was looking for a safe harbor to land in after her marriage fell apart. With a toddler in her arms and another baby on the way, Jackie found a run-down bungalow in the busy port town of San Pedro, California, just south of Los Angeles. As Jackie settled in to her new life, she noticed that something in the 90-year-old house just didn't seem right. Things started happening: The television would turn on all by itself. Pencils leapt out of a pencil holder. Her cat would chase shadows...literally. At one point, Jackie even thought she saw a disembodied head floating near her attic.

She thought she was imagining things—chalking it up to the stress of separating from her husband, being in a new place with few friends, and being pregnant. Besides, even if she wanted to, she couldn't afford to move again. So Jackie had her baby and maintained an uneasy truce with...whatever it was. But by late summer 1989, the activity started getting out of control.

FOUL SPIRITS

The house took on a nasty stench. Weird sounds emanated from the attic. Late one night, she looked into her baby daughter's bedroom and saw what seemed to be a "grayish, decaying" old man sitting cross-legged on the bed. He looked right at her, and then disappeared. A few days later, she saw the other ghost again: the floating, disembodied head. It could only be seen near the attic, and it too looked decaying. And it had mean, penetrating eyes.

Jackie's neighbor, Susan Castenada, was there the night that an orange, viscous liquid started oozing out of a light switch, and tiny balls of light flew through the house. "You need someone to come in here and help you," she said. Jackie said she could handle it, but Castenada made a call anyway. She telephoned a UCLA parapsychologist that she'd seen on television, Dr. Barry Taff.

In 2009 Connecticut police raided a home to break up an alleged canary-fighting operation.

THE ATTIC, PT. I

On August 8, 1989, Dr. Taff's team arrived at the house, including professional cameraman Barry Conrad and his friend, photographer Jeff Wheatcraft. A former elementary school principal, Wheatcraft was a skeptic but came along because Conrad told him it might be fun.

While the video camera rolled, Jackie told her story. The team was fascinated by her account but a little frustrated that none of this so-called activity was happening when the camera was rolling. So Wheatcraft decided to check out the attic. He went into the laundry room, climbed up onto the washer, opened the trap door in the ceiling, and pulled himself up. He later said he felt a little unsettled up there, as if someone were watching him. He started snapping some pictures while the others waited below. "Suddenly, without warning, all of us heard a scream," recalled Conrad. "Jeff bolted down from the attic! He held out his trembling hands: 'My camera! It pulled the camera from my hands!'" *Now* the team was excited. And Jackie, though relieved that they finally believed her, was a little put off by their enthusiasm. But Taff reassured her that they were there to help. "It's fearful of something," she told them. "It doesn't want you to be here."

THE ATTIC, PT. II

Whatever *it* was in the attic, it was making a lot of noise. It sounded, they said, like someone was stomping around up there. But regardless of the noise, Wheatcraft wanted his $1,200 camera back, and Conrad wanted to film a ghost. They climbed back up. Looking around with a flashlight, they noted that there was no other way in or out and that the room was empty, except for an old, wooden fruit box in the corner. Conrad started filming, but his camera went dead. He replaced the batteries, but it still wouldn't work. Meanwhile, Wheatcraft found his camera lens—it was behind the trap door, standing on its end, as if it had been placed there. It didn't have a scratch. But where was the rest of the camera? He finally saw it…sitting in the fruit box. How'd it get there? He didn't know, but he slowly reached in and retrieved it.

Both men were ready to get out of there, but first Wheatcraft wanted to flash off a few shots. Just as he took the third picture, a foul stench overtook them. "It's behind me," he said. Then, he said, something pushed him hard in the back, nearly causing him to topple down through the trap door opening. As the two men scrambled down, they noticed three large glowing lights in the attic. Once they reached the safety of the kitchen, Conrad's video camera started working again. They didn't need any more convincing. There was definitely *something* in that house. And it was angry.

THE ATTIC, PT. III

Over the next month, the activity intensified—doors and cabinets opened and closed. The TV suddenly turned on and blared at full volume. Pictures fell from the walls. Lights and shadows passed through the house. Conrad spent a lot of time trying to film what he could, but he couldn't be everywhere at once, so he missed most of the activity. One night when he wasn't there, Jackie told Conrad that the ghost pinned her to the floor for several minutes. Then it threw a full can of Pepsi at her head. She couldn't take it anymore. On September 4, she called Conrad and left a frantic message: "It takes my fear and gains energy from it. The more scared I get, the stronger it gets." Conrad and Wheatcraft, along with another photographer, Gary Boehm, showed up around 1:00 a.m. and found Jackie and her two children waiting for them on the front porch.

The men wanted to go in, but Jackie thought they'd come to get her out of there, and pleaded with them not to go into the house. They went in anyway. Boehm was anxious to check out this attic he'd heard so much about. Wheatcraft was hesitant but willing—he hadn't been back since the night he was pushed. Conrad refused to take his camera up there, so Wheatcraft and Boehm went up into the attic without him.

At first, they didn't feel anything weird in the dark room, so they decided to leave. Then came three loud snaps, followed by a muffled scream from Wheatcraft. Boehm snapped some pictures so he could see. The flash revealed Wheatcraft pinned face-first against the slanted wall with his legs wrapped awkwardly around a support beam. Jackie yelled from below: "Come down! Come down! I told you what this thing was capable of!"

HANGED OUT TO DRY

Boehm rushed over and discovered that Wheatcraft had a length of clothesline wrapped around his neck. He was actually *hanging* on a nail from one of the rafters. And he was completely unresponsive. Boehm couldn't untie the knot but was able to bend the nail and get his friend down and out of the attic. Finally back in the kitchen, Wheatcraft regained his senses but had a nasty headache and severe rope burns around his neck. The clothesline was tied in what they later determined to be a "seaman's knot."

The final straw came later that night, when Jackie discovered a bit of the strange, orange goop that had come out of the walls… on her baby's forehead. On several previous occasions, she'd told the spirit: "I demand you stay away from my kids!" And until that night, it had. But now, according to Jackie, "It was saying, 'I can do what I want to.'" She knew as long as she stayed there, she'd never be able to escape whatever it was. It even haunted her sleep: In a recurring nightmare, Jackie was a young man, standing on the San Pedro docks. She was hit on the head with a lead pipe and then held underneath the water. Jackie could feel the life being pulled out of her as she struggled to wake up. She knew that this ghost was telling her how he had been murdered.

TIME TO LEAVE
The next day, Jackie started looking for a new place to live, but she was nearly broke and had to tough it out for a few more weeks. Meanwhile, the investigation continued (although Wheatcraft never set foot in the house again). Reviewing his video from the previous night, Conrad saw balls of light flying above Wheatcraft's head. They seemed to follow him around the house.

Jackie didn't care what they saw on the video: She just wanted out. She and her husband agreed to try to patch things up, so she packed her stuff, put the kids in his truck, and they moved 300 miles north to the tiny town of Weldon, California. "I thought I had left the ghost back in San Pedro," she said. "I thought everything was going to be okay."

But would it? Well, you've probably guessed that because there's a Part II (page 399), the answer is no.

In China, "World Wide Web" translates as "10,000 Dimensional Web in Heaven and Net on Earth."

LOWER EDUCATION

*It's real good to no that in this crazy world that our childrens is all
getting topnotched educations so they can be moe intelligenter.
U can cholk that up to some grate teechers!*

SNACK TIME

"Whoever eats this dead fly, I will give them an 'A' on tomorrow's test," said an algebra teacher (not named in reports) at Oak Ridge High School in El Dorado Hills, California, in November 2009. Most of the kids cringed, but a student named Stephen Zeldag took the dare…and swallowed the fly. That night, Zeldag didn't study, thinking he'd earned a free pass, and the next day, he got only 9 out of 46 problems correct. The teacher held up his part of the bargain by writing, "Here is your A," on the test paper…but he put an "F" in the gradebook. "I really didn't think he was joking," said Zeldag. At last report, a school investigation was pending.

GIVE 'EM A SHOT

In May 2009, every student who attended the junior prom at Warwick High School in Lititz, Pennsylvania, was given a commemorative shot glass. "We couldn't afford to give out anything as extravagant as picture frames or money clips," said a member of the prom committee, which included students and several adults. Assistant principal Scott Galen said that he never knew what the kids would be given; on the order form he approved, it just said "prom souvenirs." School officials acknowledged that giving out shot glasses to high school students "might have sent the wrong message" and promised, in the future, to find out exactly what they're approving before they approve it.

LUNCH AND SIGHTSEEING

Mary Segall, a high-school choir director in Phoenix, Arizona, was put on administrative leave for taking 40 students to lunch following a class trip in December 2009. She claimed that the restaurant she chose was the only one downtown that could accommodate such a large group. "Nonsense," said the school's principal. "This is

a big city; there are plenty of eateries downtown to choose from."
So which restaurant did Segall take the kids to? Hooters.

TOO SOON?

In April 2007, a drama teacher at South Park School in Vancouver, British Columbia, had her 6th- and 7th-grade students reenact the Virginia Tech massacre, the worst school shooting in U.S. history—which had occurred only a few days earlier. After receiving numerous complaints, the school's principal agreed that it was a "totally inappropriate lesson." The teacher (not named in press reports) countered that the exercise was merely designed to "give the kids an opportunity to address their feelings about violence."

CREATING A CONTROVERSY

In 2008 John Freshwater, a public middle-school science teacher from Mount Vernon, Ohio, used the classroom's high-frequency generator for a totally different kind of science lesson: He burned crosses onto several students' arms. He'd been reprimanded before for teaching creationism and refusing to remove a copy of the Bible from his classroom, but the branding incident was the last straw—he was suspended without pay. A friend of Freshwater defended him: "With the exception of the cross-burning episode, he is teaching the values of the parents in the Mount Vernon school district."

SHE SAID A MOUTHFUL

To inspire girls to work harder, in January 2010, administrators at Crosby Middle School in Hitchcock, Texas, brought in a motivational speaker named Shirley Price, a local woman who had overcome physical handicaps to earn a doctorate. But, according to school superintendent Mike Bergman, "Somehow, Shirley got it in her head that students were having sex on campus and went into a profanity-laden speech about sexual-type things"—including, reportedly, graphic tips on various sexual techniques. Bergman later sent a letter to the students' homes apologizing for the "off-target and objectionable" speech. Price maintains that her comments were taken out of context, and that she merely told the girls to abstain from sex. But that didn't satisfy many parents, who demanded the school give their girls counseling. Said one mother: "She violated my daughter's innocence!"

WEIRD TOURS

*When you get tired of ordinary vacation stuff like buffets
and beaches, why not check out something new—like
shootouts, cesspits, and the U.S. Border Patrol?*

PARIS SEWER TOUR

There aren't many tours that begin with the question,
"Everyone have their nose plugs?" But starting in 1867,
tourists in Paris could take a stinky boat ride on an underground
river of moldy cheese, half-eaten baguettes, cigarette butts,
and...other stuff. Sadly, the boat tours were put to an end in 1975,
but today, for only $3 U.S., you can take a walk through the Paris
Sewer Museum, which covers 500 yards of the city's 1,300-mile-
long sewer system. From the top of a metal grate, you get a bird's
eye view of the sewage itself. But that's not all—you'll also see the
tools of the trade, including a "flusher trolley," a "two-ball traveling cleaner," a gas mask, and the new state-of-the-art computer
monitoring system. At the end of this "tour of doody," you can go
to the restroom to really be part of the action.

ILLEGAL U.S. BORDER CROSSING TOUR

To take this tour, you'll have to travel 700 miles south of the U.S./
Mexico border to Parque EcoAlberto, a park owned by the Hñahñu
Indians in the state of Hidalgo. For about $18, you and your "fel-
low immigrants" (actors) take a four-hour nighttime trek through
the desert over steep hills and across dry river beds until you reach
the (fake) U.S. border. All the while, "border-patrol" officers (more
actors) chase you and shoot guns loaded with blanks. Your mission:
to reach the "U.S. border" first, at which point the guards swear at
you in Spanish before giving you a ride back to where you started.

THE SERVANT GIRL ANNIHILATOR TOUR

In 1884 and '85, a serial killer terrorized the streets of Austin,
Texas, raping and murdering nine people, many of them servant
girls. Though several suspects were arrested, no one was convicted,
and the real "Servant Girl Annihilator" was never found. This 90-
minute tour will take you to every spot where a victim's body was

Costa Rican baseball factory workers earn about $2,500 a year. Average MLB player: $2.5 million.

discovered. However, none of the victims' houses are still standing, so the tour is basically a grisly history lesson while you look at empty lots. Price: $15.

RIO SLUM TOUR

A popular new tourism trend in Rio de Janeiro, Brazil, and other South American cities is "reality tours," where visitors trek though slums and shantytowns. One of the first of these "poorism" trips is the Favela Tour through Rio's largest shantytown, Rocinha. Organizer Marcelo Armstrong says it will be an "illuminating experience if you look for an insider point of view." Visitors can see armed men who work as guards for drug traffickers, but the tour is mostly an opportunity to help the local economy by shopping at neighborhood markets and food stalls.

L.A. GANG TOURS

"It's a terrible idea. Is it worth that thrill for 65 bucks?" asks Los Angeles City Councilman Dennis Zine, who doesn't understand why anyone would willingly travel into the most dangerous neighborhoods in L.A. "There's a fascination with gangs," counters Alfred Lomas, former member of the Florencia 13 gang, who started L.A. Gangland Tours in 2010. But it's more than just a way to spend a Saturday afternoon; Lomas says that he wants the public to see that the "mean streets" are not as mean as they might think (although passengers must sign a waiver absolving L.A. Gangland Tours of any liability should they get hit by a stray bullet). "We can either create awareness and discuss the positive things that go on in these communities," said Lomas, "or we can try to sweep it under the carpet." After paying, you'll board an unmarked charter bus and head out past the graffiti-covered walls of skid row, passing such landmarks as the Central Jail and the L.A. River (where *Terminator 2* was filmed). Then you'll travel to the Florence-Firestone neighborhood, the birthplace of the Crips. The tour is conducted by tattooed former gang members—who take extra care not to upset *current* gang members. "We ain't saying, 'Look at them Crips, look at them Bloods, look at them crackheads,'" said Frederick "Scorpio" Smith, an ex-Crip. Councilman Zine still doesn't like it: "You can go to a gang movie for a lot less money and not put yourself at risk."

OUT-OF-THIS-WORLD RELIGIONS

*What if one of these "fringe" belief systems is correct—and
the Supreme Being is a creature from another world?
Well, we at the BRI support our alien overlords!*

Religion: Raëlism

History: In 1973 French auto-racing journalist Claude Vorilhon changed his name to "Raël," which he says means "messenger," after he was visited by a 25,000-year-old alien named Yahweh. The alien told Raël, he says, that he had been chosen to tell the people of Earth the truth about…well, everything. Today Raël has an estimated 50,000 followers worldwide, mostly in Canada, France, South Korea, and Japan.

Beliefs: Raëlians believe that all life on Earth was created via genetic engineering by a super-advanced race of alien beings called the *Elohim*. They've sent several prophets to Earth, including Buddha, Moses, Jesus, Mohammed, and the alien Yahweh, to help humans evolve into a more advanced state. Reaching that state will also require genetic engineering and cloning, and when we're ready, the Elohim will come to reveal their message of peace, reverence for science—and sexual freedom—to all.

Extra: Raël claims that in 1975, Yahweh took him to an orbiting spa just outside our solar system, where he got a massage and aromatherapy treatment. Then he had dinner with Jesus, Buddha, Moses, and other prophets. After dinner, Raël went to his apartment, where he made love to several attractive female robots.

Religion: Universal Industrial Church of the New World Comforter

History: The UICNWC was officially founded in 1973 by Allen Noonan, who was born in 1916 in Britt, Iowa. Noonan says, however, that his story really begins in 1947: While working as a sign painter in Long Beach, California, he claims, he was taken out of his body and beamed up into a "Galactic lightship," where he was given his assignment as the clairvoyant channel of the Archangel Michael. (Which is why he changed his name to Allen Michael.) He had another alien encounter in 1954, moved to San Francisco's Haight-Ashbury district during the 1960s, started a commune, and in 1973 had yet another alien encounter, after which he founded the UICNWC. Nobody knows for sure how many followers he has today; the sect is centered around a Santa Rosa, California, commune with less than a dozen members, though there are more believers living elsewhere.

Beliefs: Michael is recognized by his followers as "an incarnate spiritual master from Galactica, a God conscious soul dedicated to serving humanity." His religion he founded is a mishmash of hippie counterculture, New Age spirituality, the Bible, Eastern philosophy, Marxism, and, of course, UFOs. Michael and his ordained ministers are still hard at work channeling ancient galactic beings and spreading their wisdom via books, recordings, and an extensive Internet presence. (They even have their own YouTube channel.)

Religion: The Order of the Solar Temple, or *Ordre du Temple Solaire*

History: The OTS was founded in the 1980s by a Belgian man named Luc Jouret. He'd been interested in occultism for decades, and convinced a number of people that he and fellow occultist Joseph Di Mambro were reincarnations of members of the medieval Order of the Knights Templar. At its height in the 1990s, OTS had several thousand members and active lodges in Switzerland, Canada, and Australia.

Beliefs: OTS beliefs center around far-right-wing ideology—members of an earlier, non-UFO version of the sect were believed to be former Nazis. It also combines mystical Christianity, homeopathic medicine, Freemasonry, and the belief that a messiah—Di Mambro's daughter, Emmanuelle—would save the human race by taking true believers to a planet that orbits the star Sirius. They're also a doomsday cult; they believe that the rest of humanity will be destroyed after the faithful are removed to that other planet. Their story took a dark turn in 1994 when nearly 100 members in Canada and Switzerland died. Many of them, including Jouret, Di Mambro, and "messiah" Emmanuelle, committed suicide, while others were murdered. The cult lives on, though, and has between 150 and 500 members worldwide today. However, due to their violent past, they are regarded as a criminal organization in several countries.

Religion: ZetaTalk

History: ZetaTalk got its start on the Internet chat site of the Institute for the Study of Contact with Non-Human Intelligence (ISCNI) in January 1993. That's when one chatroom member, Nancy Lieder of Wisconsin, revealed that she was in contact with alien beings called Zetans from the Zeta Reticuli star system, approximately 39 billion light years from Earth. She'd been a "contactee," she said, since childhood. Over the next couple of years, Lieder drew a following that grew into the thousands.

Beliefs: Lieder's writings quickly became popular—and more and more alarming. In 1995 Lieder wrote that the comet Hale-Bopp, which was discovered that year (and would go on to become one of the brightest comets of the 20th century) didn't exist. The Zetans, she said, had informed her that the comet was a myth cooked up by the "Majestic 12," or "MJ12," a secret group of scientists and world leaders, to hide the real truth: In May 2003, a massive object called "Planet X" would pass very close to the Earth, reversing our magnetic poles and wiping out all life on the planet. Lieder became an Internet and late-night radio-show sensation, and her followers grew in number (as did her detractors, mostly astronomers). When May 2003 came and went with no life-ending catastrophe, Lieder and her supporters claimed that she knew it all along—it was a lie the Zetans told her to fool Earth's world leaders (the mysterious MJ12 again) and prevent them from enslaving the human race. Lieder now says Planet X will destroy life on Earth sometime before 2012.

Extra: If that's not nutty enough, Lieder says she's given birth to more than a dozen children—*hybrid* children—fathered by aliens.

*　　　*　　　*

"Babies have big heads, big eyes, and tiny little bodies with tiny little arms and legs. So did the aliens at Roswell. I rest my case."

—**William Shatner**

Of the top 10 largest celebrity diamond engagement rings ever given, three were given to Liz Taylor.

CRAZY COOKBOOKS

*Some cookbooks, like Julia Child's, are perennial
bestsellers. And then there are these.*

The I-Can't-Chew Cookbook

The 99-Cent-Only Stores Cookbook

Mini Ketchup Cookbook

Cooking in the Nude

The Eat-A-Bug Cookbook

The What Would Jesus Eat Cookbook

Cooking to Kill: The Poison Cookbook

The Cannabis Cookbook: Over 35 Recipes
for Meals, Munchies, and More

Regional Cooking From Middle-earth:
Recipes of the Third Age

Mini-Mart à la Carte

Cooking With a Serial Killer:
Recipes from Dorothea Puente

Dining by the Stars: An Astrology Cookbook

Manifold Destiny: The One! The Only!
Guide to Cooking on Your Car Engine!

101 Things to Do with Ramen Noodles

The Testicle Cookbook: Cooking with Balls

Every April 1st, San Francisco's First Church of the Last Laugh holds a "St. Stupid's Day" parade.

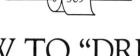

HOW TO "DRESS" A CHICKEN

Every night we have food on our plates—but we have no idea how it got there. Our grandparents have a word for that: crazy.

BACKGROUND
Just a few short generations ago, it was common for people in rural areas to raise—and slaughter—their own chickens. And cities still had open-air markets where vendors sold live chickens, which they butchered in front of the customer. Today supermarket chickens come tidily pre-"dressed," wrapped in plastic. So while this might make you a little squeamish, for better or worse, this is how you prepare a chicken.

WHAT YOU NEED:
A large pot of water, a bucket, pliers, a sharp knife, a traffic cone, and a live chicken.

HOW IT'S DONE:
1. Is your chicken ready to be eaten? If it's a chicken bred for this purpose, it should be between six and eight weeks old.

2. Don't feed your chicken for its final 24 hours—it makes the slaughter less messy. (There will be far less semi-digested food in its stomach and far less digested food in its intestines.)

3. Take an orange rubber cone—the kind used by road crews—and cut off a chunk of the wide end so it's about 9" tall. Nail this, small side down (like a funnel), to a wall or post, about 18" off the ground. Place a bucket underneath.

4. Heat up a large pot of water to about 160°F. This will be used to loosen the chicken's feathers and make plucking them much easier.

5. Catch your chicken. They're fast and don't want to be caught (obviously), so you have to catch it off-guard. Sneak up behind it

---

NASCAR superstitions: peanuts, the color green, and women in the garage are all bad luck.

and grab it by the legs. Lift it off the ground, holding it at arm's length.

6. Stuff the chicken in an empty burlap sack (like a feed sack). This calms down the chicken.

7. While the chicken is in the bag, hold it against your body with one arm. With your free hand, find the chicken's neck through the burlap. Pull down on it, then bend upward very quickly. You'll hear a snap, and the chicken's body will reflexively flap its wings, even though it's now quite dead.

8. By its feet, pull the chicken out of the bag and stick it headfirst into the inverted cone so that its head pokes out of the bottom hole, directly over the bucket.

9. Hold the chicken's head in place in the palm of your hand. Hold the sharp knife in your other hand. With one fast stroke, cut the chicken's jugular vein (where the head meets the neck).

10. Allow the blood from the chicken to drain into the bucket. When the chicken stops moving completely (even though it's dead, its muscles may continue to pulse), pull it out of the cone.

11. Holding the dead chicken by its feet, dunk it in the hot water, immersing the whole thing. Swirl it around for 10 to 15 seconds.

12. Place the chicken on a clean table. Starting near its feet, wipe your hands up the chicken's body toward the head. This should release most of the feathers.

13. Continue wiping to remove the feathers. If there are any stragglers—especially the small pin feathers—you can take them out with a small pair of pliers.

14. With your knife, cut off the head and feet.

15. Spread the chicken's legs and in between, slice into its under-carriage. Remove the chicken's innards (go on, reach in there) and cut into pieces: two legs, two thighs, and a split breast.

16. Dredge in flour, dip in an egg wash, dredge in flour again, and fry in a skillet full of oil.

17. Serve with biscuits.

CUTTING-EDGE MEDICINE

The idea of "thinking outside the box" is almost clichéd. But in the case of these medical researchers, it's absolutely appropriate.

DO RABBITS REALLY NEED THIS KIND OF HELP? In November 2009, Anthony Atala, director of Wake Forest University's Institute of Regenerative Medicine in North Carolina, announced that his research team had made a medical breakthrough: They successfully grew rabbit penises in their laboratories. Not only that, the scientists implanted the penises onto rabbits that had damaged sexual organs. Result: The rabbits developed erections, and when placed with females...well, they did what rabbits do, and were even able to father baby rabbits. The new technique involves taking specific cells from rabbit penises, spraying them onto a frame made of collagen (the main protein found in animal connective tissue), soaking the structure in growth-inducing hormones, and "growing" the new organ in a special oven. It was, of course, for a very good cause: "One of the major challenges that we find is babies who are born with inadequate organs," Atala said, "and right now there are not a lot of options." His work may also lead to growing new organs—of various kinds—for humans in the not-too-distant future.

LET'S GET NAKED!

In 2009 biologists at the University of Rochester in New York announced that they may have solved a longstanding mystery involving a bizarre species of rodent: the naked mole rat. The rats, found in East Africa, have little to no hair, can live as long as 30 years, and—this is the mystery—don't seem to get cancer. In fact, they're the only animal known to science that doesn't. In 2009 the Rochester team announced that they may have figured out why: Naked mole rats have a gene that makes the cells in their bodies "claustrophobic," meaning that if cells start multiplying uncontrollably—the defining characteristic of cancer—the gene stops the multiplying long before a tumor can form. "It's very early to speculate about the implications," say lead researchers Vera Gorbunova and Andrei Seluanov, "but if the effect of this gene can be simulated in humans, we might have a way to halt cancer before it starts."

QUICK—WHERE'S THE REMOTE?!

In 2005 Ged Galvin, 55, of Barnsley, England, suffered horrific injuries when a car collided with his motorcycle. One injury affected his ability to use the bathroom: "The doctors did several operations to repair the sphincter in my bottom," Galvin said, "but they didn't work. They told me I'd have a colostomy bag for life." But they were wrong. In 2009 doctors performed a complex procedure: They took a muscle from Galvin's knee, wrapped it around his sphincter, fitted the muscle with electrodes, and programmed a remote control to contract and expand the muscles. "Now, when I want to go to the loo," Galvin explains, "I use the remote control. They call me the man with the bionic bottom. My gratitude to the surgeons is endless because what they have done is a miracle." He also said he's fine with the fact that the muscles in his bionic bottom will have to be replaced every few years. (No word on whether he ever gets it mixed up with the TV remote.)

*　　*　　*

PHOTO FAKERY

The Image: In 2005 a photo of a kidnapped African-American soldier was posted on the Internet. He was sitting in the sand against a wall with his hands behind his back. On the wall behind him is a flag with Arabic writing on it. The barrel of an assault rifle points toward the man's head from off camera. Underneath the picture is a statement: "Our mujahedeen heroes of Iraq's Jihadi Battalion were able to capture American military man John Adam after killing a number of his comrades."

The Truth: The U.S. military wasn't missing anyone named "John Adam." After a few hours of confusion, someone noticed that the "soldier" looked a lot like "Special Ops Cody," a toy action figure only available at Army and Air Force Exchange Service stores in the Middle East. (Only a few hundred of the African-American version of the dolls were made.) Though the photo didn't do much to help the Jihadist effort, it did help the toy's value skyrocket from $39 to several hundred dollars on eBay.

THE ONE MILLION GUESSES QUIZ, PART II

We're back…with a few more quiz questions that we're pretty sure you won't be able to answer in a million guesses. (For Part I, turn to page 80.)

STORY: In March 2009, Julia Grovenburg of Fort Smith, Arkansas, got pregnant. Two and a half weeks later, she got what?

ONE MILLION GUESSES LATER: Pregnant again with a second child. Normally, hormones released after conception and throughout pregnancy stop the release of eggs from the ovaries, preventing a woman from becoming pregnant while she's already pregnant. However, in what doctors say is an extremely rare phenomenon known as *superfetation*—of which there are only 10 known cases in history—Grovenburg actually conceived a second baby more than two weeks after becoming pregnant the first time. The discovery was made in June, when doctors performing an ultrasound found two fetuses in different stages of development in her womb. (No word yet on the outcome of the pregnancy.)

STORY: In August 2009, a British dwarf performing at the Edinburgh Festival in Scotland had to stop his show mid-act and go to the hospital. What happened?

ONE MILLION GUESSES LATER: His penis became glued to a vacuum cleaner. The festival is known for its odd performances, and Daniel Blackner, also known as "Captain Dan the Demon Dwarf," has a particularly odd act that he performs with a vacuum cleaner and a…special attachment. But this time the attachment had broken before the show, and he'd used extra-strong glue to fix it. It hadn't dried by the time he did his act…and it took a trip to the hospital to get the device removed. "It was the most embarrassing moment of my life," Captain Dan said later.

STORY: Scientists at the Primate Research Center at Japan's Kyoto University reported in 2009 that while they were studying

---

Mental health professionals are twice as likely to kill themselves as other people are.

macaque monkeys at a shrine in Thailand, they'd seen several females teaching their babies to do what?

ONE MILLION GUESSES LATER: Floss their teeth with human hair. For years, monkeys at the shrine have been known to pull out the hair of visitors, sit down with it, and spend several minutes running a strand of hair through the gaps in their teeth. That's surprising enough, but the Kyoto researchers followed the activities of seven adult females, all with one-year-old babies, and found that a young monkey would sometimes sit in front of its mother and watch her intently as she flossed. While the baby was watching, the mother would exaggerate her flossing motions, opening her mouth very wide, cleaning the same spot several times with obvious motions, all while looking at the young monkey. They were, the researchers said, teaching the kids how to floss. "These findings suggest," said lead primatologist Nobuo Masataka, "that education is a very ancient trait in the primate lineage."

STORY: Firefighters in St. Petersburg, Florida, received a call in 2009 that a man was bleeding from his face not far from the fire station. Two firemen jumped into their rescue vehicle, hit the lights and sirens, and when the garage door opened, they did what?

ONE MILLION GUESSES LATER: They ran over the guy they were rushing to help. Ted Allen Lenox, a 41-year-old homeless man, was lying on the ground directly in front of the bay doors, police said, and the firefighters couldn't see him over the hood of their 10-ton rescue vehicle. They stopped when they felt a "bump," then got out and treated Lenox on the scene and later drove him to the hospital. Lenox, who'd been drinking, eventually recovered from his injuries. One of the firefighters told reporters, "We should have just walked out the door and looked."

*   *   *

BONUS QUESTION

Q: What are "Super Lemon Haze," "Vanilla Kush," "Triple Zero," "Grey Area Crystal," and "Royal Jelly"?

A: Winning strains of marijuana at the 2009 Cannabis Cup in Amsterdam.

Celebriphilia is an abnormally intense desire to have a romantic relationship with a celebrity.

THE WORLD'S MOST DANGEROUS BAND

Marilyn Manson, Alice Cooper, Ozzy Osbourne—those "wild children"
of rock 'n' roll are downright tame compared to the craziest musical act we've
ever heard of. Murder, suicide, and sheep heads are all part of the package
with the Norwegian "black metal" band known as...Mayhem.

DISILLUSION

In the early 1980s, a radical underground music scene was forming in Europe. As far as these young musicians were concerned, rock was too tame, punk had gone mainstream, and the supposed "Satan-worshipping" heavy-metal acts like Black Sabbath, Dio, and KISS were all faking it. So, with no bands that were "heavy" enough for their taste, these young people made their own music that reflected their bitter attitude toward...well, everything. The two most prominent styles to emerge from the scene came to be known as "death metal" and "black metal." To the untrained ear, both sound pretty much the same—blisteringly fast tempos; distorted guitars; screeching, unintelligible vocals; morbid lyrics (when you could hear them); and elaborate, gruesome stage acts. But of the two, black metal was the most melodic...and the most blasphemous.

THE GATHERING

One of the pioneering bands of black metal was an Oslo band called Mayhem. Formed in 1984, the original lineup consisted of guitarist/vocalist Øystein Aarseth (also known as "Euronymous"), bassist Jorn Stubberud ("Necrobutcher"), and drummer Kjetil Manheim. After going through a few singers ("Messiah" and "Maniac"), Mayhem was joined by Swedish vocalist Per Yngve Ohlin, who adopted the nickname "Dead."

Dead was *the* quintessential black-metal singer: He buried his clothes for weeks underground to give them a "grave" scent; he slashed his own skin during performances; and, for inspiration, he inhaled rancid air from a plastic bag containing the decomposed remains of a crow. In 1990 Dead and the rest of Mayhem moved

---

The vibrations caused by cranking up the bass on a car stereo can cause your lungs to collapse.

into a house together to work on their first full-length album, *De Mysteriis Dom Sathanas*—a Latin phrase that loosely translates to "Lord Satan's Secret Rites." During those album sessions, a style emerged that would come to define black-metal music. According to *Dark Legions* magazine:

> [The music] was metamorphosing into a sleeker, melodic variant with more dynamic change in the songs, producing different "settings" to tell a tale, somewhat like a micro-opera in harsh guitars and howling vocals. Similarly, the band's appearance went from t-shirts and jeans to black clothing, black boots, and black-and-white facepaint, or "corpsepaint," to make them all appear dead.

THE SPLINTERING

Life in the Mayhem house was as intense as the music: Dead, who continually battled depression, didn't get along with Euronymous. And on April 8, 1991, Euronymous came home to find Dead dead—with slit wrists and a self-inflicted gunshot to the head. (Next to him was a suicide note that read, "Please excuse all the blood.") Before calling the police, however, Euronymous ran to the store and bought an instant camera...and then photographed Dead's body in a variety of positions. (One of the photos later found its way onto the cover of Mayhem's bootleg live album, *Dawn of the Black Hearts*.) According to legend, Euronymous also kept chunks of Dead's scattered brain and mixed them into a stew, and used bone fragments from his skull to make necklaces that he gave to musicians whom he "deemed worthy."

The well-publicized tragedy gave a huge boost not only to Mayhem's popularity but to all of black metal. "People became more aware of us after that," said Necrobutcher, the bassist. "It really changed the scene." But the "scene" became too much for Necrobutcher to handle, and he soon quit the band.

THE REFORMATION

But Mayhem lived on...for a while. Singer Attila Csihar took over for Dead, while Varg Vikernes ("Count Grishnackh," named after a *Lord of the Rings* villain) stepped in on bass. But once again, there was trouble in the band—Count Grishnackh, who suffered from paranoid delusions, became convinced that Euronymous was secretly conspiring to torture and kill him. On August 10, 1993, less than a year after joining the band, Grishnackh went to Euronymous's apartment and stabbed him 23 times, killing him.

The ensuing murder trial put Mayhem in the news again. And the trial revealed that not only did the bassist kill the guitarist, but Grishnackh was also responsible for a spate of infamous church-burnings that had plagued Norway for the past few years. He was sentenced to 21 years in prison. (He was released on parole 15 years later, in 2009.)

THE SHEEP OFFENSIVE

It seemed that with two members dead and one in jail, Mayhem would never rock again. Not so—in 1995 Hellhammer got a lineup together to start anew, this time with guitarist Rune "Blasphemer" Eriksen and original member Sven Erik "Maniac" Kristiansen on vocals. He even lured Necrobutcher out of retirement to play bass. Soon after, Mayhem *finally* released *De Mysteriis Dom Sathanas*—an album that had been stalled amidst all of Mayhem's mayhem. That was followed by *Wolf's Lair Abyss* in 1997 and *Grand Declaration of War* in 2000. Mayhem were back in business—and were now a bona fide legend in the black-metal world. They managed to stay below the radar of the mainstream press... for a time.

But in 2003 the band made headlines again. During a show in Bergen, Norway, Maniac was cutting up a dead sheep on stage—a ritual that had become a regular part of their act—when its head somehow catapulted into the crowd, hitting 25-year-old Per Kristian Hagen. The sheep's head knocked the young man to the floor, and he ended up with a fractured skull. Hagen filed assault charges against Mayhem. "The whole thing was an accident," claimed Blasphemer (although he added, "but maybe it *would* be an idea for another show"). In the end, Hagen dropped the charges and the band had weathered yet another storm.

LONG DIE ROCK

With the band members now in their 40s, Mayhem is still at it. They made the news again in 2009 when they were arrested for trashing a hotel room in the Netherlands. And though they don't expect everyone to like their music, they don't want to be thought of as just a gimmick. According to vocalist Attila Csihar, "It took us 20 years of doing this before people realized we weren't joking."

...which now leads them through the hotel's lobby.

THE OBITS

Some real-life newspaper obituaries written by the loved ones (and not-so-loved ones) of the dearly (and not-so-dearly) departed.

"**William Donaldson,** who died on June 22 aged 70, was described as 'an old Wyke-hamist who ended up as a moderately successful Chelsea pimp,' which was true, though he was also a failed theatrical impresario, a crack-smoking serial adulterer, and a writer of autobiographical novels."

—*Daily Telegraph* (U.K.)

"**Dolores Aguilar,** born in 1929 in New Mexico, left us on August 7, 2008. Dolores had no hobbies, made no con-tribution to society, and rarely shared a kind word or deed in her life. I speak for the majori-ty of her family when I say her presence will not be missed by many, very few tears will be shed, and there will be no lamenting over her passing. There will be no service, no prayers, and no closure for the family she spent a lifetime tearing apart."

—*Vallejo Times-Herald* (New Mexico)

"**Jim Adams,** 53, tired of read-ing obituaries noting others' courageous battles with this or that disease, wanted it known that he lost his battle as a result of simply being stubborn and not following doctor's orders. He was sadly deprived of his final wish, which was to be run over by a beer truck on the way to the liquor store to buy booze for a date. He loved to hear and tell jokes and spin tales of grand adventures he may or may not have had. In lieu of flowers, he asks that you make a sizeable purchase at your favorite watering hole, get rip-roaring drunk, and tell the stories he no longer can."

—*Casper Star-Tribune* (Wyoming)

"**Dorothy Gibson Cully,** 86, died peacefully, while in the loving care of her two favorite children, Barbara and David. At the time of her death, Dot's daughter Carol and Carol's husband, Ron, were attending a 'very important conference' at a posh Florida resort. After learning of the death, they rushed home 10 days later. Dot's other chil-dren—dutifully at their moth-er's side helping with the funeral parlor notice, the hospice notification, revising the last will, etc.—happily picked up the considerable slack of the absent former heiress. Contributions to the hospice are welcomed. Opinions about this obit are not."

—*Raleigh News & Observer* (North Carolina)

"**Sally Baron,** age 71, of Stoughton, died Monday, Aug. 18, 2003. She took care of her family, especially Slugger, who got around better than he should have after a debilitating mining accident in 1969. Memorials in her honor can be made to any organization working for the removal of President Bush."

—*Capital Times* (Wisconsin)

"**Roosevelt Conway** passed away April 2, 2005. In 1966 he came to Los Angeles, where he met and fell in love with his wife, Pee Wee. She's a damn good mother who was faithful and devoted to her man, 'too devoted.' She got a wake-up call. They parted. She never went back. But she never stopped caring and doing good things for him. Like now, he didn't have an insurance policy. But Pee Wee made it possible. She made sure he is having a good proper burial service right now. She will help anyone long as they are not playing games. It's time for people to start giving back to her and stop calling on her so much."

—from a memorial-service brochure, Inglewood, CA

"**Patrick Pakenham,** 68, was a talented barrister and the second son of the 7th Earl and Countess of Longford; but his boisterous nature and bouts of mental illness rendered it impossible for him to sustain his position at the Bar, and he retired after 10 years' practice. During his appearance before an irascible and unpopular judge in a drugs case, the evidence, a bag of cannabis, was produced. The judge, considering himself an expert on the subject, said to Pakenham, with whom he had clashed during the case: 'Come on, hand the exhibit up to me quickly.' Then he proceeded to open the package. Inserting the contents in his mouth, he chewed it and announced: 'Yes, yes of course that is cannabis. Where was the substance found, Mr. Pakenham?' The reply came swiftly, if inaccurately: 'In the defendant's anus, my Lord.'"

—*Daily Telegraph* (U.K.)

THE SHIPPING NEWS

Weird stuff on boats, ships, and at sea. (Sorry, no pirates.)

THE GOOD SHIP *IRONY*

In April 2009, British environmental activists Raoul Surcouf and Richard Spink set out on an awareness-raising journey to Greenland's melting polar ice cap. Their ship: the *Fleur*, a 40-foot carbon-neutral yacht that operated with solar panels and an onboard wind turbine. But weather proved their undoing: Hurricane-strength winds and high waves destroyed the solar panels and the ship's generator. After the *Fleur* capsized a third time, Surcouf and Spink put out a call for help. The environmentalists seeking to raise awareness of the damage caused by fossil fuels were rescued by the *Overseas Yellowstone*, a 113,000-ton oil tanker.

WATERSPORTSCAR

A car is meant for driving on land; a boat is meant for water. And the equipment inside each is specifically designed for its purpose. But that didn't stop Marco Amoretti and Marcolino De Candia from trying to modify their pink Maserati sports car—nicknamed "Miriam"—for sea travel. It stayed afloat, too. Filled with plastic floatation aids, it moved through the water slowly, propelled by an outboard motor. After the two had traveled five miles from the port of Bocca di Magra, Italian coastal police caught up with them and ended the car's planned trip around the entire coast of Italy. (It wasn't Amoretti and De Candia's first voyage: In 1999 they traveled from the Canary Islands to the Caribbean, a distance of 3,000 miles across the Atlantic Ocean, in a modified Ford Taurus.)

IT'S MORE THAN I CAN BEAR

Marty Descoteaux left his motorboat idling for just a minute on Elliott Lake in Ontario in July 2006. While his back was turned, a bear emerged from the adjacent forest and climbed into the boat. The lumbering animal then bumped the boat's throttle, suddenly sending it into a rapid spin. Descoteaux bailed, jumping into the lake. The bear wasn't as smart: He remained on the boat as it spun wildly. After a few minutes, the boat hit a rock, sending the bear flying off the boat and into the lake.

In India's traditional Gotmar festival, participants throw rocks at each other. (It was banned in 2009.)

NUTTY NUPTIALS

*Four weird weddings, one brief marriage, and one
deadly proposal. All in the name of love.*

FOREVER MINE

In December 2006, 10 couples, all dressed in traditional Chinese wedding attire, descended 1,000 feet underground to get married in the dust-ridden pitshaft of a coal mine in Shanxi Province, China. The Datong Coal Group held the mass ceremony to show the public that the country's coal mines weren't as dismal and dangerous as recent news stories had made them out to be (at the time, a miner fatality occurred nearly every day in China).

WHITE WEDDING, BLACK FRIDAY

On Thanksgiving night in 2009, hundreds of bargain-hunters were lined up in the rain outside of a Best Buy store in Allen Park, Michigan, waiting for the doors to open the next morning for "Black Friday," the biggest sale of the year. Among the tents and other makeshift shelters was a white RV. Under its awning, Edward Burbo (wearing dress pants and a black tuxedo T-Shirt) married Jennifer Dykstra (wearing a white sweater and skirt with brown snow boots). The couple had decided to get married there because camping out for the sale was an annual tradition for them. "Everyone said, 'You're getting married at Best Buy? In line? For real?'" said Burbo. The newlyweds found some great deals the next morning.

STRONG ROOTS

In December 2006, hundreds of well-wishers traveled to the remote Indian city of Malda to celebrate the marriage of two banyan trees, the trunks of which had grown wrapped around each other in a "loving embrace." The "wedding" took place after a rash of deaths and burglaries in the region; people hoped that if the two trees were married, they might ward off evil spirits. "The trees can save us," said one attendee. The bride and groom were decked out in garlands and cloth.

Sesame Street's Bert & Ernie have been questioned about their sexual preference in interviews.

SEE THAT TRAIN A-COMIN'

In August 2009, a bride named Lin Rong, from China's Jilin Province, walked down the aisle…in a wedding dress whose train was 1.4 miles long. The lengthy train, which took three hours to unroll in a large city park, was the idea of the groom, Zhao Peng, who'd heard about a similar bridal train in Romania that was nine-tenths of a mile long. Zhao was determined to set a new world record. "I do not want a cliché wedding," he said, so he spent 40,000 yuan ($5,800) on the train. And although Zhao's bride was delighted with his gesture, his family wasn't. "It is a waste of money," said his mom.

POOR LITTLE GUYS

One night in 2009 on a moonlit beach in Hilton Head, South Carolina, a young man proposed to his girlfriend by placing 150 candles inside waxed bags that were arranged in the shape of a heart. She said yes, they kissed, and then they walked arm-in-arm to their rental home…and left the candles burning. Meanwhile, 60 newly hatched loggerhead sea turtles had just emerged from their nest on the beach. Driven by instinct, they began their scramble down to the moonlit ocean. But the candles were brighter than the water, so the hatchlings were drawn to them instead. Those that didn't die of exhaustion were eaten by crabs. The next day, authorities tracked down the lovebirds and informed them that during the threatened turtles' hatching season, it's illegal to use any artificial light on or near the beach after 10:00 p.m. The couple didn't know, and were reportedly "remorseful." No charges were filed.

KEEPING UP WITH HARVY

In 2009 Kristin Georgi, 22, married 84-year-old Joe Harvy, a wealthy—and very busy—owner of a successful lumber company. Their marriage lasted only a few months. Why? "He was very hard for me to keep up with," complained Georgi. "When you climb onto your own jet for the tenth time in four days…ugh! And we were only in each place for a day and a half. It was a bit too fast-paced for me." Harvy eventually filed for divorce and is now looking for a new bride who can keep up with his busy lifestyle.

Can you type? You're 5 times more likely to write a NY *Times* bestseller than date a supermodel.

THINGS YOU DIDN'T KNOW

Or at least we're pretty sure you didn't.

Thing You Didn't Know: When you're having surgery performed on your buttocks, you should definitely not fart.

Story: In April 2008, 30-year-old Jorgen Olsen of Hammershoj, Denmark, was anesthetized and on the operating table, having a growth removed from his buttocks with a device known as an electric knife—an instrument that cuts tissue with a super-heated spark. The surgery was under way...when, in his sleep, Olsen farted. The knife ignited the fart. And even worse, Olsen was lying on a surgery cloth laced with disinfectant—*flammable* disinfectant—which quickly burst into flames. When Olsen awoke, he was being treated for burns on his buttocks and surrounding areas. He missed nearly two months of work...and sued the hospital for an undisclosed amount of money.

Thing You Didn't Know: Gardening is bad for your eyes.

Story: A 66-year-old woman was digging in her garden in suburban Sydney, Australia, in April 2009 when she accidentally flicked some soil into her eye—along with a small leech. The quarter-inch-long creature wriggled up under her eyelid and did what leeches do best—it attached itself to the inside of her eye and began sucking blood from it. After the woman's husband was unable to remove it, they rushed to a hospital. Doctors were concerned that if they pulled the leech out, its head might remain in the woman's eyeball, so they rinsed the eye with saline water (leeches don't like salt). It worked, and the leech detached itself, but not before it had tripled in size. As a souvenir, the doctors gave the leech to the woman before she left.

Thing You Didn't Know: You should never, ever throw away your mother's old mattress.

Story: In July 2009, a woman in Tel Aviv, Israel, identified only as

Annat, decided to do her mother a favor and throw out her old, tattered mattress and buy her a new one. When her mother found out what she'd done, she told her daughter that for decades, she'd been stuffing her life savings inside the mattress—there was more than $1 million in cash in it. The two women notified authorities, and a massive search of the city's dumps began—complete with security guards to keep treasure hunters away. But after weeks of digging through garbage, the old mattress was never found. Annat told reporters, "Mom said, 'The heart is crying, but, you know, we could have been in a car accident or had a terminal disease.'"

Thing You Didn't Know: If you've been unlucky enough to lose a large part of your skull, don't worry—it may grow back.

Story: In the 1950s, Gordon Moore of Hexham, England, was in a horrific car crash in which the front of his skull was crushed from just above his eyes to nearly the top of his head. The damaged portion of his skull had to be removed, and doctors replaced it with a large titanium plate. In 2009, more than 50 years later, doctors removed the plate to treat an infection—and were astounded to find that his skull had regrown underneath it. "They took the infected plate out," Mr. Moore told the BBC, "and found I had grown a completely new skull underneath, so they just stitched me up." Doctors said that such a thing is so rare that they could find only one similar occurrence in history. Bonus: The new skull bone even had a crease where the metal plate was dented in a minor car accident years earlier.

Thing You Didn't Know: Fatty foods can clog a lot more than just your arteries.

Story: Officials in Seattle, Washington, reported in 2009 that fatty foods are also clogging up the city's sewer pipes. Just as it does inside human arteries, the glop hardens, builds up, and then backs up—causing stinky bubbles to infiltrate residents' sinks and toilets. Most of these deposits come from restaurants, which collectively wash thousands of greasy dishes every day. However, according to Seattle's pollution-prevention coordinator, Julie Howell, "One thing that has been a real surprise is that there is much bigger residential component than people might think"— meaning much of the grease comes from households.

THE WORLD'S GONE LAZY

These actual products are for people so lazy they can't even fini

PROBLEM: Pancakes are *so* hard to make. First you have to read the directions on the box. Then you have to mix the dry ingredients with the wet ingredients. Then you have to grease a pan. Then you have to fry the pancakes. That's seven minutes of your life…gone!

SOLUTION: The Chefstack Automatic Pancake Machine does all the work for you. Simply pour in a "batter pouch," turn it on, and the machine makes and stacks pancakes in 30 seconds. But it's only for *real* pancake lovers—it costs $3,500.

PROBLEM: When you use a pair of scissors, you have to move your thumb and forefinger slightly apart and then back together again, and then again, and again, and again…

SOLUTION: Try Whizzers! Perfect for the 21st-century lifestyle, they're battery-operated, automatic scissors that cut while you guide. (It's actually a motorized knife.)

PROBLEM: You're hungry, but that delicious cake is all the way over on the other side of the table. Come here, cake!

SOLUTION: The Extendable Fork. It's just like a normal fork, except that it telescopes out to 18 inches, long enough to reach across the table without having to get up.

PROBLEM: Making a peanut butter and jelly sandwich is hard work. First you have to spread the peanut butter on a piece of bread; then you spread the jelly on another piece of bread. And don't even get us started on how hard it is to put the two together.

SOLUTION: Goobers. Made by Smuckers, it's a jar filled with alternating columns of peanut butter and grape jelly. And if sticking a knife into that is *still* too much work, Smuckers also makes UnCrustables: preassembled PBJ sandwiches (with the crusts cut off).

PROBLEM: Playing "fetch" is a great way to spend some quality time with your pooch, but what if you're too busy, or there's something good on TV?

SOLUTION: The GoDogGo Fetch Machine. Like a miniature tennis ball machine, it shoots balls a few dozen yards away so your dog can chase them. If the dog brings them back and drops them into the bucket, the machine shoots them again. And you don't have to miss a second of *Survivor*!

PROBLEM: Losing weight requires exercise, which requires movement, which requires getting up off the couch.

SOLUTION: The Vibro Power Belt lets you burn fat while sitting down. How? The belt "rigorously massages the skin and underlying tissue to get circulation moving and break up deposits." The jury's still out on whether it works, but at least you can make a game of it: Eat some pork rinds, turn on the Vibro Power Belt, and let the two battle it out.

PROBLEM: Stirring your coffee or hot chocolate can be hazardous. If you get too rambunctious, it can spill and burn you. And if you stir a lot, there's always carpal tunnel syndrome to worry about.

SOLUTION: The Chunky Mug is a cup that looks like a cow and has a built-in agitator that automatically stirs your beverage for you. Just press the button, and your stirring worries are over!

PROBLEM: Licking an ice cream cone involves moving your tongue up and down, in a circle, side to side, up and down, in a circle, side to side...and you've barely made a dent.

SOLUTION: The Motorized Ice Cream Cone does all the work. Simply place your ice cream cone into the green plastic receptacle, and it will slowly rotate the cone for you. All you have to do is stick out your tongue, and the ice cream comes to you.

*　　*　　*

"Progress is made by lazy men looking for easier ways to do things."
—**Robert A. Heinlein**

THE MAYAN PROPHECY

If you're reading this before December 21, 2012, your time on this planet may be limited. If you're reading this after that, you've either survived the apocalypse, or it never happened. Either way, congratulations!

COUNTDOWN...
Have you heard the news? We're all gonna die...or else we're all gonna become superhuman. Either way, it's supposed to happen around December 21—the winter solstice—in 2012. Who says? The ancient Mayans, whose civilization in Mexico and Central America reached its zenith from A.D. 250 to 900.

The Mayans were remarkable astronomers. Without the benefit of instruments like telescopes, they charted the movements of stars and planets over centuries, and were eventually able to predict celestial events like equinoxes, solstices, and eclipses with staggering accuracy, even into the far distant future. Those skills, combined with a developed counting system and a written language, allowed them to create very accurate written calendars, including one that tracked a 365-day year, and a "Long Count" calendar that tracked much longer periods of times. That one, according to some theorists, foretells big trouble.

END OF THE LINE
The Long Count calendar divides enormous lengths of time into "eras," each of which is roughly 5,125 years long. The era we're currently in begins on the Mayan creation day, a date astronomers and other scientists have translated to our calendar as August 11, 3114 B.C., and ends on December 21, 2012.

None of this would mean anything to us today if Mayan hieroglyphic writing hadn't been deciphered. Archaeologists had been trying to decipher it for centuries before the first major breakthroughs occurred in the 1950s. Soon after that, they started writing about the Long Count calendar and the significance of its "end date" in December 2012. And in 1966 Michael Coe, one the most noted archaeologists studying the calendar, wrote in his book *The Maya*, "Our present universe [will] be annihilated when the Great Cycle of the Long Count reaches completion." Take that

In Bahrain, a male gynecologist must examine a woman with a mirror; he can't look at her directly.

dire bit of news, run it through the 1960s and 1970s New Age movements—and you get some truly weird theories.

THE AGE OF AS-WEIRD-AS-US

• In the mid-1970s, California writer Terence McKenna used a complex system of mathematics, Chinese philosophy, and a lot of psychedelic drugs to develop his "Timewave Zero" system, which he claims can predict when especially significant events will occur around the world. And he says his analysis pointed to a profound "cosmic awakening" in 2012...on the exact same date the Mayan calendar ended. "You may not believe that I didn't know about the Mayan date when I made this prediction," he said, "but I didn't."

• In the 1980s, José Argüelles, in his book *The Mayan Factor*, describes a 25-year "harmonic convergence" leading up to December 21, 2012, at which time we'll experience an evolutionary upgrade from human to superhuman. The date will mark the end of a Mayan World Age and the beginning of a New Age. People will become more intuitive—and even telepathic. (Woo-hoo!) However, only the enlightened ones will be able to adapt. Everyone else, Argüelles says, will be taken away on "silver ships."

• In 1995 a Wisconsin woman named Nancy Lieder—who claims to communicate with aliens from a world called Zeta Reticuli—said that an enormous "Planet X" is going to enter Earth's "orbital zone" and knock the planet off its axis, causing an apocalypse. When? May 27, 2003. When that didn't happen, she changed the date to December 21, 2012. (You can read more about Nancy "I want to believe!" Lieder on page 307.)

• In the 1990s, John Major Jenkins wrote a book titled *Maya Cosmogenesis 2012*, in which he claims that Mayan "skywatchers" were able to observe and track the "Precession of the Equinoxes," a celestial cycle that began about 26,000 years ago. It will lead to a point when "Earth and the winter solstice Sun align at the same point at the center of the Milky Way." Jenkins called this the "Galactic Alignment" and says it will happen on...December 21, 2012. "It will provide the opportunity for the rebirth of creation," Jenkins says.

• Richard C. Hoagland, known mostly for talking about conspiracies and UFOs on late-night radio, claims that Earth's "torsion fields" are out of balance. And if we don't fix them, he says, life as we know it will end…on December 21, 2012. He claims the Mayan Long Count calendar also contains instructions on how to survive the coming disaster, and says the government has been misleading the public about it since the 1940s. According to Hoagland, several so-called natural events—the 2004 tsunami in Indonesia, Hurricane Katrina in 2005, and the 2010 earthquakes in Haiti and Chile—were actually botched attempts to fix the torsion fields.

• Authors Patrick Geryl and Robert Bast go even further, claiming that both the Mayans and the ancient Egyptians were actually from the lost continent of Atlantis. After a catastrophe sank Atlantis, the survivors spread out across the planet to preserve their knowledge for use by future generations, including how to survive the 2012 disaster. Unfortunately, that particular bit of information is written in an unknown language, and as of yet, it hasn't been deciphered.

BACK HERE ON EARTH

So should we all start stocking up on duct tape, canned foods, and flashlight batteries as soon as possible? Sure—why not? But in the meantime, real scientists say it's all a bunch of hooey. Whatever it is the Mayans may have thought about the winter solstice of 2012, there is no conclusive reasoning that suggests anything either cataclysmic or wonderful is going to happen. In fact, NASA has even issued an official statement on the subject:

> "Nothing bad will happen to Earth in 2012. Our planet has been getting along just fine for more than four billion years, and credible scientists worldwide know of no threat associated with 2012."

Spoilsports. (See you in 2013…hopefully.)

*　　*　　*

SOUNDS LIKE FUN!

New Jersey's Action Park amusement park became so run-down and accident-prone during its 1978–96 existence that local doctors who treated customers' injuries nicknamed it "Traction Park," "Accident Park," and "Class Action Park."

…if the abduction results in a close encounter of the "fourth kind"—an alien baby.

MEMBERS ONLY

*Emergency-room workers have all sorts of disgusting stories
having to do with...well, private parts. (Warning:
These stories aren't for everyone.)*

A TREE GROWS IN GRANNY

An elderly North Carolina woman arrived at the ER saying she had green vines growing in her "virginny," as she quaintly called it. An exam and a few X-rays confirmed her story: It was a vine, and it had sprouted...out of a potato. The woman explained that her uterus had *prolapsed*, or fallen out (a condition not uncommon in elderly women), so she'd popped in a potato to hold it up—and forgotten about it.

BAD KITTY!

A woman brought her unconscious boyfriend into the ER in a panic and explained that she'd found him lying in the bathtub. Doctors noted a large lump on the man's head...and some curious scratches on his scrotum. As they were trying to determine what happened, the man woke up and told his story: He'd been cleaning his tub in the nude, and while kneeling to scrub the drain, he didn't realize that his swaying testicles had drawn the attention of his cat. The cat pounced, and the man jumped in pain...then hit his head on the tiles and knocked himself out.

WIENER DOG

In a fit of depression and self-loathing, a middle-aged man did the unthinkable—he cut off his own penis. The urologist at the ER believed he could reattach it if it was found, but time was running out. So a police officer rushed to the man's house to look for it. There, he heard a choking sound coming from the man's poodle. After a brief struggle, the officer was able to wrench the man's missing member from the dog's mouth. Sadly, it was too damaged to reattach, but the cop was given a citation for service "above and beyond the call of duty."

In 2008 a man who claimed the drug Mirapex caused his gambling habit won an $8 million lawsuit.

MMMM...CHEMICALS

Boy, this food tastes good! Uh-oh. Taste isn't everything. Turns out food manufacturers use more than 3,000 chemicals to make their products look better and last longer. Here are a few.

ACESULFAME-POTASSIUM

Found in: Baked goods, chewing gum, pudding, gelatin, diet soda, chewable medications

The Dangers: It's also called acesulfame-K, or ace-K (K is the chemical symbol for potassium). Never heard of it? It's an artificial sweetener roughly 200 times sweeter than sugar. The U.S Food and Drug Administration allowed this chemical to be added to diet soft drinks in 1988. Animal testing by the German company Hoechst suggests that the additive may cause cancer. Large doses of *acetoacetamide*, a byproduct of the sweetener, were also shown to affect the thyroid in rats, rabbits, and dogs. According to the non-profit Institute of Food Technology, adequate human trials have not yet been conducted.

FD&C RED #40

Found in: Sodas, candy, toaster pastries, cheese-flavored chips, and children's vitamins

The Dangers: The most widely used food dye, Red #40, was originally manufactured from coal tar; now it's mostly made from petroleum. A 2007 study found that it causes increased levels of hyperactivity, aggressive behavior, attention deficit disorder, and lower IQs in children. The British Food Standards Agency has also linked it to migraines in adults. Red #40 is banned in Denmark, Belgium, France, Switzerland, and Sweden but is widely used in the United States.

2-PHENYLPHENOL

Found in: Citrus fruits

The Dangers: 2-phenylphenol is a preservative marketed under the trade names Dowicide, Torsite, Preventol, Nipacide, and many others. Its primary use is as an agricultural fungicide, applied to most commercially available oranges, limes, lemons,

---

In 2003 biologist K.W. Moeliker published a study on the existence of homosexual necrophiliac ducks.

and grapefruits, after the fruit has been picked. Eye contact can cause severe irritation and burns, with possible eye damage. A 2002 study in Holland has linked 2-phenylphenol to hyperactivity in kids.

SODIUM BENZOATE
Found in: Fruit juice, carbonated drinks, pickles
The Dangers: Manufacturers have used sodium benzoate (and benzoic acid) for a century to prevent the growth of microorganisms in acidic foods. They seem to be safe, though they can cause allergic reactions in some people. The problem: When sodium benzoate is mixed with ascorbic acid (vitamin C), the combination can form benzene, a chemical known to cause leukemia and other cancers. In the 1990s, the FDA asked companies not to use benzoate in products that contained ascorbic acid. Even so, many still do.

SODIUM NITRITE
Found in: Bacon, hot dogs, lunchmeat, smoked fish, corned beef
The Dangers: Meat processors use sodium nitrite because it gives cured meat an appetizing red color (without it, hot dogs would be gray). Adding nitrites to food can lead to the formation of small amounts of potent cancer-causing chemicals (*nitrosamines*), especially in fried bacon. Several studies have linked nitrites with various types of cancer. "This would be at the top of my list of additives to cut from my diet," says Christine Gerbstadt, a spokesperson for the American Dietetic Association.

DIACETYL
Found in: "Butter"-flavored microwave popcorn and margarine
The Dangers: Small amounts exist in real butter, but the levels are much higher in processed butter-flavored foods. Although low levels are considered safe, workers in popcorn factories learned the hard way that prolonged exposure to diacetyl causes obstructive lung disease, which can be fatal. Following a lawsuit by the workers and widespread publicity about "Popcorn Worker's Lung" in 2007, most American food manufacturers switched to safer ingredients.

HYDROLYZED VEGETABLE PROTEIN (HVP)

Found in: Soups, hot dogs, lunchmeat, sauce mixes

The Dangers: Also known as "natural flavor," "soy protein," or "textured vegetable protein," HVP is vegetable (usually soybean) protein that's been boiled in hydrochloric acid and chemically broken down into amino acids. Used to enhance the flavor of food, it contains MSG, which has been shown to cause adverse reactions in some people. According to FDA rules, foods made with HVP do not have to be labeled as containing MSG.

POTASSIUM BROMATE

Found in: White flour, bread, rolls, and other baked goods

The Dangers: This additive is used to increase the volume of bread. Most bromate breaks down to form harmless bromide. However, bromate itself is proven to cause cancer in animals. It has been banned virtually worldwide, except in Japan and the United States. In 1999 the Center for Science in the Public Interest petitioned the FDA to ban bromate—but the petition failed. Only one state in the U.S. requires a cancer warning on the label of products containing bromate: California.

A LOSS OF APPETITE

So what *can* you eat that's 100% safe? Fruits and vegetables? Maybe, but most of them are sprayed with pesticides. Frozen vegetables? A lot of them are disinfected with formaldehyde. How about a yummy bowl of ice cream? Okay, but remember what makes it so creamy: a chemical called *arboxymethylcellulose*, which in one study produced tumors in 80% of the rats it was tested on. Bon apétit.

* * *

A BREATH OF STALE AIR

In the Netherlands, after a nationwide ban on tobacco smoking in bars and restaurants took effect, many patrons missed the nostalgic atmosphere that can only come from a smoke-filled lounge. To capitalize, a Dutch special effects company, Rain Showtechniek, sells (for about $900 U.S) a cigarette smoke machine that provides that "haze of yesteryear" without any unhealthy side effects.

Bats can be taught to do tricks.

HOLY CR*P!

News from the wild world of...religion.

• **In May 2006,** Clara Jean Brown, 62, of Daphne, Alabama, was standing in her kitchen praying for her family's safety during an intense thunderstorm. Just as she finished the prayer and said "Amen"...the kitchen blew up. A bolt of lightning had hit the ground across the street, traveled the length of an underground water pipe, and blasted a hole through the floor of her kitchen, sending concrete flying around the room and knocking her over. The house was severely damaged; Ms. Brown was okay. (Amen!)

• **Early-morning service** in a Catholic church in Rennertshofen, Germany, was disrupted on New Year's Day, 2001, by strange noises. Someone went to investigate—and found a man and woman having sex upstairs in the church's gallery. The couple fled, but a church employee recognized the man: He was a local police officer. The 26-year-old cop was suspended and faces three years in prison for "disruption of religious practice."

• **In front of** the Metro South Church in Trenton, Michigan, a series of strange signs began appearing in 2009—signs that said "Metro South Church sucks" and "Metro South makes me sick." Who made the signs? Satan. Not really—they were *signed* "Satan," but they were actually put up by the church. It was all part of an "edgy" ad campaign meant to attract younger people. "Jesus," Youth Pastor Adam Dorband said, "wants us to be creative."

• **Reverend Canon** David Parrott of London's St. Lawrence Jewry Church (a 17th-century Anglican church built near what was once a Jewish ghetto), asked his parishioners to bring their electronic communication gadgets—laptops, BlackBerrys, and so on—to church one Sunday in January 2010. Parrott had people pile them up on the altar—and then he blessed them. "By Your blessing," he intoned, "may these phones and computers, symbols of all the technology and communication in our daily lives, be a reminder to us that You are a God who communicates with us and who speaks by Your word." People were also asked to hold up their

---

A new scientific field, *neurotheology,* **studies what happens to the brain during a religious experience.**

cell phones during the blessing (although they had to be turned off first).

• **Officials from** the Russian Orthodox Church called police in November 2008 with an unusual complaint: One of their churches had been stolen. A 200-year-old church northeast of Moscow had been abandoned for a few months before a planned reopening. But while the church was closed, local villagers had dismantled it brick by brick and sold the pieces to a local businessman for one ruble each (about four cents U.S.). "Of course, this is blasphemy,' a church official said. "These people have to realize they committed a grave sin."

• **Reverend Dan Willis** of Lighthouse Church of All Nations in Alsip, Illinois, saw attendance at his church grow from about 1,600 to more than 2,500 in just five weeks in 2009. How'd he do it? At the end of each of the church's three Sunday services, Willis held a lottery—if he drew the number corresponding to your seat number on the pew, you won a prize of $500. (Two runners-up won $250.) Willis said he wanted to help out the congregation during these economically difficult times.

• **Nick Wallace,** 22, of Oxford, England, was born with muscular dystrophy. He told the nuns at the Douglas House hospice that he wanted to lose his virginity before he died. So Sister Frances Dominica helped Wallace arrange a date with a "sex worker" he found in a magazine ad (she went to his house when his parents weren't home). Afterward, Wallace admitted, "It was not emotionally fulfilling, but the lady was very pleasant." Sister Dominica defended setting up the date: "I know that some people will say, 'You are a Christian foundation—what are you thinking about?' But we are here for all faiths and none."

• **In November 2009,** the Church of God in Christ, one of the largest black churches in the U.S., ordained Johnny Lee Clary, 50, making him a minister. What made the event notable? Clary is not only white—he's a former Imperial Wizard of the Ku Klux Klan. After converting to Christianity, he left the KKK in 1990 (he had belonged to it since he was 14). Now he travels the world preaching against the evils of racism.

Der Waah! A German study found that within a week, newborn babies begin to cry with an accent.

DISORDER IN THE COURT

As "officers of the court," you'd think lawyers would consider it their duty to make the simple decisions that are necessary to get the legal process going. And usually they do. But not in these cases.

ROCKY RELATIONSHIP

Dispute: In a 2006 case between a utility company and an insurance company, two Tampa, Florida, lawyers for each side contested nearly every single thing that the other side did for more than a year. They couldn't even decide where to depose witnesses, even though their offices were in the same building. The plaintiff's attorney, David Pettinato, eventually filed a motion asking the court to pick a location, but Judge Gregory Presnell refused, noting that the attorneys ought to be able to resolve the matter "without enlisting the assistance of the federal courts."

Solution: Judge Presnell told them to meet on the front steps of the courthouse and "engage in one game of rock, paper, scissors." The winner would get to pick the deposition site. Presnell was widely criticized by members of the legal community, who thought his ruling invited public ridicule. But Matti Lesham of the USA Rock Paper Scissors League thought the judge made a wise decision. "When someone uses this great game to adjudicate any kind of dispute," he said, "it is a positive moment for the world."

DEFIANT TODDLERS

Dispute: In 2008 the state of Rhode Island and the town of Charleston, Rhode Island, were on the same side of a complicated Indian land case, but for months could not agree who would argue the case before the U.S. Supreme Court. Only one lawyer per side is allowed. The state wanted their lawyer, Theodore Olson (he argued and won the *Bush v. Gore* case for George W. Bush). Charleston preferred its own attorney, Joseph Larisa, who'd been

---

with the case for ten years. A motion was filed to allow both lawyers to appear; it was rejected.

Solution: Larisa suggested a coin toss—which both the governor and the state attorney general rejected. Governor Donald Carcieri's lawyer then suggested two coin tosses, one between Larisa and Olson and, if Larisa won, another between him and the attorney general (giving Larisa only a one in four chance of winning). Larisa rejected that plan. A spokesman for the attorney general's office called Larisa a "defiant toddler" and said, "The only thing that has made this the controversy that it is is Joe Larisa's ego." In the end, Larisa decided to back down and let the state have its pick...but only after being promised a seat at the counsel table.

BORDER PATROL

Dispute: *Waggoner v. WalMart Stores* was a wrongful-death suit. Ruth Waggoner alleged that the corporation was liable for the death of her 88-year-old husband, who was hit by an automatic door at one of its stores. Waggoner's attorney wanted to depose a WalMart representative, but the parties couldn't agree on where to do it. Waggoner and her son wanted it held in San Antonio, Texas; WalMart preferred its hometown of Bentonville, Arkansas. The decision eventually went to Judge James Nowlin.

Solution: "Surely," wrote the Texas judge, "the Defendant's corporate representative, a resident of Arkansas, would feel great humiliation by being forced to enter the home state of the legendary Texas Longhorns, who have wrought havoc on the Arkansas Razorbacks with an impressive 55–21 all-time series record. On the other hand, the Court is sympathetic with Plaintiff's position. Plaintiffs might enter Arkansas with a bit of trepidation as many residents of Arkansas are still seeking retribution for the 'Game of the Century,' in which James Street and Darrell Royal stunned the Razorbacks by winning the 1969 National Championship. Because the Court is sympathetic to both parties' positions, it has found a neutral site, intended to avoid both humiliation and trepidation of retribution." Judge Nowlin directed that the deposition be taken on the steps of the federal building that sits on the Arkansas-Texas border...and that each party remain on their side of the state line.

(OVER)BOARD GAMES

Board games are big business, and each year hundreds are released,
some hits…and some misses. Here are some of the misses.

Is the Pope Catholic? (1986) This game combines goofy, satirical humor with trivia questions about the doctrine and history of the Catholic Church. The ultimate object is to become pope, which you do by correctly answering trivia questions and earning rosary beads. But don't drink too much wine or spend all of your church's money on candy!

Orgy (1967) If you wanted to get in on the freewheeling sexual pursuits of the 1960s without *really* getting into them, you could buy the game of Orgy… which isn't an orgy at all, but a simple drinking game. Couples take turns pouring wine (or whatever liquid they want) out of a genie lamp called a *porron* into each other's mouths. The couple with the fewest spills wins.

Proud to Be Me! (1991) This game is supposed to make kids feel good about themselves by answering probing questions printed on cards, such as "Why do you love your family?" Then they get to read affirmations like "I am a good person." Naturally, there are no winners or losers in Proud to Be Me (because losing would make you feel bad about yourself).

Chutzpah! (1967) Marketed to Jewish people—or to those who enjoyed Jewish stereotypes—Chutzpah!'s object was to hoard money that you could then spend on teeth-capping or a move to Florida.

Pain Doctors (1996) This "Game of Recreational Surgery" was sort of an Operation for the '90s. Players portray mad doctors and vie to keep the patient healthy enough so that they can perform unnecessary elective surgery, as determined by drawing random "surgery cards."

Grade Up to Elite Cow (1986) Produced by the British Beef Association to teach kids how beef is processed and graded, the game encourages players to compete at breeding and selling the highest-quality cattle. It begins with a bull-semen auction.

43% of psychiatrists say they would self-medicate if they were depressed. 16% say they have.

FAT CITY

The media keeps telling us that the rate of obesity is skyrocketing in the United States. But the residents of one city really take the cake—and the ice cream, the donuts, the bacon bits...

W**E'RE NUMBER ONE!**
After the Centers for Disease Control (CDC) released the results of a 2008 study on obesity and related illnesses, the Associated Press crunched the numbers and singled out "America's unhealthiest city": Huntington, West Virginia. The area's 284,000 people lead the nation in obesity rates, heart disease, diabetes, and several other unhealthy conditions.

Located in the foothills of the Appalachian mountain range, Huntington has an economy that was centered around coal mining and manufacturing until the 1950s. But as those labor-intensive, calorie-burning jobs moved elsewhere, the fabric of the town changed. Joblessness and poverty have been on the rise ever since.

One thing that hasn't changed: the local diet. Fatty, fried, unhealthy (and totally delicious) food was—and still is—popular in Huntington. The deep-fried meats famous in the Southern U.S. and the fat-rich recipes brought over by English and German immigrants still make up the majority of the diet (they use lots of gravy). Because Huntington's economy is now comprised mostly of service-sector office jobs, those calories don't get burned off in the mines or at the factories anymore. Instead, they turn to fat. (Ironically, Huntington's largest employer is the healthcare industry.)

ABOVE AVERAGE
Huntington beat just about all of the CDC's national findings::
• National adult obesity rate: 34 percent. Huntington: 46 percent.
• National rate of adults who say they "never exercise": 25 percent. Huntington: 31 percent.
• National rate of adults who smoke cigarettes: 18 percent. Huntington: 25 percent.
• National rate of senior citizens who have no teeth: 30 percent. Huntington: 48 percent.

Noah's ark? In 2007 a deserted ship was discovered near China. On board: 5,000 live rare animals.

CLOGGED

Perhaps most telling of all, a quarter of older adults in the Huntington area have been diagnosed with coronary heart disease, characterized by fatty buildup in the arteries. That's two and a half times the national average. They also have higher rates of type 2 diabetes, which is caused by poor diet and inactivity. Here are two more alarming statistics *not* found in the CDC's report:

• Huntington is home to 200 pizza parlors—more than the number of gyms and health clubs in the *entire state* of West Virginia.

• The number of McDonald's restaurants per capita in U.S. is about one per 20,000 people; Huntington's rate is triple that.

When residents don't crave pizza or the Golden Arches, they can go to local favorite eateries, such as Big Loafer, Cam's Hams, DP Dough, or Fat Patty's. And every summer, the people come out en masse for the annual Hot Dog Festival.

THE SKINNY

Not surprisingly, all this negative press didn't go over too well in Huntington. When asked to comment on the CDC's findings, Mayor David Felinton (who weighs 233 pounds) said, "We've got more important things to worry about down at City Hall." Others complained that the CDC study was unfairly skewed against rural communities. According to a local doctor, Harry Tweel, there's a stubborn cultural mindset also at work: "People here have an attitude of 'You're not going to tell me what I can't eat. My parents ate that and my grandparents ate that.'"

Another local doctor, Thomas Dannals, is attempting to get his friends and neighbors off the couch and outside for some actual exercise, but it's been difficult. He announced plans to hold a marathon and triathlon on the same weekend as the hot dog festival, and has also been working to get an exercise trail built. But because of the 2008 recession, he hasn't been able to get much funding for either project.

The recession may have had other repercussions as well, as many Huntington residents blame the city's poor health on the faltering economy. "It needs to pick up first so people can afford to get healthy," 67-year-old Ronnie Adkins told a reporter…as he sat on the smoking porch of Huntington's Jolly Pirate Donut shop.

REALITY SHOWS, PART II

*More stories of behind-the-scenes betrayal, corruption,
and cheating on America's favorite reality shows.*

THE BIGGEST LOSER (NBC, 2004–present)
Premise: Obese people compete to lose the highest percentage of body weight. The winner takes home $250,000.
Story: First-season winner Ryan C. Benson claimed producers left
him out of a reunion special because he publicly admitted that he
fasted and dehydrated himself for the show until he was urinating
blood. Another contestant confessed to self-induced dehydration,
and two others were taken to the hospital after collapsing from
heat stroke during a one-mile race. Kai Hibbard, runner-up in Season 3, said she and other contestants would drink as little water as
possible the day before a weigh-in and, when the cameras were off,
would work out in heavy clothing to sweat off the pounds. Health
experts say that these are unhealthy ways to lose weight.

SURVIVOR (CBS, 2000–present)
Premise: A group of strangers are marooned at a remote location.
They must form "tribes" in order to survive and compete in various challenges. The winner receives $1 million.
Story: Although the producers claim they try to find "regular people" to compete, *Survivor*'s casting director, Lynne Spillman, says
that out of the thousands of applications they receive, very few
meet their two main requirements: good looks (like models) and
the ability to perform in front of a camera (like actors). So Spillman often hires model/actors—or, as she calls them, "mactors."
She admits that of the 19 contestants who competed in 2007's
Survivor: Fiji, 18 were recruited from talent agencies.

EXTREME MAKEOVER (ABC, 2002–07)
Premise: "Ugly ducklings" are transformed into "beautiful swans"
via changes in wardrobe, makeup, exercise…and plastic surgery.
Story: In 2005 contestant Deleese Williams filed a lawsuit against
Extreme Makeover. According to Williams, the producers forced
her sister to make false and cruel on-air remarks about Deleese's

appearance…something that made her sister feel so guilty that she later committed suicide. After a year of negotiations, Williams and the show's producers settled for an undisclosed amount.

EXTREME MAKEOVER: HOME EDITION
(ABC, 2003–present)

Premise: A down-on-their-luck family gets a free new house.

Story #1: Knowing that more people tune in when the family's plight is *very* sad, producers circulated an internal e-mail (which was later leaked to the press) instructing casting agents to look for "skin cancer, Lou Gehrig's disease, and muscular dystrophy." If a family had more than one child with Down syndrome, they were prime picking, as were those with a child who'd been killed by a drunk driver. The biggest find: a family with a kid suffering from *Progeria*, the "little old man disease."

Story #2: Five African-American kids—Charles, Michael, Charis, Joshua, and Jeremiah Higgins—were left orphans when their parents died in 2004. They were taken in by two Caucasian members of their church, Firipeli and Lokilani Leomiti. But the boys discovered later that it was all a ploy by the Leomitis to get on the show and win a free addition to their house. After the episode aired in 2005, the couple allegedly kicked the boys out. The siblings sued ABC and the Leomitis for fraud and emotional distress. The kids lost the case after ABC's lawyers argued that the five boys were only contracted to be "guests" in the Leomitis' home (which doesn't explain why, on the show, five bedrooms were added to the house).

THE BACHELOR (ABC, 2002–present)

Premise: Twenty-five women compete for the affections of a handsome, rich bachelor, who proposes marriage to the winner.

Story: According to contestant Jeannette Pawula, "The producers know that alcohol ignites emotions, and you get better responses for TV." Before the cameras rolled, she said, the women were given several glasses of wine. Then, if the sparks didn't fly, the cameras shut off and trays of shots were carted out. "If you combine no sleep and no food with lots of alcohol," said contestant Erica Rose, "emotions are going to run high and people are going to act crazy."

The hairy frog breaks its own bones and pokes the ends through its skin to create defensive claws.

I WAS BLIND, BUT NOW I SEE

The lesson here: Never give up hope (and get a second opinion).

I WAS (NEARLY) BLIND... In 1941, when Malcolm Darby of Rutland, England, was two years old, he contracted measles and was left with extremely poor eyesight. Throughout his life, he had to wear thick eyeglasses and could barely see. Then, when Darby was 70, he suffered a stroke. A blood clot lodged in his brain and required surgery.

BUT NOW I SEE. When Darby woke up after the operation, he couldn't speak, but he could see a nurse in his room carrying a newspaper under her arm. And he saw not only the nurse, but the words printed in the newspaper, clear as day...without his glasses on. Doctors said that it's not uncommon for patients to *lose* their eyesight after a stroke, but it's extremely rare for anyone's eyesight to improve. Darby has since recovered and is enjoying his new lease on life...except for one thing: "Before the stroke, I could speak French, and now I just can't get a word of it out."

I WAS DEAF... Emma Hassell was perfectly healthy—until she had a miscarriage in 2002 and was told that she may never be able to conceive another child. Then, two years later, the 21-year-old British woman got engaged. While getting ready for her engagement dinner, Hassell went upstairs to take a shower when she noticed that her hearing was "muffled." She heard a loud pop—and then couldn't hear anything at all. "I remember shouting down to my mum that I was deaf," she said, "but I don't know how it happened." Doctors didn't, either. They found nothing physically wrong with her ears. Their conclusion: It was psychosomatic. Hassell tried hypnotherapy, counseling, and acupuncture, but she remained completely deaf. For the next six months, she and her fiancé struggled to adjust to her handicap. A week before Christmas, Hassell visited her doctor, who had great news for her: She was pregnant!

BUT NOW I HEAR: That evening, Hassell was home alone

watching *Will & Grace* on television. As she was reading the closed-captioned subtitles, it seemed like she could actually hear the words. She thought her mind was playing tricks on her. Then she started banging on a table and realized she *could* hear. Elated, she phoned her fiancé: "I can hear! I can hear!" He remained silent. "Now is not the time to be speechless," she said. Doctors are still at a loss to explain how Hassell lost her hearing...and how she got it back. "I'd been dreading Christmas," she said, "but not anymore!"

I WAS (HALF) BLIND... While Don Karkos was serving on a Navy tanker in World War II, an explosion sent shrapnel flying into his face. When he woke up in the hospital, he was told that his right eye was permanently blind. Doctors offered to remove it, but Karkos said they might as well keep it in there "for looks." He returned to his home in Maine and started a family. Having one functioning eye was difficult (he often bumped into walls and other people), but Karkos managed. By the time he was in his 80s, he was still working, tending horses at Monticello Raceway in New York. One day in 2006, he was in the stable adjusting some equipment on a horse named My Buddy Chimo. "I reached underneath his chest," he recalled. "And when I did, my head was right next to his. All of a sudden, Chimo turned and he whacked me one on the head, and that was it." It was the hardest that Karkos had been hit since the explosion in 1942.

BUT NOW I SEE. Karkos spent the rest of the day in a haze; nothing seemed "right." And that night, as he was walking down his hallway, he realized why. He put his hand over his good eye...and he could still see. "Holy s***!" was all he managed to say. The incident became known as the "Monticello Miracle," and My Buddy Chimo has become a star—people come to the track just to touch him. "I'm getting him a big bag of carrots for Christmas," Karkos said. "Do you know what a doctor would have charged for this?"

I WAS DEAD... In January 2008, doctors told the family of 65-year-old Raleane "Rae" Kupferschmidt that she was brain-dead. It had been three weeks since she'd suffered a massive cerebral hemorrhage, and her vegetative state showed no signs of improving. In keeping with her wishes, a feeding tube was removed and life support was turned off. Given only hours to live, Kupferschmidt was taken to her Lake Elmo, Minnesota, home to die. She lay in her bed while her family gathered and made funeral arrangements.

BUT NOW I LIVE: To keep her mother hydrated, Kupferschmidt's daughter, Lisa Sturm, wet her lips with an ice cube…and the old woman started sucking on it. "I knew suckling is a very basic brain-stem function," said Sturm, "so I didn't get real excited. But when I did it again, she just about sucked the ice cube out of my hand. So I leaned down and asked, 'Mom, are you in there?'" Her mother quietly replied, "Yes." Sturm nearly fell over in shock. Kupferschmidt was rushed back to the hospital, where doctors drained blood from her skull to relieve pressure on her brain. Within a few weeks, Kupferschmidt was walking on her own and living a normal life again. She remembers almost nothing about her coma, except for: "Angels. They were here to help me, to help me get over this."

I WAS PARALYZED…In 1988 David Blancarte of Manteca, California, wrecked his motorcycle and ended up in a wheelchair. The former boxer and dancer went into a deep depression, but still managed to move on with life, eventually marrying and having a family. Then, 21 years after his accident, Blancarte, 48, was reportedly bitten by a poisonous brown recluse spider in his California home.

BUT NOW I WALK. The bite sent Blancarte to a hospital, where a nurse noticed his legs twitching. After he was treated for the bite, the nurse enrolled Blancarte in a physical therapy program…and he slowly learned to walk again. A local TV station latched onto the story and within weeks, headlines all over the world read: "SPIDER BITE HEALS PARAPLEGIC!" News anchors hailed it as a "medical miracle" that "offers a ray of hope to others who are paralyzed."

ACTUALLY…The spider bite (which was never even confirmed—brown recluses don't live in California) had little to do with Blancarte's recovery except to get him to the hospital, where the astute nurse noticed that the nerves in his legs were still working. And, adding insult to recovery, the media frenzy attracted the attention of police—who arrested Blancarte on an outstanding warrant for domestic abuse. But at least he learned to walk again, which is nice.

A computer program designed to grade school essays gave Ernest Hemingway a failing grade.

WEIRD, WITH A SIDE OF ANIMALS

Some real-life news stories—of the odd variety—with some animals thrown in (sometimes literally).

VERY JACKIE CHAN

Verity Beman and her husband, Beat Ettlin, were sleeping peacefully in their home in Canberra, Australia, one night in March 2009 when a six-foot-tall kangaroo crashed through their bedroom window and landed on their bed. "It leaped in, this martial-arts kind of figure," Beman told reporters the next day. "It was very Jackie Chan." The kangaroo began thrashing around the house. Ettlin, in a frantic effort to get it outside, grabbed the animal in a headlock, dragged it to the front door, and threw it out. Beman said it was a good thing her husband was from Switzerland, because an Aussie would have never attempted to get a kangaroo in a headlock. "They would be fully aware of the risk," she said. She added that she was very proud of her husband's brave actions. "I called him my hero," she said. "My hero in undies."

DOES THIS FISH TASTE CORPSEY?

A newspaper reporter in the city of Agartala in northeastern India decided to go undercover in 2009 to investigate a rumor about the city's trade in *hilsa* fish, a local delicacy. The reporter pretended to be a fish trader who needed space to store a load of hilsa he'd just bought in neighboring Bangladesh. He received an offer from one of the city's hospitals, where employees said they could sell him space to store the fish in the morgue…in cooling boxes…alongside human cadavers. Other traders had been storing fish with dead bodies for years, they told him, before the fish were delivered to the city's many street markets. They insisted that it was much cheaper than conventional storage methods, which saved the fish traders money, and it also brought in some extra cash for the hospital's employees. The reporter's exposé caused an outcry. "It is absolutely disgusting," state Health Minister Tapan Chakrabarty said, promising that an investigation into the morgue-stored fish would begin immediately.

RABBITS: THE HORROR

In October 2009, Swedish newspapers reported that several thousand rabbits were shot every year in parks in the capital city of Stockholm. That's not uncommon for large cities with rabbit overpopulation problems, but they also reported something that most of Stockholm's citizens were unaware of: Once they were killed, the rabbits' carcasses were frozen, shipped to the city of Karlskoga in central Sweden...and incinerated as fuel in the city's heating plant. The heat generated by the thousands of dead rabbits helps to heat homes in the area. Animal rights groups, the reports said, were calling for an end to the bunny-burning.

RABBITS: THE HORROR RETURNS

On the South Island of New Zealand, the town of Waiau (population 400) has a different way of dealing with its dead rabbits: a throwing contest. Kicking off the town's three-day pig-hunting festival every October is the "dead rabbit throw," in which local children compete to see who can throw a dead rabbit the farthest. The town banned the contest in 2009 after receiving complaints from the Society for the Prevention of Cruelty to Animals. One angry resident defended the rabbit toss, claiming that the ban was "political correctness gone mad." An SPCA representative disagreed, saying the event sent the message to kids that dead bodies were a "form of entertainment." The ASPCA person asked, "Do you throw your dead grandmother around for a joke at her funeral?"

*   *   *

CHRISTIANIDDLY-DIDDLIANITY

According to *Christianity Today*, the name that most U.S. college students associate with Christianity is Jesus Christ. Who's second? Is it Mother Theresa? Billy Graham? The Pope? Nope. It's Ned Flanders, Homer's church-lovin' neighbor on *The Simpsons*.

In Australia, wearing hot pink pants on Sunday afternoon is illegal.

QUICK FIXES

Bob Dylan sang, "There's a brand-new gimmick every day, just to try and take somebody's money away." (And that was before informercials.)

COMPLAINT: "I can't stop eating these tasty, fatty treats!"
SOLUTION: Aroma-Trim
EXPLANATION: To curb your appetite, just hold the plastic Aroma-Trim whiffer under your nose. It smells just like human vomit, instantly turning that sweet treat into an object of disgust. As one satisfied infomercial participant exclaimed: "Now I don't even *want* to finish that donut!" Price: $49.95 (instruction booklet and VHS tape included).

COMPLAINT: "My eyelashes are thinning out!"
SOLUTION: Latisse
EXPLANATION: Designed to combat the effects of *eyelash hypotrichosis*, a condition characterized by thin or inadequate eyelashes, Latisse is a prescription-only chemical solution. Just use the applicator to dab some Latisse onto your thinning lashes, and you'll be rewarded with a miraculous burst of new eyelash growth. But be careful: If your aim is off, small hairs may start growing from the inside of your eye, or from your forehead, your cheek, your chin, your elbow, or any other part of your skin touched by... Latisse. Price: $150 for 1 bottle and 60 applicators.

COMPLAINT: "My bust is so large that my car's seat belt cuts into me!"
SOLUTION: Tiddy Bear
EXPLANATION: The Tiddy Bear is a small stuffed animal that looks like a spread-eagle Beanie Baby. You attach it to your car's shoulder belt via a strap on its back, then slide the Tiddy Bear until its face rests between your breasts. According to the manufacturer, it relieves pressure on the bust and shoulder. Price: $14.95.

COMPLAINT: "I need a tan for my hot date tonight, but I don't have time to go to a tanning salon!"

It's easier for a person with a severe mental illness to get arrested than to get treatment.

SOLUTION: Comodynes Self Tanning Wipes for Face and Body

EXPLANATION: Reportedly used by "Christina Applegate, Lindsay Lohan, and the entire cast of *Friends*," these towelettes soaked with a mild skin dye will tan you up in just two to three hours. Do they work? Kind of, according to one online review: "I had to use two for my legs, one for my arms, and one for my torso and most of my back. I used up a half of the box for one application. In a few hours, I saw color develop. It wasn't perfect, but it wasn't orange, either. But still, not a disaster." Price: $12.99 for an 8-pack.

COMPLAINT: "I want a butt like J-Lo's, but mine sags!"

SOLUTION: The Brazilian Butt Lift

EXPLANATION: This reverse-liposuction procedure, invented by cosmetic surgeon Ricardo Rodriguez, harvests extra fat from your stomach or neck. Then the fat is spun in a centrifuge until it's "purified." After that, according to Dr. Rodriguez, "The process involves hundreds of fat injections, designed to fill the upper quadrant of your buttocks with fat so that the butt appears lifted and perky." Price: $16,000 to $18,000.

COMPLAINT: "I want a face-lift, but I can't afford one!"

SOLUTION: Rejuvenique

EXPLANATION: If you don't mind temporarily looking like Jason from the *Friday the 13th* movies, then try Rejuvenique. This battery-operated facial mask (with eyeholes) sends electric shocks into your face muscles, causing them to contract and ultimately tighten up. According to its inventor, George Springer, wearing the Rejuvenique mask is "like doing eight sit-ups a second with your face." Price: Four easy payments of only $49.75 (9-volt battery included).

COMPLAINT: "I've got no hair on the top of my head!"

SOLUTION: Ronco's GLH

EXPLANATION: GLH stands for "Great-Looking Hair," and it's easy to apply. Just spray it on your bald spot, and *voilà!*—you have a brown spot that kind of looks like hair when viewed from across the street. Price: $19.95.

FUNERAL HOME HORRORS

It's a good thing these people aren't in charge of taking care of the living.

A VERY PERSONAL EFFECT

In 2009 a New Mexico woman died in a car accident in Utah. Her body was taken to the Serenicare Funeral Home in the nearby town of Draper, and then was transferred to the DeVargas Funeral Home in Espanola Valley, New Mexico. Not long after the woman's burial, her family received a package from one of the funeral homes containing her "personal effects." They looked inside, and there, along with Grandma's wallet, jewelry, and scarf, was her brain…in a plastic bag with her name and the word "brain" printed on it. The family sued both of the funeral homes. "No loved one's brain," their lawyer said, "should ever be part of those belongings." The owner of the Utah funeral home said that it wasn't uncommon for brains to be shipped separately from bodies after accidents, but he had no explanation for why one might be shipped to a family. The lawsuit has yet to be settled; the brain has since been buried with the woman's body.

RECYCLING GONE BAD

In summer 2009, a mass grave that contained hundreds of corpses—and appeared to be recently dug—was discovered on the outskirts of the historic Burr Oak Cemetery in Alsip, Illinois. After an investigation, four cemetery workers were arrested for digging up more than 200 bodies and reselling the plots they were buried in. The cemetery was closed for four months while authorities combed through spotty records and old photographs of headstones—some dating back to the 1800s—to return the departed to their rightful resting places. "It's going to be a day-by-day, grave-by-grave situation," said one official. Among those buried at Burr Oak: music legends Willie Dixon and Dinah Washington; former heavyweight boxing champ Ezzard Charles; and Emmett Till, whose 1955 murder helped launch the Civil Rights movement.

Actual therapy animals: Sadie the "bipolar assistance parrot" and Richard the "agoraphobia monkey."

WATCH YOUR STEP

"Sometimes when families asked for their ashes back, the plastic container was too small," says a disgruntled former employee of Co-op Funeralcare in Dunfermline, Scotland. So instead of finding a larger container, workers allege that the funeral home's manager, Bob Aitchison, directed them to mix the extra ashes with sand and spread them on a handicapped-access ramp to prevent people from slipping in wet weather. (Some of the remains, reportedly, had even been tracked into the office.) Other charges against Co-op Funeralcare: After the staff lost the ashes of one deceased person, Aitchison gave the grieving family the unclaimed remains of someone who'd been dead for 50 years. And coffins that had been sold as "new" had actually been used to transport bodies, then cleaned up with felt markers and air fresheners.

ONE FOR THE ROAD

When Tito Vasquez's body didn't show up for his funeral in Bogotá, Colombia, friends and relatives went looking for him. Hours later, they finally located the corpse several miles away, in the back of a hearse...which was parked in front of a motel bar. The hearse driver apologized and explained that he had gotten "distracted" after stopping in for a beer on the way to the funeral.

*　　*　　*

ANOTHER SACRED TRADITION BITES THE DUST

According to the U.K.'s Bereavement Register, the most popular song at English funerals in 2009 was "Goodbye My Lover" by James Blunt. Also making the top 10 were funeral standards such as Elton John's "Candle in the Wind" and the Righteous Brothers' "Unchained Melody." However, the Register also conducted a survey of the top ten "alternative" funeral songs in England. That list included Monty Python's "Always Look on the Bright Side of Life," AC/DC's "Highway to Hell," "Ding Dong, the Witch is Dead" from *The Wizard of Oz*, Queen's "Another One Bites the Dust," and Sid Vicious's raucous cover of Frank Sinatra's "My Way" (which may in fact lead to even more funerals in the future—see page 413).

Although it's illegal, there is a thriving black market in Italy for a cheese containing live maggots.

FLIGHT 297

*What exactly happened on this airline flight in 2009? It's
one man's story against the airline's story—with a
lot of other parties confusing it even more.*

TERROR ON THE TARMAC

In late November 2009, Tedd Petruna, a NASA employee
from Texas, wrote an e-mail to his friend describing something that happened to him on board a Houston-bound plane as
it was taxiing to its runway in Atlanta. Petruna wrote that he
was sitting in first class on AirTran Flight 297 when "a group of
11 Muslim men in full attire peppered themselves throughout
the plane." They walked around despite being told to sit down,
took pictures of fellow passengers, and talked loudly to each
other in Arabic. Two of the men in the back of the plane were
even watching a pornographic film on a camcorder. From
Petruna's e-mail:

> They are only permitted to do this prior to Jihad. If a Muslim man
> goes into a strip club, he has to view the woman via mirror with
> his back to her. (Don't ask me…I don't make the rules, but I've
> studied.) The 3rd stewardess informed them that they were not to
> have electronic devices on at this time. To which one of them said
> "Shut up, infidel dog!"

TAKE 'EM OUT

Petruna and, as he wrote, "another Texan" got up and started
wrestling with two of the men. Petruna yelled, "You WILL sit
down or you will get off this plane!" After the Texans got the Arab
men back in their seats, "Three TSA [Transportation Security
Administration] officers and four cops burst into the plane, and the
11 men were escorted away." Then the plane returned to the gate,
where all of the luggage was removed but the passengers remained
on board. A little while later, all 11 men got back on board and
quietly took their seats. But the flight crew was visibly shaken—
they refused to fly with the men, so they were replaced by another
crew. The passengers, led by Petruna, also refused to fly, so the captain cancelled the flight. Petruna concluded: "The terrorists want-

ed to see how TSA would handle it, how the crew would handle it, and how the passengers would handle it. The threat is real."

START SPREADING THE NEWS

Petruna's friend who received the e-mail, Gene Hackemack, forwarded it to his friends with this message added to the beginning: "In my opinion, the Muslims are all getting very brave now, since they have one of their own in the White House...Thank God for people like Tedd Petruna." From there, the story was reprinted on several right-wing news sites. "The Project 9.12," a Web site run by Fox News commentator Glenn Beck, hailed Petruna as a hero. Right-wing blogger Debbie Schlussel said that Petruna confirmed to her on the phone that the events happened as he said they did. Schlussel wrote: "WAKE. UP. AMERICA. We are under siege."

THE AIRLINE'S DENIAL

As the story gained more traction in the press, AirTran released a point-by-point rebuttal that basically said that Petruna made the whole thing up. According to the airline:

• The men allegedly watching porn were in the back, so there was no way Petruna could have known what they were doing.

• There were 13 men in the group, not 11. They sat throughout the plane because they were unable to book seats near each other.

• They were not adorned in "full Muslim attire"—they were dressed "like any other passenger."

• At no time did TSA or law enforcement officials board the plane, and there were no altercations with other passengers or crew. (And the flight was not cancelled, just delayed.)

• A replacement flight crew did take over. AirTran explained that this is a common practice due to delays and scheduling conflicts. (None of the flight crew talked to reporters, nor did any of the 13 men in question, whose names weren't released in press reports.)

• Tedd Petruna's connecting flight to Atlanta was late—he arrived 26 minutes *after* flight 297 boarded. "After conducting additional research, we have verified, according to flight manifests, that Theodore Petruna was never actually on board the flight."

IT'S A CONSPIRACY!

AirTran's denials only prompted allegations from the right that it was covering up the incident because it didn't want to offend Muslims. Another passenger, a Texas chaplain named Keith Robinson, accused AirTran of letting the men back on so they wouldn't sue (the airline had recently settled a lawsuit by a Middle Eastern man who was kicked off a flight for acting suspiciously). But Robinson wasn't actually on the plane either. He was, however, at the gate when the flight crew deplaned afterward: "You could tell something was going on," he told a Houston news station. "The feeling that I have from what I observed is there was intentional intimidation. It was almost an ethnic bullying situation. By putting the men back on board, AirTran decided it was better to emotionally traumatize the remaining passengers on Flight 297 for the remainder of the flight."

Making the story even more complicated, two passengers who were actually on the plane confirmed AirTran's story. Nancy Deveikis, who was sitting behind one of the Arab men, said the whole thing was a "big miscommunication"—he was just looking at pictures. The flight attendant grew frustrated because he didn't speak English, so she took his camera away from him. It was then that the man's friend, who was sitting nearby, offered to speak to TSA as the man's interpreter to clear the matter up. Another passenger told reporters that Petruna is "living in a fantasy world."

PETRUNA'S REVISION

Petruna said he never expected his story to be forwarded all over the Internet. He refused to answer reporters' questions but insisted that he was on that plane. However, he said that he "embellished" many of the facts in his e-mail to impress his friend. He admitted that the men weren't wearing Muslim attire and they weren't taking pictures of people. Still, he maintains that AirTran isn't telling the complete story, either. He declined to say anything else because he's "in the middle of a lawsuit about this right now." But according to an AirTran official, the airline hasn't received a subpoena from Petruna or his lawyers.

The Federal Aviation Administration said it found no evidence of safety violations. After a brief investigation, the TSA ruled it a "customer-service issue." As far as AirTran is concerned, the matter is closed.

IT'S A RECESSION!

In 2008 the world was jolted by a steep economic downturn.
And, as these stories prove, when the money starts
slipping away, people tend to go nuts.

THE PENSIONERS GANG

Six German retirees, all in their 70s, collectively lost $3 million after their financial advisor, James Amburn, invested their money in a Florida real estate deal that went bad. Enraged, the six elderly men attacked Amburn outside his home, hit him on the head with a walker, wrapped him in duct tape, put him in the trunk of a car, and drove him to the basement of one their homes. Once there, the pensioners (including two retired doctors) chained Amburn up, beat him, burned him with cigarettes, and demanded that he get their money back...or they'd kill him. Amburn almost escaped on the second day when he was let outside for a cigarette. But as he was running down the street, his kidnappers shouted that he was a burglar. The neighbors kept their distance; Amburn was recaptured and dragged back inside. He agreed to pay them with his own money, so he wrote out a fax for a cash transfer—but on the bottom he scribbled a coded message for help. After four days in captivity, Amburn was rescued by police. After a doctor checked out the kidnappers (they were tired after all the activity), they were hauled off to jail.

FOLLOWING THE ECONOMY OFF A CLIFF

Chinese newspapers reported in Febrary 2009 that a "Mr. Fan," a successful business owner, had five mistresses. But after the economy tanked, he could afford only one. So Fan decided to hold a "Best Mistress" contest. He hired an instructor from a modeling agency to help judge which of his girlfriends possessed the most beauty—and the most talent at such tasks as singing and guzzling alcohol. The winner would receive a free apartment, a monthly allowance of $738, and of course, Mr. Fan's affections (when he wasn't with his wife). But after the contest was over, one of the losers, a woman named Yu, graciously offered to take her four competitors and soon-to-be-former lover on a sightseeing jaunt. She drove

---

Studies show: Weightlifters can handle heavier weights when working out in blue gyms.

them up a scenic mountain road…and off a cliff. Yu was killed in the crash, and all of the passengers were badly injured. Police initially ruled the crash an accident until Yu's parents showed them her suicide note. In the ensuing scandal, Fan was forced to shut down his business and pay compensation to Yu's parents for her death. All four mistresses left Mr. Fan. And his wife—who, until then, hadn't known about the other women—sued for divorce.

BLONDES TO THE RESCUE

Of all the nations in the European Union, Latvia may have been hit the hardest by the recession, with frightened, suddenly penniless citizens rioting in the capital city of Riga. A group called the Latvian Blondes Association came up with a unique way to beat back the financial gloom: Under a banner proclaiming "Make the World a Brighter Place," hundreds of blonde women dressed in pink and white marched through Riga, accompanied by an orchestra and a fleet of well-dressed lapdogs. It was all part of "Blonde Weekend," which also featured a golf and tennis tournament. Organizer Marika Gederte declared the event a success, saying, "People need positive emotions, especially in hard times." She insisted that there was no discrimination against brunettes or redheads, and she is hoping to make the Riga parade an annual event.

MAKING CRIME PAY

• In Nigeria, where motorcycles are a popular form of transportation, a new law requires riders to wear helmets. The money collected from violators would be a boon to the cash-strapped nation, but many cash-strapped riders can't afford to pay the tickets…or even buy helmets. Result: Riders have started wearing cooking pots on their heads, as well as dried gourds and hollowed-out pumpkins.

• A Michigan postal carrier, John Auito, fell behind on his mortgage. To save his home from foreclosure, he stole postage stamps and then sold them on eBay at a 15-percent discount. Business was so good that Auito had sold $20,000 worth of stamps before authorities caught up with him. He was arrested for stealing government property.

• Another effect of the recession: more bank robberies, especially during the holidays. Just before Christmas in 2009, a stout Santa

Claus, dressed in his trademark red suit (along with dark sunglasses) entered a bank in Nashville, Tennessee. When a teller asked him to remove the shades, Santa pulled out a gun and told her to fill his Santa sack with cash. He then drove away and was never found. Bank workers reported that the man was very "jovial" and had told them that times were tough, and he was robbing the bank because "Santa has to pay his elves."

THE RECESSION IN BRIEF

Retail sales plummeted in 2009. Among the hardest-hit items: men's underwear. Apparently, say retailers, the less underwear they sell, the worse the financial prognosis. Men just don't seem to replace their boxers and briefs when times are tight. (Uncle John can confirm this.)

VIRTUAL RELIEF

• In Tokyo, workers suffering from financial frustration can head to "The Venting Place" in a busy shopping district. For a small fee, customers can smash china cups and plates against a concrete block.

• Are you tired of seeing phrases like "rising unemployment," "growing foreclosures," and "increasingly cash-strapped"? There's a Web site called Recession Blocker that automatically filters out those kinds of phrases from news articles so you don't have to keep reading them over and over.

• There's another Web site called Shoot the Banker. People who are angry with their banker can fire a robotic paintball gun that shoots real paintballs at a live actor playing the role of a wealthy, arrogant bank owner.

*   *   *

TWO WEEKS' NOTICE

In September 2008, Alan Fishman was appointed CEO of Washington Mutual bank and received a $7.5 million "signing bonus." Just 17 days later, the bank collapsed and was temporarily taken over by government regulatory bodies. Fishman was no longer needed, but his contract with WaMu guaranteed him $11.6 million for a premature exit. So, for just over two weeks on the job, Fishman netted $19.1 million.

John Wheeler coined the term "black hole" in 1967, two years before the first black hole was discovered.

A BODY OF CASH

Need some extra cash? You could get a second job or sell off your CD collection. Or you could try selling something a bit more…biological. Sound yucky? Don't let that put you off—it's a serious business.

BLOOD BANKS. Technically, it's illegal to sell blood. You're actually selling "plasma"—the yellowish base of blood that transports nutrients to your body's cells. Blood banks collect plasma from donors (18 million people donated in 2008) and then sell it to hospitals, which use it for transfusions. So how do you go about selling your blood? Find a blood bank (they're often in the seedier part of town, or near a college), and pass the screening. Drug users are excluded, as is anyone who's gotten a tattoo in the past year—it's a hepatitis risk. Blood banks also don't accept anyone with a communicable disease (for obvious reasons) or major health problems. You'll relax on a reclining chair while a medical technician sticks a needle in your arm. Thirty minutes later, you'll be one fluid bag of plasma poorer, but about $30 (and a glass of juice) richer.

SPERM BANKS. They may elicit chuckles, but sperm banks are a very important part of helping women or couples conceive children when they are not otherwise physically able to do so. And it's a $75-million-a-year industry. Sperm banks and fertility clinics don't accept just anybody—donors have to be pretty impressive guys for strangers to want to use their chromosomes. Standards vary, but most facilities want men who are healthy, have a relatively clean family medical history, are at least 5'10" tall, and are college-educated. Average payout: around $100 per "donation."

EGG BANKS. Eggs are harvested from a woman's ovaries and are used to conceive a child by combining them with donated sperm, then implanting one in the mother-to-be's uterus. The most sought-after donors are women between the ages of 18 and 32 who are in generally good health and have a clean family medical history. The donor takes daily hormone-booster shots for a month. Then, at a clinic, she's sedated and 10–15 eggs are extracted via a large needle. It's a much more physically taxing process than sperm donation, so the payout is much larger: as much as $10,000.

In 1987 Peoria, IL, paid a PR firm $60,000 to help counter its image as America's most average city.

THE JACKSON 7

Michael Jackson had 7 letters in both his first and last names. Born in 1958 (19 + 58 = 77), he was his parents' 7th child. His two biggest hits stayed at #1 for 7 weeks. His three biggest albums each produced 7 top 40 hits. He signed his will on 7/7/02. Exactly 7 years later his memorial was held on 7/7/09. Here are 7 more strange stories surrounding the death of the King of Pop.

1 EERIE PREDICTION. In January 2009, the *National Enquirer* ran this headline: "MICHAEL JACKSON IS DYING, HAS ONLY SIX MONTHS TO LIVE, PALS FEAR." According to the story, Jackson was battling a rare genetic disorder that required him to undergo a lung transplant in order to save his life, but his health was further deteriorating because of an addiction to painkillers and alcohol. A source close to Jackson said at the time, "It's tragic. His condition is just so far gone, I'd be surprised if he lasts six months." (He lasted five months.)

2. BUG ZAPPERS. According to the family's lawyer, Brian Oxman, Jackson was terrified in spring 2009 that "people would kill him to somehow try to take control of the Beatles back catalogue." Jackson owned a share of the $1 billion publishing rights to the inventory of Beatles' songs. Just four days before his death, Jackson reportedly told a close friend, "I'm better off dead. I don't have anywhere left to turn. I'm done."

3. A THRILLER OF A CONSPIRACY. Shortly after Jackson's death in 2009, his older sister, LaToya, claimed that Michael was murdered: "Not just one person was involved, rather it was a conspiracy of people who didn't have his best interest at heart." A month later, the L.A. County Coroner ruled the death a homicide, caused by a lethal combination of drugs. Police focused their investigation on one of those people in Jackson's inner circle, his physician, Dr. Conrad Murray…who had allegedly administered Propofol, a powerful anesthetic, to Jackson shortly before his death. (Was MJ's death a murder? Stay tuned to a future *Bathroom Reader* to find out.)

4. VIRTUAL CONFUSION. Jackson's sudden end sent shock waves across cyberspace: Only seconds after his death was

---

announced, traffic doubled on the microblogging site Twitter, temporarily shutting it down. Google's search engine was similarly inundated, causing the service to issue an error message when users entered Jackson's name. (Google's computers interpreted the surge as an attack from hackers.) The confusion led many to believe the news was a hoax. After gossip blogger Perez Hilton wrote, "Jackson is lying or making himself sick," several mainstream news sites reported that. Some actual hoaxers used the confusion as an opportunity to spread rumors about other celebrity deaths, including a claim that actor Jeff Goldblum was killed in a fall while filming a movie in New Zealand. (He wasn't.)

5. BAD LEGISLATION. A few days after Jackson died, U.S. Rep. Sheila Jackson Lee (D-TX) proposed a nonbinding resolution that honored the King of Pop's contributions "to the world on behalf of America." At Jackson's memorial, Lee held up a copy of the resolution and promised it would be debated on the House floor. However, when she arrived in Congress the following week, the resolution was met by jeers on both sides of the aisle, including Speaker of the House Nancy Pelosi, who said that the bill would "open up contrary views that are not necessary at this time." (In other words, Jackson's highly publicized legal problems would have made it controversial.) Undaunted, Lee promised, "We will work with this legislation as long as necessary." It was never passed.

6. THE NOSE KNOWS. For years, fans have wondered if Jackson's nose was his own—or was it a prosthetic? That question may have been answered when it was reported that someone had stolen the artificial appendage while Jackson's body lay in a Los Angeles morgue, leaving behind, according to press reports, "a small, dark hole surrounded by bits of cartilage" in the deceased singer's surgically altered face. Police have yet to find the nose.

7. SPACE ODDITY. There were hundreds of tributes to the fallen singer in summer 2009, but here's one that never came to be: The Iowa State Fair had originally planned to feature a butter sculpture of Jackson performing his signature "Moonwalk" dance. The idea was nixed after 65% of 100,000 voters rejected it in an online poll. The butter sculpture was replaced with one commemorating astronaut Neil Armstrong's *actual* moon walk.

...devoted 93% of their air time to covering the story.

CRIMINALLY ODD

Featuring a reincarnated cat, a crook with image issues, a getaway driver who couldn't drive, and heroic tobacco juice.

KIDNAPPED!
In April 2009, James Williams's mother received some startling text messages on her cell phone: "we have ur son"; "pay $250 or we kill him"; "wire $ to the walmart in milwaukee"; "dont call cops." She did call the cops, and when they traced the calls, they found Williams, 23, a few miles away in Kenosha, Wisconsin. He was sitting in his mother's van—alone—feverishly texting more ransom messages to her. James was arrested and sentenced to 60 days in jail and one year's probation.

BURNED!
Sharon Shelton, 66, the second ex-wife of Gerald Shelton of Madison, North Carolina, sent a cryptic, letter to Gerald's third ex-wife: "If you want to get even with him, burn the house down." Ex-wife #3 turned the letter over to the police, so Sharon decided to do it herself: In October 2009, she broke into Gerald's house, poured gasoline on his coffee table, lit it up, and ran away. Luckily, Gerald had a large, plastic spittoon on the coffee table—and the heat melted it, causing tobacco juice to spill out and extinguish the fire. Sharon was charged with attempted arson.

INCARCERATED!
In 2009 Peter Koenig, a convicted bank robber serving five years in a German prison, went to court for the right to receive visits...from his cat, Gisele. Koenig, a practicing Buddhist, believes Gisele is the reincarnation of his mother. "I know it is mummy," he told the British newspaper *The Telegraph*. "She looks after me just the way she did. I need to see her like other prisoners see their wives and children." The request was refused. "While we respect the religious freedom of individuals," the judge said, "the accused has not been able to furnish proof that his deceased mother has been reborn in a cat." (The judge added that Koenig could always just write letters to the cat.)

A company called Drink Safe Texas sells bar coasters that test drinks for date-rape drugs.

DISARMED!

Four men from Essex, England, robbed a jewelry store in September 2009. They ran outside and jumped into a waiting car driven by their friend, 18-year-old John Smith. One problem: Smith has no arms below his elbows, so his fellow crooks had to help him steer and change gears. They made it 30 miles before they lost control of the car and crashed. All four were arrested. Said Smith's mother, "Because of his naïveté, he did not fully accept that by sitting in the car he was actually involved in the burglary."

BURGLED!

A man broke into a home in Woodbridge, New Jersey, in May 2009, and left not only richer but better looking and with fresh breath, too. In addition to $500 in cash, the crook took some Life Savers candies but left behind the razor he had shaved with (and some whiskers in the sink). He also left behind a pair of smelly black socks. Police are still looking for the man.

BOOKED!

When Paul Baldwin was arrested for assault in New Hampshire in 2009, he didn't have to be told where to go or what to do at the Portsmouth police station—he knew the drill. Why? He'd been booked there *152 times* before on various charges including felony theft, lewdness, arson, and shoplifting. At his trial, Baldwin told the judge that he didn't need a lawyer because, "I've been in this courtroom more than you have." (He went to jail.)

ESCAPED!

In 1987 Phillip Arnold Paul murdered an elderly woman because he believed she was a witch. He claimed that voices in his head made him do it, and was acquitted by reason of insanity and then locked up in Eastern State Mental Hospital in Washington. He tried to escape once, but was quickly captured. Other than being a flight risk, Paul was considered a "model patient." So one day in 2009, staff decided to include him in their annual supervised field trip to the Spokane County Interstate Fair. Not surprisingly, Paul escaped. "It's outrageous that security was so inept that a guy who's officially regarded as criminally insane was able to just slip away from the group," said state Rep. Matt Shea of Spokane Valley. At last report, Paul's whereabouts were still unknown.

DEADLY FLORIDA

Good thing it's pretty in the Sunshine State. At least the view will
be nice as you try to outrun all of these dangerous things.

AFRAID OF LIGHTNING?

Then don't go to Florida. A study conducted from 2004 to 2007 by the American Meteorological Society found that people are more likely to get struck by lightning in Florida than anywhere else in North America. The state averages 35 lightning injuries and seven fatalities per year, and "Lightning Alley," a hot spot that spans central Florida from Tampa to Titusville, receives an average of 50 strikes per square mile per year. And right in the middle of Lightning Alley: Disney World. Even with lightning rods strategically placed throughout the park, a quick-moving storm in 2003 caught animal handlers by surprise at Disney's Kilimanjaro Safaris attraction. Before they could move the animals to safety, a lightning bolt killed a 12-foot-tall giraffe named Betsy. Also located in Lightning Alley: Universal Studios, SeaWorld, Daytona Beach, and NASA's Kennedy Space Center, where they launch spaceships.

AFRAID OF ALLIGATORS?

Then don't go to Florida. Although the Florida Wildlife Department insists that alligator attacks are rare and seldom fatal, incidents are on the rise. Protected by law, the alligator population has grown from 300,000 in 1967 to nearly two million today. And more and more, those gators are colliding with humans encroaching on their natural habitat. Result: a drastic increase in fatal attacks (three people were killed by gators in one week alone in 2006). Because there are no plans to reinstitute alligator-hunting and few plans to curb development, we're likely to see more deadly gator encounters in the years to come.

AFRAID OF SHARKS?

Then don't go to Florida. Just a short drive from Disney World is New Smyrna Beach, the shark-bite capital of the world. According to the 2008 International Shark Attack File, 32 of the 59

---

16 of the top 20 U.S. cities most often hit by hurricanes are located in Florida.

unprovoked shark attacks worldwide occurred in Florida—and New Smyrna Beach accounted for 21 of them. Most attacks occur at Ponce de Leon Inlet, where two rivers meet before emptying into the Atlantic Ocean. The confluence creates a smorgasbord for sharks looking for an easy meal: murky water from tidal flushing loaded with plenty of baitfish. The inlet also has some of the best and most consistent surf on the East Coast and, consequently, lots of surfers. In 2008, 57% of New Smyrna's shark victims were attacked while surfing.

AFRAID OF CROSSING THE STREET?
Then don't go to Florida. A 2008 study by Surface Transportation Policy Partnership found that four of the top five most dangerous U.S. cities for pedestrians are in Florida. The national average for pedestrian deaths is 11.8% of all traffic deaths, but Florida topped out at 16.9%. America's most dangerous city for pedestrians: Orlando.

AFRAID OF RIDING A BICYCLE?
Then don't go to Florida. It's also the most dangerous U.S. state for cyclists, with 113 fatalities in 2008. (That's more than the #2 state, California, which has nearly twice as many people.) Why so dangerous? A lack of adequate bicycle lanes is one reason, but most Floridians agree that many drivers there just don't like bike riders. According to Scott Gross, manager of Open Road Bicycles in Avondale, Florida: "People are very nice to cyclists in other parts of the world, but around here they just want you off the road."

AMUSED BY DUMB CROOKS?
Then, by all means, go to Florida. Though it ranks in the top 15 states for assault, burglary, robbery, homicide, and car theft, some of our favorite dumb-crook stories come from the Sunshine State. Like this one: In 2009 a man burst into a home in Riverview, Florida, forced the residents into a bathroom, and proceeded to steal prescription drugs, cash, and some electronics. Fortunately, the man was easy to identify. When the victims were called into the police station to look at suspect photos, they pointed at one and said, "That's him!" How did they know? Because on the 19-year-old robber's left cheek was a large tattoo of the state of Florida.

NEWS FROM THE THROWN ROOM

Sometimes you're so mad, you just want to throw something...
like a waffle. Or a plate of food. Or a jellyfish.

Thrower: Keith Edward Marriott
Thrown: Several jellyfish
Story: In September 2009, sunbathers at Madiera Beach, Florida, saw Marriott, 41, as he seemed to be struggling in the surf. When they ran into the water to save him, he jumped up and started throwing jellyfish at them. Witnesses said he repeated the stunt several times, each time throwing jellyfish at people who ran to help him. He was arrested and charged with disorderly intoxication.

Thrower: Crystal Samuel of Manning, South Carolina
Thrown: A waffle
Story: Samuel and some friends were waiting for a takeout order at a Waffle House restaurant early one morning in May 2009. Her friends got their meals, but Samuel was still waiting, so her friends started eating. A waitress told the group that they couldn't eat from takeout containers in the restaurant. Samuel explained that she didn't have her food yet, but the waitress told her they all had to leave. An argument ensued—and Samuel threw a waffle at the waitress. They both went outside, and the waitress walked to her car...and took out a gun and shot Samuel in the arm. The waitress, Yakeisha Ward, was charged with assault and battery with intent to kill. Samuel told reporters she thought the incident showed that the restaurant had "bad customer service."

Throwers: Three police officers in Gainesville, Florida
Thrown: Eggs
Story: One night in November 2008, three off-duty cops were out drinking until around 2:00 a.m. when they decided to do something stupid: They went to a convenience store, bought four dozen

eggs, and drove to a part of town known to have a high concentration of prostitutes and drug dealers. The cops then cruised the streets and threw eggs at people. They were finally pulled over by another off-duty cop, who recognized them because he'd pulled them over once before—for doing the same thing. After an investigation, the officers were given a written warning. (The citizens of Gainesville can sleep soundly now.)

Thrower: William Singalargh of Whakatane, New Zealand

Thrown: A hedgehog

Story: Singalargh, 27, was arrested in June 2008 after getting into an argument with a 15-year-old boy. During the confrontation, Singalargh reportedly grabbed a hedgehog (no word on where he got it) and threw it at the kid. The porcupine-like creature struck the boy's leg, causing several punctures and severe swelling. Singalargh was fined $500 for simple assault—the original charge of assault with a deadly weapon was dropped when the hedgehog was determined "not deadly enough."

Thrower: Andrew Mizsak Jr. of Bedford, Ohio

Thrown: A plate of food

Story: In May 2008, Mizsak and his father, Andrew Sr., got into an argument at the dinner table over young Andrew's messy bedroom. The junior Mizsak threw a plate of food across the table and "made a fist" at his father when he was told to clean it up—and the father called 911 on him. But when police arrived, the senior Mizsak told them that he didn't want to press charges against his son. Why? "I don't want to ruin his political career," he said. Andrew Mizsak Jr., who was a member of the Bedford school board, was 28 years old and lived in his parents' basement. "I know this looks bad," Mizsak Jr. told reporters.

Thrower: Douglas Jones, 57, of La Quinta, California

Thrown: Golf balls, tennis balls, and cans of fruits and vegetables

Story: In 2007 park rangers in Joshua Tree National Park in Southern California began finding golf balls near roads in the park—lots of golf balls. It continued for more than two years, during which between 2,000 and 3,000 balls were found. In August 2009, rangers finally solved the mystery when someone spotted

Douglas Jones throwing golf balls out of his car as he drove through the park. Jones immediately confessed, saying that he threw the balls to "leave his mark" and to honor deceased golfers. Park rangers said that Jones also threw cans of food, which he claimed were intended for people who became stranded. He was cited for abandoning property, littering—and unauthorized feeding of wildlife.

Thrower: Taesani

Thrown: A rock

Story: A woman identified only as Ms. Kim went to a South Korean police station in 2009 to report that someone had thrown a rock at her. Who threw it? Taesani, an elephant at a Seoul zoo. Kim told officers that on a trip to the zoo, she'd noticed the elephant picking up a stone with its trunk, didn't think much about it, turned around—and felt the rock suddenly hit the back of her head. Police investigated the incident, but there were no witnesses, and it happened outside the view of surveillance cameras. No charges were filed against the elephant.

*　　*　　*

TWO CRAZY PRODUCTS

Julie Jackson from Dallas, Texas (who once worked as an intern on Mister Rogers' Neighborhood) invented two products that have us scratching our heads (and our cats' heads, too).

• **Subversive Cross-Stitch Kits—$20:** They look just like the sweet embroidery samplers that Grandma used to make, except these kits (fabric, thread, pattern, embroidery hoop, and two needles) lets you make cross-stitch patterns that spell out vulgar messages, including "Homo Sweet Homo" and "Shut Your Whore Mouth."

• **Wigs for Cats—$50:** As presented in her book *Glamourpuss: The Enchanting World of Kitty Wigs*, Jackson (along with photographer Jill Johnson and her Siamese cat, Boone) show off the many colors and styles of cat wigs. You can choose from Pink Passion, Bashful Blonde, Electric Blue, and Silver Fox.

Both of Jackson's products have been huge sellers.

PANTS ON FIRE

These people can't handle the truth!

CRIME SPREE
A Panama City Beach, Florida, man called 911 from a store in 2009 and said that he'd been robbed: He was getting into his car after leaving the store, he said, when a man "dressed in black" hit him and took $100 in cash from him. Police watched the store's surveillance video and saw the "victim" walk out of the store, sit in his car for a while, then go back inside to call 911. When confronted, the man admitted he lied…because he was afraid to tell his wife that he'd spent the $100. He was arrested.

SURE, THAT WILL WORK
In August 2009, more than 100 friends and family of cancer patient Trista Joy Lathern, 24, held a benefit in her honor at a tavern in Waco, Texas. They raised more than $10,000 for her… and she used the money to get breast-augmentation surgery. Lathern had lied to her family and friends about having cancer (she even shaved her head so she'd look like she'd undergone cancer treatment). When the hoax was found out, Lathern told police she wanted the boob job…in order to save her marriage. Her husband filed for divorce shortly after her arrest.

A DAY OFF (FROM THINKING)
Aaron Siebers, 29, of Denver, Colorado, used a small knife to stab himself in the legs, arms, and upper body one day in November 2009. He then called police and said that he'd been attacked by three men who were either Hispanic…or possibly skinheads. Police questioned his story, and Siebers finally admitted that he'd faked the attack. Why? Because he didn't want to go to his job at a video store. He was arrested.

SHE'S A LIAR (WHEW!)
A woman wearing a bandanna over her face posted a video on an Internet site in January 2010 in which she claimed that she had

HIV/AIDS—and that she had infected more than 500 men in Detroit, Michigan, with the disease. And, she said, she planned to infect more, because she wanted to "destroy the world." Within a few days, more than half a million people had watched the video. Detroit police were able to quickly identify the woman: Jackie Braxton, 23, a Detroit adult-film actress. After she was arrested, she admitted to making the video—and said it was a hoax. (She volunteered to take an HIV test, and it came back negative.) Braxton said she started the hoax to raise awareness about AIDS. Police decided she had not committed a crime.

Bonus: Braxton apparently *did* raise awareness in Detroit: Michael McElrath, a spokesman for the city's health department, said that after the video went viral, the number of men who went to clinics for HIV testing in Detroit more than doubled.

WHO ARE THESE GUYS?

A customer walked into Goomba's Pizzeria in Palm Coast, Florida, in 2009 and demanded his money back: His calzone, he said, hadn't been made properly. The owner of the pizzeria jumped over the counter and pistol-whipped the customer. Police were called, and the restaurant's owner, Joseph Milano, was arrested. The victim, Richard Phinney, was taken to the hospital. A few weeks later, police learned that Joseph Milano wasn't really Joseph Milano; his name was actually Joseph Calco—and he was a New York mobster who was in the Witness Protection Program. He was supposed to be lying low—and it was illegal for him to have a gun. Calco was arrested.

Bonus: A few weeks after finding out that Milano had lied about his identity, police found out that the victim, Richard Phinney, had lied about his, too—when the real Richard Phinney came forward and reported that his identity had been stolen. The victim's real name: Jack Kilburne, who was wanted for failure to pay child support. He was also arrested.

*   *   *

"Everything great in the world is done by neurotics; they alone founded our religions and created our masterpieces."

—Marcel Proust

The "naked recreation and travel" industry has grown by 233% in the past decade.

JUST PLANE WEIRD

Crazy tales of flying high—and not flying at all.

HIGH FLYIN'

The control tower at a small airport in Schoengleida, Germany, received a perplexing call over the radio in September 2009: "Where the bloody hell have you hidden yourself?" the pilot demanded. When the controller asked the pilot to identify himself, he replied only with, "Come on, I know you're down there!" It took a few more questions to determine that the 65-year-old Cessna pilot had had several drinks before taking off and was still drinking while he was flying. The controllers dispatched a rescue helicopter to find him and guide him to the runway. During the search, the pilot sang songs, told a mother-in-law joke, and urged them to hurry up because he had a party to go to. The helicopter finally found the inebriated pilot, who sang more songs as he followed it home. He actually made a decent landing, but then stumbled out of his plane and drove away. Airport authorities alerted police, who caught him a few miles later. He's been banned from driving a car or flying a plane ever again.

FLYING FRACAS

In 2009 a fistfight broke out in the cockpit of an Indian Airlines flight bound for New Delhi and then spilled out into the main cabin. According to witnesses, the male co-pilot, a male purser, and a female flight attendant were "slugging it out" in front of everyone. The purser was apparently defending the honor of the flight attendant, who'd complained that the co-pilot had tried to hold her hand. When she refused, he pushed her into the cockpit door "with such force that she started bleeding." The purser said that the pilots became abusive when he confronted them. The pilots later blamed the fight on the purser. An airline official called the incident "shocking."

WOULD YOU GET ON BOARD?

"People got off the plane and were kissing the ground and praying. There were little girls sobbing." That was the scene described by one of the passengers preparing to board a Thomas Cook Airlines plane on the Spanish island of Mallorca in 2009. Making the London-bound passengers even more nervous: the announcement instructing them to disregard their seat assignments and crowd together in the back of the plane. (The jet's rear loading door was jammed, and their luggage could only be stored in the front cargo bay.) The final straw: As the arriving passengers walked into the airport, several warned, "Don't get on that plane! It was the worst flight ever!" Not wanting to act as ballast, 71 people refused to board and booked flights on other airlines. The remaining passengers had a rough but otherwise uneventful flight to London.

GROUNDED

A wingless Boeing 737 got stuck in traffic on a crowded street in Mumbai, India, in 2007. How'd it get there? The decommissioned plane was being towed to New Delhi when the truck driver took a wrong turn. A low bridge blocked the way, and the road was too narrow for the truck to turn around. So the driver got out, walked off, and didn't return. The massive fuselage sat on the busy street for the rest of the day...and the next day, and the day after that. Local business owners complained that the behemoth was blocking access to their shops; others appreciated all of the tourists who came out to gawk at it. A week later, in the middle of the night, it disappeared. There was no official word on who finally took the plane, or where it ended up.

WAKE-UP CALL?

For 79 tense minutes, air traffic controllers couldn't make contact with a Northwest Airlines jet carrying 144 passengers from San Diego to Minneapolis in 2009. Fearing the worst, the military readied fighter jets to intercept the plane. After the airliner had overshot its destination by 150 miles, the captain finally radioed to traffic controllers that everyone onboard was okay. The tower asked, "Do you have time to give a brief explanation of what happened?" "Just cockpit distractions," said the pilot. "That's all I can say." So what *did* happen up there? After the plane landed safely, the pilots claimed they'd been going over scheduling issues on their laptops and lost track of the time. Aviation experts were skeptical; one said it was "more plausible that the pilots had fallen asleep."

Bad car-ma: When exposed to traffic noise, zebra finches are more likely to cheat on their mates.

SCIENCE ON THE EDGE

*Bicycles that pedal for you, robot fish, crime-fighting
leeches—the world of science has it all.*

THIS FISH TASTES FUNNY

In 2009 computer and electronic engineering scientists at
the University of Essex in England announced that they'd
created a new kind of fish: a *robotic* one. The faux fish are about
five feet long and look and swim like real fish—so they won't scare
real fish—and are fitted with complex sensors that detect hazardous pollutants in water, such as oil from a leaking ship or
pipeline. They're set to be released for a test run in 2011 in the
port of Gijon, Spain, where they will swim around, gathering information that will be sent to a control station via wi-fi technology.
The robots are even programmed to return to "charging areas"
every eight hours to get their batteries recharged. If the test run is
successful, robo-fish may soon be swimming in rivers, lakes, and
oceans all over the world.

THE LEECH OF YOUR WORRIES

In 2001 two men broke into the home of 71-year-old Fay Olsen
on the Australian island of Tasmania, tied her to a chair, "poked
her with sticks," and robbed her of $550 ($504 U.S.). Police
found no evidence at the scene except for a leech—fully
engorged with blood from a recent meal—on the floor. Officers
checked the woman and themselves for signs that the leech had
been attached to one of them, and determined that it must have
fallen off one of the robbers. DNA samples were taken from the
blood in the leech. Seven years passed. In 2008 a 56-year-old Tasmanian man was arrested on drug charges and a routine DNA
sample was taken from him and cross-checked against a database.
It matched the DNA taken from the leech. Peter Alec Cannon
eventually confessed to the seven-year-old crime and was sentenced to two years in prison. (His accomplice was never appre-
hended.) Tasmanian police said that, to their knowledge, it was
the first time DNA from a leech had assisted in solving a crime
anywhere in the world.

WHEEL TAKE IT

At the Copenhagen Climate Change conference in December 2009, engineers from the Massachusetts Institute of Technology announced the release of their "Copenhagen Wheel"—a bicycle wheel they hope will revolutionize bike riding around the world. Features: When you're pushing hard on the pedals to go uphill, sensors activate a small, powerful motor in the wheel's hub to help you along. And the battery that powers the motor is constantly being recharged as you ride. In addition, the wheel communicates, via wireless Bluetooth technology, with an iPhone application on the handlebars to let you know your speed, direction, distance traveled—even traffic and smog conditions. Best of all: You can just buy the wheel—it fits on virtually any bike.

HEADS OR HELMETS

Which is safer: riding a bike with or without a helmet? It might not be as clear as you think. Dr. Ian Walker of England's University of Bath published the results of a 2007 study in the journal *Accident Analysis & Prevention*. Walker, an avid cyclist, fitted his bicycle with sensors that could detect how close cars came to him as they passed him, then rode through the city for a couple of months—with and without his helmet on. During that time, he was passed by more than 2,300 cars. Result: Overall, cars, trucks, and buses passed his bike at a distance of about four feet. But drivers passed 3.35 inches closer, on average, when he wore his helmet than when he didn't. "This study shows that when drivers pass a cyclist," Walker wrote, "the margin for error they leave is affected by the cyclist's appearance." The reason, Walker says, is probably because drivers feel more comfortable when passing a helmeted biker rather than a helmetless one, so they may actually be more dangerous to bikers wearing helmets. (Statistics, it must be noted, still show that non-helmeted bikers are *much* more likely to be seriously injured or killed in an accident.)

Bonus: Walker occasionally wore no helmet and a long brown wig while biking, giving him the appearance, he said, of a woman. Result: Cars gave him an extra 5.5 inches of room.

* * *

"Life is just a bowl of pits." —Rodney Dangerfield

Can you? A lab/golden retriever mix named Shadow can water ski, snow ski, and scuba dive.

WEIRD BRITISH HITS

The English are used to bad weather and eating tomatoes
for breakfast. So it sort of makes sense that they'd
like these goofy novelty songs.

Artist: The Outhere Brothers
Song: "Boom Boom Boom"
Story: American hip-hop group the Outhere Brothers
have had a string of huge hits in England. And almost all of them
have related, in some way or another, to butts and bathroom
humor—often graphically. For example, their #1 hit "Boom Boom
Boom" includes the lyric "put your booty on my face." Other
notable hits include "Gimme My Sh*t," "Pass the Toilet Paper,"
and "Pass the Toilet Paper '98."

Artist: Crazy Frog
Song: "Axel F"
Story: In 2005 the cell-phone ringtone producer Jamba! introduced its new advertising mascot, Crazy Frog—a grotesque, bug-
eyed cartoon frog with a sinister smile. The character proved so
popular that the company released a remix (attributed to Crazy
Frog) of the 1984 *Beverly Hills Cop* theme song "Axel F." The song
was already a synthesizer-driven instrumental; Crazy Frog's version
sounded like a high-pitched cell-phone ringtone version of it. The
song became a smash hit, going to #1 in the U.K. and throughout
Europe. It also became one of the bestselling ringtones of all time
in England.

Artist: Rage Against the Machine
Song: "Killing in the Name"
Story: In the U.K., watching to see which song will be #1 on
Christmas is an annual pop-culture event. From 2005 to 2008,
the Christmas #1 was the song performed by the winner of the
British talent show *The X Factor*. Tired of the fact that the show
had developed such a strong influence over the pop charts, two
music fans named Jon and Tracy Morter began a campaign via

Susie Rewer of the U.K. knitted a 5-foot-long scarf—while running in a marathon.

Facebook in 2009 to steal that year's Christmas #1 spot. They chose the most inappropriate tune for Christmas that they could think of: "Killing in the Name," a profanity-laced diatribe against the American government by the leftist rock band Rage Against the Machine. Paul McCartney, Dave Grohl of Foo Fighters, and more than 750,000 Facebook users publicly endorsed the campaign. Christmas came…and Rage Against the Machine had the #1 song in England, bumping *The X Factor* winner Joe McElddery to #2.

Artist: Chef
Song: "Chocolate Salty Balls (P.S. I Love You)"
Story: The TV cartoon comedy *South Park* is just as popular in the U.K. as it is in the U.S., and this song appeared in the 1998 episode "Chef Aid." Chef (voiced by soul singer Isaac Hayes) bakes his homemade confections, "chocolate salty balls," to sell at a fund-raiser. The whole song is a string of double entendres— Chef really *is* singing about baked goods when he croons "Say, everybody, have you seen my balls? They're big and salty and brown." On Christmas 1998, "Chocolate Salty Balls (P.S. I Love You)" hit #1 in the U.K.

Artist: The Cheeky Girls
Song: "The Cheeky Song (Touch My Bum)"
Story: Pop singers Gabriela and Monica Irimia, 20-year-old Romanian twins who'd been trained in opera and ballet, appeared on the British TV talent show *Popstars: The Rivals* in 2002. They didn't win—the judges thought they were terrible singers, and one called their woeful attempt "cheeky." But since the twins were attractive and at least memorable, offers for record deals began to pour in. Just a few weeks after their losing appearance on *Popstars*, "The Cheeky Girls" signed with Multiply Records and released "The Cheeky Song (Touch My Bum)," a thumping electronic/dance song with lyrics made up almost entirely of the repeated, tunelessly sung phrases "cheeky girls," and "touch my bum." "The Cheeky Song" peaked at #2 on the British pop chart.

MANIMALS!

Hey! You got your sheep in my DNA! Well, you got your DNA in my sheep! Two great parts of nature that go great together. Or do they?

SO LONG, SPIDER-MAN

In 2009 senators Sam Brownback (R-Kansas) and Mary Landrieu (D-Louisiana) introduced an interesting piece of legislation: the Human-Animal Hybrid Prohibition Act. Just like it sounds, the bill would have made it illegal for scientists—mad or otherwise—to create creatures that are part human and part... something other than human. The reasoning went, if you made a "catwoman" in your basement laboratory, you could go to prison for 10 years and be fined up to $1 million. (Though that would be totally worth it.)

The bill was mostly laughed at, and it never made it to the Senate floor for a vote, but, as silly as it seems, it's not as far-fetched as it might sound. All around the world, scientists are hard at work trying to do just what the bill sought to outlaw. Here are just a few, and the creatures they've created.

I Am the Egg-Cow-Man: In April 2008, a team of scientists at Newcastle University in England extracted an unfertilized egg cell from a cow, removed its nucleus—where most of a cell's DNA resides—and replaced it with the nucleus of a cell taken from another animal. They then gave the egg a tiny electric shock, which "activated" it, meaning that the inserted DNA began to do its work, and the cell started dividing. In other words, it was alive. And the DNA they inserted into the cow egg was *human* (taken from a skin cell). The Newcastle scientists had successfully cloned a human-animal hybrid, possibly for the first time in history. (There have been a handful of unverifiable claims since 2003.) Did it go on to become a cow with hands and feet? Or a human with horns and hooves? No—the cells stopped dividing after about three days. But the team hopes to repeat the experiment and get an egg to keep dividing for about six days—at which time it should begin creating embryonic stem cells (ES cells), the "building block" cells found in embryos that go on to become more than 200 different types of cells in the body. The cells would be almost completely human—they'd have 99.99% human DNA and only .01% cow DNA. But, if successful, the procedure would allow scientists to skirt around laws forbidding or restricting the use of "normal" human embryos for stem-cell production. The scientists performing such experiments say they would never allow the cow-human hybrids to divide for more than a few days, and would never implant such an egg into a cow and attempt to bring it to term.

I Squeak, Therefore I Am: Stanford University professor Irving Weissman and a team of researchers have created mice with brains that are part human. Hoping to learn more about brain cancers, Weissman extracted human embryonic brain stem cells—the kind that go on to become various types of brain cells—and injected them into the brains of adult mice. The cells survived and even traveled to different areas of the brains and matured into different types of brain cells. (The researchers created special markers that allowed them to keep track of the injected human cells.) The tests resulted in mice with brains whose cells were about 1% human. The next step: inject human brain stem cells not into *adult* mice but into fetal mice still in the womb. That, Weissman says, would result in mice that have much higher human brain content...perhaps as much as 100%. Before moving ahead, Weissman went to Stanford's ethics department to make sure he wasn't crossing any lines. Law professor Hank Greely, chair of the school's ethics committee, gave the study the go-ahead with one condition: If the mice started showing any humanlike behaviors, they'd have to be destroyed immediately.

I'd Like Some Mutton and a Little Liver: In March 2007, Professor Esmail Zanjani of the University of Nevada-Reno announced that he had successfully injected sheep fetuses with human stem cells. The result: sheep that grew organs that were part human. Some had livers, for example, that were made up of as much as 40% human liver cells. Zanjani hopes the research may one day lead to sheep being raised only for the human organs in their bodies—which could be transplanted into humans who need them. The scientists could conceivably create sheep that are tailor-made for specific people. For example, a sheep could be injected with your bone marrow in order to grow organs suitable just for you.

Zanjani insists that the work is ethical and medically necessary, and that the sheep are not monsters. "We haven't seen them act as anything but sheep," he says.

Piggy, Bloody Piggy: Jeffrey Platt, director of the Mayo Clinic Transplantation Biology Program in Rochester, Minnesota, performed similar human stem cell injections into fetal pigs, and now has a group of pigs that have pig blood cells *and* human blood cells running through their veins. But it gets weirder: Some of the blood cells are both. Their DNA contains both human and pig genes. Platt hopes the work might lead to pigs being raised for their human blood and organs, but there are several hurdles, including the fact that some porcine (pig) viruses can be passed on to humans.

Just Call Me "Babe": Human/animal hybrids are actually nothing new. If you know anyone with an artificial valve in their heart, then there's a good chance you already *know* a human/animal hybrid. Thousands of people each year receive heart valves harvested from either pigs or cows. That, technically, makes these people hybrids.

BONUS

Evan Balaban, a behavioral neuroscientist at McGill University in Montreal, has produced *bird-bird* hybrids: He took brain cells from embryonic quails and transferred them into the brains of embryonic chickens. When the chickens later hatched and grew up, they didn't "cluck" or "cock-a-doodle-doo" like normal chickens…they trilled like quail. And they bobbed their heads just like quail do. Balaban said the work upended the long-held belief that these behaviors are learned, showing conclusively that they are not only hard-wired—but that they can be transferred to entirely different species.

* * *

FOUR ACTUAL BAND NAMES

- Test Icicles
- The Tony Danza Tap Dance
- Black King Acid and the Womb Star Orchestra
- Gay for Johnny Depp

Q: What do you get when you cross a turkey with an octopus? A: Drumsticks for everyone!

FATHER OF THE PARANORMAL

The name Charles Fort may not ring any bells, but chances are you're familiar with his work. Without him, the world might never have heard of blood raining from the sky, the Bermuda Triangle, or spontaneous human combustion. And he brought his strange stories to us through years of obsessive research—and a filing system made of shoeboxes.

THE SCRIBBLER

Charles Hoy Fort was a writer who made his living selling short stories to literary magazines in the early 1900s. But it wasn't much of a living: Though Fort had a knack for spinning yarns, the magazines didn't pay well, and he didn't sell enough stories to keep afloat. His wife, Anna, was the real breadwinner; she worked long hours in a hotel laundry to make ends meet while Fort sat at home, scribbling out stories at the kitchen table.

Fort was a bit of a hermit, and he didn't think he had enough life experience to base his stories on his own adventures. So he compensated by spending long hours at the New York Public Library, researching the details he needed to make his stories interesting and believable. Whenever he had trouble concentrating, he'd go to the library and do more research.

WRITER'S BLOCK

In time the trips to the library became a sort of crutch: Fort would struggle with his stories for an hour or two in the morning, then give up and head off to the library, where he'd spend the rest of the day randomly reading books, newspapers, and magazines from around the world, all the while taking copious notes.

By 1912 writing had become such a struggle that Fort put his stories aside entirely. He now spent all of his time at the library, compulsively researching anything and everything that struck his fancy, with no particular goal in mind other than to satisfy his own curiosity.

He still took plenty of notes. Before he left for the library each morning, he used a ruler to carefully tear pieces of scrap paper into

What do groundhogs, woodchucks, and marmots have in common? They're all the same critter.

neat 1½" by 2½" strips. He'd stuff his pockets full of them, and by the time he returned home later in the day, he'd have hundreds of new handwritten notes ready to be filed away. He lined the walls of the couple's tiny Hell's Kitchen tenement flat with hundreds of cubbyholes made of shoeboxes and stored his notes in them; over the next couple of years, he amassed a collection of over 40,000 individual strips of paper, each of which he carefully dated, cross-referenced, and filed, using more than 1,300 different subject categories. (If you've ever been to Uncle John's house, you know that he and Fort have a lot in common.)

NO WORRIES

How long would *you* have slaved away at a hotel laundry to support a scribbling, unproductive pack rat like Fort? Anna Fort labored from 1906 to 1916 to keep a roof over her husband's head, and she might have had to keep at it much longer if one of Fort's uncles hadn't died in 1916 and left the pair enough money to live on for the rest of their lives. Anna could finally quit her job, and Fort was free to pour himself into his research without having to worry about making a living again.

As Fort sifted, sorted, shuffled, organized, and reorganized his notes, he began to notice things that no one had ever noticed before. He started making these connections as early as 1912, when he first began having trouble writing his short stories.

CRITICAL MASS

Fort "was drawn to apparent anomalies—strange phenomena that defied neat classification," biographer Jim Steinmeyer writes in *Charles Fort: The Man Who Invented the Supernatural*. "He started to discover them everywhere, prying them out of established journals and histories. After years of collecting—idly arranging and rearranging objects, phrases, or information—he now began to notice patterns. Odd patterns."

Of course, Fort lived in an age when there was no Google, Wikipedia, or other Internet tools to help people collect and organize tens of millions of pieces of information, free of charge. Those powerful tools were nearly a century away. But Fort's strange system of cross-referenced notes was the next best thing.

For instance, Fort read that people living along the shores of the Mediterranean Sea saw strange, blood-red rain falling on March 6, 1888, and again 12 days later. "Whatever the substance may have been, when burned, the odor of animal matter from it was strong and persistent," Fort noted.

But few if any people realized that a year earlier in Cochin, China, "there fell...a substance like blood, somewhat coagulated," as Fort's notes described it. And nine years before that, in Olympian Springs, Kentucky, "flakes of beef" fell from the sky on an otherwise clear day.

In an age before radio, television, jet travel, or the Internet, when even the news wires were still in their infancy, each of these peculiar occurrences was almost by default an *isolated* incident: The people who experienced it were unlikely to know that it might have also happened somewhere else.

THE FORT-O-NET

Fort was a human search engine—a living, breathing Google. It wasn't until someone like him came along, someone willing and (thanks to his wife and uncle) able to spend more than 20 years sifting through books, journals, magazines, and newspapers, taking copious notes, and sorting the information, one piece at a time, that anyone realized that strange, unexplained events such as these were as numerous as they were.

When Fort came across an account of "a large ball of fire" that rose out of the sea off the eastern coast of Canada on December 22, 1887, then hovered in the air for five minutes before vanishing, he made a note of it. Then he filed it in the shoebox that contained his notes on similar incidents, such as the account of three "luminous bodies" that rose out of the Mediterranean on June 18, 1845, and hovered within sight of the sailing ship *Victoria* for 10 minutes before disappearing.

When he read of the case of 77-year-old Barbara Bell of Blyth, England, whose badly burned remains were found in a room where nothing else had burned and nothing had been found that could have caused the fire, he filed it with other cases of "spontaneous combustion," including that of a woman found burned to ashes in her bedroom in Paris in 1869. "Bedclothes, mattresses, curtains, all other things in the room showed not a trace of fire," Fort noted in that case. "A burned body in an almost unscorched room."

Chevy Chase was expelled from college for taking a cow to the third floor of a campus building.

Reading articles, taking notes, sorting slips of paper, stuffing them into shoeboxes—it was all simple enough. But because no one had ever done it before, Fort's contribution to popular culture would be profound.

JUST THE FACTS

It would take some time before Fort figured out how best to put his scraps of paper to use. As if the peculiar incidents he collected weren't strange enough, the conclusions he drew from them were even weirder. In 1915 he wrote a book titled X, in which he argued that a strange force that he called "X," emanating from Mars, was somehow controlling events on Earth. In 1916 he wrote a book titled Y, in which he speculated on the existence of a hidden civilization, which he called "Y," of blond Eskimos at the North Pole. Neither book ever found a publisher, which frustrated Fort so much that he burned both manuscripts. Only pieces of them survive today.

Had Fort continued to peddle his looney theories, he would likely be forgotten today, just another crackpot lumped in with the flat-Earthers and the people who believe the pyramids were built by space aliens. But he eventually concluded that the tidbits of information he was collecting were interesting enough in their own right that no theory tying them together was needed. Eventually, he published four books on the paranormal, *The Book of the Damned* (1919), *New Lands* (1923), *Lo!* (1931), and *Wild Talents* (1932). In them, Fort presented his readers with the strange phenomena he'd dug up over the years, accompanied by plenty of commentary and speculation...but no definitive answers. He left it up to the reader to connect the dots.

NOW REPEAT AFTER ME

Fort cited his sources in his books so his readers could look up the material themselves if they wanted to. The flakes of beef that fell in Kentucky? He directed his readers to articles in *Scientific American* and *The New York Times*. The ball of fire that rose out of the sea near Cape Rose could be found in the December 22, 1887, issue of the science journal *Nature*.

By challenging his readers to think for themselves and directing them to the source material they would need to do their own

research, Fort gave his books a power they would not otherwise
have had. It's one reason why they're still in print today, and why
Fort is considered "the father of the paranormal."

IT IS WRITTEN

Thanks to Fort, when a civilian pilot named Kenneth Arnold saw
some mysterious flying objects over Mt. Rainier in Washington
State on June 24, 1947, people who wanted to know more had
somewhere to go. They went to Fort's books—and there they read
about many similar incidents, including reports of several sightings
of a cigar-shaped craft with butterfly wings in the skies over Colorado, Texas, Nebraska, Iowa, Missouri, Wisconsin, Illinois, and
Indiana during the first three weeks of April 1897.

The objects Kenneth Arnold saw over Mt. Rainier weren't
shaped like cigars. They were shaped like flat discs—his was the
first modern sighting of *flying saucers*. Regardless, the public paid
attention. Fort had laid the groundwork for Arnold's sighting to be
taken seriously. The modern UFO age had begun.

In 1964 a writer named Vincent Gaddis wrote a magazine article about ships and aircraft that seemed to have mysteriously vanished in an area of the Atlantic bounded by Florida, Puerto Rico
and Bermuda. Gaddis thought back to Fort's description of "a tri-
angular region in England" that he said was home to a dispropor-
tionate number of reports of strange events. Remembering that
Fort had called the area the "London Triangle," Gaddis named his
region the "Bermuda Triangle," and another icon of the paranormal was born.

MIXED REVIEWS

But not everybody was a fan of Fort. Writer H.L. Mencken said
Fort was "enormously ignorant of elementary science," and H.G.
Wells called him a "damnable bore" who "writes like a drunkard."
The New York Times panned *The Book of the Damned* as a "quag-
mire of pseudo-science and queer speculation" that would render
the average reader "either buried alive or insane before he reaches
the end." Even Fort's beloved New York Public Library catalogued
The Book of the Damned under "Eccentric Literature" rather than
nonfiction. That made him so angry that he burned his 40,000
notes and stomped off to London for six months, where he sat in

Work related? Sarah Michelle Gellar, star of *Buffy the Vampire Slayer*, has a fear of graveyards.

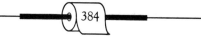

the reading room of the British Museum…and began amassing a new and equally impressive hoard of notes that he would use to write his three later books.

Despite the bad reviews, Fort's books found a large and appreciative audience, and fans soon began writing to him about odd occurrences in their own communities. In 1931 an admirer founded the Fortean Society to promote his work, but Fort refused to join. He took a militantly agnostic approach to his odd phenomena: He believed that it was important to keep an open mind and was as contemptuous of the people who accepted the strange accounts at face value as he was of the "orthodox" scientists who dismissed them out of hand. He feared the Society would become a magnet for the true believers—"the ones we do not want," as he put it. "I wouldn't join it, any more than I'd be an Elk."

STILL FORTIN'

A lifelong skeptic who was deeply suspicious of authority, Fort may have hastened his own death in the early 1930s when his health began to fail and he refused to place himself under a doctor's care. He lived long enough to see publication of *Wild Talents*, his fourth book on the paranormal. But just barely; by the time an advance copy was rushed to his hospital bed on May 3, 1932, he was too weak to hold it. He died later that night, at the age of 57.

To this day, Fort's legacy lives on in the International Fortean Organization (INFO), which is descended from the society Fort refused to join. And there's also the magazine *Fortean Times*, still dedicated to tracking reports of strange phenomena. True to Fort's memory, they present the material as objectively as possible, without taking sides. "They offer the data," as Fort once said about his own books. "Suit yourself."

*   *   *

TROUSERS BE DAMNED

On January 10, 2010, nearly 5,000 people in 44 cities in 16 countries all took off their pants and rode the subway as part of the ninth annual No Pants Day. The biggest turnout—3,000 pantless participants—was in New York City during a heavy snow storm.

Charles & Sandra McKee spent $250,000 turning their home into a replica of the Munsters' house.

COWABUNGA!

Cows just kind of do what they do;
They stand in fields and graze and moo,
But they also do other things
that make us stop and say, "Ooh!"
So here are some cow stories, strange but true.

I'M OK, YOU'RE OK. BUT WHAT ABOUT THE COW?

One morning in January 2005, traffic backed up on Interstate 4 near DeBary, Florida. The cause: A cow was standing in a swamp beside the road...and she appeared to be sinking. Concerned drivers called the Highway Patrol, who quickly determined that the cow wasn't in danger, but was merely grazing in the two-foot-deep bog. The officers left, but the worried calls kept coming in, so they went back out and put up an electronic sign on the shoulder that read: "THE COW IS OK." Shortly after the officers left, however, the cow wandered off...but the sign remained.

Now motorists were really confused: What cow was okay? Was this some kind of spiritual message, or news of some event they hadn't heard about? Those were just a few of the questions the Highway Patrol received over the next few hours. And as more and more drivers slowed down to look for the nonexistent cow, a second, larger traffic jam ensued. Officers eventually went back out and removed the sign.

UDDER CHAOS

In December 2009, an Englishwoman arrived home in Blagdon, Somerset, to discover smashed roof tiles in her yard and serious damage to the top of her house. Fearing that someone had tried to break in, she called the police, who assessed the damage and started knocking on neighbors' doors to inquire if they had seen anyone suspicious. William de Cothi, a teenager who lived next door, had seen the whole thing. He'd looked out his second-story window, he said, and a cow was standing on top of the woman's slanted roof. The sight was so odd that he'd even taken a photo. Police determined that the cow must have jumped onto the roof at its lowest point—an impressive six feet off the ground—then walked around for a few minutes, broke a few tiles, and jumped off again.

A MOO-MOO HERE AND A ROAR-ROAR THERE

Jack McDonald's landlady had a cow. Her name was Apple (because she liked to eat apples off a tree on the property). One day in 2008, a black bear wandered into Apple's field in Hygiene, Colorado, and climbed up Apple's apple tree. Apple ran to the tree and mooed sternly at the bear. It climbed back to the ground and the two animals stared each other down—and even touched noses for a brief moment. Then Apple mooed loudly and chased the bear away. McDonald described the confrontation as "hilarious."

FIRE IN THE HOLE

A Dutch veterinarian was fined 600 guilders (about $240) for starting a fire that destroyed a farm near the town of Lichten-voorde. The vet had been trying to demonstrate to a farmer that his cows were passing too much gas and, to make his point, he used a lighter to set fire to one of the cow's farts. The cow became, according to newspaper reports, a "four-legged flamethrower," and ran around frantically, setting hay bales on fire. The flaming cow (which, amazingly, was unharmed) caused more than $80,000 in damage.

COWLICKS

Jerry Lynn Davis's house must taste very good. In 2009 one of his neighbor's cows stuck her head through a fence next to Davis's residence in Rogersville, Tennessee, and started licking the house. It licked the paint off the walls, ripped off a screen, broke a window, and tore down a rain gutter, all by licking. The cow's owner agreed to move the fence back a few feet, and Davis tried to get his insurance company to pay for the damages (which exceeded $100), but was informed that his policy did not cover "acts of cow."

*   *   *

Cowboy proverb: Always drink upstream from the herd.

Studies show: Cows that have names produce more milk than cows that don't.

THE RICKROLL

*Internet fads come and go, but this is the only one we know
of that breathed new life into a nearly forgotten pop
star's career. Have you ever been "Rickrolled"?*

BACKGROUND

In May 2007, a user on the Internet forum 4chan posted what he claimed to be a link to the trailer for the new video game *Grand Theft Auto IV*. But the link didn't take users to *Grand Theft Auto*; it took them, inexplicably, to a YouTube video of "Never Gonna Give You Up," the 1987 hit by British pop singer Rick Astley.

Over the next year, the prank began popping up all over the Internet—people would send their friends (or post on Web sites) links to news stories, videos, or anything interesting that someone might want to see. But, of course, the link always went to "Never Gonna Give You Up." Perhaps you were one of the 30 million people who got "Rickrolled."

ROLLING ON

Rickrolling was one of the most talked-about items on the Internet in 2008 and '09.

• As an April Fool's Day prank in 2008, YouTube replaced all of its videos—more than 100 million of them—with "Never Gonna Give You Up."

• In June 2008, political Web sites and blogs reported the uncovering of an amateur video secretly shot of future First Lady Michelle Obama delivering a bitter, antiwhite racist rant. When the video was finally presented it was…"Never Gonna Give You Up."

• Shortly after the House of Representatives convened in January 2009, Speaker of the House Nancy Pelosi placed a video on Congress's official YouTube page, promising a look at the day-to-day proceedings in her office. It was no such thing—Pelosi "catrolled" the world, and the link led to a video of a few cats playing in her Washington office. Then Pelosi Rickrolled the catroll when, halfway through the cat video, the footage abruptly changed to "Never Gonna Give You Up."

ASTLEY'S COMET

But then the Rickroll jumped from viral Internet videos into the real world.

• In September 2009, pranksters at the Massachusetts Institute of Technology managed to scale MIT's Great Dome and surround it with white scaffolding. Then they hung up seven giant musical notes—the opening notes to "Never Gonna Give You Up."

• The Cartoon Network enters a float in each year's Macy's Thanksgiving Day Parade. In 2008, at the height of the Rick-rolling fad, their float featured people dressed as characters from the show *Foster's Home for Imaginary Friends*. The characters danced and sang to the theme song from *The Courtship of Eddie's Father* ("People, let me tell you 'bout my best friend") until a door on the float suddenly burst open and Rick Astley emerged. As the monsters continued to dance, he performed "Never Gonna Give You Up" live, bewildering spectators and the TV crew covering the event.

• The Ikee worm, an aggressive computer virus, affected thousands of iPhones in Australia. It replaced the device's wallpaper image...with one of Rick Astley.

• In the spring of 2008, the New York Mets held an online poll to pick a rallying song to play at home games. The Mets Web site was flooded with five million write-in votes for "Never Gonna Give You Up." (The Mets decided not to use the song.)

*   *   *

BUTTERFLY.NET

Here's another crazy Internet fad: "The Exploding Penguin." It began as a five-second video clip of a penguin spontaneously combusting at a South Korean zoo, but in 2007, it started to appear on Internet message boards. People posted it when they wanted to express that something they read or saw was "mind-blowing," or when they wanted to make fun of other message board-users for getting into a silly but "explosive" debate. Want to see the original footage of the exploding Korean penguin? (Warning: It's graphic.) Go to http://tinyurl.com/2g9mqh.

"Insanity is often the logic of an accurate mind overtasked." —Oliver Wendell Holmes

FROG SUCK, WYOMING

...and other U.S. towns with crazy names.

Greasy, Oklahoma

Big Rock Candy Mountain, Vermont

Chocolate Bayou, Texas

Spuds, Florida

Ham Lake, Minnesota

Toast, North Carolina

Two Egg, Florida

Goodfood, Mississippi

Eek, Alaska

Frankenstein, Missouri

Embarrass, Wisconsin

Gripe, Arizona

Lame Deer, Montana

Goat Town, Georgia

Viper, Kentucky

Candy Town, Ohio

Yeehaw Junction, Florida

Index, Washington

Monkey's Eyebrow, Kentucky

Lorida, Florida

Bumblebee, Arizona

Shake Rag, Georgia

Cow Island, Louisiana

Bob Acres, Louisiana

Assawoman Bay, Maryland

Frog Suck, Wyoming

Mary's Igloo, Alaska

Buddha, Indiana

Camel Hump, Wyoming

Buttzville, Pennsylvania

Whiskey Dick Mountain, Washington

Disappointment, Kentucky

Weiner, Arkansas

Goobertown, Arizona

Wimp, California

Beans Corner Bingo, Maine

Zap, North Dakota

Static, Tennessee

Fireworks, Massachusetts

It, Mississippi

Eternity, a morgue-themed restaurant in the Ukraine, is shaped like a giant coffin.

"ALCOHOL WAS
A FACTOR"

"O God, that men should put an enemy in their mouths to steal away their brains! That we should, with joy, pleasance, revel, and applause, transform ourselves into beasts!" —William Shakespeare, Othello

DEPARTMENT STORE COWBOYS
Clinton Evers and John Carelock decided to go shopping at the El Dorado, Arkansas, Walmart one day in 2009—on horseback. Sheriff's deputies tried to stop them after they rode into the parking lot, but the pair went inside the store—still on their horses—as the cops gave chase. The horses galloped through the food aisles, forcing customers to scatter. Police quickly reined in Carelock, but Evers galloped out of the Walmart and into the woods before he was finally caught. According to police, "Alcohol was a factor."

GLASS HOLE
A homeowner in Buchanan, Wisconsin, woke up late one night in 2009 to the sound of breaking glass. He looked outside and saw that there was broken glass in the street. The next day, police investigators visited local auto-glass shops to see if anyone had come in needing a new car window—and found a customer named Andrew J. Burwitz, whose car police traced to the glass. When questioned, Burwitz admitted that he'd decided to do a drive-by shooting at the home of his ex-girlfriend's family...but he forgot to roll down his car window before firing his gun. Burwitz was arrested. According to police, "Alcohol was a factor."

ASSAULT AND WOMBAT-TERY
In March 2008, police in Motueka, New Zealand, received a bizarre call: "Help me!" a man was shouting, "I'm being raped by a wombat!" The officers found that strange, because wombats don't live in New Zealand (they live in Australia). They were about to race to the scene when the man called back and said, "No worries, mates. I'm alright now. He's gone." Police went there anyway, and

found Arthur Cradock, 48, who told them it was a false alarm: "I'll retract the rape complaint from the wombat, because he's pulled out. Apart from speaking Australian now, I'm pretty all right, you know. I didn't hurt my bum at all!" The cops arrested Cradock for wasting their time. He was sentenced to 75 hours of community service. According to police: "Alcohol was a factor."

THAT'S NO WAY TO GO

A 28-year old man (unnamed in press reports) went to a hospital in 1997, babbling that he wanted to kill himself; his head and chest were covered with bruises. The man told the doctors that he took several nitroglycerin pills and threw himself against a wall in an attempt to make the nitroglycerin explode. He also admitted that, along with the pills, he'd drunk a fifth of vodka. According to police, "Alcohol was definitely a factor."

YOU CAN DEPEND ON IT

In August 2008, Graham Nickerson, 27, was camping in Cape Sable Island, Nova Scotia. At some point in the night, he went to go pee in the woods, took off his pants, and then couldn't find them again. After searching the forest in a haze to find them, Nickerson broke into the home of a 92-year-old woman (who wasn't there) and found an adult diaper. He put it on and then passed out. The elderly woman returned home the next morning to find Nickerson still asleep on the floor, and still wearing one of her diapers. She called the authorities and Nickerson was arrested. Say it with us: "Alcohol was a factor."

A WEE NIP

A few nights before Christmas in 2009, four-year-old Hayden Wright woke up at 1:00 a.m., snuck into the kitchen of his home in Chattanooga, Tennessee, and drank a beer (which can get a preschooler quite drunk). Then Hayden, beer in hand, wandered through the neighborhood, went up to a neighbor's house, found the door unlocked, went inside, found the Christmas tree, and started opening presents. When police finally found Hayden (empty beer can in hand), he was wearing one of the gifts: a brown dress. The boy was taken to a hospital, where his stomach was pumped. According to his mom, "He wants to get in trouble so he can go to jail because that's where his daddy is."

CRAZY DECISIONS FOR $200, ALEX

Do you get upset by people in charge abusing their power? Or when they're ruled by political correctness? This won't help.

Background: Former British army soldier Paul Clarke, 27, found a sawed-off shotgun in a garbage bag in the garden of his home in the city of Surrey in March 2009.
What he did: He took the gun to the local police station and turned it in.
Crazymaker: Clarke was arrested for illegal possession of a firearm. And in November 2009 he was found guilty by a jury—and faced a five-year prison sentence. He was given a 12-month suspended sentence instead, fortunately, but still has the felony conviction on his record.

Background: Nicole Mamo, 48, the owner of a job-recruitment firm in Borehamwood, England, put an ad for a hospital cleaning person on the British government's job Web site, Jobcentre Plus, in January 2010. The ad said that applicants must be "reliable and hard-working."
What she did: Mamo checked the Web site the next day, and saw that the ad wasn't there, so she called to find out why.
Crazymaker: She was told the ad couldn't be run—because asking for "reliable" people was discriminatory. "I placed the advert on the Web site," Mamo said, "and when I phoned up to check I was told it hadn't been displayed because they could have cases against them for discriminating against unreliable people. I started to laugh. I said, 'That's crazy!'" After the story made news around the world, embarrassed government officials changed their minds and the ran. "Reliability is important to employers, as it is for Jobcentre Plus," a spokesperson said, "and we welcome ads seeking reliable applicants."

Background: In October 2007, Boston, Massachusetts, lawyer

Woody Allen says he has morbid fears of sunshine, kids, crowds, and anyplace outside Manhattan.

Simon Glik, 31, was walking down the street when he saw three police officers trying to extract a plastic bag from the mouth of a teenager.

What he did: Glik thought the officers were using excessive force, so he pulled out his cell phone and started recording the incident with the phone's camera. One of the officers asked Glik if the camera recorded sound as well as video. Glik said it did.

Crazymaker: Glik was arrested. The charge? Illegal electronic surveillance. Turns out that Massachusetts, like many other states, is a "two-party consent" state, meaning that all parties to a conversation have to agree to have the conversation recorded. Such laws are meant to protect individuals from having their phone conversations recorded without their permission—not to stop people from openly recording something happening on a public street. But there's more: Glik was also charged with disturbing the peace (for recording the incident) and aiding the near escape of a prisoner. Police dropped the "aiding the escape of a prisoner" charge, and a Boston judge dismissed the other two charges. "Photography," the judge said, "is a form of expression which is entitled to First Amendment protection, just as the written or spoken word is."

Background: Lieutenant Jeffrey Boyle had been a member of the Chicago Fire Department for more than 20 years.

What he did: In 2006 he pleaded guilty...to arson. He had set eight fires in and around the city over the course of several years. No one was injured in any of the blazes, but two did cause significant damage to a school. Boyle claimed his behavior was related to a problem with alcohol. He served two years of a six-year sentence. When Boyle turned 50 years old in 2008, he applied for his pension from the fire department. Understandably, officials with the fire department's retirement board said, "No way."

Crazymaker: Boyle sued, saying that he was off duty when he set the fires and therefore deserved the pension—and in November 2009 a Chicago judge overturned the board. Convicted arsonist Jeffrey Boyle now gets $50,000 per year from the Chicago Fire Department and will continue to do so for the rest of his life.

MORE BIG NEWS

*With the obesity epidemic expanding, expect generous helpings
of stories like these. (For Part I, turn to page 235.)*

TRIMMING THE FAT

After the 2009 holiday season, more than 5,000 people were kicked off the dating Web site BeautifulPeople.com because they'd put on extra pounds. The site began in 2002 as a more selective alternative to dating sites that "allow just anyone to join." Only 20% of applicants to BeautifulPeople make the grade and, according to the site's founder, Robert Hintze, "vigilant members" demanded action after some users posted photos of themselves during the holidays in which it was clear that they had "let themselves go." An e-mail was sent to rejected members, inviting them to reapply when they were "back to looking their best" and even recommended boot camps where they could shape up. Hintze was unapologetic: "Letting fatties roam the site is a direct threat to our business model and the very concept for which BeautifulPeople.com was founded."

EXTRA BAGGAGE

In 2009 United Airlines became the latest U.S. carrier to announce that heavier patrons would have to purchase an extra seat if they were too wide for one seat and couldn't be relocated next to an empty one. United officials explained that they received hundreds of complaints per year from passengers who'd "had to share their seat with an oversized guest," so United joined American, Continental, Delta, and Southwest in making "customers of size" pay extra. The policy riled many critics, who complained that airline seats are already too small. Surveys, however, found that a vast majority of people were in favor of the rules, including 80% of 18,000 people polled by MSNBC.

PUT OUR MONEY WHERE YOUR MOUTH IS

In 2009 in Britain—where one quarter of adults are obese—the National Health Service implemented a trial program called "Pound for Pound," in which participants can earn up to £425

70% of airline passengers polled say they'd rather have onboard wi-fi access than a meal.

($680) for losing 50 pounds. The company in charge of running the study, Weight Wins, upped the stakes to a maximum of £1,000 for a loss of 150 pounds, "to be achieved and maintained over two years." Participants in the program lost an average of 14.4 pounds after six months, which, according to officials, compared favorably to other weight-loss programs. That finding was backed up by a study in the December 2008 issue of the *Journal of the American Medical Association* that found that people who had financial incentives were five times more likely to be successful at dieting than those who did not.

ON THE OTHER SIDE OF THE SCALE

In January 2008, the Mississippi state legislature introduced House Bill 282, which would prevent restaurants from serving "any person who is obese based on criteria prescribed by the state health department." The bill's co-sponsor, Republican State Rep. John Read, acknowledged that, at 230 pounds, he might be among the more than 30% of Mississippians affected by the ban. "I'm trying to shed a little light on the number-one health problem in Mississippi," he explained. Restaurant owners and advocacy groups opposed the bill. According to the Obesity Action Coalition, "Studies have demonstrated that discrimination, ridicule and stigma against the obese do not lower obesity rates. Instead, the opposite is true. Those who are the victims of stigma or discrimination are more likely to engage in unhealthy eating behaviors." J. Justin Wilson, a research analyst representing the restaurant industry, put it more bluntly, "What's next? Will waitresses soon be expected to make sure we eat all our veggies?" Democratic State Rep. Steve Holland, chairman of the House Public Health and Human Services Committee, pronounced the punitive measure "dead on arrival at my desk." True to his word, the bill died in committee that summer.

* * *

"It's not my fault I'm fat. Cakes are nice, and they have them in supermarkets."

—Ricky Gervais

Per capita, the U.S. has 66 times more prosecutions than France.

ZOO ATTACKS

If you think about it, it's kind of crazy that we make animals live in cages so we can gawk at them. Even if you don't think it's crazy, the animals do.

DO NOT FEED (YOURSELF TO) THE BEARS

In 2009 a man in Switzerland decided he wanted to have a close encounter with some bears. So the 25-year-old scaled a 20-foot fence at the Bern Park bear enclosure, where Finn, a four-year-old brown bear, pounced on him. In order to free the man, police shot Finn with fragmentation bullets. Zoo officials said there was an outpouring of sympathy...for Finn. (Both man and bear fully recovered.)

OUT OF THE FRYING PAN

One day in January 2008, a Golden Retriever got off its leash and darted in through the main gate at the Memphis Zoo. Workers chased the dog, but it jumped a barrier...and landed in the tiger enclosure. A 225-pound female Sumatran tiger pounced on the 50-pound dog and held it in her jaws for several minutes while keepers blasted airhorns and shot off fireworks to distract her. Finally, the tiger let go, and the dog made a full recovery. A zoo spokesmen explained that the tiger enclosure was built to keep the animals from getting out, not to keep animals from getting in: "You can jump *off* a cliff, but you can't jump *up* a cliff."

BUT THEY'RE SO CUTE AND CUDDLY

Zhang Jiao, 28, was tossing a stuffed panda back and forth with his young son at the Beijing Zoo when the toy went over a barrier and landed in the enclosure of Gu Gu the (real) giant panda—who was famous for having bitten two people—a curious teenager and a drunk man. In spite of Gu Gu's reputation, Zhang jumped the barrier to retrieve the toy. Gu Gu, who weighs 240 pounds, wasted little time attacking the intruder. "The panda didn't let go until it chewed up my leg and its mouth was dripping with my blood," said Zhang after zookeepers used tools to pry apart the animal's jaws. "The panda is a national treasure," Zhang added, "and I love and respect him, so I didn't fight back."

CELEBRITY DIETS

Oh, those crazy celebs. They don't even eat food like the rest of us.

MARTHA'S VINEYARD DETOX
The Diet: For 21 days, you ingest nothing but "live juices and enzymes" contained in fruit drinks, herbal teas, vegetable broth, and supplements. Bonus: You also get a colonic and a coffee enema each week.
Celebs Who've Tried It: Madonna and supermodel Gisele Bündchen

JOSHI'S HOLISTIC DETOX
The Diet: This non-dairy, wheat-free, gluten-free diet bans all alcohol, sugar, tea, milk, coffee, red meat, potatoes, tomatoes, and most fruit (except bananas), in an effort to avoid acidic and "toxic" foods. What's left? Mostly grains, raw and steamed vegetables, eggs, chicken, and fish. You also get herbal supplements, colonic irrigations, acupuncture to curb sugar cravings, and weekly sessions of reflexology from Hollywood's self-described Health Guru, Nishi Joshi.
Celebs Who've Tried It: Gwyneth Paltrow, Kate Moss, Cate Blanchett, and Ralph Fiennes

MASTER CLEANSE
The Diet: Invented in the 1940s and popular in the 1970s, the Master Cleanse (also called the Lemonade Diet) is back. You drink a mixture of maple syrup, water, cayenne pepper, and fresh lemon juice for 10 days—no solid food allowed. Result: You're free of harmful cravings for alcohol, tobacco, coffee, tea, and drugs.
Celebs Who've Tried It: Mariah Carey, Beyoncé, Vince Vaughn, Angelina Jolie, Jared Leto, Anne Hathaway, Gwyneth Paltrow, Ashley Judd, and Jay-Z

FACIAL ANALYSIS
The Diet: Kate Winslet promotes this naturopathic plan that

Drug lord Joaquin Guzman was *Forbes* magazine's 41st-most-powerful person in the world in 2009.

analyzes your skin, hair, and eyes to determine your food and mineral deficiencies. There are six "face archetypes." One example: "Ruled by the thyroid gland," the symptoms of which are dry skin, fluffy hair, and bulging eyes. Foods to avoid? Chocolate, mangoes, and red wine. Foods to eat? Asparagus, cucumbers, oats, and potatoes.

21-DAY CLEANSE

The Diet: Oprah Winfrey underwent this 21-day "Jump-Start" cleanse in which you cut out all animal products, gluten, caffeine, sugar, and alcohol. You also practice "conscious eating," which means that in choosing your food, you must first consider its environmental impact, and whether or not any animals were harmed at any point in its cultivation (such as the use of pesticides). Ultimate goal: to achieve "spiritual integrity."

Other Celebs Who've Tried It: Pamela Anderson, Casey Affleck, Andre 3000, Alicia Silverstone, and Natalie Portman

BABY FOOD DIET

The Diet: How do you eat only 600 calories a day? Replace one or more meals with baby food. According to super-skinny fashion designer Hedi Slimane, who created the diet: "The less I chew, the better."

Celebs Who've Tried It: Jennifer Aniston, Lily Allen, Reese Witherspoon, and *Desperate Housewives's* Marcia Cross

MORE STRANGE CELEBRITY DIETS

• Victoria Beckham's daily intake is edamame (baby soybeans in the pod), strawberries, a few prawns, and lettuce, along with two pints of algae or a seaweed shake.

• Mariah Carey believes that purple foods keep her from getting wrinkles. Three days a week, she eats only foods such as grapes, plums, and beets.

• Christina Aguilera follows a 7-Day Color Diet regimen in which she eats one type of food per day, based on color or texture. The colors: white, red, green, orange, purple, yellow, and rainbow!

THE HAUNTING, PART II

When we left Jackie Hernandez in Part I of this ghost story (page 297), she had finally escaped the terror of that San Pedro house...or so she thought.

YOU CAN RUN...BUT YOU CAN'T HIDE

Not long after Jackie arrived in Weldon, her husband left her. Once again, she found herself alone in a new town. But she wasn't really alone. It started with a familiar pounding noise coming from the shed behind her trailer at night. Jackie recognized that sound. Then two of her neighbors got the scare of their lives when they were carrying a TV into her house and a face appeared on the screen. When they described its "evil eyes," Jackie knew whose face it was. Then one evening when she was in her baby daughter's room—Jackie turned around and the bedspread caught fire for no apparent reason. Had she not been there...

On April 13, 1990, the investigators got a phone call. Jackie was hysterical. Barry Conrad and Jeff Wheatcraft immediately jumped in their car and drove to Weldon. They arrived around midnight, but of course the house was quiet. Conrad turned on his camera and conducted some interviews. Nothing happened. So Jackie had an idea: "Let's use a Ouija board and see if we can get it to talk to us." The investigators weren't too keen on the idea. It wasn't that they believed the stories that a Ouija board could somehow "open the door" for evil spirits; they thought it was just a toy. Still, they agreed to give it a try.

THE CONVERSATION

Conrad trained his camera on the Ouija board while Jackie and a neighbor looked on. Wheatcraft and Conrad sat at the table with the board placed between them. Then the camera shut off. Conrad got up and turned it back on. And it shut off again. Just like that first night in the attic, he couldn't get it to work. So although there were four witnesses, there was no camera to record what happened next. Here's what they reported.

Shortly into the séance, the room grew very cold. As the two men asked questions, the pointer moved from letter to letter, sometimes with their hands upon it, other times by itself. It spelled out its answers while Jackie wrote everything down.

> **Q:** Are you really a ghost?
> **A:** YES
> **Q:** How many ghosts reside among the living?
> **A:** PHANTOMS FILL THE SKIES ABOVE YOU

While Wheatcraft and Conrad tried to make sense of the response, the table began to shake. Then a candle went out. Then another one went out. They resumed the session.

> **Q:** Where did you die?
> **A:** SAN PEDRO BAY
> **Q:** Did you drown?
> **A:** NO, I WAS HELD UNDER WATER
> **Q:** Did you live in the San Pedro house?
> **A:** MY MURDERER
> **Q:** Why do you follow Jackie?
> **A:** ENERGY

As the night went on and dawn approached, the spirit revealed even more: He died in 1930, and he hanged Jeff Wheatcraft because "YOU HAVE THE LIKENESS OF MY KILLER." Then Conrad asked, "Is there anyone in this room that you hate?" The letters spelled out: "J-E-F-F".

And then, wrote Conrad: "For in a furious few seconds, Jeff and chair were levitated off the floor and hurled backwards into the trailer wall. The impact was so great that the entire trailer shook as Jeff toppled to the floor, unconscious." Petrified, Jackie quickly took her two kids out of the house. Conrad was able to rouse Wheatcraft and get him to safety as well. Knowing that she couldn't escape the spirit and that there was nothing left for her in Weldon, Jackie and her two children went back to San Pedro to stay at a friend's house.

NAMES TO THE FACES

"The majority of paranormal cases aren't worth pursuing," explains Barry Taff. "There's a lot of invention, a lot of embellishment, and a lot of outright fraud." But Jackie Hernandez's ordeal was different. "This is is the first case, out of more than 3,000 that I've been on, where the phenomenon went after the researchers." It even followed Wheatcraft and Conrad back to their L.A. apartment, taunting them by—among other things—turning on the stove burners and placing scissors under their pillows. Wheatcraft said he was even pushed again.

DOCK OF THE BAY

So who was this malevolent spirit? After the séance, Conrad looked through old newspapers and found an article dated March 25, 1930, about a young sailor named Herman Hendrickson who was found dead in the water at the San Pedro docks. He had a large gash on his head, and foul play was suspected, but there were no witnesses. So police ultimately ruled the death accidental, believing that he probably slipped, hit his head, and drowned. When Jackie read the article, she felt right away, "That's him."

And what about the other ghost—the old man? Jackie believes she found out during the summer of 1990, after she moved back to San Pedro. While staying at her friend's house, she saw a bright light outside one afternoon. Jackie followed it to a graveyard a few blocks away from her old house. It seemed to hover above the grave of a man named John Damon. "It went around and around the grave and just disappeared," she recalled. Jackie later learned that her old house had been built by that same John Damon.

MOVING ON

Barry Conrad produced a documentary movie about the case called *An Unknown Encounter: A Haunting in San Pedro.* He also wrote a book about it. Barry Taff, still in the paranormal business, says he's never seen a case like this one, before or since. He doesn't know why or how this entity was so focused and so powerful, but he believes that it was somehow "feeding off the negative energy emanating from Jackie" in those troubled times. "One theory is that the environment can somehow store information," he said. "And under the proper circumstances the information is reconstructed so that you can feel it, see it, or hear it.

Jackie Hernandez settled in an apartment in San Pedro. (She had it blessed by a priest before she moved in.) Then she started repairing her life. As things got back to normal—and she stopped bringing the investigators around—the "activity" grew quieter and quieter over the next couple of years. Today, she still lives in San Pedro, and claims that although she hasn't been attacked since the early 1990s, the ghost of Herman Hendrickson still makes its presence known to her every once in a while. And at last report, Jackie's old house is still haunted. The present owners have said that no previous tenant lasted more than six months.

CONCLUSION

To date, no one has ever been able to produce video proof of a haunting. Yet with the Jackie Hernandez case, everyone involved took and passed lie detector tests. In addition, the investigators captured footage of what appear to be floating balls of light, including one that can be clearly seen flying *into* Jackie's head. Video experts and insect experts have examined the footage—as well as the still photographs—and all said the same thing: "These are not bugs or reflections or anything else that can be easily explained away. They're like nothing we've ever seen." That's not all. Conrad filmed objects that moved on their own, as well as "something" dripping out of the wall. When Taff took the liquid to the forensics lab at UCLA to be tested, it was determined to be human plasma.

So why isn't the San Pedro case the "smoking gun"—the one that makes everyone believe in spirits? "The problem is," admits Taff, "these days, anything can be faked. So it's not truth beyond a reasonable doubt."

And the search for the proof of ghosts continues.

*   *   *

PERSISTENCE SQUARED

A 22-year-old British man, Graham Parker, bought a Rubik's Cube in 1983 at the peak of the puzzle toy fad's popularity. He started trying to solve it, and kept trying...for 26 years. Finally, in 2009, at age 48, Parker solved it. "I've missed many important events," he said, "and I've had wrist and back problems from spending hours on it, but when I clicked that last bit into place, I wept."

The yolk of an ostrich egg is the largest single cell in the world.

O CANADA...

...glorious and weird! O Canada, we stand on weird for thee...

Police in Langley, British Columbia, issued a warning to men in the city in October 2009: be on the lookout for a "serial testicle kicker." Police said a woman in her late teens or early twenties had walked up to several men in the city and, without warning, kicked them in the groin. One man, 22-year-old Anthony Clark, had even lost a testicle to the woman. "I just want to know what her problem is," Clark said.

A man whose car ran into a ditch while being chased by police in southwest Ontario in February 2010 ran across a shallow river to hide his tracks—and then jumped into the snow and covered himself up to hide. Officers couldn't find him until they brought in a canine unit. The man was arrested...and taken to a hospital to be treated for hypothermia...hours later.

Robert Medwid, 39, and Sabrina Lonsberry, 32, of Red Deer, Alberta, won the Canadian national lottery in January 2007, taking the $13.8 million jackpot. Medwid chosen the winning numbers based on the weather in Scarborough, Ontario, where the numbers are drawn. "I decided to research the climate, humidity, and snowfall on draw nights in Scarborough," Medwid said, "and I chose my numbers based on that information." Winning numbers: 5, 9, 14, 31, 37, and 46. (Brrr!)

Bela Kosoian, 38, of Montreal, Quebec, was arrested in 2009. Her crime: not holding a handrail on an escalator in a subway station. (She was busy digging in her bag for change when ordered to hold the rail, and refused.) She was handcuffed, taken to a holding cell, and finally released with a $100 ticket for the handrail offense and a $320 fine for obstructing justice. Said Kosoian, who left the Soviet Union years ago to live in Canada, "Stalin may be dead, but Stalinism lives on."

In August 2009, three men from Cudworth, Saskatchewan, took a video of themselves illegally shooting ducks on a pond—from their car—and put the video on YouTube. They were arrested within days, fined $5,000 each, and banned from hunting for three years. One of the men, David Fraser, 30, tried to explain the incident by saying they'd only recently moved to Saskatchewan from Toronto...where the only birds they'd ever seen were seagulls and pigeons.

David Dauphinee, 52, and his brother Daniel Dauphinee, 51, both retired officers with the Royal Canadian Mounted Police, were arrested in 2001 after throwing dozens of onions, apples, and oranges at police officers from a 19th-floor hotel room window in Winnipeg. When police got to the room, the two men—who were drunk—jumped into bed together and pretended to be asleep. When asked for their names, police said the older brother "barked, like a large dog." The two were convicted of assault with a weapon (the fruit and vegetables) and sentenced to two months in prison.

In 2008 Catherine McCoubrey, 25, of Winnipeg, Manitoba, stabbed her boyfriend in the heart...accidentally...while attempting to carve a heart shape into his skin with a large knife, which he had asked her to do while they were having "rough sex." She pleaded guilty to assault and was given three years of probation. The boyfriend nearly died, doctors said, but made a full recovery.

A Toronoto gym owner named Rick Evans applied for the vanity license plate "KICK-BUTT" in 2009. However, the review board rejected because it "condoned violence and contained sexual subject matter." Ironically, Evans's first license plate choice was "BUTT-KICK"...which wasn't available because someone else had successfully applied for, and received, the plate.

Juanita Stead, 36, of eastern Newfoundland, went to a hospital on New Year's Eve 2008 with abdominal pain. She and her husband Terry both thought she was passing a kidney stone. Doctors took X-rays, but could see no evidence of a kidney stone...they could, however, see a baby in her belly. "I told him he had the wrong X-ray file," Stead said. Six minutes later, she gave birth to a 7-pound, 12-ounce boy. Stead, who'd had another child two years earlier, had no idea she was pregnant—she hadn't experienced any morning sickness, and her menstrual cycle continued normally. "Honest to God," her husband said, "I just don't have words to explain it." (Little Nicholas is doing just fine.)

Japanese embassies have a 24-hour hotline for Japanese tourists suffering from severe culture shock.

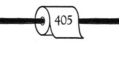

JACKASSES

MTV's show Jackass *(2000 to '02) featured a group of young men performing dangerous and disgusting stunts. Of course it was a huge hit. But for some die-hard fans, just watching it on TV wasn't enough—they had to live it!*

SPITFIRE

Jackass was created in 1999 by a 27-year-old writer and out-of-work actor named Johnny Knoxville, who came up with a novel idea for a magazine article: To test the effectiveness of different defensive weapons, he would purposely get himself shot, tasered, and pepper-sprayed. A skateboarding magazine liked the idea, but suggested it would be funnier if Knoxville filmed all of the tests. He did, and they ended up in a skateboarding video called *Big Brother Number Two*, which became hugely popular. Knoxville and his friends (including director Spike Jonze) shopped the idea of an amateur stunt show to several networks. MTV outbid Comedy Central for the rights, and *Jackass* premiered in 2000.

I CAN DO THAT

Fans immediately took to the show's no-holds-barred stunts. In one infamous episode, Knoxville donned a flame-retardant suit, attached raw steaks to his body, had himself tied to a giant rotisserie spit, and was set on fire. But at least two of the 4.9 million viewers who saw the stunt didn't heed the warning to "not try this at home." In January 2001, Jason Lind, 13, of Torrington, Connecticut, went into his backyard, doused his hands and pants in gasoline, and a friend lit his pants on fire. Unfortunately, Jason left out the most important part—the *flame-retardant suit*. After jumping into the snow trying to smother the flames, he ended up with second-degree burns to much of his body. His friend was arrested for reckless endangerment.

A few weeks later, 12-year-old Thomas Hitz sprayed bug repellent on his hands in a friend's backyard in Lake Mary, Florida. He was then lit on fire and ended up jumping into a swimming pool while his friends laughed. Thomas also was severely burned.

EXCUSES, EXCUSES

The two incidents made headlines, especially after the boys' families claimed it was MTV's fault. "I don't blame myself," said Thomas Hitz. "I did it because I saw it on *Jackass* and I was copying the show." (His mother described him as "very intelligent.") The Hitzes appeared on *Good Morning, America* and insisted that MTV should cancel *Jackass*. Senator Joe Lieberman agreed. In an open letter to MTV, he wrote, "Either cancel this exploitative and degrading show or eliminate the stunts that could be dangerous if imitated by children."

At first, MTV bosses held their ground: "While we don't accept responsibility, obviously we feel horrible when a young person does something to hurt themselves," they wrote in a statement. "We take great care to air our shows responsibly. *Jackass* airs with a TV-Mature rating, with written and verbal warnings throughout the show." They also pointed out that the episode had featured three minutes of footage showing Knoxville's safety precautions.

In the end, however, MTV moved *Jackass* to a late-night slot and limited the stunts the cast could do—which upset fans as well as the performers, some of whom quit. The show ended its run less than a year later, and Knoxville and his cohorts went on to make a string of successful *Jackass* movies. "It's a real primal thing, watching someone get hurt," said Knoxville. "It's funny and accessible. I should quit, but man, we have so much fun!"

MORE JACKASS-INSPIRED IDIOCY
Both of the burned boys made full recoveries. But they weren't the only ones who tried the "home version" of the show.

• A 16-year-old Wisconsin teen copied a stunt in which a *Jackass* crewmember ran up and stole a taco from the hand of a worker at a drive-through. However, unlike on the show, this particular fast-food worker held onto the taco and ended up with a broken arm.

• Four Scottish men in their 20s were arrested in 2004 after performing a fake kidnapping in which one of the men stumbled out of a car in a supermarket parking lot with a black plastic bag over his head, screaming for help. The men told police they were recreating a scene from *Jackass* because it was "funny."

• In 2006 a 22-year-old British man copied a stunt from the first *Jackass* movie. While his friends watched, he got down on all fours and launched a firework known as a "Black Cat Thunderbolt"... out of his rectum. (Rectum? It damn near killed him!)

HOAXERS

*Why are people so quick to believe any old story they're told? Simple:
Because this world is a crazy place, and crazy things happen all
the time. Here are two classic hoaxes, and one recent one.*

THE ICEBERG COMETH

April 1, 1978, was a gloomy, overcast day in Sidney, Australia. But that didn't stop hundreds of people from going
to the harbor to await the arrival of local entrepreneur Dick
Smith, owner of Dick Smith Foods. He'd promised to show up in a
barge hauling an iceberg. Then, he said, he was going to break up
the massive iceberg and sell the pieces as "dickcicles"—ice cubes
made from pure Antarctica water. A lot of the onlookers figured it
was just a big April Fool's Day joke and Smith wouldn't show up
at all. But then, off in the distance, they could see the barge…and
it really was hauling an iceberg. A few minutes later the *Dickenberg I*, as a local DJ dubbed it, floated into Sydney Harbor.

And then it started to rain.

Within minutes, the "iceberg" was revealed for what it really
was: a floating platform slathered in a ton of shaving cream.
Unfazed, Smith docked and gave everyone cold drinks (the ice
cubes came from the barge's beer cooler). He later said the stunt
was worth a million dollars in free advertising.

THE LADY VANISHES

On March 29, 1950, a blonde, buxom actress named Nicole Riche
was starring as a kidnapping victim in the noir play *No Orchids for
Miss Blandish* at the Grand Guignol Theatre in Paris, France.
Between Acts I and II, stagehands witnessed Riche pick up a note,
read it, and then run out the backstage door. She never returned
for Act II. Theater manager Alexandre Dundas canceled the rest
of the performance and called the police. Investigators found the
note—which Riche had dropped on the floor—and suspected kidnapping. A massive manhunt commenced.

Headlines across Europe told the "life imitates art" story of the
beautiful woman who was abducted while starring in a play about
a beautiful woman who gets abducted. Two days later, Riche, still
wearing the negligee and fur coat she had worn on stage, stumbled

into the Pigalle district police station and told her story: Two men had dragged her into a car and driven her to a hideout outside of Paris, where they berated her for being in an immoral play, and had then left her in the woods. She said she'd found some "kind Gypsies" who gave her a ride back to Paris, but when pressed for a description of her abductors, all she could say was that they were "Puritans." Police chief Marcel Cambon smelled a rat, so he kept pressing her for the truth, and Riche finally came clean: It was a hoax orchestrated by Dundas to drum up publicity for his financially strapped theatre. Riche had to pay a fine for creating a public nuisance…but the play drew much larger audiences after the fake abduction.

THE BIG FAT LIAR

In November 2009, General Felix Murga, head of Peru's Criminal Investigation division, held a national press conference: "There is a horrible crime being committed in the jungles." A gang called the *Pishtacos*—named after a mythical Peruvian creature who kills people for their body fat—was kidnapping and killing people for their body fat. A police drawing depicted racks of human carcasses strung up like sides of beef. The Pishtacos, he said, were selling bottles of the fat for up to $60,000 per gallon. The story made headlines; no one in the Peruvian press was talking about anything else. But then that was the whole point. Before that, everyone in Peru *had been* talking about another scandal, in which a police "death squad" illegally executed 46 criminals. It dominated the news…until the fat story. And then people began to question *that* story. Reporters cited a prominent plastic surgeon who noted that "human fat has no value." And police in Huanaco, where the Pishtacos were supposedly based, had never even heard of the fat-stealing gang until General Murga's press conference.

A few weeks later, the Peruvian daily *La Republica* reported that the fat story was a complete fabrication—nothing more than a "grease screen." The press immediately went back to reporting about the death squads, demanding an explanation of the government cover-up. After initial denials, Peru's chief of police, Miguel Hildago, finally acknowledged the hoax with an announcement that General Murga had been fired for "sullying the reputation" of his department.

LOUD NOISES!!!

*On page 266, we told you about some of the more common sources
of noise pollution—car stereos, loud parties, and Wiccan priestesses.
Here are a few more stories full of sound and fury.*

CRAZY COMMERCIALS

You're curled up on the couch watching your favorite TV
show. Something really dramatic happens, the scene fades
to black, and before you know it, your television erupts into loud
music, glaring colors, and some announcer yelling, "There's never
been a better time to buy a Toyota!" To curb this annoyance, in
2009 Rep. Anna Eshoo (D-California) introduced legislation
called the Commercial Advertisement Loudness Mitigation act,
or CALM, which will fine stations for airing "excessively noisy or
strident" commercials. But even if the law passes, it may prove
hard to enforce. That's because in the United States, the FCC
already controls how loud a station can broadcast. TV shows
rarely, if ever, reach the maximum level. Advertisers, however,
push the entire 30 seconds to the highest level. "If someone sets
off a camera flash every now and then, it's one thing," writes
Spencer Critchley in *Digital Audio* magazine. "If they aim a steady
spotlight into your eyes it's another, even if the peak brightness is
no higher."

OH, THE iRONY

The Apple iPod was designed to be an "instrument of solitude,"
where the listener can retreat to his or her library of music while
not forcing it upon others. But a 2007 *Associated Press* article
reported that people who don't own the devices have complained
to Apple that the iPod itself is a growing source of noise pollution.
That's because the listeners who put the little ear buds on—while
on a bus or plane, or in their cubicle or a waiting room—are often
unaware that the tinny sound can be heard by anyone within
about 10 feet. "Like the cell phone," said the article, "the iPod
can foster a sense of apathy when the user is among strangers. It's
easier to blow off social norms—and channel Justin Timberlake
during rush hour—when you don't know whom you're irritating."

A Hunch, Inc., political survey found that Conservatives prefer Colby cheese. Liberals like Brie.

GOING GREEN THE LOUD WAY

Farmers in Massachusetts have been furious since a taxpayer-subsidized solar panel factory was built on nearby land in January 2009. The plant is so noisy that, according to the *Boston Herald*, "Their horses have ulcers, the ducks have disappeared, and a dog has started gnawing off doorknobs." Said one farmer, "Imagine tuning your radio to a station that gets only static. Then imagine having to listen to that 24 hours a day, seven days a week. That's what we are living with. It's like our tax dollars are being used to torture us." The plant has since hired a "noise specialist" to try to figure out how to dampen some of the sounds (after the factory was threatened with fines of $1,000 per day). A spokesman apologized, but said that making solar panels is a "loud business."

A WAKE-UP CALL

In a recent study conducted by Imperial College London, scientists measured the heart and brain activity of people who lived near four major European airports (including England's Heathrow, which has had a long history of noise-pollution controversy). Every time a plane flew overhead, the subjects' blood pressure went up, even when they were asleep. It wasn't just the jet engines that did it: Whenever any significant "noise event" occurred—described as 35 decibels or more (a passing car with a loud engine, or drunk people shouting in the street)—the subjects' blood pressure raised to dangerous levels. And there was a direct correlation: the louder the noise, the higher the blood pressure. That makes for restless nights, which leads to stressful days.

THOSE DAMN KIDS!

An 82-year-old German man was fed up by an annoying song coming in through his window. It happened in the morning, the afternoon, and the middle of the night. He kept yelling out his window for the neighborhood kids to shut up, but the song would start playing again. It was so annoying that he finally called the police—who instantly solved the case. How? An officer found a greeting card on the man's windowsill. It was the kind that has a tiny speaker inside and plays a song every time the card shakes... which happened every time a breeze came in through the window. The man was "happy, relieved, and a little embarrassed."

Poll results: One in three iPhone owners has ended a relationship via text message.

I HAD MY BABY IN A...

Pregnancy offers so many novelties: stretch marks, mood swings...and the
chance to give birth to a slimy little human in the unlikeliest of places.

POST OFFICE
Sonia Marina Nascimento went to a post office in Wisbech,
England in May 2009 to buy some minutes for her mobile
phone—when her water broke. Postmaster Paul Childs, 58,
jumped into action and moved Nasciemento from the lobby and
into an office. Then, before an ambulance could arrive, Childs, his
wife Helen, and an employee delivered a baby girl. "It was jolly
good," Childs said to reporters afterward. "She hadn't even been
having contractions. She dropped her jeans and out it popped."
Childs weighed the baby on a post-office scale. "She weighed 5
pounds, 15 ounces," he said. "We worked out that that's the equivalent of an £8.22 first-class parcel."

SHRIMP BOAT

In August 2007, shrimp boat skipper Ed Keisel was 30 miles off
the coast of Texas when his cook, Cindy Preisel, went into labor.
Keisel grabbed a roll of paper towels and a first-aid book and got
ready. But there was trouble: The baby came out breech, or feet
first. "I'm no doctor," Keisel said, "but even I knew that's not supposed to happen." He stayed calm, but there was more trouble:
The umbilical cord was wrapped around the baby's neck. "So I did
the only thing I could," the skipper said. "I waited for a contrac-
tion, and then slid my fingers in around the top of his head and
scooped him out." But now the newborn wasn't breathing. Keisel
cleared the baby's nose and mouth and gently performed CPR.
After an agonizing 25 minutes, the boy sucked in air, turned red—
and started bawling. "I was so happy and relieved," Cindy Preisel
said. "It's hard to put into words." She named the boy Brian, after
his father—a crewman on the boat—and gave him the middle
name Edward, after the skipper who delivered him.

JET PLANE

Nicola and Dominic Delemere of Scunthorpe, England, took a

Spivey's Corner, North Carolina, hosts an annual festival to "revive the lost art of hollering."

flight from London to the Greek island of Crete in August 2007. Nicola was six months pregnant, far from full term. But at 30,000 feet, her water broke and she went into contractions. There were no doctors on board, so while the pilots turned the plane around, flight supervisor Carol Miller and a passenger delivered the baby—which weighed only one pound, one ounce. The tiny baby boy wasn't breathing, so the quick-thinking Miller used a straw to clear fluids from the newborn's lungs, gave him mouth-to-mouth resuscitation, and massaged his heart until the plane landed at Gatwick Airport. The boy was rushed to a hospital, where doctors said he'd gone too long without oxygen and had almost certainly suffered brain damage. They were wrong: Four months later, little Alfie Delemere was home and was expected to be just fine. And the airline offered the whole family a free flight.

TREE

In February 2000, Sofia Pedro of Mozambique was about nine months pregnant when the Limpopo River flooded. To escape the rising waters, she, her two children, her mother-in-law, and several of their neighbors climbed a large tree—and were all trapped there for the next three days as the flood raged. On the third day, Pedro went into labor. Thinking fast, her mother-in-law tied Pedro to a branch with a blanket, then caught the baby when it arrived—with the floodwaters six feet below them. Just then, a rescue helicopter appeared overhead and a medic was lowered down. He cut the baby's umbilical cord and hoisted baby and mom to safety. Everyone in the tree survived the disaster.

McDONALD'S RESTROOM

Danille Miller was working the night shift at a McDonald's restaurant one night in December 2007 in Vancouver, Washington, when she suddenly ran to the restroom. A co-worker followed her in, asking if she was okay. Miller said something felt wrong, but she wasn't sure what. Within a few minutes, she had her answer when she began giving birth to a baby. This was a shock—because Miller had no idea that she was pregnant. Her equally shocked co-worker told someone to call 911, then helped deliver a six-pound baby boy. Mom and baby (later named Austin) were transported to a nearby hospital, and both were fine.

Roto-Rooter contest prize: The "Pimped-Out John," a toilet with built-in mini-fridge, TV & laptop.

KILLER KARAOKE

"And now, the end is near..." is the opening line of the song "My Way." Alas, in some karaoke bars in the Philippines, that's not just a lyric but an eerily accurate prediction.

HE DID IT HIS WAY

In 1968 Frank Sinatra invited 27-year-old singer/songwriter Paul Anka to dinner, where Sinatra revealed that he was thinking of retiring from the music business. He asked Anka to write a farewell song for him. Anka already had a tune—he liked the melody of a song called "Comme d'Habitude" ("As Usual") that he'd heard while vacationing on the French Riviera. He did not like the self-pitying French lyrics about living in a loveless relationship, however, so he got the composers' permission to write new English lyrics for it.

Anka began the lyrics that very night. As he worked, he tried to make it a song about Sinatra's life, written from Sinatra's point of view, heavy with swaggering bravado. He finished at 5:00 a.m. and flew out to Las Vegas to sing it to Sinatra. The song: "My Way." It became the archetypal later-Sinatra song, so much so that Sinatra didn't retire. It became one of the most popular, most recorded songs of all time, and a staple of karaoke bars around the world. But in one country, the Philippines, the song has taken a dark turn.

ALL YOU NEED IS DEATH

The "My Way Killings" is what Philippine newspapers call them. Nobody really knows how many people have been killed during a karaoke performance of the song, but in early 2010, the *New York Times* reported that there have been "at least a half-dozen" deaths in recent years. (The *Asia Times* estimates that the number is in the dozens.) Some of the cases include:

- A singer in a San Mateo bar who ignored a heckler who complained that the guy was singing out of tune. Midway through the song, the heckler pulled out a .38-caliber pistol and shot the performer in the chest, killing him instantly.
- Faced by hecklers, another singer took the initiative and shot

two audience members, killing one.

• A "Sinatra-loving crowd" reportedly rushed the stage en masse and beat a singer to death for his poor performance of "My Way." The situation so spooked employees and patrons that many karaoke bars removed the song from their machines, and families banned it from their sing-along gatherings.

As an inexpensive form of entertainment in a relatively poor country, karaoke has become an important part of Philippine culture. It's hard to escape the sound of somebody singing along to synthesized music—you can hear it in bars and nightclubs, at family gatherings, even on the street or in malls, courtesy of coin-operated kiosks. And apparently singers take their performances seriously, taking offense at audience inattention or heckling; hardcore audiences can get ugly when someone steps up to the mike unprepared or out of tune.

MY WAY OR THE HIGHWAY

But what puts "My Way" into its own category of karaoke danger? Observers suggest two possible reasons:

1. It's sung too often. On any given night, a bar-hopper in the Philippines would likely hear "My Way" performed several times, enough to drive a music lover to despair even if it was sung well. When sung badly...well, get ready to duck.

2. Because of its arrogant lyrics. The lyrics brag about being a tough guy who follows his own course, implying that anybody who doesn't is a loser. Perhaps Sinatra could get away with it, but when a taxi driver sings those lyrics, some listeners just want to pop the guy, or at least put him in his place.

THE END IS NEAR

In a hot, crowded bar, in a desperate society with millions of illegal handguns, it's easy for irritation to boil up into murderous rage. Many Manila karaoke bars have now banned the singing of "My Way" to protect patrons from alcohol-fueled fights. (Even Sinatra grew to hate it. After performing it in 1984 at London's Albert Hall, he was heard muttering "I can't stand that song.") Although "My Way" is one of the most played at funerals and is even quoted on gravestones, Sinatra chose another of his songs as his epitaph: "The Best Is Yet to Come."

Beer, sawdust, and used diapers are all being considered for use as alternative fuels.

DOCTOR, NO!

So far, we've made you afraid to fly (page 370), afraid to call the police (page 223), afraid to send your kids to school (page 301), and afraid to vote (page 178). And now we're going to make you afraid to go the hospital. (Sorry.)

ALWAYS GET A SECOND OPINION
In 1989 a man identified as Mr. C was told by doctors at Western General Hospital in Edinburgh, Scotland, that he had Huntington's disease, an incurable brain illness. The news shocked his family and they prepared for the worst—the onset of symptoms and his eventual death. The diagnosis affected all of their lives: His wife and one of his daughters terminated their pregnancies for fear of passing on the hereditary disease, and another daughter quit school because of the stress. But by 2007, Mr. C hadn't developed any symptoms, so doctors tested him again...and discovered that he never even had Huntington's. "We are deeply sorry for the anxiety caused to Mr. C and his family," said a hospital spokesperson. A lawsuit is pending.

DO YOU FEEL A DRAFT?
Johanna L., a 78-year-old retiree, checked into the Hochfranken-Klinik in Münchberg, Germany, in March 2008 to have knee surgery. But when she woke up in the recovery room, her knee hadn't been operated on...and she felt a strange breeze blowing up the back of her gown. She called a nurse, who informed Johanna that she had been given an artificial anus. Apparently, there was a records mix-up: The patient who was suffering from severe incontinence got knee surgery; Johanna got that patient's new anus. She sued the hospital, and the doctors were suspended.

SMILE—YOU'RE ON CANDID CAMERA
In 2008 at a hospital in the Philippines, officials were forced to apologize to a 39-year-old patient. Why? Because after he checked in to have a "canister of perfume" removed from his colon (no

report on how it got there), the medical team assigned to remove it decided to film the procedure—and then uploaded it onto the Internet. The film, which featured doctors and nurses laughing around the patient's unconscious body and cheering when they finally extracted the canister, became a hit. A hospital spokesperson later said that cameras and cell phones had been banned from operating rooms, and added that while it was acceptable at a teaching hospital to allow young doctors and nurses to watch an operation, it had been "a violation of ethical standards" for them to spray the perfume at the end.

HE TALKS TOO MUCH

Eighty-year-old Tom Talks of Rochdale, England, was walking his dog in July 2008 when he tripped and broke his ankle. Doctors at Fairfield General Hospital put his leg in a plaster cast and sent him home. But the cast was too tight. "Every day for a week, I begged them to release the pressure," said Talks. "It felt like my leg was trying to burst out of its skin." They refused to loosen the cast...until Talks collapsed in agony. That convinced them to examine him...and they discovered an infection so severe that part of his leg had to be amputated. Afterward, Talks suffered a heart attack and developed kidney problems. His grandson, Karl Sanderson, said, "This is the 21st century—we should not be in a situation where someone might die because they fracture their ankle!" At last report, Talks's family had filed a formal complaint with the hospital.

BRAINLESS SURGEONS

In the span of a few months in 2007, neurosurgeons at Rhode Island Hospital made a rash of unusual—and similar—errors: They operated on the wrong side of patients' brains three different times. Two of the patients barely survived; one died a few weeks later. Rhode Island's Department of Health fined the hospital $50,000 and assured the public, "We are extremely concerned about this continuing pattern." The state ordered the hospital to develop a checklist to remind the brain surgeons to verify that they're cutting in the right place before they start cutting.

In 2006 Toys for Tots turned down a donation of talking Jesus dolls, but later changed their minds.

DARK COMICS

Comic books and superhero stories like The Dark Knight *and* Watchmen *have taken the genre through some unusual twists and turns. Here are a few that were even more twisted.*

Superman: At Earth's End (1995)

This comic book is set about 500 years in the future, after humanity has been all but destroyed by an apocalyptic disaster. Superman is still around, but he's a very old, mentally ill, homeless person with a long white beard. The U.S. is now run by the DNA Diktators, twin clones of Adolf Hitler who want to exterminate what's left of the human race and start over with a "master race." So they send out evil Batman clones and flying robots to find and kill any remaining humans. Superman tracks down the Hitler twins, kills them, retrieves Batman's corpse from the cloning lab, and then sets it—and himself—on fire.

Spider-Man: Reign (2006)

Now 60 years old, Spider-Man (or Peter Parker) is retired from crimefighting and works as a florist. He's not doing too well—he vomits, hallucinates, and cries a lot, all signs of inconsolable grief. Why the grief? Because the love of his life, Mary Jane, died of cancer after a mysterious, prolonged exposure to radiation. Only he knows the truth: Because he was bitten by a radioactive spider as a young man—which gave him his spidey-superpowers—his bodily fluids constantly emitted radiation. Then he married Mary Jane and, after years of doing what married people do, his own super body gave Mary Jane cancer...and killed her.

Civil War (2007)

After the Incredible Hulk flies into a rage and kills 28 people one day in Las Vegas, the government passes the Superhuman Registration Act, requiring superheroes to check in with the government and divulge their true identities. The superhero community splits into two camps on the issue. The anti-registration contingent is led by Captain America, who is executed for treason by the pro-registration side, led by Iron Man, who hires an army of supervillains to hunt down noncompliant superheroes. Dozens of Marvel Comics characters get involved in this satire of the paranoia and ratcheted-up security measures in the U.S. since 9/11, the Patriot Act, and the Abu Ghraib scandal.

The Punisher Meets Archie (1994)

The Punisher, who made his debut in the 1970s, is one of the darkest superheroes in comic-book history—a vigilante who avenges the deaths of his family (who accidentally witnessed a mob hit) by torturing and brutally murdering any criminal he can get his hands on. Meanwhile, Archie is the squeaky-clean "all-American teenager" who hasn't changed much since his introduction in the 1940s. In this comic, the Punisher is looking for Red, a drug kingpin who's hiding out, posing as a gym teacher in Archie's high school…and who also happens to look exactly like Archie. After a series of mistaken-identity gags involving Archie and his friends, the Punisher gets ahold of Red (and nobody dies).

The Ultimates (2003)

In this update of the '60s superhero team the Avengers, the main characters are Quicksilver and Scarlet Witch, fraternal-twin superheroes (male and female, respectively). But this brother and sister are bound not just by their family ties or common special powers; they're also…romantically involved. The Ultimates is believed to be the first incestuous-twin superhero comic book. And why the attraction? Quicksilver says he's drawn to Scarlet Witch because she "reminds him of his mother." (Eww!)

*   *   *

MORE BACON-RELATED PRODUCTS

- bacon-flavored lollipops
- bacon-flavored breath mints
- bacon air freshener
- bacon ice cream
- bacon tape
- bacon bandages
- bacon-infused personal lubricant

About 1% of the static on a TV tuned between stations is a relic of the Big Bang.

THE YEAR OF LIVING FESTIVELY

Want to have the most fun year of your life? If you've got the time, the money, and a spirit of adventure, we've found 12 of the world's most bizarre festivals, gatherings, and sporting events for you to attend.

JANUARY: Camel Wrestling Championship, Turkey
Description: You're standing among a crowd of thousands of cheering fans. The main event begins when two elaborately saddled bull camels are walked to the center of a dirt field. Then, to get them in the mood, a lavishly decorated female is paraded in front of them. The animals' nostrils flare, their saliva froths, and the little bells on their humps jingle as they trip, push, and sit on each other in a battle for dominance. A winner is declared when one of the animals falls down or runs away. But more often than not, the camels just stand there. Or they *both* run away. Or their handlers become so worried that their prized animal will get injured that they pull it from the competition.

History: This pastime has been a tradition throughout Turkey for centuries, but is now limited mostly to the region bordering the Aegean Sea. The annual championship takes place in Selçuk every winter during camel mating season.

Don't miss: The owners trash-talking each other during the pre-fight camel parades through the city. But watch out for saliva and urine—anyone within 10 feet of a camel is at risk of getting hit with one of these projectiles.

FEBRUARY: Ivrea Carnevale, Italy
Description: Your next stop is the largest food fight in Italy, held annually in the town of Ivrea a few days before Lent. You and about 10,000 other "rebels" are divided into nine "combat teams." Then you run through the streets throwing oranges at each other and at hundreds of "aristocrats," who defend themselves from chariots and balconies. By the end of the battle, the peels and pulp blanket the town's streets in a foot-deep layer of orange goop.

The small town of Las Nieves, Spain, is home to the annual Fiesta of Near Death Experiences.

History: According to legend, a 12th-century maiden named Violetta fought back against the tyrannical ruler Count Ranieri when he tried to clain the "right" of the local duke to sleep with every new bride on her wedding night. In the struggle, Violetta decapitated him. Upon hearing the news that the hated tyrant was dead, the townspeople stormed the castle and threw rocks at the guards. Afterward, an event was held annually to reenact the rebellion—some participants played the castle guards, others played the rebels, and they all ran around and threw beans at each other. In the 19th century, imported oranges became the preferred weapons.

Don't miss: Not only is participation free, so is the food. Locals serve regional specialties such as *fagioli grassi* (beans boiled with sausages and pork rinds), cod with polenta, pastries, and Italian wines.

MARCH: Hokitika Wildfoods Festival, New Zealand

Description: Ever eaten fried lamb testicles? You and about 15,000 other tourists can sample that and other "gourmet" foods at this feast provided by Hokitika's "Coasters" (people who live on the thinly populated west coast of New Zealand's South Island). The menu is different every year; past feasts have featured grasshopper bruschetta, smoked eel, "huhu grubs" served on toothpicks, and, for dessert, wasp larvae ice cream followed by mealworm Jell-O shots. What will they serve next year? It could be just about anything.

History: During New Zealand's 1860s gold rush, the Coasters learned to make do with whatever protein-rich foods they could find. In 1990, to celebrate the 125th birthday of the town of Hokitika, a winemaker named Claire Bryant came up with the idea of a festival that honors the diverse local fare.

Don't miss: The gorgeous sunsets, live music…and mimes.

APRIL: Beltane Fire Festival, Scotland

Description: Every April 30, also known as the Eve of May, thousands of people gather near Calton Hill above Edinburgh and wait for the sun to go down. As it does, a fire is lit that will provide the spark for the dozens of ritualistic fires to follow. Then there's a procession—an actor dressed as the "May Queen" emerges from the ground, and hundreds of performers march together as thousands of drums beat in unison. The May Queen is brought to her King, the "Green Man." As darkness falls, more players perform dramatic reenactments of the lives of ancient gods and goddesses. It all culminates with a giant bonfire, and everyone dances the night away.

History: Although this particular festival—the largest of its kind in the world—is only about 30 years old, the Gaelic festival of "Beltane" dates back thousands of years, as farmers celebrated the end of winter by lighting bonfires to honor the fertility of the land. In the late 1980s, a group of musicians formed the Beltane Fire Society, a nonprofit organization that puts the festival on every year.

Don't miss: A chance to participate as one of the performers. Contact the Society a few months ahead of time to join in.

MAY: Mike the Headless Chicken Days, Colorado

Description: The town of Fruita celebrates its most famous historical figure, Mike the Headless Chicken, with an annual weekend of fun and chicken. First there's a lawnmower race, followed by fried chicken. Then a classic car show, followed by chicken tenders. There's also a chicken dance, followed by more chicken.

History: As longtime *Bathroom Reader* fans may know, Mike the Chicken's neck went under farmer Lloyd Olsen's axe in 1945. Miraculously, the rooster lived for 18 months *after* his head was chopped off (he still had a brain stem, and his keepers fed him by dropping liquefied food down his neck). Mike became famous and toured the U.S. and abroad as a star attraction. "Mike's will to live remains an inspiration," it says on his official Web site. "It's a great comfort to know you can live a normal life, even after you've lost your mind." Mike died in 1947.

Don't miss: The "Run Like a Headless Chicken 5K Race."

JUNE: Toe Wrestling Championships, England

Description: Each June, competitors assemble in Staffordshire to lock big toes and try to force their opponent's foot off of a custom-made podium known as a "toesrack." If you think you can go toe-to-toe with one of the sport's superstars, such as Alan "Nasty" Nash or Paul "Tominator" Beech, it's free to join the competition. All you need are clean feet and strong ankles.

History: Toe wrestling was invented in the 1970s by a group of bored pubbers at Ye Olde Royal Oak Inn in Wetton, Derbyshire. Today it's an internationally recognized sport, attracting big-name sponsors such as Ben & Jerry's Ice Cream.

Don't miss: Also in June and just a few hours' drive away is the annual Summer Solstice Festival at Stonehenge, a celebration that's much larger and, in many ways, weirder—but features little, if any, toe wrestling.

JULY: Boryeong Mud Festival, South Korea

Description: At this festival, you can frolic in the mud with more than 1.5 million revelers in the coastal city of Boryeong. The six-day celebration attracts as many foreigners as locals, making it not only the largest festival in Korea, but also one of the biggest in the world. Enter the Mud King contest, enjoy a mud massage, ride on a mud slide into a giant tub of mud, and when you're done, take a mud shower.

History: This festival was founded in 1998 to take advantage of the town's unusually silty soil. Because it isn't suitable for agriculture, marketing-savvy civic leaders concocted a plan to push the mud's beauty benefits. With high concentrations of germanium and other minerals, Boryeong mud is said to be great for the skin and hair.

Don't miss: The opportunity to take some of Boryeong home with you in the form of mud soap, mudpacks, and mud cosmetics for sale at the festival.

AUGUST: Burning Man, Nevada

Description: Each year during the week before Labor Day, nearly 50,000 people gather in the Black Rock Desert, a flat tract of fine sand 80 miles north of Reno. But don't expect to be able to buy supplies there; the only things for sale at Burning Man are coffee and bags of ice, both available at what's known as "Center Camp." Everything else—food, water, fuel, tents—you have to bring yourself. You'll also need some very sturdy tent poles to keep your homestead secure during one of the inevitable dust storms and wind gusts that often blow over 50 mph. And during the day, the temperature regularly tops 100°F; at night, it can drop down to the 30s. Why put yourself through all of that? To see mechanical fire-breathing dragons lurch by on hydraulic legs, or take a ride on

---

a life-size clipper ship sailing over the sand, or just get to know the thousands of artists, performers, and ordinary people who make Burning Man an annual pilgrimage. Plus there are 24-hour dance parties, live music from all over the world, a Thunderdome (just like the one from *Mad Max*), and the ceremonial burning of the 40-foot-tall Man on Saturday night.

History: In 1986 two friends from San Francisco, Larry Harvey and Jerry James, went to a nearby beach and built an 8-foot-tall wooden man—and a wooden dog—and burned them. Inspired by the crowd that had gathered to watch their "spontaneous act of radical self-expression," they did it again the following year. More people came. The next year, even *more* people came. Finally, it got too big for the beach. After a long search, in 1991 the organizers moved the event to the Black Rock Desert.

Don't miss: The chance to take part in Burning Man's "gifting society." Bring extra trinkets and supplies to give away to other attendees.

SEPTEMBER: Sputnikfest, Wisconsin

Description: Enjoy the fried cheese, cold beer, and friendly people dressed as big-eyed aliens, and see local celebrities get soaked in the "Splashdown" dunk tank.

History: Around 5:30 in the morning on September 5, 1962, hundreds of early risers in northern Wisonsin reported a spectacular sight: dozens of bright, burning objects streaking throught the clear dawn sky. Around the same time, two patrolmen in the town of Manitowoc noticed a strange object in the middle of a street: a 20-pound chunk of metal that had embedded itself in the pavement. They went to remove it—but it was too hot to touch. It turned out to be a piece of *Sputnik IV*, a Russian satellite that had gone off course shortly after it was launched two years earlier, and had finally disintegrated in the skies over Wisconsin. In 2008 the town decided to turn the odd incident into a reason for a celebration—and Sputnikfest was born.

Don't miss: The tinfoil-suit fashion show, the "Miss Space Debris" beauty contest, and for the kids, the Alien Autopsy Room.

OCTOBER: Phuket Vegetarian Festival, Thailand

Description: Squeamish? Then stay far, far away from this festival.

Every autumn, Chinese and Thai religious devotees called *Mah Song* parade through Phuket's streets in trance-like states, their bodies pierced with, among other things, bicycle wheels, saw blades, and metal skewers of varying sizes—all protruding into and out of their arms, legs, noses, lips, ears, and eyebrows. There's also hot-coal firewalking and a ladder made of sharpened blades. Why? The Mah Song believe that those who are truly devoted feel little, if any, pain, and aren't left with scars. You don't have to participate in the self-mutilation, but like the Mah Song, you're asked to adhere to a vegetarian diet all week. Luckily, that's not hard because the festival's food is excellent.

History: In the 1820s, when Phuket tin miners and their families were suffering from a malaria epidemic, a traveling opera company from China came to the area. The singers also caught malaria, but for 10 days, they ate nothing but vegetables and performed religious ceremonies. To the surprise of the miners, the performers recovered from the illness much more quickly than the locals did. The opera singers taught the rituals to the townspeople, and within a year the malaria epidemic had ceased. The festival keeps the tradition alive today, though it's unclear how the self-mutilation became part of the festivities.

Don't miss: The ear-plug vendors. In addition to being one of the world's most unusual festivals, it's also one of the loudest. Drums and firecrackers are sounded all week long to scare away evil spirits.

NOVEMBER: The Quiet Festival, New Jersey

Description: One of the activities at this low-key festival in Ocean City: hearing a pin drop. You can also try your hand at a group whispering session, enter a yawn-off, and take as many naps as you like. It's one of the smallest and most obscure festivals in the world (only a few dozen people participated in 2009), and also offers silent movies, a sign-language choir, and mimes.

History: "I've been tired for about 40 years now," says Mark Soifer, 72, who organized the first Quiet Festival for stressed-out people in 1989. "I feel uniquely qualified to represent the millions of tired folks in this nation and the world." By day, Soifer works as Ocean City's publicist, but he's also the president of the National Association of Tired People (NAP), which sponsors the event.

Don't miss: The "windchime symphony."

Oxford scientists have discovered a way to implant artificial memories in the brains of fruitflies.

DECEMBER: Night of the Radishes, Mexico

Description: Each December 23rd, this pre-Christmas celebration features the most elaborate radish sculptures in the world. Skilled artisans gather in Oaxaca City for *La Noche de Rábanos* to show off their pink-and-white sculptures of saints, Nativity scenes, conquistadors, and animals. And these are no ordinary radishes, but giant ones, some measuring 1½ feet long and weighing seven pounds. The festival lasts only one night because after that, the artwork starts to rot.

History: Spanish monks brought radishes to Mexico in the 16th century and encouraged the locals to grow them—and also to carve them. The elaborate veggie sculptures have been a tradition ever since. The Night of the Radishes officially began in 1897, thanks to Oaxaca's mayor, Francisco Vasconcelos Flores, who wanted to preserve this unique cultural heritage (and sell more radishes to tourists).

Don't miss: After the judging has ended and a champion radish-artist has been named, fireworks light up the sky.

WELCOME HOME!

Congratulations! Now that you've dodged camel spit in Turkey, splattered your friends with oranges in Italy, devoured fried lamb testicles in New Zealand, danced around the Maypole in Scotland, run around like a chicken with your head cut off in Colorado, wrestled toe to toe in England, frolicked in the mud in South Korea, sailed on a ship through the Nevada desert, performed an alien autopsy in Wisconsin, traversed hot coals in Thailand, made windchime music in New Jersey, and sculpted a radish saint in Mexico, you can take a month or two off.

Or...you could catch a quick flight to Russia and participate in a truly surreal New Year's party: At Lake Baikal, the world's deepest lake, a hole is cut into the ice and divers haul the New Year Tree more than 100 feet below the surface. After you get your picture taken with Russian folk heroes Father Frost and the Ice Maiden, you plunge into the depths where you'll celebrate the night SCUBA-dancing among the sparkling lights of the New Year Tree.

Then you can dry off, warm up, fly home...and take that well-deserved sabbatical.

Michael Jackson & Raquel Welch had something in common: Both reportedly bathed in bottled water.

ODDS AND ENDS

With the emphasis on "odd."

• **In September** 2008, Santiago Cabrera woke up in his Fresno, California, home when he "felt something hit him in the face," according to the subsequent police report. He looked up to see "an unknown male bent over him. The male continued to strike him in the face and head area with a sausage." The assailant—who really *was* hitting Cabrera with a sausage—then took off his pants and ran out of the house. Police found the man's identification in the pants he'd left behind, and Antonio Vasquez Jr., 21, was arrested a short time later. "I tell you," said Fresno police officer Ian Burrimond, "this was one weird case." (The sausage couldn't be used as evidence; amid the confusion, Cabrera's dog ate it.)

• **Prena Thomas** of Lakeland, Florida, has something unusual in her freezer: a 33-year-old snowball. She made it in 1977 during a rare Florida snowstorm and kept it as a memento. "It's just like a little pet," she says, and she occasionally takes it out of the freezer to look at it.

• **British television** personality Myleene Klass, 31, was appearing on the reality show *I'm a Celebrity, Get Me Out of Here!* in Costa Rica in 2009 when she had to call for help one night from her hotel room. The problem? She'd sprayed herself with insect repellent, which had reacted with the varnish on the bed's wooden frame—and one of her hands had gotten stuck to the wood. Staff had to slowly peel Klass off the frame to free her (which was, many agreed, more entertaining than the reality show).

• **Jonathon Guabello**, 29, of Fort Myers, Florida, and his girl-friend came home from a bar one night in October 2008. Guabel-lo wanted to have sex, but his girlfriend wasn't in the mood...so Guabello shot himself in the arm twice, then tripped over the oven door, hit his head, and passed out. His girlfriend called the police; Guabello was arrested for threatening violence and firing a weapon in an occupied dwelling, and faces several years in prison.

Two men burst into a home in Plant City, Florida, late one night in December 2008. One of the men held a knife to the throat of the homeowner...and demanded an eggbeater. The homeowner found an eggbeater and gave it to him. Robert Eugene Thompson and Taurus Deshane Morris were arrested a short time later on burglary and aggravated assault charges. The eggbeater was found in Thompson's back pocket and returned to the victim.

In January 2010, police arrested Carlos Laurel, 31, and Andre Hardy, 39, on drug charges in Kingston, Pennsylvania. Police reports noted dryly that Laurel and Hardy had 50 bags of crack cocaine in their possession.

Adeel Ayub, 30, a stocker at a supermarket in Preston, England, was arrested in 2009 for, among other things, licking a raw chicken in the store. A coworker filmed the chicken-licking, the video ended up on YouTube, and Ayub was arrested. He was later sentenced to two months in prison.

A farmer named Luis Alfonso Sanchez was treated at a Colombian hospital in December 2009—after he castrated himself so that he wouldn't cheat on his wife. She had refused to have sex with him, he told doctors. "When I saw that I could no longer count on her," he said, "I made the decision to cut my testicles off because I am a Christian and did not want to go look for another." He also said that, as a farmer, he had castrated many animals, so he thought it was no big deal. "He's been looked at by the urology department," a hospital spokesman said, "and they found a complete absence of the testicles." They added, however, that his wounds had become infected.

In January 2010, lawyer Jeffrey Denner stood up in court in Woburn, Massachusetts, and told the judge that his client, Eben Howard, on trial for assault, was mentally competent to stand trial. His client suddenly jumped out of his seat, accused Denner of putting poison in his cranberry juice, and attacked him. Courtroom security had to restrain him. "Perhaps," Denner said later, "I spoke too hastily." The trial continued at a later date.

The total number of counterfeit U.S. $50 and $100 notes passed and seized in 1990: 1,240,840.

IT'S TOO LATE...

...to contemplate. The world's already gone crazy.

"The weird and the stupid are becoming our cultural norms, even our cultural ideal."
—**Carl Bernstein**

"The world today doesn't make sense, so why should I paint pictures that do?"
—**Pablo Picasso**

"The human race's prospects of survival were considerably better when we were defenseless against tigers than they are today when we have become defenseless against ourselves."
—**Arnold J. Toynbee**

"Perhaps in time, the so-called Dark Ages will be thought of as including our own."
—**Georg Lichtenberg**

"Ninety-nine percent of the people in the world are fools, and the rest of us are in great danger of contagion."
—**Thornton Wilder**

"There is no salvation in becoming adapted to a world which is crazy."
—**Henry Miller**

"Maybe this world is another planet's Hell."
—**Aldous Huxley**

"You can't make up anything anymore. The world itself is a satire. All you're doing is recording it."
—**Art Buchwald**

"It's not the end of the world, but you can see it from here."
—**Pierre Trudeau**

"I think the people you should worry about are the ones who say, 'Everything is fine.'"
—**Parker Posey**

"The world just doesn't work. It's an idea whose time is gone."
—**Joseph Heller**

"The optimist proclaims that we live in the best of all possible worlds, and the pessimist fears this is true."
—**James Branch Cabell**

"We do not have to visit a madhouse to find disordered minds; our planet is the mental institution of the universe."
—**Johann von Goethe**

A WORLD GONE...SANE?

Maybe Earth isn't quite as cracked up as it's cracked up to be.

EVERYTHING'S COMING UP ROSES

"We are living in the most peaceful moment of our species' time on Earth," according to Harvard University psychologist Steven Pinker. Using models based on modern hunter-gatherer societies, Pinker theorizes that if we all lived like our pre-agrarian tribal ancestors, death rates from violence would be around 2,000 percent higher. During the 20th century alone (which included two world wars), instead of the 100 million lives lost due to conflict, the number would have been closer to two billion. In short, people just aren't killing each other the way they used to.

The rate of state-based conflicts (wars) worldwide has declined since the end of World War II and has dropped 40 percent since 1992. On February 15, 2003, in 800 cities around the world, 20 million people protested against the impending invasion of Iraq. Although the protests didn't stop the war, *Guinness World Records* lists it as "the largest anti-war demonstration in history."

On a smaller scale, says Pinker, cruelty-as-entertainment is almost gone. Our ancestors flocked to see convicted criminals hanged, beheaded, or burned at the stake. The Romans routinely threw Christians to the lions before thousands of cheering spectators. But public executions rarely occur today, and when they do, they're condemned by the world community.

NEW AGE THINKING

So when did humanity start evolving into a softer, gentler race? Pinker points to the Age of Enlightenment in the 17th century. One of the by-products of the newfound reasoning in which superstition gave way to science was that people began to develop more empathy for each other. In today's "Age of Information," it's easier than ever before to know about people on the other side of the world, which also leads to increased empathy. Western-style democracies, which rely on cooperation rather than conflict, have also contributed significantly to the sharp decline in violence. There were 20 democratic governments worldwide in 1946; in 2005 there were 88.

The 1-inch-long vampire moth feeds on the blood of elephants.

EVEN MORE POSITIVE REINFORCEMENT

According to the Millennium Project, an international think tank, there could be even more reason to be hopeful about the future:

• Thanks in large part to emerging technologies, global literacy rates are way up and are expected to rise. In 1970, just 63 percent of people over the age of 15 were literate, compared to 62 percent today. One billion people now have access to information technology and that number is expected to rise, too.

• Population growth, which is currently putting a strain on the world's resources, will begin declining by 2050. By 2100, there will be one billion fewer people than there are today. The alternative forms of energy that are starting to be implemented on a wide scale should provide more than enough power for them to thrive.

LOOK ON THE SUNNY SIDE

So if the world is actually becoming safer, smarter, and nicer, what accounts for all the gloom and doom on the news? "Better reporting," says Pinker. He calls it a *cognitive illusion*: "The easier it is for us to recall specific instances of something, the higher the probability we will assign to it." In other words, when we see violence and political discord all over television, we assume it's happening *everywhere*. To combat it, says Pinker, adopt a glass-half-full attitude: "We tend to view things by how low our behavior can sink as opposed to how high our standards have risen."

So maybe all the crazy stuff in this book is the exception, not the norm. But to be honest, we hope the world doesn't go *completely* sane—because it just wouldn't be as much fun to write about.

*   *   *

PERHAPS YOU SHOULD DISREGARD THE ABOVE

In 2007 a 21-year-old Seattle woman was arrested for assaulting a man in a karaoke bar after his rendition of Coldplay's "Yellow." A witness reported that the woman shouted, "Not that song, I hate that song," before telling the victim that his "singing sucked" and then running up and punching him twice in the face. After she was arrested, the woman head-butted a police officer several times before she was finally subdued and handcuffed.

After Japan's biggest bank heist ($5.4 million), the bank got a thank-you note from the robbers.

UNCLE JOHN'S BATHROOM READER CLASSIC SERIES

Find these and other great titles from the *Uncle John's Bathroom Reader* Classic Series online at **www.bathroomreader.com**. Or contact us at:

Bathroom Readers' Institute
P.O. Box 1117
Ashland, OR 97520
(888) 488-4642

THE LAST PAGE

FELLOW BATHROOM READERS:
The fight for good bathroom reading should never be taken loosely—we must do our duty and sit firmly for what we believe in, even while the rest of the world is taking potshots at us.

We'll be brief. Now that we've proven we're not simply a flush-in-the-pan, we invite you to take the plunge: Sit Down and Be Counted! Log on to *www.bathroomreader.com* and earn a permanent spot on the BRI honor roll!

If you like reading our books...
VISIT THE BRI'S WEB SITE!
www.bathroomreader.com

- Visit "The Throne Room"—a great place to read!
- Receive our irregular newsletters via e-mail
- Order additional *Bathroom Readers*
- Read our blog

Go with the Flow...

Well, we're out of space, and when you've gotta go, you've gotta go. Tanks for all your support. Hope to hear from you soon. Meanwhile, remember...

Keep on flushin'!

Praise for *The Younger Wife*

"Completely compulsive. Sally Hepworth delivers with this stay-up-late, one-more-chapter gem."

—Jane Harper, *New York Times* bestselling author

"Smart, suspenseful, brimming with secrets. This is Sally Hepworth at her unputdownable best."

—Kate Morton, *New York Times* bestselling author

"An immersive, propulsive tale."   —*Good Morning America*

"Hepworth is back with another thriller that will have you muttering 'just one more chapter' to yourself at 1:00 A.M."

—*E! Online*

"*The Younger Wife* is a page-turner, bursting with suspense and tension, up to the conclusion, a shocker sure to leave the reader with questions: Did he, or didn't he?"   —*New York Journal of Books*

"A warped tale [that] boasts Jane Harper's multilayered characters and Liane Moriarty's wealthy suburban world saturated with lies and deceit. With each domestic thriller, bestselling Hepworth shines brighter and draws in more readers."   —*Booklist*

"Hepworth weaves the struggles of dementia, sexual assault, anxiety, and domestic abuse into the lives of realistic, likable characters that readers will be rooting for."   —*Library Journal*

Also by Sally Hepworth

The Secrets of Midwives

The Things We Keep

The Mother's Promise

The Family Next Door

The Mother-in-Law

The Good Sister